Obligation in Exile

Obligation in Exile
The Jewish Diaspora, Israel and Critique

Ilan Zvi Baron

EDINBURGH
University Press

© Ilan Zvi Baron, 2015, 2024

Edinburgh University Press Ltd
13 Infirmary Street
Edinburgh EH1 1LT
www.euppublishing.com

First published in hardback by Edinburgh University Press 2015

Typeset in 11/14 Sabon by
Servis Filmsetting Ltd, Stockport, Cheshire, and
printed and bound in Great Britain by
CPI Group (UK) Ltd, Croydon CR0 4YY

A CIP record for this book is available from the British Library

ISBN 978 0 7486 9230 9 (hardback)
ISBN 978 1 3995 3696 7 (paperback)
ISBN 978 0 7486 9231 6 (webready PDF)
ISBN 978 0 7486 9232 3 (epub)

The right of Ilan Zvi Baron to be identified as author of this work has been asserted in accordance with the Copyright, Designs and Patents Act 1988 and the Copyright and Related Rights Regulations 2003 (SI No. 2498).

Contents

Acknowledgements	vii
Preface	x
Foreword to the Paperback Edition	xvi
Introduction	1
Situating Israel: The Jewish Diaspora and Israel Today	11
A Question of Obligation	24
Methodology	30
Book Outline	36
1. The Limits of Political Obligation	41
Introduction	41
What Is Political Obligation?	43
Obligation and Security	53
Liberalism and the International in Political Obligation	58
The Particularity Principle	61
Conclusion: Why Obligation?	67
2. Power and Obligation	71
Introduction	71
Power in the Particularity Principle and Political Obligation	73
Max Weber: Power and (Political) Obligation	76
Power and the Political Obligation Literature	81
Power and Transnational Political Obligation: Arendt and the Disassociation of Power from the State	85
Power and Questions of the Self	104
The Muscle Jew: Power, Politics and Identity in Theory and Practice	113
Conclusion	118

3. Between Zion and Diaspora: Internationalisms, Transnationalisms, Obligation and Security — 123
   Introduction — 123
   Transnationalism — 124
   Liberalism, Obligation and Jewish Internationalism — 132
   Diaspora–Israel Transnationalism: Between Zion and Diaspora — 136
   Israel and Diaspora Security — 144
   Conclusion — 154

4. From Eating Hummus to the Sublime — 156
   Introduction — 156
   The Loyalty Problem — 160
   The Authority and Legitimacy Problem — 163
   From Hummus to the Sublime — 167
   Conclusion — 191

5. Obligation and Critique — 193
   Introduction — 193
   Critique and Transnational Political Obligation — 197
   Toward an Immanent Critique of Zionism — 202
   Conclusion: A New Diaspora/Israel Relationship — 212

Conclusion: Obligation in Exile, Critique and the Future of the Jewish Diaspora — 217

Appendix — 224
Notes — 231
Bibliography — 268
Index — 288

Acknowledgements

As with most research projects, this work owes a considerable amount to the support and generosity of many people. The theoretical idea behind this book started when I was a graduate student, and became the basis of my post-doctoral research. I would, therefore, like to thank my PhD supervisor, Hidemi Suganami, for encouraging me to pursue research on obligation and international politics, and the late Fred Halliday for his mentorship and support when I was a post-doctoral fellow at the Institut Barcelona D'Estudis Internacionals (IBEI). I would also like to acknowledge IBEI for providing me with the research funding that supported the initial fieldwork. I was very lucky to have a great group of colleagues when I was in Barcelona, especially Karsten Frey and Gemma Collantes-Celador, who helped me out a great deal by introducing me to new literature and always had the time for our regular and much-needed coffee breaks.

My current academic home, in the School of Government and International Affairs at Durham University, has been a supportive environment in which to pursue this topic and to be given the chance to test out various elements of it. I would in particular like to thank Peter Stirk, who offered advice on various theoretical problems encountered, and John Williams, who similarly offered not only advice but time, having read and commented on both an early paper draft in which I tested out some of the more abstract elements of the paper and the entire book manuscript. I also want to thank Jeroen Gunning, who helped me to improve my interview skills, and to Jim Piscatori, for his enthusiasm for this project and for pointing me in the direction of interesting literature. I have also benefited from friends in other parts of the University. Yulia Egorova was especially kind in listening to me talk about this project and in reading various portions of it, and Susan Frenk, principal of St Aidan's College, has been especially generous in supporting Jewish Studies research at Durham.

I have also been fortunate enough to have had the opportunity to discuss various elements of this project with scholars from multiple continents, who have all been generous and supportive. I have benefited greatly from conversations with John Horton, Brent Steele, Gabi Sheffer, Ronald Zweig, David Engel, Bethamie Horowitz, Jonathan Boyd, Brian Black, Keith Kahn-Harris, and David Feldman. In addition, Piki Ish-Shalom has been an excellent sounding board on more than a few occasions, and generously showed me the error of my ways by highlighting some of the faults in earlier manuscripts. I take full responsibility for any consequences arising from my not having followed all of his advice! I want to thank Daniel Levine, whose encyclopedic knowledge of Jewish Studies, Political Theory and International Relations probably means that he should be writing this book instead of me. I also wish to thank Simon Glezos, a friend since our undergraduate days, who at an ISA conference in San Francisco listened to me ramble on about this project.

The book was finished while I was a visiting assistant professor in the History Department at the University of British Columbia. Being at UBC proved to be invaluable in allowing me to find both the time and the resources to complete this manuscript. I would like to thank Christopher Friedrichs for his support, Richard Menkis, who was my sponsor at UBC, and Jocelyn Smith, who helped me get set up at UBC, sorting out my IT and library access, and providing me with an office.

This book would also not have been possible without the time given by the multiple people interviewed for this project. A list of all those who participated is provided in the Appendix. Let me thank everybody who shared their time and thoughts with me, in some instances on multiple occasions. This book would not have been the same without their generosity and honesty. There are a few people, however, who made the interviews possible but do not appear in the list. In New York, thank you to Aaron and Melissa. I have known both for many years, but they exceeded any expectations of generosity in opening up their home for a lengthy period of time so I could conduct fieldwork. Thank you very much. The same is true of my relatives in Israel, and I thank Guy and Avital in particular for their unwavering hospitality and generosity. And of course, thank

Acknowledgements

you to Sony and David, who hosted me for three months during my stay at UBC.

But of course, this book would never have been possible without the love and support of my wife Yael, who, in a break from tradition, managed not only to read the entire draft of this book, but actually enjoyed it!

This book is dedicated to my grandfather, Hillel Meyerhof, who passed away in 2002. I hope he enjoys it.

Preface

This project follows from two experiences. The first one is academic, and I should perhaps not admit that it is the minor force behind the project. When I completed my PhD on obligation and war, I was dissatisfied with how the political obligation literature I had been reading did not seem to take identity particularly seriously. Identity was always present in some form, but usually only in a very vague and general sense in references to membership or citizenship. It appeared that the different life experiences that accompany different identities do not matter for the problem of political obligation, which seemed odd to me. A theorist of political obligation would at this point stop me and point out that the problem of political obligation is not supposed to address such issues, that it is concerned with why citizens accept the obligation to obey the law, and that it addresses a category of life in which identity only matters in a general sense. Citizens are expected to obey the law regardless of gender, ethnicity, age, religions, sexual orientation or class.

Nevertheless, residents, citizens or otherwise, experience the law differently, and considering that there could not even be a theory, let alone a problem, of political obligation without people being recognized as having and feeling that they have specific political obligations because of who they are, dismissing the complexity of identity is not something to be done with an analytical sleight of hand. More problematically, what concerned me as a multidisciplinary type of person most of all was how obligations that are political are different for particular identity-groups, and how political theory could help address this question with regard to the lived experiences of an identity-group. I started to think about political obligation as if obligations could be considerably different for women, for minorities, and for diaspora populations. In addition, I also questioned what made the obligations political. At this point

Preface

it became clear that I was no longer thinking about political obligation in the traditional sense in which the term is used. Providing a theory that was appropriate became a driving force behind this book and, academically speaking, in the process this book ends up addressing and contributing to literatures in political theory, diaspora studies, transnationalism, international political sociology, Jewish Studies, and possibly Israel Studies as well.

However, the greater force behind this book has been a personal journey that I am still in the process of making. I started writing this preface while sitting in a café at Tel Aviv University, waiting for a meeting in the nearby Museum of the Jewish People, *Beit Hatfutsot*. I had not been there for quite a few years, and the research for this book was taking me back to places that I had travelled to in the past, and am now re-visiting. At this point it should be obvious that this book is largely a product of a reflexive research project, and my activities with others on reflexivity encouraged me to clearly articulate the personal journey behind this book. Brent Steele and Jack Amoureux have been especially crucial in supporting this work, as have many others including Piki Ish-Shalom, some of whom were generous enough to listen to me present work on this book. I remember presenting a paper about transnational political obligation at the International Studies Association in San Francisco. During the question period, Brent Steele asked me to explain more about the role of power, because I had been quite brief in my presentation and had not mentioned any names. But just before I could state my reliance on Hannah Arendt, he said, "And don't say Arendt!" Sorry.

Growing up in the West Coast of Canada meant that geographically I was far removed from the land where my mother was born. She was born in Israel, and as I grew up this connection was always very important to me. The connection was double because my paternal grandfather also had ties to Israel, although in his case he never lived in Israel but in Palestine. He ran away from home and eventually ended up in the British Merchant Marines and then the Australian Commandos in the Second World War. But he returned to Palestine briefly, and was involved first-hand in the smuggling of weapons and refugees into Palestine. I thus grew up with Israel all around me. On my mother's side I had a communist grandmother, on my father's side a grandfather involved in the infamous Altalena episode, who was a friend of Begin and had fond memories of the people who were most likely responsible for the King David bombing in Jerusalem in July 1946. Ideological commitments to Israel ran across all spectrums in my family and I ended up attending a socialist Zionist camp modeled on the Labor Zionist Movement.

For a few summers as a kid I went to a kind of pseudo-kibbutz on Gabriola Island, a small island in between Vancouver Island and the mainland. This camp, *Mahane Myriam*, is part of a wider movement, *Habonim Dror*, and with *Habonim* I went to Israel twice. Once for a summer and once, after high school, for a year. I was, it is fair to say, a highly indoctrinated young Zionist, and I almost made *aliya* to Israel twice, the first time before I went to university and then again when I finished my MSc degree at the London School of Economics. I ultimately did not move to Israel (why I did not is a story for a different book), but what did stay with me is the question of how we are to explain the commitments that Jews in the Diaspora feel for a country that we do not live in, and where we do not pay taxes (although many buy Israel bonds and donate money to relevant organizations), do not serve in the army, and do not vote. I would bet that for most Diaspora Jews, Israel is an idea with a place to back it up.

It may be my academic training, but the certainty that once commanded a loyalty to support Israel has become a question about what kind of loyalty is at stake. The usual Zionist and Jewish Peoplehood arguments for Diaspora connectivity with Israel all sound fairly reasonable when articulated clearly, but are also not that difficult to challenge and, consequently, doubt is not hard to come by. A close friend who did end up immigrating to Israel eventually left to find that many Diaspora Jews had, as he told me, questionable if not troublesome views about Israeli politics. For scholars of diaspora studies, this sociology is not surprising, but what it reveals and what is not altogether clear is how exactly Diaspora Jews understand their relationship with Israel. While I used the terms "commitment" and "loyalty" above, these are possible descriptions of the relationship and not an explanation about it.

As I contemplate the questions of obligation, commitment, or perhaps other related terms such as loyalty, allegiance and duty, I am still sitting in Tel Aviv University and I can hear Israeli singers practice for the upcoming 65th anniversary of Israel's founding. I will, in 2013, be in Israel for both *Yom HaZikaron* and *Yom*

Hatzmaut, and thus be able to indulge in some Israeli myth-making and nation-building. The greatest myths, however, and the ones that speak the most to me, are the little ones about what it means for there to be a Jewish country. In some ways, what is the most telling is when I arrive in Israel and find everything to be Jewish courtesy of the language. Sitting in a *sherut*, a kind of mini-bus taxi service, and seeing a fire extinguisher that looks just like all other extinguishers I have ever seen but with all the text written in Hebrew, the warnings and the instructions, invites a curious feeling. I am not sure if it is pride, the feeling of finally being at home, curiosity, or perhaps some kind of fetishism (which, to be honest, is the most likely), but the feeling is strong. Yet it is also not possible to divorce this feeling from knowing of all the violence that has taken and continues to take place in order to produce a Hebrew fire extinguisher for a Jewish country. Ultimately, it may be a good thing that there are such devices, because there will no doubt be many fires to put out.

Israel's first national poet, Hayim Nahman Bialik, is known to have said that the Jewish people would enter the community of nation-states as normal members when Jews are able to procure services from Jewish prostitutes. I am not so sure about the merits of this target for recognizing Jewish arrival. In my world, it is the fire extinguisher. Hopefully, this book will help make better sense of the roles that the Diaspora has and could have in responding to fires and the potential for fires in Israel. But ultimately, I hope that this book will contribute to a wider discussion about what it means to be Jewish in the age of Israel, and of what discourses contextualize the political ties that frame the Diaspora's relationship with Israel. As such, this book is also designed to fill a gap in the contemporary literature that I am surprised exists.

The vast majority of the texts out there about the Diaspora and Israel are either historical or designed to advance a political agenda. It is amazing to me that there are so few contemporary texts that seek to understand in detail the character of the politico-cultural relationship that exists between the Diaspora and Israel. There are texts that speak to a more religious audience and that address the issue of how to place Israel in contemporary Judaism. While I do not address religious argument as such in this book, I did interview a lot of rabbis, because they often hear and speak to the concerns of their communities about Israel. Yet, what is interesting is that perhaps the main theological issues about the Israelization of Jewish identity rarely came up in religious, theological or spiritual terms. The few times it did were in response to the order of God, Torah and Israel. Outside of this religious question, which is beyond my area of expertise, the recent texts that I have discovered that do touch on the issue of the political culture of the Diaspora/Israel relationship do so in passing, or only as a chapter in a larger commentary.

A historical outlook on the literature, however, paints a different story. Before the State of Israel existed there was a huge literature about the political spaces in which Diaspora Jews should act, of how Diaspora Jews should respond to Zionism and its alternatives, which ranged from Jewish socialism to Diaspora Jewish nationalism to full assimilation. Yet there are no such texts any more. The answers appear to have been provided and so debate has closed, and been replaced with a kind of false multiple choice question where there are multiple answers, but few "correct" ones. The choices now have to do with the type of connection to Israel a Diaspora Jew has, with each choice carrying different political, ethical and social implications. Yet this scenario presumes that Diaspora Jews are comfortable with the choices open to them. I would suggest that many Diaspora Jews are not, and I am not here speaking only about those who vocally engage in public Israeli criticism. Rather, I am speaking more generally, as my sense is that in the Diaspora there is a progressive and ongoing process of enquiry about how Diaspora Jews are to identify themselves culturally and politically in the age of Israel.

It can be a deeply troubling experience to feel uncomfortable in one's own skin, to dislike the options available. There is nothing self-hating about feeling uncomfortable with a series of options which you had no part in making, but which are imposed. Thus, what is a Jew to do when, simply as a Jew, you are expected to support without too much public criticism or debate a country that may be heading toward theocracy, and even if it is not does not represent a moral model unto the nations of how to act in the face of adversity? Alternatively, what is a Jew to do when the sociological framing of Jewish Diaspora identity remains tied to the dichotomy between Israel and Diaspora, when both are no longer what they were, when it is not clear where either is heading or how the two continue to be related. It is partly for these reasons that there is a small but growing literature in Jewish history that seeks to reclaim these lost voices of Jewish politics because today there seem to be no other options. Thus, in historical research there are texts that speak to this gap. What is needed is a historically informed but contemporary critique. This book provides such a critique.

As such, this book is designed to open up discussion about the Diaspora and Israel. It is not the point of this book to tell Jews what they should believe or how to act. The point is to reveal some of the contradictions and tensions that frame the Diaspora experience with regard to Israel, and how we can begin theoretically to understand this experience in a post-Zionist age, when Israel's existence is no longer in such doubt, when it is harder if not impossible to view the Diaspora as empty and devoid of any value, and when the Diaspora/Israel relationship is in the process of changing. The theoretical sections of this book are thus a contribution to trying to think differently about the political relationship and the political geography between Diaspora and Israel.

Before I begin, however, I would like to offer some advice to the reader, and I hope that doing so does not come across as presumptuous. There are at least two ways in which the reader can read this book. One is to read it cover to cover. This reader will have an interest not just in Jewish identity in the Diaspora, but also in theoretical academic debates and the question of what is meant by transnational political obligation and how this type of obligation differs from traditional notions of political obligation. Chapters 1 and 2 in particular involve some close readings of political theory texts and my own theoretical contributions, neither of which will interest everyone (although the section on the Muscle Jew will probably be of wider interest). Another way to read this book, for the reader primarily interested in Diaspora Jewish identity, the Israelization of Diaspora Jewish identity and the relationship between Diaspora identity and Israel, is to skip these primarily theoretical chapters without guilt.

Foreword to the Paperback Edition

I have always been interested in how Diaspora Jews (like me) navigate their relationship with Israel. It was an effort to better understand that relationship that led to this book. In it, I deploy the language of political obligation because, to be honest, I did not know where else to turn. Elsewhere, I introduced the idea of diasporic security (which is close to what is now termed vicarious security) to explore the twofold dynamic of diaspora populations feeling the violence back "home" while also somehow being held responsible for it, and this book sought to expand on that discussion. Conceptually, however, theories of security did not seem appropriate despite their relevance, and theories of long-distance nationalism are problematic due to the antisemitic history regarding accusations of dual loyalty. I needed a different conceptual framework. I ended up exploring the idea that a diaspora people can feel obligations that are political, but which theories of political obligation do not consider. To put this another way, why not use the words "political obligation" to mean what they suggest, obligations that are political?

While I settled on obligation, and I'm still unsure if it was the best choice, what I did not consider is that while Jews may feel an obligation to Israel, others attribute to Jews a responsibility. I did not consider the question of responsibility. That was a mistake.

It was a mistake in two ways. First, because of how diaspora Jews are often treated as though we can be held responsible for actions taken by the Israeli state. Second, because we can feel responsible to something – Jewish peoplehood and the place that Israel holds for the past, present and future of the Jewish people – without being responsible for something – such as Israeli policy. This distinction and the importance of exploring the meaning of responsibility has become even more important in the past few months.

Foreword to the Paperback Edition

Since October 7th, 2023, and Israel's subsequent military response, both antisemitism and Islamophobia have been on the rise, and, of particular significance for this book, Jewish identity and Israeli security policy are intertwined with an intensity that has not been felt for a long time.

On October 7th Hamas launched a brutal attack against Israel. The attack was vicious, more like a massacre. Human Rights Watch is conducting its own investigation into the attack and is working on a report. Civilians were decapitated, raped, murdered, shot, blown up. There was evidence of people's limbs being cut off. The numbers at last count are that approximately 1200 Israelis were killed and over 240 were taken hostage. What took place on October 7th was, in my view, evil.

The brutality and shock of the attack meant that Israel's response was going to be harsh. Israeli security strategy has always been about deterrence, and that should Israel be the subject to attack it would respond with deadly force in order to deter future attacks. Without rendering judgement about this strategy, Israel's failure to protect its citizens on October 7th meant that Israel was highly likely to respond with overwhelming force. Regardless of one's views about Israel's ongoing military occupation of the Palestinian people, the war crime of collective punishment inherent in Israel's siege of Gaza since the 7th, and Israel's disproportionate and seemingly indiscriminate use of force that has left over 30 000 Palestinians killed since Israel started bombing Gaza, it was deeply disturbing to see how quickly signs of unmitigated solidarity with the Palestinians started to appear immediately after the 7th. To be clear: I am not questioning the moral case for supporting Palestinian rights. Rather, the question is whether or not supporting Palestinians means celebrating or justifying the October 7th massacre?

Scholars I knew and respected, student unions, colleagues in my professional labour union, and Palestinian activists treated the massacre as a moment to celebrate Palestinian resistance. UN Women, in their statement on October 13th, barely mentioned anything about what appears to have been a systemic strategy to rape women by Hamas. Do Israeli women's rights matter less than those of Palestinian women? I, like so many others, found these zero-sum responses deeply disturbing.

The question of victimhood, of who is the greater victim, and of the righteousness that we attribute to victimhood are themes that I explore in the book, especially in my interview with Rabbi Brechner who raises precisely these points. We should be able to highlight the different victims without undermining the respective victimhood of either group or trying to claim some kind of righteousness of being the greater victim. Horrible as it sounds, victimhood is also more than crude body counts. There is a tragic abundance of trauma in this conflict that, one would hope, would enable compassion to transgress ideological certainty.

Yet, all too often the discourse around this conflict prevents that kind of reflection from taking place.

There are a lot of reasons why that is the case, but one of them has to do with perspective. Often, Israelis want to focus on the present, on terrorism, security, and the future, whereas Palestinians are concerned about the injustices of the past and their historic displacement. Focusing on the past creates a challenge insofar as if we refuse to acknowledge Israel's military victory in 1948, and then again in 1967, we are potentially questioning the very right of the State of Israel to exist and its right to self-defence. However, I do think that we can recognise Israel's right to exist like any other sovereign state in the international community and still hold it to account for its own crimes against the Palestinians.

The underlying problem, as I see it, is that when we discuss Israel and the Palestinians, there is an overwhelming impulse to find that the greater blame is on the other side. It is their fault. Moreover, accompanying this moral blame is a moral certitude in our own righteousness. Justice is on "our" side. These are questions about responsibility. Yet, the reality is that there is a lot of fault and blame to go around.

Surely there should be a place to recognise the rights and aspirations of the Palestinian people without either calling for the destruction of the State of Israel or celebrating mass murder? My answer is obviously yes. And yet, the moral compass of many treated the massacre by Hamas as a moment of triumph. Jewish lives (although not all who were killed were Jewish) seem to matter less than Palestinian ones, and antisemitic attacks have increased as Israel's attack against Gaza – and a rising Palestinian death toll – continues.

We've seen this attitude play out across protests in Canada, the U.K. the United States, France, and elsewhere. The lesson seems to be that Jews can be held responsible for Israel's action, and although we can be held to account it appears that Palestinian solidarity means not holding Hamas responsible for their violence, but celebrating their ostensibly "progressive atrocity," and dismissing their inhumane cruelty.

However, Hamas is not a benevolent association. They are a brutal, violent terror group, who has no time for minority populations (forget women's rights or any rights for LGBTQ people). What does it mean to support Palestinians without supporting Hamas' rule in Gaza? Alternatively, what does it mean to support Israel without supporting its military occupation or, in the past few months, the bombing and the war in Gaza?

In this book I explore how debate about Israel matters for Jewish identity. I discuss how open debate about Israel in Jewish communities is often problematic because it is difficult to identify when debate crosses the line into antisemitism. The legacy of Jewish communities not confronting this challenge directly, and often failing to support or at least acknowledge different viewpoints about Israel respectfully created a longer-term problem. Israel was ostensibly supposed to help bring the Jewish people together, and instead it has been tearing Jewish communities apart.

I argue that one of the reasons why debate about Israel is so divisive is because at issue in such discussions is not so much Israel, but Jewish identity. This dynamic has a clear demographic angle, with older generations being more inclined to support Israel unilaterally, and younger generations being either uninterested (it's too divisive and complicated so why get involved) or more likely to side with Palestinians due to Israel's aggressive security policies. The important decolonisation agenda also plays a role here. Israel is one manifestation of a settler-colonial state. The normative inference follows from how the decolonial agenda means questioning Israel's right to exist. In this vein, we've seen multiple news stories emerge of young Jewish activists finding themselves more comfortable waiving Palestinian flags than Israeli ones. I suspect that the debate about Israel in Jewish communities is changing in a way that is likely to change the role that Israel poses for future generations of Diaspora Jews.

This book does not provide answers to negotiating Jewish diaspora politics in light of the October 7th massacre and Operation Swords of Iron. But it was my best effort to try to make sense out of the often paradoxical and confusing ways that Israel informs Diasporic Jewish identity.

Introduction

I grew up with a strong attachment to a country that I did not know very well. Nevertheless, as I learned more about Zionism and Jewish history I became a committed Zionist (albeit one who felt that logically, if I argued for the right of Jewish self-determination, I could not simultaneously reject the right of self-determination for the Palestinians). What eventually came to interest me was how I was to explain this connection with Israel, a country I could not vote in, did not live in and whose language I was not fluent in. I eventually encountered the view that to be a Jew meant supporting Israel, that being a good Jew meant being a Zionist. But over time this position became increasingly problematic. I found it difficult to explain the connection, one that seemed to come with an obligatory duty to support Israel, or at least an obligation to feel a connection to Israel. Questions arose about what it meant to support a country whose political future I have no say in as a Diaspora Jew. The questions became all the more pronounced the more I learned about Israel's history. Many Jews feel the same way, and often are uncomfortable with what such an obligation can mean, in no small part because of concerns over being identified with Israel because of one's Jewish heritage or because of the overwhelming significance that Israel has come to have for Jewish identity.

Israel's significance is matched by how much is published about Israel. Increasingly, this literature is not only about trying to explain Israel's wars, the military occupation or other parts of its history, but about the relationship between Diaspora[1] Jewry and Israel. One influential critique of this relationship is Peter Beinart's 2010 article in the *New York Review of Books*, where he commented on the failure of American Jewry to engage in any healthy debate about Israeli policy and about what it means to be a liberal American Zionist. One of the more telling passages in the article occurs when he writes:

> Morally, American Zionism is in a downward spiral. If the leaders of groups like AIPAC and the Conference of Presidents of Major American Jewish Organizations do not change course, they will wake up one day to find a younger, Orthodox-dominated, Zionist leadership whose naked hostility to Arabs and Palestinians scares even them, and a mass of secular American Jews who range from apathetic to appalled. Saving liberal Zionism in the United States – so that American Jews can help save liberal Zionism in Israel – is the great American Jewish challenge of our age.[2]

What lies behind this critique is the question of what it means to be a liberal Diaspora (American) Jew and have a connection with Israel. In the same piece Beinart writes: "Not only does the organized American Jewish community mostly avoid public criticism of the Israeli government, it tries to prevent others from levelling such criticism as well."[3] The consequence of this has been a detachment of young, non-religious, liberal Jews from Israel. They are just not that interested. But for Beinart and many others, this itself is a serious problem. They should be interested. They should care. Jews should care. At which one might ask, why?

As I tried to answer this question the word "obligation" kept coming to mind. The common answers usually have to do with how Israel is the only Jewish state, how it is an important place historically, how it plays an important part for Jewish peoplehood, and so on. These seem to be good answers. However, the Diaspora is also important historically. Why lessen its significance in relation to a country that, when it was in the process of establishing itself, had to force Jews to immigrate because not enough Jews wanted to go to, let alone fight in, Palestine?[4] Jerusalem has always been an important religious and cultural city for the Jews, but does that justify the human rights violations toward others? What about the alternative Zionist discourses that can be found in the works of Hannah Arendt, Martin Buber, Judah Magnes and others? Why not take alternatives more seriously? Does the Jewish historian Simon Dubnow's Jewish nationalism no longer have any relevance? Do all the Jewish critical voices about Zionism need to be silenced or marginalized simply because Israel exists? At what peril has been the all-too-often uncritical acceptance of Louis Brandeis' view that to be a good Jew means becoming a Zionist?

In the opening paragraph of the first chapter of one of the few best-sellers about theoretical physics, Stephen Hawking, who in 2013 attracted some controversy by boycotting an Israeli conference,[5] writes:

> A well-known scientist (some say it was Bertrand Russell) once gave a public lecture on astronomy. He described how the earth orbits around the sun and how the sun, in turn, orbits around the center of a vast collection of stars called our galaxy. At the end of the lecture, a little old lady at the back of the room got up and said: "What you have told us is rubbish. The world is really a flat plate supported on the back of a giant tortoise." The scientist gave a superior smile before replying. "What is the tortoise standing on?" "You're very clever, young man, very clever," said the old lady. "But it's turtles all the way down!"[6]

For each of the traditional answers explaining Israel's significance for Diaspora Jewry, there is always another turtle, many of which were revealed by the so-called revisionist historians. These historians, such as Avi Shlaim and Benny Morris, among others, contributed widely to challenging many of the traditional answers, and the many myths that underpinned Israel's moral stature as a place Jews everywhere could be proud of. The pride is still there, but so too are grave concerns, and not just about the military occupation or that Israel is not so innocent after all, but about Israel potentially becoming a Jewish theocracy.

There is without doubt great intensity surrounding the Jewish Diaspora's connections with Israel, which have to do with how Israel has come to function as an important part of Jewish identity. Historically, however, Israel's significance has not always been as pronounced as it has become. In particular, the catalyst that publicly revealed the extent of Israel's importance for Diaspora Jewry was the Six Day War in June 1967.

Jacqueline Levine, of the American Jewish Congress, has said that "Israel made us all stand a little taller in 1967."[7] Not only did Jews stand taller, they also gave, and at an unprecedented level. The scope of Diaspora generosity was staggering:

> A United Jewish Appeal luncheon which netted $15,000,000 in fifteen minutes, individuals who took bank loans or cashed in life insurance policies in order to make contributions, young children who rang doorbells and donated their savings, contributions from Jewish soldiers in

Vietnam ... The International Ladies Garment Workers Union purchased $1,000,000 in Israeli bonds; Mount Sinai Hospital in New York offered to pay the salary of doctors who went to serve in Israel.[8]

By the war's end, over a million US dollars had been raised.[9] In order to help the Israeli economy recover from the war, the United Jewish Appeal in the USA raised in six months $307 million, "more than double the UJA's total for the entire year before."[10] There are even stories of Jews liquidating their bank accounts and mortgaging their homes in order to donate.[11]

H. H. Ben-Sasson also highlights the role played by the Six Day War in solidifying Israel's place in modern Jewish identity and Jewish history:

> The most profound change [in the relations between Israel and the Diaspora] occurred as a result of the Six Day War, when it transpired that Israel was standing alone and that her sole ally was the Jewish people throughout the world. The demonstrations organized by Diaspora Jews, their volunteering to fight, their generous response in mobilizing funds, their grave concern for Israel's fate reawakened the sense of a common destiny. In the Diaspora, there was a resurgence of interest in Judaism and in Jews, their culture and history ...
>
> The Yom Kippur War, despite its different outcome, did not change this basic tendency. Most Israelis, as well as most Jews in the Diaspora, began to realize that the factors uniting Jews all over the world were more numerous and more binding than they had assumed – and perhaps even more binding than the founders of the Jewish national movement themselves had ever imagined.[12]

The general conclusion is that Israel is what binds the Jews together. That the bond was cemented out of a war is in itself significant, as it contributes to the militarized notion of power that political and revisionist Zionism held as crucial in remaking the modern Jew and which has since become one cause of Diaspora alienation. Nevertheless, a great bond was formed,[13] which remains. Stephen J. Whitfield, in the final chapter to David Biale's edited three-volume work *Cultures of the Jews*, writes:

> After the Six Day War of 1967 support for Israel became the *sine qua non* of [American] Jewish communal affairs and leadership, so that an

agnostic or even an atheist became more acceptable as an attribute of, say, a synagogue president than an anti-Zionist.[14]

The idea that the president of a synagogue need not have any religious leanings but must be a Zionist is in some ways amusing, although mainly tragic, but it accurately reflects the extremity to which support for Israel has come in defining Jewish identity.

As in politics, however, active Diaspora participation in Israel-centered activities is probably not as widespread as could be inferred from the role it plays in the construction of Jewish identity.[15] In some ways, it does not matter that it is a relatively small number in the Diaspora who speak out on behalf of Diaspora/Israel relations. Israel may be a regular topic of discussion over dinner, but this has not translated into widespread political engagement even though Israel's existence has significantly redefined the meaning of contemporary Jewish Diaspora identity. The amount of news-space, in the Jewish media and elsewhere, taken up with Israel most likely misrepresents the extent to which everyday Jews actively involve themselves in Israeli activism. However, it accurately reflects just as it constructs the extent to which Israel has come to inform contemporary Diaspora identity.

Israel's importance for Jewish identity is a sociological factor to take seriously. But why is Israel so important and what does its importance mean? How are we to explain the character of this connection? What are the limits of this connection?

These are not new questions, and some tentative answers can be found in David Vital's short book from over two decades ago, *The Future of the Jews*. Vital, who has written extensively on Zionism, modern European Jewish history and international relations more generally, argues that the Diaspora and Israel are heading in different directions.[16] The book is in some ways out of date, but in others Vital raises core points that remain relevant. One of the main claims in the book is that what the authorities in Israel say or do impacts the "lives and fortunes" of Diaspora Jewish communities.[17] Vital identifies defense policy first and foremost, but also public policy regarding marriage and divorce.[18] Significantly, he highlights the importance of "the question to what extent, and in what sense, policy made by the government of Israel is in fact and in principle policy for Jewry as a whole."[19] He recognizes that there is a connection between Israeli policy and Diaspora public life, pertaining to security and representation, but the connection is not always clear.

Note for example, how not too long ago the Israeli Ministry of Foreign Affairs affirmed Israel's centrality for world Jewry and Israel's role in helping to strengthen and protect the Jewish Diaspora:

> World Jewry, in recognition of the centrality of Israel in Jewish life, participates in building the country, through social, political and financial support, as well as by coming to Israel, making it their home and adding their particular skills and cultural backgrounds to the Israeli mosaic. A long tradition of mutual aid among Jews is manifested in a multifaceted network of organizations designed to cater to hundreds of Jewish-Israeli interests. For its part, Israel constantly seeks to strengthen the Jewish communities and its bond with them by helping those in need, promoting Israel-oriented activities, Hebrew language study, economic opportunities and visits of groups and individuals to Israel.
>
> The State of Israel actively attaches high importance to the security of Jewish communities all over the world.[20]

These kinds of political statements mask more than they reveal. First, world Jewry does not view itself as existing to support Israel. Second, it is self-serving for Israel to define itself both as central to all Jewish life and as providing security for all Jewish communities. Third, it provides a revision to the original Zionist negation of Diaspora by identifying a history of mutual aid and in suggesting a strong connection between Diaspora and Israel that the Jewish State values and recognizes. The extent to which Israeli policy actually reflects this revision in practice is open to debate since the wide range of Diaspora voices regarding Israel cannot all be responded to, and as those voices are not of Israeli citizens, there is a political structure that legitimates selective hearing with regard to which areas of Diaspora concern Israel responds to.

Further complicating the issue is that there exists much greater Jewish diversity in a religious sense outside of Israel than inside, which leads to significant political battles. In this vein, the Ministry also lists on its website the role of the World Zionist Organization, that serves as the liaison between Israel and the Diaspora, and the Jewish Agency, an organization that plays a crucial role for *aliya*[21] and other Diaspora activities geared toward fostering greater connection with Israel. The Agency's chairman is Natan Sharansky. The neo-conservative Sharansky has held multiple posts in the Knesset, including Minister of Industry and Trade, Minister of Internal Affairs, Deputy Prime Minister, Minister of Housing and Construction, and Minister of Jerusalem Affairs. In his role as chairman, he has been very active in trying to prevent Jewish assimilation.[22] He also came to the defense of the Jewish women's group, Women of the Wall, who argue for equal religious rights for women to pray at the Wailing Wall in Jerusalem.[23]

For Vital, the point is that while the Diaspora/Israel relationship is a strong one, or at least an emotionally intense one, there is a significant difference between Diaspora Jewry and Israel. The stronghold of Jewish Orthodoxy in Israel is one example. However, he frames the question in different terms that are quite revealing, as he writes:

> Still, national loyalty (and its consequent obligations to state, country, and legitimate government) as a matter of primary, *which is not to say exclusive*, obligation in all but utterly exceptional circumstances remains an accepted sociopolitical imperative in virtually all modern societies . . ."[24]

Note how he recognizes that there exist other types of political obligations than those defined by citizenship. In addition, while he makes a distinction between loyalty and obligation, he suggests that loyalty leads to obligation, and that this loyalty *qua* obligation exists in all modern societies, not just states. The mention of societies is important, because he continues a few lines later:

> But what constitutes exceptional circumstances? That hard question is certainly one that admits of no simple answer. Moreover, the particular matter of Jewish loyalty to Israel, or to Jewry as a whole, cannot fail to be in many ways much more complex than a straightforward conflict between obligations to country of residence and citizenship, on the one hand, and obligations (if any) to community and kin, on the other, would normally suggest.[25]

This statement is key. It is not the question of exceptional circumstances that matters, but what kind of obligation it is that explains the loyalty *qua* obligation that exists between the Diaspora, Israel, and world Jewry, respectively. It is trying to get to grips with the character and quality of this relationship that animates the theoretical content of this book.

Vital correctly points out that the boundaries of Jewry are not clear. "Jewry has no formal boundaries; its informal boundaries are subject to constant movement, change and debate."[26] He argues that the reason for the absence of such boundaries is the lack of a Jewish authority:

> There is no person, group, or institution competent to represent it in its entirety, let alone capable of doing so in practice, because, of course, there is no central authority governing it. But more: there is no agreement about what constitutes the Jewish national interest . . .[27]

This analysis remains perceptive, albeit problematic. Recently, Donniel Hartman, of the Shalom Hartman Institute in Jerusalem, has used Jewish law to attempt to answer part of this question and provide an explanation of what the boundaries of Judaism are. Hartman suggests a two-pronged "boundary policy." The first is an a priori presumption of loyalty to uphold the boundaries of the community. The second is a logical argument that he hopes will make it possible to overcome the generally intransigent divide between Orthodox Jewry and the rest. This second prerequisite is "the decision to apply the category of intolerable deviance descriptively and not prescriptively. That which is classified as intolerable must be shaped by the living reality that is the Jewish people."[28] Hartman adds a few additional features to his boundary-making theory, including that it be based on using "various *halakhic* vehicles that enable mutual accommodation."[29] In essence, his argument is about trying to present a case for the Orthodox to become less strict and more tolerant of other Jewish communities. While I am skeptical about the extent to which this goal is possible, what is really interesting is where Hartman starts with his question about Jewish boundaries:

> In cities across North America, Jews from all denominational movements unite to march together at Israel Day Parades, but those same denominational rabbis will not share a public platform or sit on a shared rabbinic council, lest it be perceived that by doing so one is granting legitimacy to the other. Jews across the globe unite, but rarely share everyday ritual and holiday services together.[30]

Note how he begins with the shared Jewish experience of participating in the Diaspora in an Israel-focused activity. In one significant way, his argument is similar to that provided by Vital. Both identify Israel as a unifying element for Diaspora Jewish identity.

Both also presume that there exists a Jewish people, a world Jewry, that has some identifiable boundaries and shared loyalties, and that these boundaries are threatened. Vital sees the threat as a consequence of Israeli and Diaspora Jews having different interests and holding different political loyalties. Hartman sees the threat in increasing Jewish intra-communal conflict. "The sad state of contemporary Jewish boundary policies," he writes, "is that instead of serving to unite the Jewish people, they merely serve to separate Orthodoxy from the rest."[31] A significant part of the problem here is the influence of Orthodox Jewry in Israel and that Israel matters hugely for Jewish identity, with Hartman regretfully acknowledging that Israel has replaced Judaism as the tie that binds.

Vital and Hartman see a similar problem, the fragmentation of modern Jewry, but they approach it from different angles. Hartman's is ultimately a *halakhic* argument, which does not concern me here, whereas Vital's is political. Where Vital's argument loses traction, however, is in his uncritical framing of political space and of how it is authority that necessarily enables boundaries.

Diaspora politics do not function according to the same assumptions about authority, politics and boundaries that guide the conventional traditions of political thought which are modeled on, in the words of Michel Foucault, "the juridical monarchy."[32] As Foucault writes, "In political thought and analysis, we still have not cut off the head of the king."[33] In the Diaspora there are multiple authorities, few spatial boundaries and a diffusion of varied power relations, and it is these unique characters of diaspora that have led to radical attempts at articulating a uniquely Jewish and diasporic ethics.[34] The Jewish nationalism of the nineteenth century equally reflects an alternative to Zionism, in this case a pluralistic view of political identity and political spaces that does not wed the idea of the nation to that of the state.[35]

Vital's assumptions about politics create some avoidable difficulties. For him, the difference between Diaspora and Israel is that they are separate worlds. There is "no symmetry," he writes, between Diaspora political life and Israel.[36] He wants to tell two stories: one of how important Israel is for the Diaspora and one of how Jews everywhere are susceptible to compulsions of loyalty and obligation to each other, regardless of citizenship. But he also claims that, "Governments, the Jewish government among them, have powers of compulsion. The great majority of Jews in Israel bear loyalty to their government. The great majority of Jews elsewhere bear loyalty to other governments."[37] Vital sees the political world divided into states, and thus while he recognizes the reality of a complex transnational relationship he cannot explain it, nor even define it, for it defies the boundaries of his international framework. For Vital, Israel has power, like a state does, while the Diaspora is powerless. However, the Diaspora is not powerless,[38] but claiming that it is provides Vital with an excuse not to pursue the more complex problem: "the particular matter of Jewish loyalty to Israel, or to Jewry as a whole."[39]

Yet Vital may suspect that his framing of the problem cannot get to a solution. Israel, he writes, is located

> at the center of one of the great international whirlpools of our time (into which Jews everywhere have been sucked to some extent), and the fear, the love, the hatred, the admiration, and the dislike it evokes variously and sometimes simultaneously – all these have tended to involve the Jews outside Israel, and beyond its formal jurisdiction, in its affairs; in spirit and in fact, for good and for ill. The government of Israel therefore sustains a relationship with world Jewry to which none of the accepted and conventional political categories are applicable, for which there are no true precedents, and which evokes joy, dismay, comfort, and dread – again variously and sometimes simultaneously – as the case may be: too weak and indeterminate a relationship for some, too strong and binding a relationship for others.[40]

As Sharansky recently told the board of governors at the Jewish Agency, "It is increasingly clear that world Jewry depends on Israel and Israel depends on world Jewry."[41] However, as J. J. Goldberg correctly and astutely points out, "'increasingly clear' it's not."[42] "Clarity" is not the word that comes to mind when trying to understand the Jewish Diaspora's relationship with Israel.

Introduction

Situating Israel: The Jewish Diaspora and Israel Today

On February 26, 2014, *The Jewish Daily Forward* published a news report entitled "Feud over Israel Erupts at Jewish Institutions." The article reported on three examples of museums and schools canceling appearances by Rashid Khalidi, Judith Butler and John Judis because of their views pertaining to Israel. The article stated:

> A debate is raging in the Jewish world about what constitutes acceptable discourse on Israel. And these events, occurring within days of each other in mid-February, seemed to underline the urgency of an issue coming to a head as never before: What speakers are appropriate at Jewish institutions that purport to be devoted to serious intellectual inquiry?[43]

The article also commented on the increasing debate on university campuses in Hillel and Jewish associations about who may speak at a Hillel event.

The issues raised in the article suggest that Jewish youth do not feel that they are educated appropriately about Israel, feeling that instead of an education they are getting an indoctrination so that they can engage in Israel advocacy. The article went on to quote Steven M. Cohen, a sociologist who focuses on the American Jewish community. According to Cohen, "the disputes will only get worse as demographic change brings in a new generation." As he said, there is

> a general shift among young people away from support for the policies of the Israeli government, albeit with support for Israel ... The conventional communal leadership in the U.S. has only two compartments. One is pro-Israel and the other is anti-Israel. So it's hard for them to understand that there's a third compartment: pro-Israel, critical of its policies.[44]

In a sense, too much debate about Israel seems to represents a threat to the conventional communal Jewish leadership that Cohen refers to. Otherwise, there would not be a story about Jewish institutions canceling public talks. In one case that the article reports on, the head of a Jewish School in New York argued that having the Columbia Professor Rashid Khalidi speak to his students was problematic because Khalidi is too much of an expert to be able to engage in a fair discussion with less educated students. I find this argument to be deeply troublesome, but personal concerns aside, the gist of the issue here appears to be that at least some supposed leaders of the Jewish community view too much debate and too much openness to ulterior views as threatening. What exactly the threat is can be a bit unclear, although it has something to do with how a positive connection to Israel is assumed to be a crucial part of contemporary Diaspora Jewish identity.

Part of the problem here is that the view from the major Jewish organizations does not reflect the growing alienation and sometimes antipathy felt by Diaspora Jews toward Israel. In interviews conducted between 2008 and 2012, it was not uncommon to hear leading Jewish representatives of the American Jewish Congress, the American Jewish Committee, and others in religious organizations, such as the United Synagogue of Conservative Judaism, either openly state or infer that there could be no greater calamity to the Jews today than if Israel were to be destroyed. In the words of Rabbi Steven Wernick, the Chief Executive Officer of the United Synagogue of Conservative Judaism, "If Israel were to disappear it would be a disaster for the Jews everywhere."[45] Israel's centrality for Jewish identity is also evident in the amount of money and resources dedicated to the Taglit-Birthright program, a program that takes young Jews to Israel in order to "strengthen Jewish identity."[46]

Israel is never far away in the Jewish world. Whether it is the European Jewish Congress or the Conference of Presidents of Major American Jewish Organizations, Israel always has a presence and has become an especially important part of Diaspora Jewish identity. Yet, Israel clearly has different meanings to different people and not all Jews respond to Israel in the same way. The American Jewish Population Survey by Pew both confirms and questions the importance of Israel for Jewish identity (Tables 1–4). On the one hand, it reveals that less than half of all Jews believe that supporting Israel is essential to being Jewish, although age and religiosity are important variables. On the other hand, it also points out how caring about Israel and having a sense of humour are both more important for being Jewish than observing Jewish law.[47]

The Pew Survey's findings generated significant controversy, although not all was deemed to be doom and gloom. As Bethamie Horowitz, a sociologist who conducted a similar population study

Introduction

Table 1 Connection to Israel

	NET Jewish	Jews by religion	Jews of no religion	Jewish background	Jewish affinity
	%	%	%	%	%
How emotionally attached are you to Israel?					
Very attached	30	36	12	21	26
Somewhat	39	40	33	37	43
Not too/not at all	31	23	55	41	30
Don't know/Refused	1	1	*	*	2
	100	100	100	100	100
Have you ever traveled to Israel?					
Yes	43	49	23	13	9
No	57	51	77	86	91
Don't know/Refused	*	*	0	1	0
	100	100	100	100	100
Is the U.S. ___ toward Israel?					
Too supportive	11	7	27	16	9
Not supportive enough	31	35	17	37	41
About right	54	56	50	40	41
Don't know/Refused	3	3	6	7	10
	100	100	100	100	100

Source: Pew Research Center 2013 Survey of U.S. Jews, February 20–June 13, 2013.
QG2, QG3, QC2. Figures may not sum to 100% due to rounding.
PEW RESEARCH CENTER

in New York in 1991, remarked, the survey offered much to be positive about and the immediately pessimistic reactions were indicative of an old joke about a Jewish telegram: "Start worrying. Details to follow."[48] Yet, the report's detailed findings were concerning enough for the Jewish Federation of North America President Jerry Silverman and Board Chairman Michael Siegal to write a response that highlighted the need to improve Jews' connections with Israel by building on the success of Birthright.[49]

What the Pew Survey demonstrates is that for American Jews, Israel remains important, although less important for some Jewish demographics than others and less important than the major Jewish organizations would like. In the UK, it is worth pointing out, a similar survey yielded a different result, with "81% of British Jews [feeling] a strong or moderate attachment to Israel."[50]

Obligation in Exile

Table 2 Attachment, attitudes about Israel

	NET Jewish %	Jews by religion %	Jews of no religion %
How emotionally attached are you to Israel?			
Very attached	30	36	12
Somewhat	39	40	33
Not very/Not at all	31	23	55
Don't know/Refused	1	1	*
	100	100	100
Been to Israel?			
Yes	43	49	23
No	57	51	77
Don't know	*	*	0
	100	100	100
Impact of continued building of Jewish settlements on Israel's security			
Helps	17	19	9
Hurts	44	40	56
Makes no difference	29	31	21
Don't know	11	10	14
	100	100	100
Believe God gave Israel to Jewish people?			
Yes	40	47	16
No	27	27	27
Don't know	5	6	3
Don't believe in God*	28	20	55
	100	100	100

Source: Pew Research Center 2013 Survey of U.S. Jews, February 20–June 13, 2013. Figures may not sum to 100% due to rounding.
"Includes those who said "don't know" or declined to answer when asked whether they believe in God. For more details, see table on belief in God on page 74.
PEW RESEARCH CENTER

The historian Noam Pianko writes that "the perceived equivalence of the State of Israel with the nation of Israel remains deeply embedded in popular consciousness and Jewish studies."[51] Intellectually and politically, Israel continues to exercise, if not an overbearing presence on Jewish identity, then a significant one. The poles of extreme Jewish attitudes toward Israel play an important role in the discourses of contemporary Jewish Diaspora life and in what it means to be Jewish. Supporting Israel is often associated

Table 3 What's essential to being Jewish?

% saying ___ is an essential part of religion (what being Jewish means to them)	NET Jewish %	Jews by religion %	Jews of no religion %
Remembering the Holocaust	73	76	60
Leading an ethical and moral life	69	73	55
Working for justice/equality	56	60	46
Being intellectually curious	49	51	42
Caring about Israel	43	49	23
Having good sense of humor	42	43	40
Being part of a Jewish community	28	33	10
Observing Jewish law	19	23	7
Eating traditional Jewish foods	14	16	9

Source: Pew Research Center 2013 Survey of U.S. Jews, February 20–June 13, 2013. Q.E5a-i. PEW RESEARCH CENTER

with being a good Jew, the inverse being that a Jew who is overly critical of Israel may be self-hating, or at least has no respect for Jewish peoplehood. These extremes play out repeatedly in public debates but also in Jewish literature.

The Man Booker Prize-winning novel by Howard Jacobson, *The Finkler Question*, reveals especially clearly the extremes of this debate, with some characters representing the support-Israel-at-all-costs stance, and others taking the Israel-is-a-human-rights-violating-racist-regime position. While these positions and the characters that hold them are in some respects caricatures, it is hard not to suspect that one of reasons for this novel winning the Man Booker Prize is precisely because a Jewish author aired out debates which many in the Jewish community feel should be kept private, and which, when articulated publicly, especially by non-Jews, are viewed as potentially anti-Semitic.

In Jacobson's novel, the two leading characters, Finkler and Libor, regularly debate Israel and the Middle East. They cannot separate their Jewish identity from the security politics of Israel, or, for that matter, from the security politics of Jewish history. Libor would often raise the Holocaust as a defense clause supporting Israel, and he would attack any Jew who is critical of Israel as being self-hating. The novel repeats this circle of debate almost endlessly. For Libor, Israel provides a "lifeboat position." As he says, "No, I've never been there and don't want to go there, but even at my

Table 4 Essentials of Jewish identity

	Remembering Holocaust %	Leading ethical life %	Working for justice/equality %	Being intellectually curious %	Caring about Israel %	Sense of humor %	Being part of Jewish community %	Observing Jewish law %	Eating Jewish foods %
NET Jewish	73	69	56	49	43	42	28	19	14
Men	70	61	51	45	39	39	24	16	12
Women	75	76	62	53	46	44	32	23	17
Ages 18–49	69	66	51	47	35	38	28	21	18
18–29	68	65	55	49	32	39	26	20	15
30–49	69	66	48	45	38	38	29	21	20
Ages 50+	77	71	61	51	49	45	28	18	11
50–64	76	73	61	50	47	43	28	18	11
65+	77	69	62	54	53	47	29	19	12
College grad+	74	73	56	54	43	39	26	15	11
Post-grad degree	73	74	57	55	41	34	24	13	11
BA/BS	74	73	56	53	45	43	28	17	11
Some college	74	63	56	44	44	45	27	21	17
HS or less	68	60	58	40	39	48	35	32	23
Orthodox	66	80	51	35	55	34	69	79	51
Ultra-Orthodox	65	78	46	25	45	33	70	82	60
Modern Orthodox	74	90	61	54	79	39	71	78	40
Conservative	78	69	58	48	58	41	40	24	18
Reform	77	75	62	52	42	42	25	11	9
No denomination	67	59	51	50	31	46	13	8	6

Source: Pew Research Center 2013 Survey of U.S. Jews, February 20–June 13, 2013. Q.E5a-i.
PEW RESEARCH CENTER

age the time might not be far away when I have nowhere else *to* go. That is history's lesson."⁵²

I heard this argument many times as I learned about Zionism, but it was not one I had heard for some time. A veteran peace activist and current volunteer also told me he had not heard this argument for some time either, and does not consider it to be an especially strong one.⁵³ Yet, a young woman who also volunteers for J Street was using precisely this argument.⁵⁴ Libor, the fictional character, is not young, and his historical consciousness would surely be different from that of a twenty-something (non-fictional) New Yorker. Nevertheless, the fictional debates in *The Finkler Question* largely replicate those taking place in the Jewish world, and do so almost verbatim, even if the arguments are not good ones.

The characters Finkler and Libor display a deep level of anxiety in their debates around Israel, so much so that it is a third party, Treslove, who is able to describe the neurosis in their debates. For Libor, the Holocaust was always central, so central that he rarely had to even mention it. "It was always possible, Treslove concluded, that Jews didn't have to mention the Holocaust in order to have mentioned the Holocaust."⁵⁵ Libor's accusations toward Finkler being a self-hating Jew also did not ring true. "Treslove had never met a Jew, in fact never met anybody, who hated himself less than Finkler."⁵⁶ Moreover, Finkler's view toward Israel was one of simultaneous disappointment (tinged with disgust) and frustration. "Treslove . . . could never quite get whether Finkler resented Israel for winning or for being about to lose."⁵⁷ For Libor the questions over Israel are one of conscience, whereas for Finkler the issue is justice. Neither of them is ever satisfied. When Finkler raises the justice question, Libor says that shame is best kept within the family, and that you can explain to your family member your shame, but you would not boycott a relative. Libor and Finkler are unable to resolve their dispute, and they both represent archetypes of contemporary debate about Israel. The other characters in the novel fit into these archetypes, modify them and supplement them. They never, however, challenge them. The terrain of the debate remains fixed between the poles of Libor and Finkler.

Occasionally, the terrain slips out of control. Finkler's son, Immanuel, gets into a fight. Finkler is led to believe that the fight was with anti-Semites. Immanuel attended a debate at the Oxford Student Union, where the topic was something along the lines of

Obligation in Exile

"This house believes that Israel has forfeited its right to exist."[58] Student unions in the UK currently have such debates. As Finkler interrogates his son, he learns that Immanuel ended up picking a fight with Jews:

> "They were Zionists. The real meshuggeners with black hats and fringes, like settlers."
> "Settlers? In Oxford?"
> "Settler types."
> "And he picked a fight with them? What did he say?"
> [Blaise, Immanuel's mother replies] "Nothing much. He accused them of stealing someone else's country . . ."
> She paused.
> "And?"
> "And practicing apartheid . . ."
> "And?"
> "And slaughtering women and children."
> "And?"
> "There is no and. That's all."
> Immanuel looked up. He reminded Finkler of his late wife, challenging him. He had that same expression of ironic unillusionedness that comes with knowing a person too well. "Yes, that's what I said. It's true, isn't it? You've said so much yourself."
> "Not specifically, to a person, Immanuel. It's one thing to iterate a general political truth, it's another thing to pick a fight with a person in the street."
> "Well, I'm not a philosopher, Dad. I don't iterate general political truths. I just told them all what I thought of them and their shitty little country and called one of them, who came up to me, a racist."
> "A racist? What had he said to you?"
> "Nothing. It wasn't about him. I was talking about his country."
> "Was he an Israeli?"
> "How do I know? He wore a black hat. He was there to oppose the motion."[59]

Finkler ends up being furious at his son for provoking this physical fight. Yet as his son points out, his argument was not that far away from Finkler's. While a significant portion of the exchange involves the complications of the father/son relationship, there are other ingredients as well. Jacobson's novel reveals the emotions and strongly held beliefs that influence Jewish affinity with or Jewish alienation from Israel, as well as the assumption that links being Jewish, in this case Orthodox, with being either an Israeli or the equivalent, which is (apparently) to be a Zionist Jew. Significantly, the phrase "shitty little country" is an allusion to a remark made by the French ambassador to London in 2001, Mr Daniel Bernard, to the then owner of *The Daily Telegraph* but now disgraced media baron Conrad Black. The novel reflects the public discourse and private assumptions that frame so much contemporary debate about Israel. In this discourse, Israel is not only never far away in the Jewish world, it also often holds an overbearing presence.

It is, however, not just the importance of Israel in the construction of contemporary Jewish identity that is at issue, but the implications of this importance. Israel-centered discussions have a tendency to steer toward the extreme and the intolerant. The existence of such groups as Campus Watch,[60] that seek to monitor Israeli-related activities, educational or otherwise, on university campuses, is one example of the kind of surveillance practices that some Jewish communities feel are necessary in order to fight the so-called propaganda war and protect their interests. Concerns over Israel take an especially important place in Jewish discourse, which ranges from extreme right-wing views to extreme left-wing views, with these often having incommensurable qualities.

In the Diaspora, one of the more public illustrations of such a debate is that between the political scientist Norman Finkelstein and the legal scholar and lawyer Alan Dershowitz. The often *ad hominem* exchanges between Finkelstein and Dershowitz are an example not just of a debate about academic integrity and academic freedom, but of how debates about Israel can take on extreme and over-inflated rhetoric, matched perhaps only by the egos of those wielding the verbal swords. Challenging Dershowitz's work in *The Case for Israel*, in *Beyond Chutzpah* Finkelstein writes:

> It can fairly be said that *The Case for Israel* surpasses *From Time Immemorial* in its deceitfulness and is among the most spectacular academic frauds ever published on the Israel–Palestine conflict. Indeed, Dershowitz appropriates large swaths from the Peters hoax. Whereas Peters falsified real sources, Dershowitz goes one better and cites absurd sources or stitches evidence out of whole cloth ... I demonstrate that it's difficult to find a single claim in his human rights chapter or, for

that matter, any other chapter of *The Case for Israel* that, among other things, doesn't distort a reputable source or reference a preposterous one.[61]

Dershowitz has responded in a variety of ways, but his claiming that Finkelstein sits comfortably with Holocaust deniers and labeling Finkelstein a self-hating Jews provides a flavor of their exchanges.[62]

The very public debate between Finkelstein and Dershowitz – which spilled over into Finkelstein's denial of tenure at DePaul University[63] – is in some ways the precise kind of extreme position that Jacobson depicts in his novel. The intensity of these debates reflects ideologically driven positions, whereby those who do not share in one's normative view of the world are participants in the destruction of how the world ought to be. Yet, at issue in debates about Israel is also something else, something more personal.

What is it, for example, about questioning Israel's human rights record that makes others think it is appropriate to call such a critic a self-hating Jew? It is all the more surprising how vitriolic and emotional these debates get in the Diaspora when we pause to consider the views from Israel. One recent poll claims that while Israelis do not view their country as an apartheid state, they would not mind if it became one.[64] Another has demonstrated that a majority of Israelis find that Israeli foreign policy is too reactive and relies too much on American support.[65] Debate about such matters in Israel is a matter of course and, while it is not always pleasant, it is in a sense more open than it is in the Diaspora where there is a tendency to challenge debate and to take extreme positions that are emblematic of not living with the consequences of one's preferred policies.[66]

If one turns to one of Finkelstein's more recent works, *Knowing Too Much: Why the American Jewish Romance with Israel Is Coming to an End*, it becomes clearer that what is taking place in the American-Jewish Diaspora is a potential crisis in its relationship with Israel. Finkelstein opens the book by quoting Rabbi Shira Milgrom, a rabbi at Congregation Kol Ami in White Plains, New York. She says:

> Once it was easy, when everyone had their head in the sand and didn't understand the situation. There are still people who want to talk only about Exodus and "the only democracy in the Middle East," but younger Jews, students, grew up on other stories, and they have a very

tough conflict between the Israel they know and their sense of Jewish ethics.[67]

Zionists have for years used the Passover celebration as a reference points for how Israel has never been far from the hearts of Jews everywhere, and the religious settler movement has taken the religious connection with Israel into a political agenda that many find disturbing and destructive.[68] Yet what Rabbi Milgrom is getting at is something different, something that Peter Beinart echoes.[69] There does exist a deep connection between being Jewish in the Diaspora and the State of Israel, but the older generation is holding on to views which are difficult to sustain and which are being questioned by younger generations.

Be that is it may, as the former editor of *The Jewish Daily Forward*, J. J. Goldberg, told me in one of our interviews, for some it is remarkably easy to understand this relationship because it is a case in point of a global diasporic community having an overriding loyalty to its homeland. Dual loyalty is one example of how such a relationship can manifest itself,[70] and has come up a few times with regard to Diaspora Jews, most recently in the Prisoner X scandal (in which an Australian Jew committed suicide in an Israeli maximum security prison where he was ostensibly being held for crimes pertaining to espionage and treason). According to Goldberg, the reason for the Mossad recruiting this man was that as an Australian he had a passport that allowed him to travel to places into which an Israeli passport would make entry difficult. Israel, among others, has used forged Canadian passports for the same reason.[71] Disturbingly, one consequence of the Prisoner X scandal has been that in Argentina Jews have recently been accused of loyalty toward Israel and disloyalty to the Argentinian state.[72] The relationship Diaspora Jews have with Israel is nothing if not fraught with uncertainty and complexity, and is often influenced by Israeli security practices and the potential implications of these practices for Diaspora Jews.

These implications can vary, from concerns about Israel making the world more dangerous for Jews to feeling that for a Diaspora Jew who does not live in Israel it is wrong to tell Israelis what to do. However, while there is a large amount of published work on Israel, and increasing numbers of works by Jewish scholars who critique Israeli policy, there is surprisingly less work on how Israel functions in the construction of contemporary Jewish identity. Most of the time, the pattern is simply to state Israel's importance, often by suggesting that Israel represents the culmination of Jewish history. An example is H. H. Ben-Sasson's edited tome *A History of Jewish People*, first published in 1969, which ends with a chapter about Israel. Apparently, Jewish history stops with Israel, since before Israel the Jews were a Diaspora people and were defined by this condition, while after 1948 they have not. A similar inference is in Irving M. Zeitlin's sociological history of the Jewish Diaspora, *Jews: The Making of a Diaspora People*,[73] which ends with the creation of the State of Israel.

The last chapter is about Zionism, with the last words of the book being about the need for peace in the Middle East. Perhaps Zeitlin ends with Zionism because anything past that point is still in the process of being written, and with the creation of Israel the Jewish Diaspora ceased to hold its unique stateless quality that had defined it for around two thousand years. Yet Zeitlin's book is recent (published in 2012), and so surely he could at least have also addressed the changing character of the Diaspora/Israel relationship since 1948. The implied suggestion from how he ends his book is that while a Jewish Diaspora remains post-1948, it is so qualitatively different from what came before that the making of the Jewish Diaspora effectively ended with Israel's creation, that emerged out of the ashes of the Second World War. Israel is, in this reading, the final stage in the Jewish Diaspora's history, which incidentally is also the claim of the famous Israeli historian Ben Zion Dinur, who wrote, "The political rebirth of Israel is the very essence of Jewish history."[74]

The preposterous nature of such an argument should be obvious, since the main Jewish communities in the Diaspora are not at risk of disappearing any time soon and cannot be defined by reference to Israel. Israel is neither the be-all and end-all of Jewish identity nor the culmination of Jewish history, as if Jews have nothing else to offer and there is no Jewish life in the Diaspora. This argument is belittling of Jewish Diaspora communities, marginalizing them and ignoring how they are important centers of Jewish life in their own right, although variations of this argument continue.[75] It is hard to believe that Zeitlin, a professor at the University of Toronto, a Jew who lives in the Diaspora, would be insulting the Jewish Diaspora. Nevertheless, the structure of his book is deeply suggestive of just how important Israel features in the making of modern Jewish identity in the Diaspora. As Arnold Eisen demonstrates, the "return" to Israel marks a significant change for a people that had previously been spatially and in some senses spiritually defined by Diaspora.[76] The assumed and argued centrality of Israel for Jewish identity is a recurring theme that I explore. It is also a theme that some have challenged. It is important, however, to remember the importance of avoiding a Whig approach to history,[77] that methodologically would emphasize the necessity of Israel and that frames any other Jewish political project, such as Jewish internationalism, as a precursor to either Jewish nationalism or Diaspora support of Israel.

What I try to do in this book is to highlight the need to think differently about the way Israel frames contemporary Jewish identity and how to understand the shadow that Israel casts on the Diaspora landscape. It is important to appreciate that accompanying Israel's importance have been equally important moves to distance a Diaspora identity from Israel, so that it remains possible to emphasize Diaspora Jewish identity without Israel.[78] This de-Israelization of Jewish Diaspora identity could be read as a return to a kind of Diaspora nationalism. The historian Simon Dubnow (1860–1941) defined this nationalism in terms of protecting Jewish identity.[79] This Diaspora nationalism was not about seeking territorial independence but about recognizing and protecting the "will to live" of the Jewish people.[80]

Nevertheless, Diaspora nationalism did not succeed along the lines hoped for by Dubnow. The nation-state model does not provide much room for a deterritorialized Diaspora nationalism, and with the creation of Israel it was only logical in the age of the nation-state that Israel would come to play a major role in the construction of Jewish identity and in public Jewish political discourse. While I do not want to make too much out of the structure of Zeitlin's book, it is worth considering why a sociological history of the Jewish Diaspora spends so little time on developments in the Diaspora in the twentieth century that are not related either to the Holocaust or to Israel. Part of the reason, I would suggest, is that it is very hard to detach the idea of Jewish identity from the history of Israel's creation and the continued presence of the Jewish State. The Jewish Diaspora is not defined by Israel, but so too it cannot be divorced from it.

Obligation in Exile

A Question of Obligation

Theories of obligation necessarily contain within them an expectation of behavior not only of the obliged but also of other people. As such, they presume an account of identity, of who these people are who are obliged in different ways. The tendency is either to explicitly link political obligation to state citizenship or to assume such a correlation. Yet, as Inderpal Grewal correctly points out, "Privileges of citizenship are extended unevenly."[81] Theorists of political obligation, however, rarely question the identity assumptions that support their theories. There is a puzzle here that warrants unpacking. The puzzle is why political obligation is seemingly unconcerned with how identity can mitigate the types of obligations that one has, and perhaps even more importantly, the types of obligations that are expected of those who are different.

It is not hard to find examples of how discourses of obligation reflect particular assumptions about specific identity-groups. On January 25, 2012, two days before Holocaust Memorial Day, the British Liberal Democratic politician and elected MP David Ward published the following statement on his website:

> Having visited Auschwitz twice – once with my family and once with local schools – I am saddened that the Jews, who suffered unbelievable levels of persecution during the Holocaust, could within a few years of liberation from the death camps be inflicting atrocities on Palestinians in the new State of Israel and continue to do so on a daily basis in the West Bank and Gaza.[82]

Within a few days he was censored by his party. He initially refused to apologize for his comments, but eventually came out with a belated and somewhat defensive apology, saying how he was not a racist and was simply making a statement of fact.[83]

Whether or not Ward's comments are anti-Semitic is not at issue. What is at issue is the correlation that he presumes exists between Jews and Israel. We might ask: what does his statement have to do with obligation? First, there is the curious judgment, one suggestive of a mild racism, that it is the Jews, not Israelis, who are the persecutors here. There is no distinction, but simply the statement of "fact" that Jews are the ones to blame. This kind of generalization neatly complements the wider discourse surrounding the so-called Jewish lobby, when it is really "Israel lobby" that is the more appropriate nomenclature. It is deeply problematic to conflate Jewish Diaspora identity with Jewish Israeli identity. There are significant sociological differences between Israeli Jews and Jews who live outside of Israel that are recognized among Jews and Israelis. For example, in 1997, an Israeli member of the Knesset, Shoshana Ben-Aviv, was quoted in a talk she gave to a Reform Jewish congregation in Canada as saying how (Jewish) Israelis and Diaspora Jews are different. Recalling this distinction, the anthropologist Jasmin Habib writes:

> Her preference was to call Diaspora Jews simply "Jews," and Israeli Jews simply "Israelis." "We are different," she insisted. "We live our lives very differently. We always have and always will. Why would you call us Jews? We are Israelis. *They* are Jews."[84]

Second, there is a kind of historical moral projectionism in David Ward's comments, also suggestive of a mild racism, that whereas Europeans were able to commit some of the worst atrocities in history, it is OK to place the Jews at a higher level of expectation and then condemn them for not living up to this higher moral standard – in essence, to hold Jews accountable today for not behaving better than Europeans have in the past. This greater expectation of Jews, or at least the correlation that is placed on the lesson of their being Holocaust victims, is that Jews should never victimize anyone else, and it is a statement that Ward has since repeated.[85] There are other points that could be raised in regard to the appropriateness of his comments, the potential one-sided nature of them, and of course the gross insensitivity of them that uses the Holocaust as a rhetorical weapon against the Jews.[86] In this sense, a disservice is done to the reality of Palestinian suffering by framing it not as a human tragedy but as a problem caused by Jews who did not learn the lessons of the attempted genocide against them.

In any case, it is deeply peculiar that it seems acceptable to publicly presume that an entire identity-group should be held to legal, political and moral account for what is taking place in a country that many of its members do not live in and are not citizens of. How is it possible to associate Jews with being responsible for the military occupation of the West Bank and the Gaza Strip? Why use the term "Jews"? Just because Israel is defined as the Jewish State, it does not follow that all Jews are responsible for what goes on there, nor that all Jews are even supportive of what goes on there. This kind of broad generalization ostensibly makes sense because of how minority identity-groups can be presumed to hold obligations that cross state borders. Ward's comments also sting because he wants to hold the Jews up to a higher standard, a standard that many Jews would probably like to achieve themselves. The reference to the Holocaust implies this higher standard, a standard, it is worth pointing out, that is sometimes also raised by Jewish authors.[87] Jews are tied to Israel, and often have obligations to Israel, just not the kind that Ward thinks that they do.

In her critique of Zionism and her exploration of ethics and Jewish identity, Judith Butler uses the term "obligation" slightly over two dozen times.[88] This may not be a large number, but if we consider that the term "loyalty" is not used once, the twenty-seven appearances are significant. In the social sciences, terms such as obligation and loyalty tend to carry specific meanings. Underlying both terms is the question of how to explain and understand those normative influences that explain how political communities are sustained. Political Science has been heavily shaped by such questions, hence the importance in political theory of why people accept the obligation to obey the law and support the institutions of the state that many find themselves attached to by being born in a particular place. Butler's choice of the term "obligation" is, as such, not random. Yet how exactly this category of obligation is to be understood is not entirely clear. On the one hand, Butler challenges the extent to which such obligations function, but on the other she also accepts that Jews either can be or are in some obligatory way connected with Israel.

For diaspora and migrant groups, where one is born is not the deciding factor in how they locate their commitments. In this regard, this book engages with previous work in the social sciences on the local and global politics of diasporas, including the work of Yossi Shain, Gabriel Sheffer, Robin Cohen, Stéphane Dufoix and Steven Gold, and in the humanities, the work of Lisa Mosses Leff in particular, whose historical writing on Jewish internationalism[89] provides a precursor to understanding today's Diaspora/Israel relationship.

Shain, who has published widely on diaspora politics more generally,[90] has identified the close political connections that exist

Introduction

between the Diaspora and Israel, particularly with regard to discourses of Jewish security. Writing about changes in Israeli political discourse, he and Barry Bristman note that in one vision, as articulated for example by Prime Minister Ariel Sharon, "Jewish solidarity and Jewish security are completely intertwined with Israeli security."[91] This trans-state security discourse that intertwines Israeli security with Jewish Diaspora security is largely a product of Zionist ideology and represents the "Israelization of diaspora security."[92] Shain and Bristman note how Jews in the Diaspora are being called on to get involved in Israeli politics, writing:

> The new call for Jewish American involvement represents a sharp break with the older Zionist idea of state security as (1) overshadowing diaspora security (including during the pre-state Yishuv period); (2) taking precedence over or controlling diaspora security (ingathering of exiles, refugees); and (3) controlling or directing diaspora voices in Israeli internal matters through a demand for unqualified support on issues of war and peace. Above all, this position represents a break from the heyday of the Oslo posture, when Shimon Peres and the late Yitzhak Rabin told the diaspora to stay away from Israeli security issues (when Jewish organizations pushed to move the US embassy to Jerusalem) and asked diaspora leaders to look after their communities' own cultural survival.[93]

Shain and Bristman do not, however, satisfactorily address the ideational and political discourses that enable such mobilizations to be felt, accepted and/or acted upon.

In this regard, part of what I aim to accomplish in this book is to help to provide an answer to the question of how Diaspora Jews are able to be treated and understood as being legitimately asked to be mobilized in ways that tie them to the State of Israel. As such, part of this book is about trying to come to grips with a puzzle noted by Judith Butler and which I share. Butler writes:

> It continues to surprise me that many people believe that to claim one's Jewishness is to claim Zionism or believe that every person who attends a synagogue is necessarily a Zionist. Equally concerning is the number of people who think they must now disavow Jewishness because they cannot accept the policies of the State of Israel.[94]

27

Butler here misses another equally concerning problem, which is, to rephrase her writing, "the number of people who think they must now disavow [any tie to Israel] because they cannot accept the policies of the State of Israel."

In this book, I suggest that one way to understand the Diaspora's relationship with Israel is to view it as a transnational political obligation. What this focus does is slightly reposition how this relationship is understood so it becomes possible to assess it more clearly and provide non-ideological critiques of it. In short, the point of this framework is to move beyond the current debates about Zionism, Diaspora support for Israel, concern over increasing disengagement by Diaspora Jews of Israel, and so on. All of these debates in some way return to the underlying position of Israeli centrality for Jewish identity without offering a clear path for evaluating critiques of this (ostensible) centrality.

By repositioning the intellectual position about Diaspora and Israel it becomes possible to better understand:

- Why debate about Israel is often so heated and contentious;
- Why viewpoints surrounding the Diaspora/Israel relationship are often incommensurable;
- What the main flashpoints of Diaspora/Israel debate are and why;
- How the role played by critique of Israel might be addressed and assessed.

With regard to the third of these, I suggest that the main flashpoints pertain to security, political practice and identity. A fourth, religion, also matters, but I do not explore it because to do so would unnecessarily confuse the political focus by obliging me to deal with how religious debates about textual interpretation and religious practice are also political.

While it might appear that some of these points are obvious, I would ask, if they are, why is there so little published about the Diaspora/Israel relationship that does not explain them? The usual texts are almost always partisan in taking a political position about how to support Israel. They rarely, if ever, explore in the abstract the relationship between Diaspora Jews and Israel. In a sense, the most sophisticated debates in this regard were by Zionists, Jewish internationalists, and Jewish nationalists in the nineteenth and early twentieth centuries. My book is, in a sense, aimed at revitalizing these types of theoretical debates.

The term "obligation" is chosen for specific reasons, one of which is that it is better than "loyalty," in part because it is more flexible, for reasons I explore in the next chapter. The phrase "political obligation" is purposely used, to enable a transnational political theory of obligation to develop, by borrowing some of the underlying assumptions in political theory that define political obligation. The development of my theory of transnational political obligation is designed to contribute to a wider debate about how to understand the relationships of Diaspora, migrant and transnational communities. In particular, I focus on how select assumptions within the political obligation literature are useful in helping us to think through transnational politics, and in the process, I set out the beginnings for a theory of transnational political obligation.

There are, consequently, two objectives to this book. One is to enable a better understanding of the Diaspora/Israel relationship and the other is to suggest a new theoretical framework for understanding transnational politics. With regard to the first of these, in addition to the points listed above, what my theory also does is reveal the significance of critique in the Diaspora/Israel relationship. In particular, I suggest that contained within the traditional framings of the Diaspora's relationship with Israel rests an immanent critique of how this relationship cannot succeed, and that, as a consequence, what is needed is a different way of thinking about both Israel and, especially, Diaspora.

Some existing literature already engages with this issue, including Caryn Aviv and David Shneer's book *New Jews*, which seeks to emphasize Diaspora Jewish identity without Israel.[95] The already-cited work by Butler and the critical text *The Question of Zion* by Jacqueline Rose are also related to critically re-evaluating Diaspora Jewry in the age of Israel.[96] Sometimes, such texts tend to be more polemical than others, such as those by John Rose and Max Blumenthal.[97] However, the point of this book is not to supplement such polemics, although I find myself in agreement with much of the argument advanced by Jacqueline Rose who questions the myths underlying the Zionist story, and illuminates the destructive potential unleashed by a historically informed consciousness of victimhood that never came to terms with no longer being a powerless victim.[98] Rather, a theory of transnational political obligation enables a critique of how normative texts about Israel function as a process in the Diaspora/Israel relationship, regardless of which position on the political spectrum one takes.

The ground provided by my theory of transnational political obligation, however, is not completely solid. Whereas theories of political obligation in the traditional sense are grounded in the existence of the state and in how sovereignty offers promises of stability and security, transnational political obligation offers no such imaginings. Its foundations, such as they are, are always moving. My argument, however, differs from Jacqueline Rose's in a few respects, including a minimal engagement with the traditional Zionist ideologues, the absence of psychoanalytic critique, and my uses of political theory and Critical Theory in providing a framework for analysis. Before proceeding, however, I will say a few words about methodology, and then provide an outline of the book.

Methodology

In his essay *Objectivity in Social Science and Social Policy*, Max Weber argues that social scientists need to disclose their position and that "there is no absolutely 'objective' scientific analysis of culture."[99] Weber did not mean that there can be no valid social science. Indeed, in the same essay he wrote, "The type of social science in which we are interested is an *empirical science* of concrete reality (*Wirklichkeitswissenschaft*)."[100] While the legacy of Weber's methodological thinking remains contested, he did point the way toward an interpretive social science.[101] His interpretivism relied on the use of ideal types, which enable the researcher to separate personal value judgments from the research process, and although I am not using ideal-type theory, the methodology used is inspired by his interpretive turn.[102] Learning from Weber, albeit perhaps by overemphasizing certain elements of his thought, this project is certainly the product of the *position* of the researcher.

There is a significant autobiographical element to this research project that cannot be avoided, which I have been upfront about. My position in this project has also made me more sympathetic to a research design that is not predicated on assumptions and metaphors that presume an objective reality. I begin from a methodological perspective that is much closer to what Michael Shapiro writes about in his famous essay *Metaphor in the Philosophy of the Social Sciences*:

> there are no "things" that have meaning apart from the human practices that are implicit in what we regard as things and ... our discursive practices are vehicles for the production of subjects and objects that participate in what are generally regarded as forms of knowledge.[103]

The empirical methodology I used is based on an interpretive ethnographic approach concerned with what the participants say, how they "say it," and with revealing shared and contested meanings about Diaspora Jewish identity and its connections with Israel. As such, the fieldwork for this project is a cross between political sociology and political anthropology. Between 2008 and 2013 I conducted over forty interviews in the USA, Canada, Israel and the UK. Interviews took place in New York City, Vancouver, Victoria, Tel Aviv, Jerusalem and London. Overall, the interviews represent a fair cross-section of different Jewish constituencies covering age, gender, the different Jewish denominations, and religiosity.

Participants were initially selected by contacting major Jewish organizations in New York and London. The selection of New York and London was partly a matter of demographics and significance. I went to New York twice to conduct interviews since it is, in the words of Caryn Aviv and David Shneer, "A new Zion of the Jewish World, with its complexity, density, and sheer cacophony of Jewish voices, institutions, and cultures."[104] New York is, they write,

> Jewish, not just because it has the largest urban Jewish population in the world, not just because it is the financial and cultural hub of the Jewish world, not just because nearly every rabbi trained in the world will spend some time there, not just because it has the best Yiddish-language study program in the world, but also because it is the place to which so many global Jews trace their histories and through which they envision their futures.[105]

In New York I interviewed rabbis, executives of major Jewish organizations, academics, political activists, former Jewish youth camp counsellors, and other important Jewish public intellectuals. Interview participants came from the American Jewish Committee, the American Jewish Congress, the American Jewish World Service, the Joint Distribution Committee, J Street,[106] the Orthodox Union, the Union for Reform Judaism, the Association of Reform Zionists of America (ARZA), the United Synagogue of Conservative Judaism, former Jewish youth camp counsellors, and young Jewish adults (aged between 25 and 35), all of whom were university graduates who had spent time in Israel. I also met with established Jewish Studies scholars in New York, who helped in setting up interviews and formulating the research and interview questions, all of which contributed to a snowballing effect that widened the scope of the interview participants and put me in contact with public intellectuals and activists.

London was also chosen for demographic purposes, as it has the largest English-speaking Jewish Diaspora population in Europe. In London, I interviewed individuals from the Board of Deputies, and the Jewish Institute for Policy Research, as well as Reform, Liberal, Orthodox and Masorti rabbis. Recent university graduates were also interviewed. I interviewed rabbis and members of Jewish organizations, but also academics.

Jews in the UK do not tend to wear their Jewish identity publicly like New York Jews do (or North American Jews in general), and so at times it was trickier to find individuals who would participate in interviews. One experience stands out in particular at an academic conference in the UK where I was presenting material related to this book. After the panel had ended, one of my co-panelists (who I had not met before) came up to me and in a very quiet voice said how he had found my presentation quite interesting and that he was Jewish. I asked this person how he would feel about talking with me about this project and possibly being interviewed, but no answer was forthcoming. The shyness this individual had about being Jewish is not uncommon in the UK, and when I started the UK-based fieldwork was not something I anticipated. Indeed, the sociology and social psychology of British Jewry is quite different from what I come from in North America – yet another sign of being separated by a common language.

Those who were interviewed sometimes spoke on behalf of an institution, but more often than not they spoke for themselves. The interviews did not include anybody from Alternative Jewish Voices or related Diaspora groups that are especially critical of, and in some cases hostile to, both Israel and the role it plays in constructing Jewish identity and Jewish community. I did not interview self-identified non-Zionists or anti-Zionists. Such individuals do not share in the transnational political obligation sentiments that I am concerned with. Rather, they react against them, but doing so is itself significant, as will become clearer later on, for I do make use of the relevant critical literature at some length in the final chapter.

Much like the historical precedent set by Jewish internationalism that was concerned with Jews in other countries, contemporary Jewish transnational political obligations are directed toward the main Jewish community outside of the Diaspora. Jews who do not share in this sense of obligation offer different, and important, ways of identifying as a Diaspora Jew. Indeed, the ambivalence that many Jews feel toward Israel is becoming an important part of Diaspora identity, and of the changing dynamics of the contemporary Jewish map.[107] Such views do play an important part in this project, and they are not ignored.

Interviews in Canada took place in Vancouver and in Victoria. Here the interviews were limited to young adults, primarily individuals who at one point were involved with *Habonim Dror*, although one rabbi was also interviewed. In addition, I participated in a large group discussion and, subsequent to this, contributed to the first Vancouver *Limmud* Jewish learning festival in February 2014. The population and cultural centers of Jewish life in Canada are not in these cities, but in Montreal and Toronto. Yet, Victoria has the oldest synagogue in Canada that has been in continual use, and Vancouver has a very close-knit Jewish community due, in part, to there being a *Habonim Dror* summer camp nearby on Gabriola Island (one of only seven such camps in North America). I attended this camp and had some inroads into the Vancouver Jewish community as a result. Here was an opportunity to interview young Jews who have, throughout most of their lives, learned to connect with Israel but who, nevertheless choose not to live there. Every one of the Vancouver Jews interviewed spent over a year in Israel, and one had made *aliya* (emigrated to Israel) but had subsequently returned to Canada.

Vancouver is often overlooked as an important city for Jews in Canada, overshadowed by Montreal and Toronto and far removed on the West Coast from the traditional Eastern political heartlands of Canada. Yet Vancouver is home to a Jewish annual arts and culture festival, *Chutzpah*, that regularly brings in Israeli dancers, and has done so for a number of years.[108] While the sample size I have used insofar as Vancouver Jewish participants are concerned is modest, this project nevertheless offers the opportunity to address this imbalance. Moreover, since there is considerable overlap between American and Canadian Jewish organizations, especially religious ones, the interviews in New York in some cases also related to wider Canadian Jewish organizational viewpoints. There is significant overlap with regard to the views held by American and Canadian Jewish organizations. Interestingly, but not surprisingly, one representative of one of the Jewish religious organizations whom I interviewed in New York is Canadian. Wider North American participation was also possible, as I did conduct interviews with individuals who live or had lived in other North American Cities, including Washington DC and Chicago.

Interviews in Israel involved employees in the Israeli Ministry of Foreign Affairs, as well as intellectuals in Israel who work in related NGOs that are concerned with the Jewish Diaspora. Most Israelis are not concerned about Diaspora/Israel relations, so for the purposes of this book it was not necessary to establish a wider interview participant pool in Israel.

The one national demographic that I feel is missing from this book are French Jews. The history of Jewish internationalism is closely tied up with the history of French Jewry and France has the largest Diaspora population in Europe. I hope in the future to explore the ongoing relevancy of this history to French Jews today, but financial and time pressures involved in this research project made it impossible to conduct fieldwork in France.

Most of the interviews were recorded, with participants given the chance to opt out of the interview at any time, and all participants were provided with an informed consent document to sign. The interviews varied in length from 30 minutes to four hours, with some participants being interviewed more than once. The discussions were fairly informal, semi-structured, and more often than not took the form of a conversation.

Methodologically, the interviews were influenced by the work of Clifford Geertz, who stresses the multiple contexts in which meaning is created.[109] Although his methodological work pertains to ethnographic fieldwork, there is a close relationship between anthropological ethnography and qualitative research in other social sciences such as Political Science and Sociology. Geertz's definition of thick descriptions has been influential beyond anthropology, for a main component of this method is to respect the narratives of participants and the contexts in which these narratives are formed in influence. Geertz, however, has been criticized for privileging the authority of the researcher.[110] This criticism has been especially important in this project, for methodologically I came to the fieldwork via a very specific language of political theory as well as my autobiographical positioning. In the first few interviews I was essentially testing the assumption that political obligation could, in a sense, be used to apply to how Diaspora Jews self-understood their relationship with the Jewish State. Yet, as I tried to test this hypothesis it became very clear that the discourses of professional political theory did not speak to how non-political theorists understand their obligatory political relationships. This finding reflects the difficulty that the political theorist George Klosko discovered when his focus group participants conflated key concepts in political obligation.[111] As a result, I had to jettison much of the terminology contained in theories of political obligation and try to identify shared meanings between what the participants articulated with regard to a relationship that involves obligations that are political. However, as I did so it became fairly obvious that I was privileging my position as the researcher and trying to fit the participants narrative into a pre-existing structure.

The resolution to this problem lay in discussing terminology with the interviewees. Having this discussion first made it possible for me to sort out the wider conceptual framework for how they understood their relationship with Israel, as well as how they understood the specifics of this relationship. In this way it was possible to distance myself as the authority and let the participants articulate their own account, using their own language. Inevitably, however, in making comparisons across the interviews and searching for common themes, the researcher does make an imprint on the interview material, exercising some authoritative and authorial intent.

The findings I present are helpful in enabling us to understand how some Jews understand their relationship with Israel, and to recognize that their experiences and knowledge claims on this issue are not unique among Diaspora Jews. I do not claim that they are representative of all Jews. Indeed, many of the interviewees were clear on this point, that they speak only for themselves and that obligations or commitments, or even a connection to Israel, are a choice for each Jew to make.

Book Outline

Chapters 1 and 2 are the main theoretical chapters, with Chapters 3 and 4 involving the bulk of the empirical material. While Chapters 1 and 2 are theoretically dense (with the exception of the section on the Muscle Jew), and will probably not be of interest to the more general reader, Chapters 3 and onwards are different on both accounts. Where there are theoretical discussions in these chapters, they are written to be more easily accessible. Chapter 5 offers a critical commentary and turns to normative questions.

Chapter 1 introduces the concept of political obligation, and begins to set out how transnational political obligation is a different type of political obligation. Both share some underlying features, including a concern with security, but they also differ in one especially significant aspect, which is the non-statist element of transnational political obligation. This difference is addressed through a critique of the particularity principle, which I begin by exploring how political obligation is concerned with security. Security is one of the features that informs transnational political obligation, and highlighting it here foreshadows subsequent explorations of security in the Diaspora/Israel relationship.

What links political obligation with transnational political obligation, other than security, is power. Theories of political obligation are heavily influenced by assumptions about power, but the literature rarely addresses power. Chapter 2 explores the extent to which a particular Weberian understanding of power shapes what is commonly understood by political obligation. I suggest that it is this understanding of power that defines what makes political obligations political. Consequently, I argue that transnational political obligations are political because they too are shaped by discourses of power. However, the power in transnational political obligation is significantly different from how it is understood in the Weberian-informed political theory literature. Consequently, I explore at some length the political thought of Hannah Arendt in order to reveal an account of politics and of power that enables the removal of the state from a theory of obligation. This discussion relies almost exclusively on Arendt's own writings and does not seek to develop the secondary literature about Arendt, of which there is a lot. Arendt is chosen here not only for her insights into a non-statist and non-sovereign account of politics and power, but because her thought has also been especially influential in Jewish critiques of Zionism. Yet, whereas most of this literature focuses on her critiques of Zionism as found in her early writings, or in a few significant remarks she made about politics, ethics and identity, this literature rarely provides a sustained explanation of her theoretical writings. Thus, I seek to remedy this shortcoming by providing a detailed introduction to Arendt's thinking about power, as doing so provides a stronger grasp of how her thought can be linked to critiques of Zionism and Israel.[112] Her thinking about power is also important because it provides a different way of understanding power relations, one that is more conducive to the role of critique. The Arendtian discussion serves as the theoretical background for my subsequent analysis, interpretation and critique.

Chapter 2, in its discussion of power, also provides one other function. In addition to Arendt, I turn to the work of Michel Foucault to help make the transition from a public account of politics and of political power to how power also informs the construction of identity and related discourses of the self. Whereas Arendt enables a disassociation of power from the spatial and juridical geographies of the state, which is necessary for a theory of transnational political obligation, she does not make the move that links discourses of power to constructions of the self and the subsequent political practices that are shaped by and in turn inform individual subjectivity. The relationship between power and the self is important because it comes up a lot in the empirical work, and this theoretical discussion sets the stage for how to interpret the empirical material. In order to begin this discussion about the self and power, I use the example of the Muscle Jew to illustrate the different ways in which power and identity are related.

Chapter 3 begins the empirical work, and explores empirically the theoretical issues raised in the previous chapters. It further develops the security linkages raised in Chapter 1 and introduces a historical precedent to today's transnational political obligation, the example of Jewish internationalism. The chapter then makes the transition from this historical illustration to today by locating how Diaspora has changed significantly with the creation of Israel.

Chapter 4 continues with the empirical material, and builds on the previous chapters by exploring different ways in which those interviewed understand the Diaspora/Israel relationship, both individually and collectively. This chapter explores, among other points, the obligation question by returning to the issue of loyalty and not obligation, but primarily it is concerned with the various ways in which Israel is understood to inform Diaspora identity and, by inference, related political practices between Diaspora and Israel. In this regard, this chapter reveals the different ways that Diaspora Jews who feel connected to Israel understand this connection, and the concerns they have about this connection.

Chapter 5, the final substantive chapter, could be described as the normative chapter. The multiple references to loyalty in the previous chapters provide a regular reminder that behind any obligations exist normative decisions, of whether or not one should accept an obligation. The political obligation literature seeks to explain an empirical condition that is explicitly normative. Most people, most of the time, obey the law; they accept the obligations placed upon them by membership in the state. In this literature, the main normative issue is already present and the challenge is to explain why people accept their moral obligations to the state. The literature is not about whether they should accept such obligations. That question pertains to the related but different question of resistance and/or rebellion. I raise these issues in earlier chapters, but nowhere in those chapters do I suggest what Diaspora Jews ought to do. I do not provide a normative argument for how Jews should act in their transnational relationship with Israel. I argue that the transnational political obligation that Jews have with Israel is to have a relationship with that country. The transnational political obligation does not direct specific actions, which is why the literature about the Diaspora/Israel relationship argues that there are different ways in which Jews should act with regard to Israel. The obligation is configured sometimes to be one of support, and at other times to be one of critique. Thus the question remains, what ought Diaspora Jews to do with regard to the obligation to be connected with, to have a relationship with, Israel?

This chapter argues that this normative question misses the more problematic issue that what underlies the transnational political obligation with Israel is the role of critique; that the normative question is not one of action but of belief. Consequently, critique

Introduction

becomes the flashpoint for the Diaspora/Israel relationship because it is where contestations are the strongest with regard to how the obligation should be manifested. More than this, however, contained with this significance of critique is an immanent critique, a hidden contradiction, that points out the unsustainability of how the current Diaspora/Israel relationship is constructed. Chapter 5 involves an examination of the role of critique, and of how critique is the primary means by which resistance to transnational political obligations is manifested. In particular, I argue that contained within the transnational political obligation between the Diaspora and Israel there exists an immanent critique that undermines the obligation itself. It is for this reason that debate about Israel is such a flashpoint, because it potentially reveals the extent to which the Diaspora and Israel are heading in different directions. This divergence could mean a major revision of what it means to be a Diaspora Jew, potentially requiring that we re-examine alternative conceptions of political space and Jewish identity that Diaspora Jews explored before the success of Zionism.

1 The Limits of Political Obligation

Introduction

Jewish Diaspora identity politics and political obligation may not appear to have any mutual relevance. Indeed, in one sense they do not because theories of political obligation do not directly address questions pertinent to minority politics. Rather, such theories treat citizens as a single group, and are in this sense not concerned with the different political experiences of minority communities. Different identity-groups are not addressed. Yet in another way, political obligation as a particular type of moral commitment and not a universal duty is deeply relevant to diaspora politics. An example that demonstrates as much is the Damascus Affair.

In Damascus in 1840, a Capuchin friar disappeared and a Jewish barber was arrested and charged with the ritual murder of the friar. The barber was tortured and after a forced confession a mob attacked the local Jewish community. The French government became involved, owing to its Middle Eastern ambitions, and supported the charges against the Jewish barber. French Jews were, consequently, placed in a difficult position. On the one hand, as French citizens they should support France's ambitions in the Middle East, but as Jews they could not stand behind their government's support of a malicious crime against Jews. Indeed, the charge against the Jewish barber revived the blood libel accusation common in the Middle Ages. In the end, owing to the involvement of a Jewish French politician, Adolphe Crémieux, and the British Sir Moses Montefiore, the Jewish prisoners in Damascus were released.[1]

What the Damascus Affair demonstrated was that a diaspora community could pose a security concern to the state because of its diasporic status, of belonging to a trans-state national community.

Moreover, it upheld the frightening accusation of dual loyalty, and it did so by presenting the minority diaspora community, in this case the Jews, as not being counted upon to uphold the interests of the state, and thus the institutions of the state. In this sense, the Damascus Affair was for French Jews at least a Pyrrhic victory. With the help of Adolphe Crémieux, the Jewish prisoners in Damascus were released. The Jews involved in the Damascus Affair were not acting for another state but for their people abroad. However, this victory was not without consequences. "The outcome was an apparent victory in humanitarian terms but . . . it was a Pyrrhic one. Thereafter, French patriots argued that love of their brethren would always be greater than the love of the French Jews for France."[2]

Dual loyalty[3] raises the relevance of political obligation for minority groups because the extent to which this accusation functions depends on whether or not the target group can be counted upon as upholding or accepting the traditional political obligations. Consequently, it is important to explain what is conventionally understood by political obligation and why it matters for security. Providing such an explanation is part of the goal of this chapter.

There is, however, another and more significant way in which political obligation is, or could be, relevant for diaspora identity-groups. If a diaspora or minority group is perceived by the state to pose a security risk because it cannot be counted upon to accept the political obligations that come with citizenship (or residence) in the polity, it is likely because it has a conflict of competing political obligations. This logic is evident in the case of spies. Thus, for example, Jonathan Pollard represents a case of someone who acted in the interests of another country, Israel, by betraying his legal obligations to his own country, the USA.

However, this model of the spy does not always work in the case of a diaspora group. In the nineteenth century, the Jews in France and Britain had no legal or political obligation to become involved in trying to save Jews in Damascus and the legal obligations to their home country were in the process of being written. Today, while there exist laws that frame the limits of transnational political activities, there is, for example, no political or legal conflict for American Jews working to support Israel by becoming involved with J Street or AIPAC. The question at issue is, did the Damascus

Affair demonstrate a conflict of political obligations? In fact, the Damascus Affair did demonstrate a conflict of political obligations, as does the political work done by Diaspora Jews on behalf of Israel, but political obligations of two very different kinds. Providing an overview of this second type of political obligation is the goal of this and the subsequent chapter.

In order to provide such a theory and illustrate how it differs from the traditional theories of political obligation, I provide a brief introduction to political obligation, focusing on some of the key theorists in this area including John Horton, George Klosko, John Simmons, Hannah Pitkin, and Margaret Gilbert. This discussion also addresses how political obligation is concerned with security, and provides a critique of the "particularity principle" of political obligation. Rejecting this principle is crucial for understanding one of the fundamental differences between conventional framings of political obligation and the different version offered here.

What Is Political Obligation?

There are a great many different theories of political obligation, and it is not my aim to explore them all here.[4] Nevertheless, it will be helpful to introduce what is traditionally meant by political obligation in order to signal where I differ from the traditional framings. The online *Stanford Encyclopaedia of Philosophy* defines political obligation as "a moral duty to obey the laws of one's country or state."[5] As George Klosko notes, theories of political obligation are designed to provide moral arguments about *why* people should obey the law or support the state.[6] In this sense, political obligation is closely tied to theories of state. In other words, there is a close relationship between the question of political obligation and the normative justification for the state.

A slightly different definition is provided by John Horton. Political obligation, he writes, is

> the relationship – that between people and their political community – with which political obligation is fundamentally concerned. The problem of political obligation is about how this relationship is to be understood and what, if anything, it implies about the responsibilities we have to our political community. In particular, it is about whether

we can properly be understood to have some ethical bound with our polity, and if so how this manifests itself.[7]

Whereas Klosko used the terms "state" and "country," Horton does not. His term of choice is "polity," which more generally refers to a political community. The implication of this word-choice could be significant were it not for the fact that Horton employs the "particularity principle" as a key part of his understanding of political obligation. This principle, which will be explored in detail shortly, emphasizes how political obligation has to refer to the country of which one is a citizen. Consequently, Horton also suggests that a general theory of political obligation does not need to explain "how everyone has a political obligation," but "should cover at least the standard case of people who acquire membership through being born into the polity."[8]

The question of political obligation is closely tied to theories of state, but while this may explain the focus *of* political obligation it does not explain what the different arguments *for* political obligation are. Indeed, there are many different types of political obligation arguments. Horton helpfully identifies five: voluntarist, teleological, deontological, anarchist, and associative.[9] What unites voluntarist theories is that they explain political obligation according to how individuals freely choose to accept a binding moral relation to their polity. The political obligation is a product of their choice. Teleological theories of political obligation explain political obligation according to consequentialist or another logical structure that is geared toward future outcome, as opposed to a past agreement. According to Horton, the difference between voluntarist and teleological theories is as follows:

> Voluntarist theories of political obligation essentially conceive of political relations in terms of individual choices or commitments, and of the polities as a form of voluntary association. By contrast, teleological theories view polities as instruments: typically, the polity is conceived as the best means to achieve a valuable end or particular benefit.[10]

The third category, deontological arguments, explains political obligation by emphasizing duty or according to a normative value. Various versions of consent theory fit into this category.[11]

Horton recognizes that this third category is not really representative of any shared philosophical group, and those theorists that he places under this category cannot be considered to belong to a single theoretical approach. Kant features briefly in this description, as does Hannah Pitkin, who, although she writes in the vein of tacit consent, is for Horton not a voluntarist, because her concern is not with whether anybody consents, but with whether they would. For her, it is not consent that matters but the basis upon which consent could be given. Horton discusses Rawls in this section because even though Rawls provides a type of consent argument, it is a hypothetical experiment. If the consent is not actual but hypothetical, it follows that the argument is not actually based on the requirement of there being situations where people consent. As Ronald Dworkin writes, "a hypothetical contract is not simply a pale form of contract; it is no contract at all."[12] Developing his discussion of Rawls, Horton places him within the deontological category of political obligation arguments based on fairness.

The fourth category refers to anarchist arguments that reject all theories of political obligation. They represent a kind of critical school of thought that does not seek to provide an alternative theory of political obligation, but argues against the merits of all existing theories. A. J. Simmons provides a leading example of this type.

The fifth category is of associative theories. In this regard, Horton writes that the term "associative" "seems to have been coined by Ronald Dworkin. By this he means "the special responsibilities social practice attaches to the membership in some biological or social group, like the responsibilities of family or friends or neighbours," and he goes on to observe that "political obligation might be counted among them."[13] What characterizes associative accounts are the features of belonging to a community. This is the argument that Horton supports. The associative account emphasizes how obligations "arise from social practices."[14] Horton writes:

> They are the obligations of family, collegiality and political community. Such obligations are not owed to everyone: they are special obligations owed to other members of a particular group or association to which we belong. But unlike special obligations that are created through voluntary choices or decisions, such as those that arise from promises or a decision to a join a club, associative obligations cannot be explained in terms of individual voluntary acts or decisions. It is this combination of

not being owed to everyone and not arising from voluntary choice that makes associative obligations different and distinctive . . ."[15]

This account is closest to what I will argue. It is, however, worth pointing out that Horton frames obligation in territorial terms. "For most people, their political obligations, as we might say, come with the territory."[16] Indeed they do, but which territory? Transnational political obligations are not territorially based in the same way, if at all. Rather, as I argue in the next chapter, it is not territory but power that is at issue, the power of identity and an account of political power that breaks the tie between political power and the territorial nation-state.

There is a sixth category of theories, theories that Horton notes do not really fit into the five, and that is those types of theories that reject the assumption that there must be only one type of theory to explain political obligation. Instead, it may make more sense to approach, as Klosko has done, political obligation as involving different principles from the different theories, although even in this multiple-principles approach Klosko still makes use of three underlying principles, that of natural duty of justice, that of the common good, and that of fairness.[17] Klosko's earlier work focused on developing H. L. A. Hart's principle of fair play or fairness[18] into a theory of political obligation, which Klosko has defined as (within the liberal tradition at least) the problem of "why some individuals should obey others."[19] Klosko's theory, however, is firmly located in the liberal philosophical tradition, with its emphasis on the individual, and his thought is also primarily applicable only to idealized liberal states. This focus, however, is in some ways a logical necessity since theories of political obligation often involve a combination of state authority with state legitimacy. A state may have the authority to compel but not the legitimacy to do so. In such cases an argument for political obligation (or for resistance) will not be the same as in a case where the state has both authority and legitimacy. Defining and limiting the scope of political obligation is part of the problem in providing a theory of it.

Indeed, as Horton demonstrates, trying to clarify what the question or problem is that political obligation is concerned with is itself part of the challenge in explaining political obligation. In her attempt at clarifying the problem of political obligation, Hannah Pitkin classifies it as a question made up of four parts:

The Limits of Political Obligation

1) The limits of obligation ("*When* are you obliged to obey, and when not?");
2) The locus of sovereignty ("*Whom* are you obliged to obey?");
3) The difference between legitimate authority and mere coercion ("Is there *really* any difference; are you ever *really* obligated?");
4) The justification of obligation ("*Why* are you ever obliged to obey even a legitimate authority?").[20]

Pitkin highlights how close political obligation is to the issue of resistance or rebellion, two practices that are specific challenges to the existing political authority. Indeed, Pitkin notes that political obligation is closely linked to the issue of authority, yet her question is about framing authority in normative terms (legitimate authority versus authority that coerces). Obligation in this account rests on tying the practices of political obligation to consent. This approach finds support in the literature that notes a distinction between political obligation in any state and political obligation in a particular state, often in liberal democratic states.[21] The problem or puzzle of political obligation is with little debate framed as a statist discourse in which the political is inevitably tied to a life made possible by living inside the sovereign state. Of course, the vast majority of human beings live in sovereign states, but my point is that our understanding of politics and of obligation does not have to remain tied to conditions of possibility that are understood to exist only after a claim to sovereign statehood has been made. In this regard not all theories of political obligation begin with an account of sovereignty, although they often end there.

In her book on political obligation, Margaret Gilbert argues that political obligation represents a puzzle: "how can membership in a political society – which seems to be something natural – be conceptually tied to obligation – which does not?"[22] Political obligation is ostensibly puzzling because of a set of assumptions about the conditions under which political life takes place, and a bias toward a temporal story that begins with the individual, leads to a society within a state, and then creates obligation. Her plural subject theory begins with a promise between individuals, reflecting a traditional methodology in liberal philosophy that begins with the individual.

Gilbert's account is especially interesting insofar as her focus is on "the relationship between individual human begins and the political societies of which they are members."[23] Unlike many other accounts, she does not begin with the state but with a political society. Since political obligation is traditionally concerned with obligations inside the state it is worth asking if a political society is the same as a state. Obviously, there are political societies that are not states. Interestingly, Gilbert provides a few examples from international relations to support this. With resonances of Hedley Bull's idea of the international society,[24] she writes:

> The type of society in question is not a mere aggregate of small social groups. It resembles certain international bodies whose members are individual nations – bodies such as the League of Nations, the United Nations, and NATO. A member of a given "inclusive" society of this type can also be a member of other such societies with a different membership – just as the members of NATO are also members of the United Nations.[25]

Gilbert, however, is not making the case that states are individuals with the same type of political obligations that individual human beings have as members of a political society. In this case, her example falls flat because states are not individuals. As Thomas Hobbes clearly demonstrated,[26] the state is not the same as an individual. Individuals do not have the same resources at their disposal and so this kind of analogy is not obviously applicable if we are trying to explain individual human behavior.[27] However, her concern is with the issue of size because what she wants to do is extrapolate from a small example to a larger case. Thus, what her example is meant to demonstrate is that there are a variety of different types of political societies, and that it is possible to be a member of multiple political societies at the same time.

I agree with Gilbert on this point. We do all belong to different political societies, and her subsequent claim that people understand themselves as plural subjects is, in a sense, also convincing. However, I disagree with her rational game theory-based approach to understanding human subjectivity and human choice,[28] as well as with how she goes about presenting what constitutes a political society. Gilbert, as Horton notes,[29] is concerned with trying to explain political obligations, not with trying to justify them. The reason for this is not that normative judgments are unimportant but that Gilbert wants to demonstrate how a society creates obliga-

The Limits of Political Obligation

tions. Hers is an associative argument. Here, however, is where I think her account has some difficulties.

Gilbert's example of how a political society comes together, and thus of how political obligations are formed, sees her relying on a situation where two people meet and decide to go for a walk together. As it happens, the two individuals know each other and agree to walk up Fifth Avenue toward Central Park in New York City. As part of their joint commitment to each other to walk to Central Park, they have a "special standing" in relation to each other that others do not.[30] Thus, for example, if one of them is walking faster the other has the standing to request this person to slow down. A stranger who decided to follow them would not have this standing. As she writes, "The standing of the participants is a functioning of their joint activity. Thus it is special not only in the sense of not being shared by people generally, but also in having a specific source, namely, the joint activity."[31] The joint action is ostensibly demonstrative of what constitutes a political society and it can provide an explanation for political obligations since "such obligations and the correlative rights are *grounded in the joint activity itself.*"[32]

A political society is, of course, more than two people agreeing to do something together. She makes it clear that the example she provides is only an example, and that the spatial limits it imposes are not necessary (people living far apart from each other can still have shared commitments). Moreover, she also argues that a political society is characterized by having political institutions, by which she means "institutions of governance."[33] The example of the two walkers is meant to provide an empirical context, although it is of course hypothetical. What she ultimately wants to demonstrate with her theory is:

> According to a central everyday conception, a political society is constituted by an underlying joint agreement to accept certain rules, rules that count intuitively as political institutions. Those who are parties to the joint commitment are the members of the political society in question, of if you prefer, they are its core members.[34]

Gilbert believes that her example of two walkers "can be generalized from the kind of small-scale example . . . to less transient and much larger and impersonal social groups, including a polity."[35]

49

As Gilbert argues, it is the forming of a joint commitment that creates political obligation. She writes: "According to the theory, an understanding of joint commitment and a readiness to be jointly committed are necessary if one is to accrue political obligations."[36] There have been a few criticisms of her argument. Richard Dagger has questioned her account as a contribution to contract theory, arguing instead that it relies less on individuals committing themselves than on membership.[37] A. J. Simmons has also raised objections to her account of joint commitments.

Simmons challenges Gilbert's argument on three points. The first is that her account of joint commitments confuses "felt obligations with genuine obligations."[38] Just because someone feels herself to be committed does not mean that this person actually has any political obligations. Second, Gilbert presumes that an acceptance to "go along with an arrangement" demonstrates a willingness to commit.[39] Simmons writes that Gilbert confuses "political acquiescence with positive, obligation-generating acts of relationships."[40] It is quite possible that committing to go for a walk does not in fact translate into future acts of agreement with the other agreeing party. The joint commitment does not provide an explanation of future acts of agreement and thus cannot provide an explanation of political obligation. Moreover, as Simmons points out, one could be cajoled into an agreement that was not entirely objectionable at the time but doing so does not entail any future joint commitments to this person or group. Third, Simmons questions how far Gilbert's argument works since the joint commitment often involves some kind of proximity or regularity of contact that is not normally the case with regard to the more general category of political obligation.

Simmons' objections are certainly plausible enough, although, as John Horton has suggested, Simmons' second critique

> presupposes that obligations could only result from what [Simmons] calls "positive obligation-generating acts or relationship." Although it is not quite clear what this expression is supposed to cover, it certainly cannot be intended to include the kind of "joint commitments" with which Gilbert is concerned. If it were, of course, it would not be an objection to her view.[41]

The strength of Simmons' critiques rest largely on whether or not one is prepared to accept his anarchist conclusion, since his approach is often to take arguments on behalf of political obligation and then set them up for failure. As evidence there is Horton's critique of Simmons, but in the same article[42] we find Simmons critiquing anti-voluntarist obligation arguments for not supporting the philosophical anarchist position, as if an anti-voluntarist argument should at least be amenable to supporting his position. Simmons' position ultimately rests on the extent to which one is prepared to accept his starting principles (presumably all of them), and it is one of his principles in particular that I take exception to and will address in the next section.

Gilbert's argument is perhaps most problematic in the analogy she uses of two people going for a walk. It makes very little sense to think that this hypothetical can stand in for the underlying element of a political society and that this kind of agreement can provide the basis for what constitutes a political obligation. Two individuals agreeing to go for a walk cannot be presumed to reflect the complexity of a political society, and nor can the supposed agreement involved in the joint commitment between the two walkers reflect the content of a political obligation. Political obligations are generally not considered to exist in a realm where there is no political authority. Yet in this agreement there is no political authority, only two people agreeing with each other to walk to a shared destination. The agreement is supposed to act like a social contract origin moment that establishes the beginnings for political authority. Nevertheless, the agreement takes place in a society, with people who already know each other, and already recognize certain expectations of conduct. There are pre-existing power relations that frame the conditions under which this agreement is made, understood and acted upon. Forms of political authority are already present in her example.

Moreover, along their journey they will be walking in a space that is inclusive of at least one larger society made of people who are not part of the initial agreement. Just because the two agreed to walk together does not mean that each of them does not also have other unspoken agreements with the strangers they pass on their journey. The expectation of the walk is that it will conform to the standards of behavior that govern how people behave in public. These standards exist independently of the two walkers, and thus these two people have to already belong to a political society in order to understand some of the ground rules involved in walking in a city. The analogy does not stand.

For Gilbert, political obligation represents both a particular type of promise and a puzzle and her book borrows heavily from a variety of sources. One of them is H. L. A. Hart.[43] For Hart, it is a mistake to conflate an obligation with a promise. As he wrote in a 1955 article on natural rights, social contract theorists are mistaken in identifying the obligation to obey the law as an example of a promise.[44] Hart suggests that while there are similarities between a political obligation and a promise they are not equivalent types of agreement, largely because a promise does not incur rights. The relationship between rights and political obligation is an important one provided that political obligation remains focused on the state and domestic law. The question of rights is, I think, of crucial importance in thinking about political obligation, but it is not as important in my theory of transnational political obligation because the content of the obligation is of a different order.

What is more important for our purposes is whether or not the problem of political obligation is in fact a puzzle of the kind that Gilbert suggests. In her account the state is natural, whereas obligations to it are not. However, it seems equally plausible to suggest the following:

1) Membership in a political community is conditioned and possibly necessary, but not necessarily natural, in which case there really is no puzzle since both the state and political obligations are socially constructed. There may be other puzzles, but not that between natural membership and unnatural obligations.
2) There are no good reasons for presuming that membership involves obligations. The anarchical position challenges the view that there are such reasons, or at minimum that there is no good explanation for having political obligations.[45]
3) It may be the other way round – that it is through obligations to others that membership becomes noticeable. In other words, obligations contextualize the possibility of membership, rather than membership leading to obligations.
4) Political obligation and membership are mutually constitutive, in which case it is illogical to argue the problem of political obligation as if it occurred after the construction or recognition of a political society, because the two emerge simultaneously.

If any of these alternatives are possible arguments, and I think they are at least plausible, it may be that the problem of political obligation is a problem for a different set of reasons, in which case it would be fruitful to rethink the meaning of political obligation. It may be that Gilbert is aware of these kinds of problems in her statist account of political obligation, for in passing she implies that it is possible to have political obligations in non-state political societies, although she does not pursue this possibility in much detail.[46]

Not pursuing this point is unsurprising. The literature on political obligation is not concerned with membership in communities that transgress sovereign borders. Obligations may, as Horton suggests, come with the territory. But what territory? What political spaces is political obligation concerned with? One answer to this question, and one of Horton's requirements for defining political obligation, is the particularity principle. Horton borrows this term from Simmons, who writes that "the problem of political obligation does not concern a number of things we might call 'political obligations.'"[47] Simmons suggests that political obligation refers specifically to those moral bonds that bind citizens in a special way to their government.[48] This tenet of political obligation is particularly important for our purposes because it does not and indeed cannot feature in my theory of transnational political obligation.

Obligation and Security

As Martin Wight famously argued, political theory is by and large concerned with political life that happens inside the state.[49] While there are notable exceptions to this,[50] and Aristotle, Augustine, Hobbes, Kant, Marx, and Hegel among many others wrote about war and the relations that exist between bounded territorial units, theories of political obligation fit within this rubric. Yet, I am suggesting that there exists a kind of political obligation that transgresses the sovereign borders of the modern state. Political obligation is not as removed from international politics as it may seem. The key concept in the political obligation literature that limits its geographical scope is called the particularity principle, but this ostensibly limiting factor also reveals how theories of political obligation are not entirely separate from international politics.

In order to explore the particularity principle and the connection that political obligation has with international politics, I mainly use George Klosko's influential text *The Principle of Fairness and Political Obligation*, because in it Klosko emphasizes the importance of security for political obligation, although Michael Walzer's work is also addressed. This focus is needed because the question "What does political obligation assume about international politics?" also requires that we ask "Why is this assumption made?" The answers to both questions have to do with the particularity principle and security. Political obligation is necessarily tied to security in at least two ways.

The first, which I address in Chapter 4, is how theories of political obligation generally accept Max Weber's definition of the state, and associate the obligation to obey the law with the state's provision of security via its monopoly over the legitimate use of force within its territory. It is, consequently, not surprising that Klosko begins both of his books on political obligation with references to Weber.[51] The second reason, which is related to the first, has to do with how a theory of political obligation can overcome one of its more significant problems, that of the extent to which all political obligations are obligatory.

One of the overarching difficulties with theories of political obligation is how limiting the obligations in political obligation are. If obligations are understood according to the tripartite definition identified by Klosko, that they are performatively generated, owed to someone or some group, and connected with rights,[52] it follows that only a very limited type of obligation can be a political one. When these three conditions are met, a political obligation is often understood to be similar to a promise or consent, since consent becomes the means by which these conditions are met, and the obligation explained and justified. Some have argued that it is not possible to meet these conditions in all cases,[53] which makes it impossible to provide a theory of political obligation, at least for existing liberal societies. Klosko, however, suggests otherwise. The solution is to use an argument based on fairness instead of consent[54] and to reframe the problem of political obligation so that political obligation is not so strictly or narrowly defined according to these three conditions. Klosko writes:

> Despite the arguments of Pateman and other theorists, the problem of political obligation, as traditionally conceived and as relevant to the

The Limits of Political Obligation

concerns of modern citizens and theorists, does not require a narrow construal of "obligation." The questions that demand answers center upon justifying obedience to political authorities, both general and specific, and explicating the qualities that render political authorities legitimate or worthy of obedience.[55]

Klosko argues that emphasis needs to be placed on the relationship that those who are obligated have with the authority that ostensibly obligates them. He suggests that the three conditions can be met, but indirectly and in a general way because the problem of political obligation is not about meeting these three conditions, but about the relationship that people have with political authority. His theory is, as such, not strictly about "obligations" but about the relationship with authority. As a consequence, the type of authority at issue becomes exceptionally important, as does the caveat that political obligations are always *prima facie*, that they are not absolute but are binding only under normal circumstances and "can be overridden by conflicting moral principles."[56]

Klosko is able to use this caveat because of the relationship people have with the authority that obligates them, since his theory is limited to liberal societies. He clearly states, "the argument in this essay rests on the distinctive premises of liberal political theory and is therefore applicable to only those societies in which these premises obtain."[57] Klosko presents this bias as unproblematic:[58]

> The premises of liberal political theory from which we proceed, moreover, are not isolated assumptions or "arbitrary commitments or sentiments that we happen now to share." Rather, they are among our most firmly held moral principles and beliefs. They are aspects of our moral experience of which we can be most certain. If a satisfactory moral view should not be presumed to be consistent with them, it is not clear where else we should turn.[59]

This uncritical predisposition has the effect of marginalizing the political element in political obligations, and also provides a greatly whitewashed version of liberal societies. However, for the moment what matters is that this liberal vision means that Klosko can treat the state in generally benign terms that enables him to apply Hart's fairness principle to state authority.

The fairness principle is in essence the recognition of benefit and of not taking advantage of public efforts committed by others. Klosko quotes Hart, who writes:

> when a number of persons conduct any joint enterprise according to rules and thus restrict their liberty, those who have submitted to these restrictions when required have a right to a similar submission from those who have benefited by their submission.[60]

The fairness principle is used by Klosko to associate the public goods provided by the state with political obligations.[61] At issue, however, is what goods the state provides that deliver the legitimacy for any political obligations. The conditional nature of political obligations as evident in their *prima facie* character means that not all obligations are to be blindly accepted (which opens the door to resistance – I will come back to this). It can only be a general kind of good that provides the underlying legitimacy. Klosko calls such goods "presumptively beneficial goods," by which he means, borrowing from Rawls, "things that every man is presumed to want."[62]

Klosko suggests that such a public good is security: "I refer to public goods such as security as presumptively beneficial because of the strong presumption that A benefits from their receipt more or less regardless of his behavior toward them."[63] He emphasizes the centrality of security repeatedly:

> obligations to obey the law are rooted in public goods supplied by government that we cannot do without. Government's most prominent role is providing security, mainly national defence and law and order, which are preconditions for all other aspects of acceptable lives ... Throughout this work, the goods on which we will focus centre upon physical security ...
>
> The class of benefits that are public goods and indispensable are quite small. I will therefore generally confine discussion to its clearest members physical security comprised mainly of national defense and law and order, protection from a hostile environment, and provisions for satisfying basic bodily needs ... .[64]

Klosko's emphasis on security is maintained in his second book on political obligation.[65] He points out how this is necessary in the liberal tradition of political thought,[66] and his theory fits within the liberal tradition. Political obligations cannot, in this account, be divorced from the state. Indeed, Klosko goes so far as to suggest that while non-state entities may provide some of the goods and services that the state traditionally does, they are unable to provide all the goods necessary for people to live acceptable lives.[67] Klosko thereby doubly ties political obligation to security: not only is security a presumptively beneficial good that is necessary for understanding the foundations of the obligatory relationship, but it is a good that only the (liberal) state can satisfactorily provide.

There exists, consequently, a strong theoretical connection between political obligation and security, but Klosko also suggests a sociological reason. As he notes in the preface to the new edition of *The Principle of Fairness and Political Obligation*, political theory research has often been influenced by wider security issues of the time. Walzer's early work on political obligation is clearly related to the moral concerns raised by the Vietnam War,[68] including the challenges posed by the draft at that time.[69] Walzer thus also links his work on obligation with questions about national security, and Klosko notes that the "political upheavals in the United States over the War in Vietnam" influenced the political philosophy literature of the time. Indeed, it was in the 1970s that works on political obligation began to increase significantly in number. According to JSTOR data on research metrics, the number of articles published on political obligation per year increases during the 1960s, and corresponds to the Vietnam War.[70]

There exist multiple connections between theories of political obligation and security, but what these connections so far all demonstrate is that the security discourses at issue are understood by the security provided by the state. Klosko's framing of security is quite broad, encompassing not just national defense but also social, economic, health, and environmental security. This framing of security is of particular interest for two reasons. First, its statist outlook follows from Weber's definition of the state, but the scope of security issues that it includes cannot always be addressed by the state as an independent entity and in some cases may actually be threatened by the state. If the state is unable, independently, to provide security in all these areas then an original reason for the focus on the state is called into question and along with it a reason for political obligation.

Liberalism and the International in Political Obligation

One of the necessary conditions for political obligation is that it involves a relationship between the citizens and their state. As George Klosko writes in the introduction to his book *Political Obligation*:

> Among the major theorists in the liberal tradition from Locke and Hume to Mill, Rawls and Nozick, there are significant differences about central issues. But all these theorists agree about the need for the state, and I believe that need for the state is central to liberalism. Questions concerning whether the state is necessary and what kind of states we require are important to political obligation, because if the state is in fact not necessary, then it is difficult if not impossible to demonstrate that we have a moral requirement to obey it.[71]

Klosko uses an argument incorporating a prisoner's dilemma or tragedy of the commons to justify a public-goods-based argument. In short, the state and only the state is capable of providing all the necessary public goods, including protection, both individual and collective, social and environmental security, a legal system, support for cultural institutions, redistribution programs, and standards regulations for food, drugs and finance, for example. Most, if not all, of these goods pertain in some manner to the multiple ways in which the state provides security. Security in its broadest sense is thus the foundation for the state and of why people have a moral requirement to obey it. To put it somewhat crudely, political obligations can be explained because of the overwhelming good of security that the state provides.

This formulation begs a number of questions, such as whether or not there are other types of security that the state cannot provide and what the wider implications are for this particular statist form of security. Klosko claims that one of the strengths of his theory is that it can help make sense of political obligations in today's world. Yet, Klosko's argument does contain some disturbing implications. The most serious of these is an uncritical acceptance of the liberal order and the illiberal politics on which it is based.

If there is no compelling moral reason based on the liberal principles of human freedom to accept the political obligations to one's government, it follows that it would be justifiable to rebel against such an illiberal government. Liberal theories of political obligation contain within them the seeds for a justification of resistance and possibly violent revolt against an unjust, illiberal government. Yet, liberal political philosophy has also tried hard to severely circumscribe such recourse to rebellion. As Kant famously wrote in his essay *What is the Enlightenment?*, think and "argue as much as you like and about whatever you like, but obey!"[72] Thomas Hobbes, for example, can be read as privileging stability over any right to rebel, although John Locke may be more tolerant of the right to resist an unlawful command and even to rebel and replace the rulers. Closer to Locke than Hobbes, Walzer argues that there is a right to rebel, so long as the disobedience "does not threaten the very existence of the larger society or endanger the lives of its citizens."[73] In essence, Walzer is suggesting that disobedience is legitimate when it is morally appropriate, that it is acceptable when in a liberal society the government pursues illiberal policies. However, this circumscribes disobedience significantly, since what if the liberal society is pursuing illiberal policies overseas? Such illiberalism is, however, not necessarily relevant as a right of disobedience because the people whose rights are being violated do not belong to the community of people who share obligations to each other. While the illiberalism of the violation seemingly overrides a liberal base for any political obligations, there is an important caveat. Walzer notes that those citizens who engage in disobedience over such issues do so with regard to a self-identified membership in the wider human community, but such a community cannot be properly understood to involve any obligations or commitments.[74] It does not follow that illiberal policies abroad can justify legitimate disobedience at home if those at home are not affected as citizens (in the conventional sense of the word).

The communitarianism in Walzer's thinking here is evident, which is not surprising as theories of political obligation are necessarily so. Nevertheless, there are international calculations which privilege stability over any right to resistance or rebellion and which political obligation theories assume. Revolutions against a government are, as the famous scholar of international relations and revolution Fred Halliday argues, never self-contained in the states where they take place, but spread and have international repercussions.[75] Consequently, a revolt in an illiberal state could impact the security of liberal states through the revolt's internationally destabilizing effects. If we accept these premises, it follows that liberal regimes would prefer above all else stable and predictable international relations,[76] and that stable borders make for good neighbors, as Walzer argues in his earlier work.[77] It is not surprising that Walzer, a political theorist of political obligation, liberal justice and international morality, would take such a view as any liberal theory of political obligation necessarily privileges the moral bounds of nation-state sovereignty and is accordingly suspicious of anything that could undermine the borders and stability of this sovereignty – and Walzer's work on obligation preceded his work on war. As such, a liberal theory of political obligation could indirectly support a liberal state's foreign policy that supports the stability of illiberal states. While Walzer's critique of political obligation was influenced by his moral concerns about an unjust war, he does not address the extent to which a theory of political obligation tolerates the existence of illiberal regimes and an illiberal foreign policy in order to protect the state that provides the goods that justify political obligations.

Moreover, as the post-colonial theory literature has argued, liberalism has had an implicit part in the spreading and legitimation of deeply violent processes, including colonialism.[78] Thus the good of security that liberal theories of political obligation describe cannot be divorced from either the support of illiberal regimes internationally in order to maintain a stable and secure international society, or the history of liberalism that justified the violence of colonialism (none of this even begins to address the discriminations and violence committed inside the state by liberal regimes against women and minority populations). In short, the security underpinning political obligation is as illiberal as it is liberal.

What this liberal bias means, and what Klosko and the other theorists of political obligation fail to address, is the extent to which their theories presume a particular type of international order, an order that is potentially contrary to their universal liberal values of human freedom, rights and dignity.[79] Regardless of whether or not liberal states are strong enough to withstand the potential international and/or global reverberations of localized resistance against illiberal forces, the historical record is that in international relations, liberal states all too often prefer stability and narrowly conceived national self-interest over human rights.[80]

The internal order that liberal theorists of political obligation use as the imagined ideal society that justifies political obligations is tied to an international order that they ignore.[81] This blindness is all the more striking when considering, for example, that Klosko uses the empirical examples of military service in Germany and Israel,[82] and a hypothetical example involving Uganda.[83] He even raises the illegitimacy and violence faced by citizens in Haiti in the late 1980s and early 1990s, and the election stolen in Panama by Manuel Noriega in 1989.[84] Yet there is nothing about how Noriega worked for a period of time for the CIA, and Klosko ignores any moral questions surrounding the invasion of Panama and its consequences. The USA's policies throughout Latin and South America, its global activities during the Cold War, and even its earlier imperialist policies in the American Hemisphere in the Monroe presidency, all attest to an illiberal liberalism in international relations that hides behind the veneer of liberal legitimacy presented by Klosko and others.

Theorists of political obligation are able to be so selective because they restrict the scope of political and normative problems that political obligation is concerned with. Assuming for the moment the independent nature of the state presumed by Klosko, his theory works only to the extent that we understand the political obligation relationship as one that exists primarily between citizens and their state. In this sense his emphasis on security is another way of emphasizing the particularity principle, which enables a domestic focus at the expense of forgetting any international illiberal implications. Indeed, both Klosko and Walzer are concerned with the security dynamics faced by citizens in their country of residence. For Walzer the question was a draft, among other things, and for Klosko the question is about the presumptively beneficial goods that can by definition only be provided by the state. Since it is the state that, as Weber reminds us, is defined by being able to provide security by holding the monopoly over the use of the legitimate force, the presumptively beneficial good of security can only be provided by the state. By emphasizing security in this way, Klosko also emphasizes the particularity principle.

The Particularity Principle

The importance of the particularity principle for theories of political obligation is demonstrated clearly by Klosko:

> An acceptable principle of political obligation must account for the strong connection between the individual and a specific political body, of which he is generally a citizen. However, this poses problems for a duty of mutual aid. If Grey is required to help people in distress, why must these be his fellow citizens as opposed to allowing him to fly off to Africa or Latin America where people are likely in far greater distress?[85]

One might add, or Jews in Paris and London helping Jews in Damascus. Two points: first, it is not entirely consistent to think that people overseas will in fact require greater aid than those locally do. Poverty may be greater in some countries than in others, but it is empirically incorrect to claim that distress primarily exists in poorer states. The greater issue here is one of choice, of being able to choose whom to help. Second, the question at issue here is one of moral responsibility more generally and of the relationship between this moral responsibility and community, as well as of the type of community. The particularity principle provides one such answer to this question.

This answer is that your primary duties are to the country in which you are a citizen. There are different ways of explaining this essentially normative principle, which emphasizes the relationship between citizens and their state above other political relationships that may also involve duties or obligations. In his article "What Is So Special about Our Fellow Countrymen," Robert E. Goodin explains one feature of this relationship in the following way: "National boundaries simply visit upon those particular state agents special responsibility for discharging those general obligations vis-à-vis those individuals who happen to be their own citizens."[86] In his account, the significance of the state is that it enables the most effective application of general duties to a particular population. David Miller provides a related argument in his article "The Ethical Significance of Nationality." His argument in this article is that "national boundaries may be ethically significant"[87] because they seemingly provide the most effective means of applying universalist principles toward particular populations, through the provision of various goods via state institutions.

It is from an influential critic of theories of political obligation that we find one of the more developed explanations of the particularity principle. In his book *Moral Principles and Political Obligations* A. J. Simmons provides a philosophical anarchist rejection of political obligation. The anarchism he presents is not an appeal or justification to rebel. He writes:

> The absence of political obligations within a community, then, will not *entail* that disobedience or revolution is justified. We will normally have good reasons for obeying the law, and for supporting some types of governments of which our own may be one.[88]

Simmons argues that there is no compelling reason for a general theory of political obligation. However, even though he rejects theories that explain political obligation, he does provide a strong explanation of a core tenet of most political obligation theories – indeed, a tenet that John Horton says is crucial.[89] At issue here is the particularity principle.

Simmons is concerned with exploring how there is no convincing account of political obligation. What he defines as the obligation to obey the law relies exclusively on the existence of positional duties. As he writes, "The mere fact that an institution exists (or set of institutions) exists, and that its rules apply to me, will not bind me to that institution."[90] It is very clear that for Simmons political obligation is closely tied to the institutions of the state, but his argument goes further, for as his exposition of the difference between obligation and duties suggests, he is concerned with a limited order under which political obligations exist.

For Simmons, obligation is "a moral requirement which satisfies" four conditions.[91] The first of these is that "the obligation is a moral requirement generated by the performance of some voluntary act (or omission)."[92] This condition differentiates duties from obligations in that an obligation requires some kind of action, what Simmons calls "special performances."[93] This is indeed an important feature of a political obligation, for what he is referring to is the internal drive or decision to accept an obligation. Obligations are a choice that individuals take on, and while they may be imposed they are by definition accepted by the agent as a special category of duty that requires self-affirmation of the obligation. The clearest way to explain the difference is by how we use the language of obligation and duty. As Simmons points out, "we 'obligate ourselves,' but do not 'duty ourselves.'"[94]

The second condition is that "An obligation is owed by a specific person (the 'obligator') to a specific person or persons (the 'obligee[s]'). Again, this distinguishes obligations from moral duties which are owed by all persons to all others."[95] This condition differentiates obligation from a universal moral imperative, for example. Obligations are specific to particular contexts, people, places and times. What this condition raises is the serious question about how we define what constitutes the limits necessary for an obligation to remain particular. Simmons' focus on this condition is on how obligations can be released. "While we 'do' our duty," he writes, "we 'fulfill' or 'discharge' an obligation."[96] What becomes especially important is how these boundaries are defined. Are they temporal, spatial, moral? There are no limitations to the acceptance of the duty other than the imposition of the duty existing. Obligation, however, has a greater conditionality since it has a larger amount of limitations imposed upon its relevance. Obligations have at least two limits: the morality of the obligation, which is to say the ability to legitimately disobey or reject it, and the fact that obligations represent a relationship between agents. There needs to be a relationship between the agents that makes the acceptance of the obligation possible. A duty, on the other hand, is not open to choice in the same way.

The third condition is one which Simmons borrows from H. L. A. Hart, and which further distinguishes an obligation from a duty. A duty is one-directional. The person who is held to have a duty does not create, by virtue of having a duty, a correlative right. An obligation, however, does. As Simmons writes, "For every obligation generated, a correlative right is simultaneously generated."[97] Simmons bases this condition on how obligations and duties do not create the same kind of rights. Duties, when they do correlate with rights, do so with rights that apply to all other people. Obligations, on the other hand, create rights that apply only to a specific person (or specific type of person, such as a citizen or group member). This difference provides yet another example of how obligations are limited in a way that raises questions about how their boundaries are constructed.

The fourth condition is that "It is the nature of the transaction or relationship into which the obligor and obligee enter, not the nature of the required act, which renders the act obligatory."[98] In other words, "Obligations are not generated by the nature of the obligatory act."[99] These are the four features that Simmons suggests separate obligations from duties, and what brings them together is the particularity of political obligations. Political obligations involve only the relationship between an individual and a particular political community. This is the particularly principle. Simmons writes: "I want to suggest that we are only interested in those moral requirements which bind an individual to one particular political community, set of political institutions, etc."[100]

Part of the importance of the particularity principle is that it separates political obligation from the obligation to obey only just governments. If the obligation were only for just governments there would be nothing to explain why we are not obligated to obey all just governments where one would be "equally constrained by the same moral bond to support every other just government."[101] At least, this is the problem that Simmons identifies. The order or type of political obligation with which he, and the literature, is concerned is generally focused on the obligation that citizens have to their state. It is not the obligation that a tourist has when she travels abroad and has to obey the laws in the land she visits that can provide an example of a political obligation, although empirically it is difficult to explain the difference faced by any individual who decides to break the law, either as a citizen in their country of citizenship or as a tourist. Nevertheless, the particularly principle is that "principle of political obligation which binds the citizen to one particular state above all others, namely that state in which he is a citizen."[102]

Problematically, Simmons is not concerned with permanent residents, since that would raise a geographical component of proximity, which he views as unhelpful. Proximity clearly makes it easier to obey the law, but it does not provide any moral reason to do so. Simmons provides an interesting critique of Lockean arguments for tacit consent since he rejects residency as a reason for justifying a political obligation. Simmons uses the example of war to emphasize how we do not view permanent residents as having the same obligations as citizens.[103] However, this example surely misses a key point.

While it is generally true that citizens are held to a different set of political obligations during a war from those permanent residents are held to, this has not always been the case, even in the twentieth century. After the Second World War, non-state agents of the Jewish settlements in Palestine conscripted Jews in the Displaced Persons Camps in Europe. In some cases they forcibly conscripted individuals who had no real citizenship as refugees to fight in a war for a country which did not yet exist and which they were not citizens of.[104] Moreover, there is nothing to say that the obligation to go to war, what Walzer called the obligation to die,[105] is an obligation that has primarily been explained by reference to citizenship.[106] What Simmons and the political obligation literature is concerned with often does not speak to the experiences of people who live with the consequences of their actions. The heuristic world in which only citizenship enables political obligations does not exist.

Any good theory has to discriminate, and in this regard the particularity principle plays an important theoretical role. However, in making it impossible to recognize that there are obligations that exist outside of citizenship and outside of the ostensibly special relationship that citizens have to their state, the particularity principle may be too discriminatory. In spite of the particularity principle it is still worth asking if it is possible to have obligations which are political and which are to a community that is not the state. Such accounts of obligation do exist, for as Walzer notes, "Obligations begin with membership, but membership in the broadest sense, for there are a great variety of formal and informal ways of living within a particular circle of action and commitment."[107] In this sense, it is possible to have a transnational political obligation, even if the statist communitarian element of the literature is dismissed.

There is, however, a communitarian element in transnational political obligation, for these obligations are also a part of membership. The political obligation literature is widely concerned with the question of membership, although because of the particularity principle it does not explore transnational or diaspora membership. The transnational and diaspora literature presumes membership but does not address the question of obligation, even when diaspora is featured as becoming a central form of membership.[108] Melissa S. Williams comes close in her critique of citizenship by defining citizenship not in terms of "shared identity but in terms of 'shared fate.'"[109] She also notes the relevance of obligation, although only in passing, and is seemingly concerned primarily with who would be considered to belong to the community and could participate in the decision-making processes of this community. The citizenship literature comes closest to addressing the questions of membership concerned here, precisely because at issue is a kind of shared

The Limits of Political Obligation

political community and culture, which crosses state borders, and which invites specific norms of behavior and commitment that are often geared toward sustaining the community. With the Jewish Diaspora, however, I do not want to get into questions of citizenship, as doing so would necessarily involve addressing at minimum whether or not it makes sense to think of there being a Jewish people (as opposed to disparate Jewish communities) and of who belongs, of who is a Jew. In the interviews, some points were raised that could be relevant to this wider question of membership and of citizenship in non-state political communities, but for ethical and methodological reasons they were not pursued. What is being assumed, however, is that the kind of transnational community in which transnational political obligations exist is not a cosmopolitan community, but one that is defined by discourses of inclusion and exclusion, of a bounded and limited membership.[110]

Conclusion: Why Obligation?

Political obligation is a significant concept within political theory. It includes a wide range of literature and sophisticated debate. Consequently, why bother critiquing it for something that the literature is not especially concerned with? Why bother challenging the statism of the particularity principle when it makes sense in the terms of what political obligation is meant to explain? Why illuminate the international security inferences contained in theories of political obligation and of the potential for it containing illiberal demand when the point is not to challenge theories of political obligation *per se*, but to provide a different account of obligations that are political, and are also transnational? The answer to all these questions is fairly simple: because it is necessary.

There exist significant political relationships across state borders carried out by or expected of minority populations. These kinds of practices and the related expectations are not new. They have been variously described by reference to transnational, diaspora or migrant communities. The case of Jewish internationalism is one such example, one that also demonstrates one of the political aspects via the relevance of dual loyalty. There are many practices of groups and individuals that are deeply suggestive of being both political and obligatory, but because they do not necessarily fit under the statist and/or legal framework for conceptual accounts of political obligation, they do not figure in the traditional framing of political obligation. Consequently, what is needed is a critique of this literature that reveals some of its hidden assumptions about international politics, and how the particularity functions so that it becomes possible to identify an alternative political discourse to replace the state.

In this sense, I am perhaps starting from a curious place – that the term should explain what the term's words suggest. Disciplinary jargon is often far removed from this type of clarity, and thus the way in which I am using the term may seem awkward, but necessary. While what is political in political obligation are the spatial and juridical structures of the state, and the relations that citizens have with these structures, the political in transnational political obligation is different.

Something similar to what I am calling transnational political obligation has been described as a trans-state relation, as opposed to a transnational one,[111] and elsewhere I have followed his usage.[112] With regard to the Jewish Diaspora, the concept of Diaspora nationalism is used by Jasmin Habib to identify the relational character of how Israel informs Diaspora Jewish identity and practice, and distinguish this kind of nationalism from one based on geographical proximity within a single territory. Yet, Habib also invokes the idea of obligation, writing:

> Although they [Diaspora Jews] do not live within the geographic borders of Israel, the narratives of the nation-state have become their narratives of belonging as a nation (as Jews). This form of diaspora nationalism is based on a sense of obligation and responsibility to preserve the collective, in memory, tradition, and practice.[113]

Obligation may only play one part in this account, but it is clearly an important part and while Habib's text is a bit short on theoretical analysis, it is clear in the empirical work she conducted that there are different ways in which obligations toward Israel can be felt and acted upon. For the moment, however, the point is that her move toward a relational politics is what matters, as in this text she is also working on exploring a political relationship that does not take place in a territorially contiguous political community.

Spatial politics are located across different categories, including international, state, city, community. The last of these easily challenges the integrity of the other three. Yet, in modern political thought there has traditionally only been one political space, that of the state. It can be difficult to think differently about political spaces and identities, and the particularity principle in political obligation is conservative in this regard. The paradigm of the state is always looming in the political imagination,[114] and although the convergence of nation with state became especially problematic for the Jews of Europe, it was especially hopeful for the Zionists.

The political aspect of transnational political obligation is different from that set up by the particularity principle. Historically, for the Jews, questions about political space and the obligations that went along with it was a major topic. Caught in between the destruction and promise contained in the merger of the state with the nation were alternatives, Jewish nationalism being one of them. Jewish nationalism was about protecting the Jewish nation in the Diaspora. It was pluralistic in its adoption of how multi-ethnic societies could coexist within the state while simultaneously belonging to a trans-state national community.[115] With the successes of Zionism and Jewish integration in the latter half of the twentieth century, this alternative has largely been forgotten, although recent scholarship has sought to bring back various alternative Jewish voices on Zionism, Jewish identity, the Diaspora and Israel.[116] What it demonstrates, however, is that it is possible to understand the identity, politics and discourses of obligation outside of the limits enforced by understanding politics to function only within conditions made possible by life under sovereignty. These are themes that will be explored in subsequent chapters, as I set out to explain a different account of politics that can shape a theory of transnational political obligation.

As Hannah Arendt famously wrote, "men, not Man, live on the earth and inhabit the world."[117] She invites us to think about politics not in terms of exclusivist nation-state models but in terms of people, of diversity and alternative conceptions of politics and of political spaces. In particular, she identifies an account of politics and of power that begins a conversation which can displace the political dominance of the state and of sovereignty. These are themes I address in Chapter 3, where I highlight how it is possible to argue for a non-statist account of obligation. In the next chapter,

Obligation in Exile

however, I continue with the international and related security elements which are contained in political obligation and which contribute to making the transition from the statist political to the transnational political.

2 Power and Obligation

Introduction

In Chapter 1, I explored the particularity principle of political obligation. This principle ties political obligation to the particular state that one is a member of, and according to John Horton, without it there can be no theory of political obligation.[1] Political membership, insofar as political obligation is concerned, thus functions only to the extent that political identity is defined by one's membership of a specific state and presumably to the state where one lives. There are some significant empirical problems with this framing that can lay doubt on the extent to which obligations to obey the law transgress state borders and the limits of citizenship, as well as the uniformity that this principle assumes with regard to the relationship each citizen has to their state – what about permanent residents, what is meant/understood by citizenship, what about tourists and their obligation to obey the law, what about the international law of extra-territoriality or extradition treaties, what about crimes against humanity, what about citizens' different experiences of the law and of institutional discrimination? – and so the particularity principle is best understood as an ideal type.

Consequently, what the particularity principle also does is enable theories of political obligation to sidestep some important considerations. One of these has to do with how the state is defined and how this definition in turn shapes what is understood by politics. In a sense, all theories of political obligation could be read as theories of state because without political obligation there would be no state, and so to explain political obligation is also to explain and justify the state. What is meant by politics then follows from this centrality of the state. However, if we look more closely at how the state is understood in some of the political obligation literature, it is not only security and other normative goods that the state provides which are used to define the state. The traditional definition of the modern state as provided by Max Weber is also used, which links the state to violence and power.

In this chapter, I suggest that power is an important and underexplored element in theories of political obligation. I then argue that there exists an alternative model of political power that is not statist and thus avoids the necessity of accepting anything like the particularity principle. Following from this discussion, which is based on the work of Hannah Arendt, I turn to Michel Foucault, who makes the important move that links power with individual identity. This combination enables two important theoretical points. The first is that it is possible to argue for an account of obligation that is political because of the power relations contained within, but which are not defined or framed by the state. In other words, while I accept the claim that politics is defined by power relations, I contest the traditional Weberian framing of what power means in this context. Second, once political obligation becomes deterritorialized in this way, it remains to explain the empirical condition of transnational political obligation. In using Arendt, this deterritorialization sets up the theoretical scope in which we can understand some of the power dynamics within transnational political obligation. What Arendt's account of power does not provide, however, is a sufficient framework for recognizing acts of power that are not visible and for appreciating how power pertains to individual senses of self and individual identity, and for this insight I use Foucault.

While my use of Foucault should not arouse any controversy, my use of Arendt is different from how she is often used, as her work is heavily influenced by the idea of the classical notion of the citizen, and so it remains statist in the sense of her being committed to the idea of a polity and to the idea that politics happens inside the policy. Yet Arendt was also deeply suspicious of some key elements of the modern state, calling sovereignty bankrupt,[2] for example. Her critiques of Zionism similarly reflect a deep suspicion of the modern state, especially when it is merged with the idea of the nation. She is sometimes used not to deterritorialize politics but to critique or redefine citizenship.[3] Nevertheless, her account of power can be read as enabling a deterritorialization of power from the state and a locating of it instead in a different political society. Using her definition of power to help define what is meant by politics, I imply that we can use her to set up an account of power that is appropriate for transnational political obligations.

The greater difficulty with using Arendt in the way I am is that it is difficult to apply her thought to an account of politics that is limited by such a specific community as a diaspora, which is certainly not the kind of political society she had in mind. In this regard, what I am not arguing is that transnational political obligations are a manifestation of an Arendtian model of politics. She was clearly no stranger to the types of political relations I am concerned with, as both her Jewish writings and her critiques of nation-state politics demonstrate.[4] Her life experience, as a Diaspora Jews and also a German refugee, clearly impacted her thinking. As such, it is not so far-fetched to suggest that it is consistent to use Arendt to help provide a theoretical formulation for what constitutes the political in the Jewish Diaspora's relationship with Israel. The Diaspora is, in this sense, assumed to be a kind of political community. Since defining the Jewish Diaspora is difficult at the best of times (is it a religious, cultural or ethnic community? How are different Diaspora communities related with each other? What empirical bonds exist across these communities? To what extent is the Diaspora experience the same for all Jews? Does it even make sense to think of the Jewish Diaspora and of Diaspora identity today?) and usually requires a general definition of Diaspora based on historical, religious and cultural similarities, adding an account of politics that links Diaspora with Israel should be acceptable.

Power in the Particularity Principle and Political Obligation

Bertrand Russell once wrote that "the fundamental concept in social science is Power."[5] His purpose in making this claim was to justify a liberal education so that citizens will not fall prey to abuses of power. His definition of power provides a forceful example of how in the liberal tradition power is often framed in negative terms. In his account:

> Power may be defined as the production of intended effects. It is thus a quantitative concept: given two men with similar desires, if one achieves all desires that the other achieves, and also others, he has more power than the other. But there is no exact means of comparing the power of

two men of whom one can achieve one group of desires and another another . . .[6]

As will become evident, his definition is similar to Max Weber's; both emphasize that power involves an ability to influence others, and as such, is empirically observable because of its causality. Neither of these claims, however, is an appropriate way of understanding the power dynamics in transnational political obligation, even though they are both influential in theories of political obligation.

Michael Mann, in his epic four-volume work on social power, identifies four sources of social power, ideological, economic, military and political, and further divides the character of power into extensive ("the ability to organize large numbers of people over far-flung territories in order to engage in minimally stable cooperation"), intensive ("the ability to organize tightly and command a high level of mobilization from the participants, whether the area and numbers covered are great or small"), authoritative ("willed by groups and institutions . . . comprising definite commands and conscious obedience") and diffused (which "spreads in a more spontaneous, unconscious, decentered way throughout a population, resulting in similar social practices that embody power relations but are not explicitly commanded").[7] The fourth of these, diffused power, is suggestive of Foucault's concept of governmentality, although the other three seem primarily suited to the more traditional framing of power employed by Weber and Russell.

There are many different theories and definitions of power. What these theories, including Russell's, tend to share is the claim that, in the words of Michael Mann, "In its most general sense, power is the ability to pursue and attain goals through mastery of one's environment."[8] This admittedly general account of power is influential in the political obligation literature, especially since much of that literature is concerned with the problem of external organizations impeding the free will of individual citizens and trying to justify or legitimize this infringement. The form of power present in such accounts involves a kind of contest between the individual will and the state.

If we read theories of political obligation backwards, and begin from the empirically observable point that the majority of people do, in fact, abide by the obligation to obey the law, then the most powerful agent is either the people who self-actively chose their course of action as free beings, or the state, that sets up the choices under which acceptable conduct is understood and is able to back up these conditions with force. Theories of political obligation necessarily imply that the state is ultimately the more powerful agent. If the theories presented a different case, they would not be theories of political obligation but of political resistance or rebellion.

Perhaps the avoidance of power occurs because theorists of political obligation are keen to avoid too much discussion of resistance. If they do so, and come on the side of explaining political obligations and possibly justifying them, they run the risk of their theories becoming justifications for *raison d'état*. What the traditional statist framing of political obligation suggests is the extent to which theories of political obligation are often variations of what could otherwise be called theories of state: theories that seek to explain and possibly justify the existence of the state with its ability to infringe upon the freedom or free will of those who live within its legal/political borders in return for it offering certain basic goods. Framed in this way, theories of political obligation are necessarily statist, and as such it could be argued that, all things being equal, they succeed to the extent that they provide a convincing account of what makes up the state, which is where the particularity principle becomes especially useful.

With the particularity principle, theories of political obligation are able to avoid lengthy discussions of power because the relation at issue is not with everybody who is subject to the laws, but only citizens or those connected to the polity in some equivalently special way. As such, power becomes too broad a concept to address, because if political obligation were approached as an example of power, it would have to pertain to everybody, and not just citizens. The particularity principle makes it possible for theories of political obligation to limit their scope, and presume an ideal-type state with ideal-type relations to its citizens. Paradoxically, however, it is the particularity principle that enables an avoidance of an engagement with power, even though the particularity principle is based on a particularly influential theory of power.

The most famous definition of the modern state is from Max Weber. He defines the state as having a monopoly on the legitimate use of violence. Weber, however, goes further than that, for his definition of the modern state is also tied to his definition of politics, and for Weber politics is about power. Theories of political obligation, consequently, should also contain a discussion about power.

Max Weber: Power and (Political) Obligation

Weber clearly sets out how political obligation and power are related. The connection between political obligation and power is outlined in Weber's famous essay *The Profession and Vocation of Politics*. Weber does not feature prominently in the political obligation literature, although there are references to his work. Klosko, for example, mentions Weber only once,[9] but the usage is illustrative. He uses Weber to help define the state, and he refers to Weber's famous definition of the state holding the monopoly on the legitimate use of force. Weber, however, has more to say about obligation and politics than Klosko's limited offering suggests.

Weber's discussion begins with an introduction to what he means by politics. At first, he uses politics to refer to almost any type of policy, but he quickly narrows his focus so that politics refers to "leadership, or the exercise of influence on the leadership, of a *political* association (*Verband*), which today means a *state*."[10] Two points emerge from this definition. First, that politics is concerned with practice that has a noticeable effect – the use of the term "exercise" is significant as it becomes important later on. Second, that defining politics in this way requires a definition of the state. What follows in his analysis is how a definition of the state leads into a discussion about the character of politics. It is at this juncture that Weber provides his famous definition, "that the state is that human community which (successfully) lays claim to the *monopoly of legitimate physical violence* within a certain territory."[11] The legitimacy of violence exists only within the state, for the state is "the sole source of the 'right' to use violence."[12] This definition helps explain some of the logic behind the particularity principle of political obligation. By defining the state in this way Weber provides a foundation for treating political life as functioning only within a given territory,[13] and the particularity principle reflects this territoriality. Weber, however, does not end his definition of politics here.

Weber continues by asking what is meant by politics, and then identifies politics as being tied to leadership in the state. The term "politics" for Weber is intimately tied to the state, or rather to a political organization. Organization is political "insofar as its existence and order is continuously safeguarded within a given *territorial* area by the threat and application of physical force on the part of the administrative staff."[14] Weber thus provides additional confirmation of the spatial character of the state, and how the state and politics are both tied to the use of violence. The concept of the state now has three components to it: a specific and demarcated geographical territory, politics as leadership, and legitimate violence. The second and third components require further clarification.

To suggest that politics is about leadership in the state, and that the defining character of the state is a legitimate right to violence, implies a correlation between politics and violence, so that politics could be about leadership pertaining to the control of violence. The state having legitimacy over the use of violence provides a further linkage between politics and violence. The state's violent character, however, does not necessarily lead to the legitimacy of violent politics or the suggestion that politics is necessarily violent. A distinction needs to be drawn between an ontological framing of politics that is concerned with establishing an understanding of what a political institution is, and a relational understanding of politics that is concerned with understanding what defines political action. In other words, Weber identifies a political space that is institutional, territorial, intimately connected with violence and political life. The ontological framing of the state defines the state's monopoly over violence as legitimate, but this legitimacy does not automatically transfer over to someone who is involved in the action or life of politics.

There is, consequently, the question of legitimacy, not of the state's monopoly of the use of physical violence, but rather of political leadership. Weber has to explore the question of legitimacy, but also provide a greater explanation of what is meant by politics. Otherwise the political can too easily become another term for legitimate violence, which is not the same as saying that what defines the state is its monopoly over the use of legitimate violence.

Politics, Weber suggests, involves "striving for a share of power or for influence on the distribution of power, whether it be between states or between the groups of people contained within a single state."[15] Political activity is further characterized as "striving for power, either power as a means to attain other goals (which may be ideal or selfish), or power 'for its own sake,' which is to say, in order to enjoy the feeling of prestige given by power."[16] These qualifications to his definition of power accomplish two objectives. First, it is now possible to more clearly identify a separation between his definition of political space, which is institutional, spatial and violent, and politics as action, which is not necessarily any of these. Second, Weber can now return to his definition of the state with an important addition. The state is not just about violence but is also about rule.

The reason why the state is also about rule is because political activity is what takes place within a political space. The state as a space may be distinguished from political action, but political action is what takes place inside the institutions of the state, and what takes place in these spaces is the pursuit of power by those who rule. Once power becomes a key feature of politics, the question of ruling over others, and thus of political obligation, becomes central. Weber's definitions of politics and of the state make it possible for him to provide what is in effect an account of political obligation. There are a few ways in which he makes this connection, but they all come down to the significance of power for politics.

Weber argues that the obligation to obey the law is another core part of what defines the state, that "the state is a relationship of *rule (Herrschaft)* by human beings over human beings, and one that rests on the legitimate use of violence (that is, violence that is held to be legitimate)."[17] The relationship between the individual and the polity is explained by having to obey rules that are backed up by the use, or threat, of force. Weber thus uses what John Horton[18] defines as political obligation as one of the fundamentals that defines the state.

It is in this regard that Charles Tilly has argued that the modern state can be likened to a protection racket.[19] There really is no choice about adhering to the rules of the state, and indeed Weber states as much: "For the state to remain in existence, those who are ruled must *submit* to the authority claimed by whoever rules at any given time."[20] The emphasis on submission is crucial here as the force of the submission is backed up by the use of violence, ostensibly legitimate. The violence is legitimate if it is carried out legitimately by the institutions of the state. Violence is not automatically legitimate simply by being conducted under the auspices of the state by one of its institutions. Weber was suspicious of non-state uses of violence and was greatly influenced by concerns about the Russian revolution.[21] He was not in the least sympathetic to Marxist arguments for revolution, even though he respected Marx intellectually.[22] Weber did not consider revolution to be a legitimate form of political change, largely because it involved upending legitimate power in the modern state, which for him was closely tied to the military.[23] What Weber suggests is that for the ruled there is no choice: they *must* submit and they must obey the authority of the state, which is not to say that there can be no political action aimed at change, just no violence or rebellion. This life of submission to authority is a part of what comes with living in a state, in a political association. It is a political life, a life characterized by power relations.

That the submission to authority is evidence of a power relation is clear for at least two reasons. First, because this life is contingent on belonging to a political association, it is closely tied to what is meant by politics. The ruled may not be engaged in politics *per se*, but s/he cannot be segregated from the effects of those who are. Those who are engaged in politics, who search for power, are part of the political establishment that legislates, enforces, or affirms the situation of rule to which the ruled must submit. The obligation contained in the phrase "must submit" is a direct reference to the power of the rulers over the ruled.

Second, this framing of necessary submission mirrors Weber's definition of power, which is done in two parts. He distinguishes two different types of power. The first is power (*Macht*) and the second is domination or rule (*Herrschaft*):

> "Power" (*Macht*) is the probability that one actor within a social relationship will be in a position to carry out his own will despite resistance, regardless of the basis on which this probability rests.
> "Domination" (*Herrschaft*) is the probability that a command with a given specific content will be obeyed by a given group of persons. "Discipline" is the probability that by virtue of habituation a command will receive prompt and automatic obedience in stereotyped forms, on the part of a given group of persons.[24]

For Weber, it is not *Macht* but *Herrschaft* that has the greatest relevance to the politics of everyday life inside the state, to political obligation. Relations of power (*Macht*) are more circumscribed in their political empirical manifestations and do not exist in the daily obligations to obey the law, but feature in extraordinary situations such as when one is faced with challenging such obligations. In this sense, *Herrschaft* depends on *Macht*, for the probability that a command will be obeyed in political relations under sovereignty functions only to the extent that if the command is resisted, there is a power (*Macht*) ready to enforce it.

State politics is about rule, and thus we see how closely aligned Weber's definition of the state is with the general concern that animates the political obligation literature. Weber does not use the term "obligation," he uses the term "rule," but the problematic is for all intents and purposes the same. Political obligation is about the relationship between the individual and the polity; it is a relationship based on accepting an authority that can create rules and expect others to accept these rules. Weber is in effect arguing that a theory of political obligation has to involve an account of power. Contemporary liberal philosophy, however, cannot accept Weber's argument, because it requires a forceful power (*Macht*) to overpower individual will regardless of consent or agreement.

That is not, however, the immediate problem. Rather, the problem is that Weber's definition of politics is too closely tied to the state and his definition of power is too limited. Weber may be trying to suggest a methodological separation between politics and non-political sociological spaces. Yet, as the urban political theorist Warren Magnusson has argued,[25] it is not so easy to separate the political from the sociological, and often the sociological ends up back at the state, because of the definition of politics. Michael Mann makes a related point in his multi-volume work on power. As he writes, "The enormous covert influence of the nation-state of the late nineteenth and early twentieth centuries on the human sciences means that a nation-state model dominates sociology and history alike."[26] The point here is not to suggest that the state is unavoidable, but rather that since we know that there are many political spaces that are not the state we should alter our understanding of politics in order to include such spaces. Weber is correct in that politics always involves power relations, but the relations may not be of the type of power that he recognizes. Moreover, if politics is about power relations, there are such relations that exist outside of the state, which means that there should be some kind of political relationship between societies across territorial states that could incorporate elements of both *Herrschaft* and *Macht*.

In this sense, Weber asks us to question what kinds of power relations exist internationally and transnationally, and if his account of *Herrschaft* resembles the problematic that political obligation is concerned with, then there should also be questions about what kind of political obligation, or relations characterized by non-statist manifestations of *Herrschaft*, exist across states and among peoples. Weber does not feature heavily in the political obligation literature, largely because of his illiberal account of politics. Yet, ignoring Weber has consequences of forgetting how closely tied the state and politics are to power, and of forgetting the need to understand how power functions as an element of political life.

Power and the Political Obligation Literature

It is a problem that power features so minimally in the political obligation literature. In accepting Weber's definition of the state, the political obligation literature ought to address his account of power as well, or at minimum explore the relevance of power for political obligation. Yet, power barely features in the political obligation literature. There is no explicit discussion of power in the main obligation texts by Klosko, Simmons, or Horton.[27] Gilbert[28] also does not write explicitly about power, and although she provides a discussion about "political power" her concern is authority, not power. One notable exception is Walzer's collection of essays on political obligation,[29] because they are almost all about power. The very titles of his chapters are more than strongly suggestive of the relevance of power for his analysis: to name but a few of them, "The Obligation to Disobey," "The Obligation of Oppressed Minorities," "The Obligation to Die for the State," "Political Solidarity and Personal Honour." Yet, the concept power does not appear once in the index even though the word appears, to my count, thirty-eight times, sometimes as a direct quotation.[30] The actual number of appearances is by itself not so important, but it is telling since the term "power" appears more than twice as often as "authority" (which also does not appear in the index), a term that may be of even greater relevance than power to his discussion. What is most telling, however, is in how Walzer uses the term "power." His usage is not consistent.

Walzer uses power as shorthand for political authority, as in the power of the sovereign, or the power of congress.[31] Contained within this usage is the idea of power as a political agent that commands and is obeyed. Whether or not the power succeeds because of its legitimacy or because of its ability to coerce varies according to the context in which Walzer uses the term. This usage that links power to state authority, or in a few instances to legally conferred authority,[32] is the most common usage in his book. Power is sometimes used to refer more generally to distributions of influence and control. Power as something that can be distributed and power as part of a structure are also recurring usages.[33] The reference to a distribution of power is evidence that power is something that can be shared, which gives power certain types of attributes that are consistent with Robert Dahl's Weberian-influenced writing on power where power can be observed and is closely tied to political authority, to being able to, in colloquial parlance, get things done.[34]

Walzer's usage of the concept of power reflects the different framings of power that Steven Lukes identifies in his famous short book *Power: A Radical View*. Using Lukes' terminology, Walzer is using both one- and two-dimensional understandings of power.[35] The one-dimensional view is what others call the pluralist view of power, and is essentially a Weberian account of power where power is relational. In the words of Robert Dahl, who adopts Weber's definition, "A has power over B to the extent that he can get B to do something that B would not otherwise do."[36] However, there is a variation in Walzer's usage since the reference to legally conferred authority is suggestive of what Lukes calls the two-dimensional view of power.[37] This view of power includes how power can function in setting the "rules of the game" that confer benefits on those who are in a position to protect their interests, and disadvantages those that are not.[38] The two-dimensional view offers the following advantages: "It incorporates into the analysis of power relations the question of the control over the agenda of politics and of the ways in which potential issues are kept out of the political process."[39] When Walzer writes about the power of citizens[40] or of self-government he is conflating the one- and two-dimensional views of power. His discussion about Socrates is evidence of this difference, for he discusses how Socrates did not have the power to overthrow the government of Athens, but that Socrates also chose not to escape his punishment.[41]

Walzer, it should be clear by now, uses power to refer both

to institutions and to individuals without distinguishing how the power of an individual is logically not of the same character as the power of an institution. The common denominator for him seems to be that both cases display the capacity for compelling the specific actions of another. Yet, there is no discussion as to how the "power" of an individual and the "power" of an institution can function in the same manner, even if they both ostensibly seem to display a similar type of relation and causal capacity.

To add further confusion, he also talks about power in something close to either a phenomenological or existential account, where it is not the ability to control the terms of debate but an emotional influence or existential concern that has power. In this usage, power is probably better understood as a kind of unseen physical force. How else are we to understand what he means by power when he writes, in a discussion concerned with Thomas Hobbes, of "the power of the fear of death (or of physical pain)"?[42]

Walzer uses the term "power" in seven different ways. He uses it to refer to (1) authority, (2) force, (3) individual power, (4) institutional power, and (5) the power to control the agenda (call it discursive power), and also to two variations of power as authority: (6) a legal account where power is explained by the capabilities enabled by law, and (7) a popular account, where power is best understood as the responsibility of individual citizens. Walzer is clearly aware that he is using the term in different ways, and he does at one point try to provide some clarity by offering a distinction between power and authority.[43] In this brief one-line distinction, he suggests that power refers to a capacity or ability to affect the behavior of others (Lukes' one-dimensional view) whereas authority is about the normative aspect of being accorded this kind of ability to influence. To be fair, his book on obligation was not written as a monograph but is a compilation of essays, and so to read it as one piece of work is slightly unfair. Nevertheless, the scope of how he uses the term "power" is interesting, since it may be a sign that power serves a large role in theories about political obligation, but that it is not clear what exactly this role is. Walzer may not be clear what he means by power, but his work is suggestive that power is significant in thinking about political obligation.

Indeed, the role of power should figure prominently in any theory of political obligation. The subjection of individuals to authoritative processes is another way of framing the moral conundrum of political obligation in such a way that it raises both the normative problems that it seeks to explain and the power relationships contained therein. As the political theorist James Tully writes:

> It is difficult to imagine a more widely held assumption of contemporary moral and political thought than that freedom consists in either the freedom from power or the freedom to act in accord with power exercised through norms validated in conditions of power.[44]

I take this to mean that one of the main issues for making sense of politics and political possibilities is to engage with how individuals and people are constituted as having powers to act and as simultaneously being restricted by other powers in the conditions of possibility for their actions. The problem of political obligation is one way of articulating the relationships in which people and individuals are both constituted as subjects having power but are also subjected to the power(s) of other people, groups, institutions, and law, of those discourses that limit and increase or sustain conditions of possibility for public life.

It is, I would suggest, impossible to argue that there is an absence of power relationships in any empirical situation that could be explained by a theory of political obligation. Political obligation, it could be argued, is largely based on there being power relationships that are able to sustain the cohesion of the political community. Power does not have to be a negative, where it is understood primarily as the ability to force someone to act against his or her will. Power relations could be understood as inevitable in any political community and even as having emancipatory potential. It is only in thinking about politics by starting with the imaginary philosophical figure of the liberal individual with a pure will that power necessarily becomes a negative. As Foucault argues, if we start elsewhere, power is not so much a negative force threatening individual freedom as an unavoidable part of (political) life.[45]

Transnational political obligation is a different type of political obligation both in its statelessness and in how power features in it. Walzer is one of the few authors who brings to the fore the relevance of power in political obligation, even if his is a confused account of power. However, when we attempt to better understand how power is central to understanding political obligation it is Max Weber who provides the clearest connection. His account of power is, like the twentieth- and twenty-first-century obligation literature, state-centric, whereas our interest in the Jewish Diaspora is not spatially orientated in this way. Why, consequently, is power so important for the transnational political obligation, how does power contribute to shaping Diaspora/Israel relations, and why start with Weber?

To take the last question first, Weber is not especially helpful, but he remains important for demonstrating how any theory of political obligation necessarily requires some conception of power. As Walzer demonstrates, there is more than one discourse of power at play in theories of political obligation. To start with Weber is to return to a key source, which in the process informs our map of which account of power is most relevant for transnational political obligations.

In the remainder of this chapter I build on how the non-statist aspect of transnational political obligation requires a different form of power, one that is appropriate to the type of practical discourses characteristic of this form of political relation. I suggest that, first, we can use Hannah Arendt to provide an account of politics that redraws power away from the state and its institutions of rule. Second, by turning to Foucault, this account of power can be supplemented by identifying how power informs individual senses of self, and how such individual self-construction can take the place of Weber's institutional framing of *Herrschaft*. This combination of thinkers also involves a logical structure. Arendt's work can be read as a critique of Weber,[46] Foucault's work on power has been argued to represent an extension of Weber,[47] and it is possible to read Foucault and Arendt as being in a dialogue with each other with regard to their respective work on power.[48]

Power and Transnational Political Obligation: Arendt and the Disassociation of Power from the State

As befits a fundamental concept in the social sciences, there exists a sizeable literature on the concept of power, with strenuous disagreements about what the concept means and how to study it.[49] While this is not the place to conduct a "bibliographic commentary"[50] concerning power, it is necessary to argue how the Weberian account of power that sits behind the scenes propping up arguments for political obligation can be radically revised so that power still refers to a kind of obligation that is political but is not statist.

There is no shortage of work on power or relevant to power that makes a move to separate power from the state, even if Political Science and International Relations, two academic fields that emphasize the importance of power, remain heavily influenced by statist thinking. Some of the most significant works on power in the twentieth century include Hans Morgenthau's work about international relations and Robert Dahl's work about American politics, both of which adopted a Weberian account of power as an observable ability to accomplish a set objective over (the possibility of) an opposition.[51]

However, because the concept of power can be used in many different ways, it has been a common move by theorists of power to suggest that there exists a singular root meaning that lies across the range of ways in which the term is used. In order to uncover the real meaning of power, all one has to do is explore the different ways in which the term is used and find a common denominator. The statist definition, as such, is only one manifestation of power's inherent meaning. Dahl provides such a claim, and in the process uses the terms "influence" and "control" as synonyms for power. In a direct response to Dahl's conflation of influence and power, Peter Morriss follows a similar linguistic method, but disagrees with Dahl nevertheless.[52]

Morriss argues that power refers to "an ability or dispositional property"[53] which can be active or latent. He uses a range of examples of how the word power is used in order to analytically arrive at the fundamental meaning of the concept. One recurring example that he uses involves the example of the power of water to dissolve sugar. This example serves as a kind of metaphor for different manifestations of power that reflect individuals affecting or effecting particular outcomes.[54] Yet, this kind of comparison betrays the fundamental flaw in such an approach to understanding power. Water does not have any power to dissolve sugar. Sugar's solubility is a property of its molecular makeup, not a power of water. Just because in English we can use the word power in such a sense does not mean that from this usage it is possible to distil a core characteristic of power. Language is much more fluid and malleable than this kind of analytical philosophy demands. The ability to use metaphors, for example, attests to how language is never an objective methodology for communication but requires interpretation in order to discover shared meaning.[55] The ability of words to miscommunicate an intended meaning provides another example.

Less analytical approaches to power have included Marxist-inspired accounts, such as the work of Nicos Poulantzas.[56] Anthony Giddens' work provides another route to theorizing about power in a political sense, but without necessarily framing the political in purely statist terms.[57] However, it is the works of Hannah Arendt and Michel Foucault that are the most helpful in understanding how power functions in transnational political obligations. In this section I spend a fair amount of time going over Arendt's account of power. This is because, on the face of it, Arendt's account of power would appear to be highly relevant to the Jewish Diaspora and to an account of political power that could apply to a transnational relationship.

Arendt's work was highly influenced by her experiences as a Diaspora Jew. She was a refugee from the Nazis, a critical Zionist, and a deeply Jewish thinker.[58] Her account of politics is a product of these influences and foreshadows the argument of Appadurai about looking to non-state spaces for politics, to what he labels ethnoscapes, but what for Arendt is appreciating the "in-between spaces" in which "all human affairs are conducted."[59] The literature on Arendt has become something of a growth industry over the years.[60] My interpretation of Arendt will no doubt attract some disagreement. Nevertheless, turning to Arendt is important because she offers some distinctions which provide a significant critique of Weber and which set up a theoretical way of conceptualizing relations of power without requiring the state or sovereignty, merely people who share a common purpose.

Arendt helps us to understand how power is distinct from authority; how power cannot be separated from the human condition of living a life among others and of not being able to choose with whom we can share our lives on this planet; and that power involves people acting together, in concert, in public. All of these points distance her account of power from the kind of Weberian theories of power that overshadow the statist political obligation literature. As Jürgen Habermas argues, while both Arendt and Weber "represent power as a potency that is actualized in action" they provide significantly different arguments.[61]

The background to Arendt's theorizing on power is complex.

For Arendt, power and politics are influenced by the importance of plurality. Her understanding of both was influenced not just by the Hungarian uprisings of 1956 and the American Revolution, both of which represented important models of political activity, but also by the totalitarian movements of the twentieth century that she saw as an attempt to destroy politics. Arendt was also concerned with the politics of progress in the twentieth century. At the height of the Cold War, she questioned what faith in human progress meant, as it ignored the technological terrors being created in a nuclear world. Technological innovation was, she claimed, outpacing moral thinking. Progress could lead humanity to its own destruction.

Technology, particularly that supporting weaponry, is often framed in conventional language as a kind of power. The power of militaries, weapons, technologies, etc. to force the will of another into submission is a common Weberian reading of power that Arendt argues against. To her, it made no sense to read power in such a destructive way, as such an account of power was ultimately based on accepting the conclusion that human creativity could lead to the destruction of humanity. It made no sense to her for power to be a totalizing force whose very meaning is based on the capacity to destroy humanity. Arendt argues that both those on the Cold War Right, the Hawks, and those on the left, the revolutionaries such as Franz Fanon and even Jean-Paul Sartre, all agreed that power is about force, a reading that she rejects.

In challenging the meaning that enables power to be jointly understood by Right and Left in the same fashion, Arendt, in one of her typical moves, alters the focus of enquiry and asks if it makes sense to read power according to a tradition that has roots in the old European idea of absolute power and the modern European idea of sovereignty. This is the tradition of Hobbes,[62] Bodin,[63] and even Weber. They located power in a discourse of sovereignty, with sovereignty being indivisible and, as Hobbes points out in anticipating Weber, legitimately being able to use force to protect order. Power is thus traditionally read as being tied to force, and it is in this tradition that we find Weber's definition of power, as well as his followers Dahl and Morgenthau, among others. This tradition continued to influence much work on power in the twentieth century.

Arendt, however, challenges this reading by pointing out that there is something new in modernity that makes this traditional account of power both insufficient and inaccurate. First, there is the implication of nuclear weapons, and of how the creation of these weapons means that power, so long as it is tied to force, becomes based on the technological ability to destroy. Second, this traditional reading of power made the term almost meaningless. Power as a concept requires at least the potential that all actors are able to act powerfully. Yet as Arendt writes in *The Origins of Totalitarianism*:

> Modern power conditions which make national sovereignty a mockery except for giant states, the rise of imperialism, and the pan-movements undermined the stability of Europe's nation-state system from the outside. None of these factors, however, had sprung directly from the tradition and the institutions of nation-states themselves.[64]

Thus, power should, ostensibly, have no meaning outside of the so-called major powers, yet clearly, those who do not constitute major powers display the ability to exert influence and have an effect. The disdain Arendt has for the traditional reading of power is based on its inherent internal contradiction and rejection of humanity.

Third, the Weberian argument relies heavily on the agency of the powerful. There is a trajectory with Weber that is almost physical in its causal character, that an action from one source can be held responsible for a specific outcome in another because of power. It is for this reason that Dahl notes how power has always been tied to the question of causation.[65] Arendt, however, suggests that this linear trajectory no longer exists in modernity. Rather, in modernity there is something new: bureaucracy, the rule of nobody. She writes of "Bureaucracy or the rule of an intricate system of bureaus in which no men, neither one nor the best, and neither the few nor the many, can be held responsible, and which could properly be called rule by Nobody."[66] In this system there can be no power, at least not according to the traditional account. The reason is that there is no clear causal link between an agent deciding on an action and that agent being able to impose his or her will on another. A bureaucracy removes this kind of direct accountability or responsibility necessary for power. This critique of bureaucracy is also a response to Weber; it follows closely from her work on totalitarianism, and was taken up largely by Zygmunt Bauman in his text,

Modernity and the Holocaust.[67] But it is Arendt's *The Origins of Totalitarianism* and her reporting of the Eichmann trial that provide the original insights for this argument.[68] Arendt makes an important point here, that power can be understood (indeed, needs to be understood) in terms that separate it from the authority of the state and its institutions of governance. In short, she is separating power from organizations of rule, and thus radically challenges the Weberian definition that ties power to the institutions of the state, including bureaucracy.

There is, she claims, a great potential danger to humanity when bureaucracies become too influential for the conduct of human life because within a bureaucracy it is the structure or system that ends up providing the legitimacy for the action. Agency and the responsibility that comes with agency are greatly diminished, and it makes little sense to approach bureaucracies as having any power. Power requires agency, and Arendt argues that bureaucracies have none.[69] Power, for a bureaucracy, is not tied to human agency but to structural possibilities.

This reading of power is perhaps too one-sided. The works of Michel Foucault, Steven Lukes and Anthony Giddens all offer different interpretations and seek to frame power as more diffuse than Arendt appears willing to do.[70] While for Arendt power is not as diffuse as required by Giddens and his theory of structuration, she does not suggest that power is somehow something static or measurable. As she writes in *The Human Condition*, "Power cannot be stored up and kept in reserve for emergencies, like the instruments of violence, but exists only in its actualization."[71] This actualization of power is something that can only happen among people.

For Arendt, human existence is characterized by a life among other (different) people, and this feature also ties the concept of power to politics. Arendt approaches a definition of power according to the character of human existence, which is political owing to the inherent plurality of humankind. What makes power political is that it exists when humans come together to act in relation with other human beings in their public lives. In this regard, the key for Arendt is in the connection that power has to public life. The potential of power is not just one attribute or characteristic that defines the concept of power; it is necessary, since for Arendt power is innately associated with the potential of the people to act together in the public realm. The potential of power is not just a conceptual abstraction but a core component of human existence and of politics. For Arendt, "Power is what keeps the public realm, the potential space of appearance between acting and speaking men, in existence."[72]

This framing of power disassociates from power many of the other concepts that are often thought of as being related to it, such as strength, force, authority and violence. Arendt distinguishes all of these terms, removing them of their importance insofar as they inform what is meant by power. These distinctions are already evident in her 1958 work *The Human Condition*, in which she writes:

> Power ... is boundless; it has no physical limitation in human nature, in the bodily existence of man, like strength. Its only limitation is the existence of other people, but this limitation is not accidental, because human power corresponds to the condition of plurality to begin with.[73]

Arendt is raising two points here. The first is a general one, that power is not physical – it cannot be measured, stored and saved for later – and even though it is related to individual being/existence it is not something that exists in individuals as independent beings, but only when individuals come together. Second, power is tied to the human condition of plurality. Plurality refers to the triple condition of equality, distinctness, and what could be called difference. The equality of plurality involves the ability of mutual understanding among different people. The distinctness of plurality is about how each person is uniquely different from any other. Arendt explains the equality and distinctness of plurality as follows:

> If men were not equal, they could neither understand each other and those who came before them nor plan for the future and foresee the needs of those who will come after them. If men were not distinct, each human being distinguished from any other who is, was, or will ever be, they would need neither speech nor action to make themselves understood.[74]

The third element of plurality is what could be termed "difference." Arendt famously explains this crucial aspect of plurality by writing about the "fact that men, not Man, live on the earth and inhabit the world."[75]

The importance of plurality for politics is evident, for "this plurality is specifically *the* condition – not only the *conditio sine qua non*, but the *conditio per quam* – of all political life."[76] For Arendt, politics and plurality cannot be divorced, but it is through power that the plurality of humankind becomes political. It is in becoming active in political life that power takes place. Power's proximity to plurality and politics is what distinguishes Arendt's account of power from many others. She develops this distinction in her later work *On Violence*, published eleven years after *The Human Condition*.

In *On Violence* she supplements her explanation by clarifying that what distinguishes strength from power is that strength, unlike power, refers to individuals, not to people. She writes:

> Strength unequivocally designates something in the singular, an individual entity; it is the property inherent in an object or person and belongs to its character, which may prove itself in relation to other things or persons, but is essentially independent of them. The strength of even the strongest individual can always be overpowered by the many, who often will combine for no other purpose than to ruin strength precisely because of its peculiar independence.[77]

It is groups of people acting together that are powerful, not any individual. Moreover, this distinction further reinforces how in bureaucracy there is no power, for a bureaucracy is not the equivalent of a group acting together, but is an organizational structure that isolates individuals from each other by removing them from the decisions produced by the bureaucracy.

Whereas strength is individual, force is distinct from power for a different reason. Power, Arendt argues, has to do with activity whereas force is physical. "Force, which we often use in daily speech as a synonym for violence ... should be reserved ... for the 'forces of nature' or the 'force of circumstances' (*la force des choses*), that is, to indicate the energy released by physical or social movements."[78] While both power and force offer an inference of potential activity, her differentiation here rests on how some attribute force to the exertion or spending of energy. Problematically, this definition does not provide an especially clear separation from power. People acting in concert in public life do expend energy, sometimes physical, perhaps as part of a social movement. In any case, the point that Arendt appears to be making is not so much that the term "force" could refer to power, but that it should not refer to power. For her, the term "force" should be reserved for other usages that share in common the underlying physicality suggested by the phrase "the forces of nature."

"Authority" is another term that is easily associated with power. For example, Talcott Parsons writes, "Authority is essentially the institutional code within which the use of power as medium is organized and legitimized."[79] The connection between authority and political power is, as Arendt points out, often presumed, but authority is nevertheless distinct from power.[80] The key point insofar as obligation is concerned, however, is not that there may not be ways in which authority and power are, contra Arendt, linked, but that in challenging this connection Arendt also questions an important aspect of political obligation.

If we take the problem of political obligation to refer to the question of why anybody accepts the obligation to obey the law, the issue of authority necessarily arises. The act of obeying is a direct consequence of a relation with authority, but Arendt argues that the conventional account that frames authority as the ability to "make people obey"[81] is misleading. Authority is, according to Arendt, not inimical to freedom, and it is not so much making people obey that is the heart of authority. That is why Arendt writes, "To remain in authority requires respect for the person or the office. The greatest enemy of authority, therefore, is contempt, and the surest way to undermine it is laughter."[82] While authority does require some kind of obedience, it is not through force or violence: "Its hallmark is unquestioning recognition by those who are asked to obey; neither coercion nor persuasion is needed."[83] This framing is distinct from power although power may contribute to the recognition of authority. That authority can be legitimate with a kind of obedience by choice, what political theorists sometimes call political obligation, means that power may be related as a source of authority, but only indirectly. Power does not provide the basis for authority, it merely functions as a process whereby authority is recognized.

This process of recognition is crucial for how Arendt frames the concept of authority, and to make her point she turns to classical philosophy. Authority, she argues, was a problematic concept for the classical philosophers Plato and Aristotle. "The word and the concept are Roman in origin. Neither the Greek language nor the varied political experiences of Greek history shows any knowledge of the kind of rule it implies."[84] Arendt suggests that for these philosophers the difficulty was in recognizing and reforming the relationship between authority and coercion. They realized that the linkage between authority and coercion was not suitable for political authority. The challenge was to devise an account of authority that was political and not based on coercion or tyranny or on a kind of household despotic model (what we could today term patriarchal despotism). Consequently:

> Authority implies an obedience in which men retain their freedom, and Plato hoped to have found such an obedience when, in his old age, he bestowed upon the laws that quality which would make them undisputable [sic] rulers over the whole public realm. Men could at least have the illusion of being free because they did not depend on other men.[85]

After the death of Socrates and in *The Republic*, Plato struggles to resolve this challenge of how to explain the basis of political authority when this authority was not based on coercion or tyranny.

The challenge for Plato, and for theories of legitimate authority, is to explain how authority does not mitigate the freedom of the people and of individuals. There is a curious paradox to this challenge, for the problem of political authority is a problem precisely because, in the free sphere of politics, there should be no authority:

> The freedom of the political realm begins after all elementary necessities of sheer living have been mastered by rule, so that domination and subjection, command and obedience, ruling and being ruled, are preconditions for establishing the political realm precisely because they are not its content.[86]

This paradox is why, with Aristotle, we get formulations about being ruled and ruling in turn and of the need for education.[87]

However, Aristotle's answer to this paradox is a response to the problems that Plato encounters when he tries to provide an account of political authority. In *The Republic* Plato turns to philosophers to rule the city, but this is in order to protect philosophy and philosophers, and not for the benefit of the city *per se*. For the philosophers, authority could come from reason and persuasion, a means devoid of physical violence. However, only the philosopher would participate in such means of persuasion; the people who make up the polity could not be presumed to also adhere to, let alone understand, the concept of rule through and by reason. People may need to be coerced. Consequently, Plato turns to a variety of examples in search of a non-violent principle of authority.[88] Most, if not all, of these examples come, however, from non-political sources.[89] They include the relations "between the shepherd and his sheep, between the helmsman of a ship and the passengers, between the physician and the patient, or between the master and the slave."[90] According to Arendt, what Plato looks for in these examples is "a relationship in which the compelling element lies in the relationship itself and is prior to the actual issuance of commands."[91]

No such element is satisfactorily found, since each example ultimately comes down to linking thought, primarily rational thought, with action, which renders the philosopher into a politician, something which, problematically for Plato, Socrates is against, at least according to Arendt.[92] Aristotle's response to these problems is to explain political authority according to the principle of being ruled and ruling in turn.[93] Aristotle seeks to explore not just the concept of political authority, but of rule, and of the different types of political constitutions, but in order to explain authority, primarily in the context of political authority, he turns to the idea of nature.

Reason, he points out, is not enough, since "men do many things against habit and nature,"[94] and consequently, education becomes crucial to guard people from being persuaded, rationally or otherwise, to act contrary to their nature and according to requirements of a political society. The challenge that Aristotle seeks to resolve is how it is possible to provide a grounding for authority in political society when people can be persuaded, sometimes by legislators, to act against their nature. Moreover, and crucially, this challenge is especially important with regard to rebellion, or in cases where the people feel treated unjustly, choose to act against the legislators, but fail to appreciate the superiority of their rulers. Such ignorance poses a considerable threat not only to unjust governments but to just ones as well. Hence Aristotle's turn to nature:

> Nature herself has provided the distinction when she made a difference between old and young within the same species, of who she fitted the one to govern and the other to be governed. No one takes offence at

being governed when he is young, not does he think himself better than his governors, especially if he will enjoy the same privilege when he reaches the required age.[95]

Nature provides the basis for authority, but it is education that replaces the need for (violent) coercion. Moreover, education serves another purpose: "For he who would learn to command well must, as men say, first of all learn to obey."[96] Aristotle alters Plato's argument that struggles with the potential contradictions between reason and rule. Aristotle grounds authority not in reason, but in age, which is natural and inevitable. Education serves to reinforce, through human activity, these natural foundations.

Such claims to nature no longer have much influence, at least not in Aristotelian terms, although the turn to education remains significant (as we will see in some of the examples in the subsequent chapters). Here Arendt identifies yet another crucial distinction between power and authority, that of justification. For Aristotle, the use of education enables a discourse by which authority is learned to be justified. However, Arendt argues that the concept of authority in politics is not yet clear with Aristotle. She suggests that it is the Romans who develop this account in ways that are important for understanding how authority is distinct from power.

For the Romans, authority is based on a combination of a deep belief in the importance of tradition, understood as a reference to the importance of founding, and a belief that education helps ensure respect for the greatness of the founders, or the guiding ancestors.[97] "Authority, in contradistinction to power (*potestas*), had its roots in the past, but this past was no less present in the actual life of the city than the power and strength of the living."[98] The Roman conviction of the importance of founding is one way to emphasize the connection between authority and authorship. It is the author as creator that confers authority. Arendt develops this point by pointing out the difference between the author, that is, the "one who [inspires] the whole enterprise," and the builder.[99] It is, she tells us, traditionally the author who remains pivotal to the meaning of the enterprise, not the actual builders. This conviction remains relevant today. We rarely remember the names of the actual builders who constructed the towering edifices of modernity in our urban landscapes. It is the architects, the authors of the buildings, who we remember. Authority, consequently, tends to look to the past.

It is not a forward-looking discourse, whereas power is. Authority derives its special character in its binding connection to the past, to, for the Romans, "the sacred beginning of Roman history."[100] The relevance of tradition for authority should be obvious, since it is in the past that authority, as a reference to original authorship, is defined. Arendt provides another argument that links authority to tradition, and in a way helps us to further understand what she means by politics and power.

In a very short essay, *On Tradition*, Arendt provides another twist in the shift in political thinking from Plato to Aristotle. This twist begins with Socrates who was uninterested in pursuing politics. The Socratic model was that the philosopher and citizen are expected to accept the laws of the *polis*, even if the decision requires an obligation to die.[101] For Plato, the fact of the city condemning the philosopher to death for corrupting the youth of Athens was a crime.[102] The solution was to protect the philosopher from the politics of the city. Plato was thus contemptuous of politics, yet paradoxically forced to provide a philosophical reason for philosophers to engage in politics. Aristotle provides a radically different approach, that of claiming the unavoidable naturalness of humans as political beings.[103] Thus, political thought, that is political philosophy, claims Arendt, begins with a specific tradition that starts with Socrates' death and the subsequent reactions to it. She writes, "At the beginning of tradition, politics exists because men are alive and mortal, while philosophy concerns those matters which are eternal, like the universe."[104] However, this schism between philosophy and politics was problematic for political philosophy. The eternal focus of philosophy made its political content deeply deficient, and it also made it difficult to connect philosophical activity with political activity. Arendt is here exploring the distinction between thinking and action, a distinction that was especially important for her.[105] This distinction may be a product of her personal relationship with Heidegger, and of her need to explain his involvement with the Nazis,[106] but it was also an important theoretical distinction that she continued to explore until the end of her life.[107]

With regard to tradition, Arendt provides two different usages of the term. Relying on one of her preferred methodologies, anamnesis, a critique based on forgetting past heritage, she returns to both Ancient Greek and Ancient Roman thought to explain the concept of tradition. The first is the tradition that led to the origins of political thought, the tradition that we find with Plato and Aristotle. The second is a "traditional" paradox: that this tradition led to the removal of tradition from politics – and led to tradition becoming important for authority and not politics, and thus not power. It is in this vein that Arendt writes:

> Thus our tradition of political philosophy, unhappily and fatefully, and from its very beginning, has deprived political affairs, that is, those activities concerning the common public realm that comes into being whenever men live together, of all dignity of their own.[108]

Amazingly, Arendt appears to be claiming that political philosophy has no tradition of politics because political philosophy originally sought to remove actual participation in politics from the concern of political philosophy. The political philosopher was concerned with being able to remove the philosopher from politics, and even Aristotle does this: "In Aristotelian terms, politics is a means to an end; it has no end in and by itself. More than that, the proper end of politics is in a way its opposite, namely, nonparticipation in political affairs."[109] The consequence of this approach to politics (and political philosophy) is that politics, and political participation, is ultimately concerned with the escape from politics. "Politics, in other words, is derivative in a twofold sense: it has its origin in the prepolitical data of biological life, and it has its end in the postpolitical, highest possibility of human destiny."[110] This paradox has meant that there is no tradition in politics because the point of politics is its escape. This paradox is especially evident in the thought of Karl Marx, who sought to explain politics in terms of an ultimate goal of escaping from a condition of politics defined in terms of class struggle. Arendt's argument is, in part, that tradition became a concern for politics in a different sense of the political, a sense of politics that was not tied to people coming together and acting in the common realm.

Arendt is deeply critical of how authority, as a concept, has come to lose its traditional meanings, and becomes easily conflated or confused with other concepts – the example of authoritarianism is just one such. She writes:

> While all the models, prototypes, and examples for authoritarian relationships – such as the statesman as healer and physician, as expert,

as helmsman, as the master who knows, as educator, as the wise man – all Greek in origin, have been faithfully preserved and further articulated until they became empty platitudes, the one political experience which brought authority as word, concept, and reality into our history – the Roman experience of foundation – seems to have been entirely lost and forgotten. And this to such an extent that the moment we begin to talk and think about authority, after all one of the central concepts of political thought, it is as though we were caught in a maze of abstractions, metaphors, and figures of speech in which everything can be taken and mistaken for something else, because we have no reality, either in history or in everyday experience, to which we can unanimously appeal.[111]

She provides a specific account of authority that it is important to understand if we are to understand her account of power. For power is easily conflated or confused with authority, and it should now be possible to explain why the powerful may have authority but authority need not be powerful.

Power is not about tradition, but it may result in authorship, in the creation of something new. Power is thus more a moment of founding and of creation than a reference to past action. Power, authorship, creation, existence, are all related, but only insofar as power is about the joining of the people in their public lives. "Power corresponds to the human ability not just to act but to act in concert."[112] None of this is to say that power is always legitimate. Power requires legitimacy, although unlike authority it does not require justification. Authority needs to be justified, whereas power "needs no justification, being inherent in the very existence of political communities; what it does need is legitimacy."[113] Here is yet another distinction, that between legitimacy and justifiability. Yet this distinction is primarily about being able to differentiate between the concepts of power, authority and violence. Authority requires justification and possibly also legitimacy; violence can also be justified, but violence can never be legitimate. It is only power that does not require justification but requires legitimacy, and the reason for this is that power can take illegitimate forms (such as, in some conditions, state security services).

The illegitimacy of power is primarily a product of the encroachment of violence into the realm of power. Arendt's exploration of violence is in large part a reaction to prevailing events in the USA and elsewhere during the 1950s and '60s, and of course of the Second World War. As a political thinker, however, she places her exploration not only in terms of the events of her time, but also in contrast to prevailing thought about power and violence.

For Arendt, violence is a means/ends category, whereas power cannot and is not characterized by this categorization. Arendt's writings on violence are primarily found in her short book *On Violence*, which along with *On Revolution*, is one of her most relevant texts for the study of international politics.[114] But it is a topic that she has explored in other writings. Unlike violence, politics cannot be understood by the means/ends category. There is no real end for politics, there is only the means, but the means are defined by the purpose of achieving this nonexistent end, which is in effect the processes of life characterized by plurality, and thus the very idea of means (which gets its meaning from its opposition to ends) is meaningless. One way to work out this somewhat convoluted framing of means/ends and politics is to recognize that for Arendt, politics is something that happens between people. Or as she writes, "Politics is based on the fact of human plurality ... *Man* is apolitical. Politics arises *between men*, and so quite *outside of man*."[115] Since it is impossible to avoid the interactions of people, of *men*, the ostensible end of politics makes no sense. There can never be such an end. It is complete nonsense to think of politics as having an end or a means – politics simply is a condition of the inevitable gregariousness or sociability of being human. Violence, however, is different.

Arendt's chief concern in critiquing the conceptual framing of violence is to challenge the influential argument that, in the words of C. Wright Mills, "All politics is a struggle for power; the ultimate kind of power is violence."[116] She also quotes Weber's definition of the state, as "the rule of men over men based on the means of legitimate, that is allegedly legitimate, violence."[117] However, she finds this formulation strange: "The consensus is very strange; for to equate political power with 'the organization of violence' makes sense only if one follows Marx's estimate of the state as an instrument of oppression in the hands of the ruling class."[118] Arendt does not accept this premise or its conclusion and points out the importance of distinguishing between violence, power, and force, a distinction which, she demonstrates, was previously noted by A. P. D'Entrèves.[119]

Key to her explanation of violence is shifting the focus onto how violence is distinct from power and force, and she already provides the grounds for this in her definition of violence as driven by the means/ends distinction:

> The very substance of violent action is ruled by the means–end category, whose chief characteristic, if applied to human affairs, has always been that the end is in danger of being overwhelmed by the means which it justifies and which are needed to reach it.[120]

This definition of violence has an affinity with Clausewitz's account of war tending toward the extreme since violence, like war, shares the characteristic of the means becoming overwhelming.[121] However, unlike Clausewitz, for Arendt the violence of war makes war inherently un-political, even though power may be involved. This complex relationship between violence and power is defined not just by the means/ends character of violence, but also by the instrumentality of violence. Unlike power, which by definition cannot be instrumental owing to its centrality for politics, violence is instrumental. Yet while violence is instrumental and defined by the means/ends category, Arendt remarks that even though they are distinct, they often appear together.

Nevertheless, the fact that violence often accompanies power does not mitigate their opposite character:

> Power and violence are opposites; where the one rules absolutely, the other is absent. Violence appears where power is in jeopardy, but left to its own course it ends in power's disappearance. This implies that it is not correct to think of the opposite of violence as nonviolence; to speak of non-violent power is actually redundant. Violence can destroy power; it is utterly incapable of creating it.[122]

In *The Human Condition*, Arendt writes that "violence can destroy power, it can never become a substitute for it."[123] Arendt is not ignorant of the great connection that exists between power and violence. Her work on revolution further demonstrates the point that violence often plays a role in revolutions but that it need not play the only role.[124] She is acutely aware of the close connection violence has with the human condition. For her, having experienced the horrors of the twentieth century, the question is not about ignoring the potential for violence but in demonstrating how violence and politics are separate. As Margaret Canovan writes, she "seems to have taken for granted that violence is a part of the human condition, although something which can, on occasion, in favourable circumstances, be kept out of politics."[125]

Consequently, contrary to the Marxist argument that views violence as offering emancipatory potential, Arendt is deeply suspicious of violence. Arendt is no utopian idealist, and so she does not suggest that violence can be eradicated from the human condition, but she does not view violence as a component of political life, and thus violence has to be distinct from power. For her, the power of the state comes from the support of the people; it is not about military capability or economic capacity, or even the institutions of the law. "All political institutions are manifestations and materializations of power: they petrify and decay as soon as the living power of the people ceases to uphold them."[126] The government of any state is dependent on the power of the people to support it, and this is one aspect that demonstrates the problems of tyranny. Tyranny, the most violent form of government, is based on the implements of violence, not the power of the people. Violence does not need numbers; it does not need people. Violence can be achieved without many people at all, but by relying on weapons and technology. It is from these distinctions, between violence, authority, force, strength and power, from the relevance of means/ends categories, instrumentality, and tradition, and, crucially,[127] from her account of politics, that we arrive at her definition of power:

> Power corresponds to the human ability not just to act but to act in concert. Power is never the property an individual; it belongs to a group and remains in existence only so long as the group keeps together. When we say of somebody that he is "in power" we actually refer to his being empowered by others. The moment the group, from which the power originated to begin with (*potestas in populo*, without a people or group there is no power), disappears, "his power" also vanishes.[128]

Power, unlike violence, requires no justification. For if power were to require justification it would be akin to demanding an explanation of the public for their participation in political life. This kind of justificatory discourse exists only in tyrannical or totalitarian

Power and Obligation

regimes, where the people are, by threat of violence, kept out of the public sphere.

There is a lot going on here with Arendt, but each of the points she raises is helpful in providing a theoretical framework for understanding the empirical material explored in the subsequent chapters. Her definition of power as pertaining to a public life, or in the words of Habermas "as the ability to agree upon a common course of action in unconstrained communication,"[129] is appropriate in understanding how Diaspora debate about Israel is illustrative of power and thus of a political process. Arendt provides a variety of intellectual tools that are useful in being able to make sense out of the chaos in the Diaspora/Israel relationship. Most importantly, however, she makes it possible to recognize that there exists a widespread form of power in the Diaspora/Israel relationship. This power is characterized by the role in which debate about Israel has become an important part of contemporary Jewish identity. There may not be an agreed-upon course of action as to how this relationship should exist, but there is no shortage of public activity in the cause of this relationship. In this sense, the transnational political obligation between the Diaspora and Israel is not one of specific practice, but of commonality, so that the obligation becomes having a relationship with Israel and in the process participating in the public life of contemporary Diaspora Jewry. It is this activity that begins to set in motion the transnational political obligation between the Diaspora and Israel.

It is not without irony that I am using Arendt to suggest that there is a discourse of obligation between the Diaspora and Israel. While Arendt was early on a kind of Zionist and clearly sympathetic to the political needs of the Jews, her work pertaining to Israel and Zionism greatly diminished over time, with her last published work of relevance being *Eichmann in Jerusalem*. The major controversy surrounding this work no doubt contributed to her deciding not to get involved in this element of Jewish life any longer and to dismiss any expectation of an obligation placed upon her by virtue of her Jewishness.

Nevertheless, the extent of the controversy reveals that Arendt hit a nerve, and that perhaps she was onto something. As such, it makes sense to return to Arendt to see how she can help understand the Diaspora/Israel relationship. Furthermore, her identification of the problematic ways in which authority and tradition are understood, and the classical reactions to defining politics, tradition and authority, all feature in the discourses that try to position the Diaspora/Israel relationship. The matter of education and of authority, of the quest for tradition, and of how these all in turn need to be appreciated as secondary to power, helps explain the problematic relationship between the major Diaspora organizations and the Jewish publics that they claim to represent or on whose behalf they act. Power and politics clearly matter in the Diaspora/Israel relationship, and as a consequence so do discourses of obligation.

Power and Questions of the Self

To participate in politics is to take on political obligations, and Arendt makes it possible to understand the role of power in such obligations. Arendt helps us to understand how power is not necessarily tied to authority and how it cannot be separated from the human condition of living a life among others and not being able to choose with whom we share our lives on this planet, and that power involves people acting together, in concert, in public. All of these are important insights that enable a distancing from the statist and Weberian assumptions about power that shadow the political obligation literature. She also makes it possible to recognize the positive element in power so that power is not about forcing another into submission. What Arendt's theory of power offers is an alternative framing for understanding how power functions in communities that are not set up according to a political order based on sovereignty and state citizenship, but are part of the human condition itself. The insights gained from her theory will become increasingly apparent in exploring the empirical material addressed in the next chapter.

What Arendt does not help us with is understanding the connection that exists between power and the construction of individual and collective identities. She suggests that identity matters, for how else could people come together to act in concert if they did not have some identity related ideational factors in common that bring them together as a heterogeneous group? Power, for Arendt, is tied to identity, but only in the sense of identity being constituted out of an engagement with plurality. Moreover, the relevance of identity to power for Arendt is mainly tied up in her public account of politics. There is no power in private, and thus private identities are ostensibly not tied to relations of power.

Arendt borrows this public/private distinction from her readings of the classical political thought of ancient Greece and of how politics was defined largely in opposition to the home life. Politics was tied to the *polis*, not to *oikos*, the home sphere. Yet, this distinction is troublesome, for a public life is often made possible by the division of labor at home. Aristotle's declaration of humans being political animals by nature is restricted to land-owning males, who are able to live a life of political participation because they can rely on slaves and women to deal with the business of daily affairs.[130] This public life reflects the ideal contemplative life that Socrates represented, which is not a life open to all, and if we believe Plato, it may even be that politics is the enemy of philosophy.[131] Political power, in the Platonic sense, is thus a necessity for philosophers so that they may conduct their own higher calling, whereas for Aristotle it cannot be divorced from a gendered division of labor, among other discriminations.

Arendt is not suggesting that the sexism of Ancient Greece or Plato's philosophical elitism are acceptable, but she is accepting the classical claim of politics being by definition an activity that happens in public, outside of the home sphere. Power, however, contra Arendt, exists in multiple spheres and not just in the public arena. Yet the type of power that exists in the home sphere complements her definition of power because, in parallel to the classical argument, the power that exist in private contributes to the conditions of possibility under which power can exist in public, even though the power that exists outside of the public arena is different from the kind of collective action that Arendt defines as power.

Outside of the public sphere, power is firmly related to the construction of identity. Power, in a sense, is identity, and identity is power. It is the power to construct a sense of self that provides the crucial connection between public and private power (if we adopt an Arendtian and classical distinction) because it is via the construction of the self that individuals are able to participate as recognizable agents in their public lives. In general, the power of identity is what feminists are getting at when they argue that the personal is political, and the power relations contained in the construction of (gendered) identity is one of the important insights that feminist scholarship provides,[132] although it is with non-hierarchical forms of power (and identity) that I am concerned here.

In *Society Must be Defended*, a compilation of his lectures of 1975–6, Michel Foucault says that the research question on power that he is interested in is not about who has power and what the person with power is thinking, but is about "what happens at the moment of, at the level of the procedure of subjugation, or in the continuous and uninterrupted processes that subjugate bodies, direct gestures, and regular behaviour."[133] Identity clearly features in Foucault's thinking about power, although it does so in a variety of ways.

According to Anthony Giddens, Foucault's interest in identity and power is primarily about the category of the body. In *Modernity and Self Identity* Giddens writes:

> Foucault has analysed the body in relation to mechanisms of power, concentrating particularly on the emergence of "disciplinary power" in circumstances of modernity. The body becomes the focus of power and this power, instead of trying to "mark" it externally, as in pre-modern times, subjects it to the internal discipline of self-control.[134]

Giddens finds fault with Foucault, accusing him of equating the body with agency. Be that as it may, Giddens is partly missing the point, for what Foucault also does is highlight an avenue along which it becomes possible to explore how discourses of power feature in the construction of identity. It is not the body that matters here so much as it is the self that is in self-control.

Foucault is widely recognized as one of the foremost thinkers about power, although this is not to say that his thinking on power is uncontroversial. Giddens takes issue with it, as already noted, and Michael Mann does not even reference Foucault once in his four-volume work *The Sources of Social Power*. The political philosopher Peter Morriss goes so far as to deny that Foucault even wrote about power, claiming instead that Foucault's writings on power are actually about *pouvoir*, the French word that means being able to.[135] The verb *pouvoir* is used to denote the action of doing something. For Morriss, *pouvoir* is not power, but evidence of power, and hence Foucault does not in fact say anything about power as such. Yet, Foucault seems to be aware of this kind of distinction. He merely suggests that an analysis of power needs to take into consideration the manifestations of what he terms "force relations" and sometimes "relations of force" as a constituent part of power.[136] Moreover, *pouvoir* can and is used to refer to politics.

Foucault, however, does not do himself any favours by simultaneously offering a theory of power while claiming that he is not doing so. While his writings on power are suggestive of a kind of theory, he explicitly states in the first volume of the *History of Sexuality*, first published in French in 1976, that he is not providing a theory of power. Nevertheless, there are at least two different accounts of power that he identifies and that do contribute to a theory about power. The first is the disciplinary mode of power that he writes about in *Discipline and Punish*, first published in French in 1975. Disciplinary power pertains to how individuals modify their own behavior and how this modification reflects shifts in how human subjectivity is understood.[137] Self-discipline is evidence of a technique of power that manifests itself in individuals governing their own behavior according to their sense of subjectivity. "Discipline," he writes, 'makes' individuals; it is the specific technique of a power that regards individuals both as objects and as instruments of its exercise."[138] He continues: "The success of disciplinary power derives no doubt from the use of simple instruments; hierarchical observation, normalising judgement and their combination in a procedure that is specific to it, the examination."[139] Thus, every time one acts according to a set of ostensibly pre-inscribed routines that are representative of a particular identity-type, one is participating in a discourse of power.

In transnational political obligation there is an element of disciplinary power, but only to the extent that individuals self-consciously act on assumptions about what sorts of behavior, conduct and beliefs are compatible with their respective claims about self-identity and Diaspora Jewish subjectivity. Every time Israel is either defended or, for that matter, challenged in public or private Jewish discourses, there is an element of disciplinary power at work. It is through such actions that individuals simultaneously act on relations of force that guide how an identity-group is presumed or supposed to act, and engage in acts of self-definition. The relations of power are both internal, in contributing to the construction of the community itself, and external in forming a part of how particular individuals who belong to particular communities act (i.e. the assumption that being Jewish involves supporting Israel or that being Jewish means supporting universal human rights and especially minority rights because of Jewish history) and through such actions contribute to defining the identity of the actor.

Disciplining power also functions in another way in transnational relations with regard to self-monitoring. There exist processes of collective self-monitoring in the Jewish community about who says what about Israel. Such processes can take the form of op-eds, book reviews, public talks, and blogs (such as MondoWeiss and the recently closed OpenZion at the *Daily Beast*, campus-watch-style activities, and public pronouncements by major Jewish organizations). There exists a public examination that takes place in the media, where Jewish authors and intellectuals are attacked or defended on the basis of their views about Israel. Claims pertinent to winning the so-called propaganda war, and the conventional wisdom among many Jews that to criticize Israel is to provide ammunition to your enemies, and that what is required of being a good Jew, or at least a synagogue president, is that you support Israel are all forms of collective and individual self-discipline. In this sense there is a power–knowledge nexus that involves the disciplining of, if not behavior, belief. This is a very different kind of power from the one that Arendt has in mind or that we find in Weber and his followers. I once sat on a synagogue hiring committee that was incredibly sensitive to any applicant's views about the Holocaust, even though we know that Holocaust memory is often used in a deeply politicized manner.[140] Manifestations of power functioning as a process of disciplining are prevalent in many walks of life, from hiring committees to public debates to claims about how different genders should act and dress.

While the techniques of power Foucault is interested in in *Discipline and Punish* pertain to the power relations of punishment, his analysis of power in this text nevertheless gives rise to some interesting avenues that are applicable to how discourses of power function in the Jewish Diaspora's relationship with Israel. These discourses are representative of a subjectivity characterized by transnational relations, of being in multiple places simultaneously and as a consequence of being disciplined to respect the connection to these different places as doing so is one of the bases for the construction of self. In this sense, Foucault is providing a reading of power that is sympathetic if not consistent with the metaphorical definition of diaspora that, in the words of Robin Cohen, involve "decoupling ... diaspora from homeland."[141]

Power and Obligation

Cohen is cynical about what he labels social constructionist theories of Diaspora, arguing that when the scope of diaspora is broadened the concept loses its meaning. What Cohen forgets is that "Because 'diaspora' is just a word, like all words, it serves only to denote part of reality, one that isn't always the same each time it is used."[142] For many Jews, Diaspora is both a condition and a metaphor, as the condition of Diaspora life has undergone radical changes since 1948 with the establishment of the State of Israel and since the 1960s with the civil rights movements. Jewish communities in North America are diasporic, but as with the history of Jewish Diaspora communities across the world, the idea that they exist as a dispersed people, wandering in exile, kicked out of their homeland, is a Zionist myth more than anything else.[143] The meaning of diaspora is a part of Jewish existence, but it is a contested meaning with implications for how Diaspora Jewish identity is conceptualized. Diaspora is, in this understanding, a technology of the self: it serves as a discourse for how Jewish subjectivity is constituted. The disciplining power in Diaspora identity is the construction of Diaspora identity. It is the knowledge of what being a Diaspora Jew means that provides the meaning for how Jews ought to behave with regard to their relations with the Jewish State.

The second account of power that Foucault provides pertains to what he terms in one of his lectures, governmentality,[144] but elsewhere is described as pertaining to relations of force.[145] This aspect of his thinking is on the surface less relevant to transnational political obligation, but in actuality complements the relevance and insight offered by his disciplinary account. What interests Foucault is how these relations of force have changed. He notes that in the Western tradition power has generally been understood with regard to "a pure limit set on freedom" and that "In Western societies since the Middle Ages, the exercise of power has always been formulated in terms of law."[146] Yet Foucault argues that this kind of juridical power based in law and related to sovereignty is significantly different from the "new methods of power whose operation is not ensured by right but by techniques, not by law but by normalization, not by punishment but by control, methods that are employed on all levels and in forms that go beyond the state and its apparatus."[147] He claims that "power must be understood in the first instance as the multiplicity of force relations immanent in the sphere in which they operate and which constitute their own organizations."[148] In opposition to theories of power that focus power into specific central points, such as sovereignty, for Foucault, power is always moving, it is "local and unstable."[149]

In *The History of Sexuality*, Foucault goes on to suggest that there are five "propositions" about power. First, "Power is not something that is acquired, seized or shared, something that one holds on to or allows to slip away; power is exercised from innumerable points, in the interplay of nonegalitarian relations."[150] Second, relations of power are immanent in a multiplicity of relations, and do not exist separately from the various relationships that people have. Third, power does not emerge out of a binary hierarchy. Fourth, power is always exercised for some purpose but is not necessarily the product of individual rationality. "There is no power that is exercised without a series of aims and objectives. But this does not mean that it results from the choice of decision of an individual subject."[151] Power is in some senses everywhere, but only where there are relations, and its exercise is always geared to some end, although the end may be the product of multiple connections. Fifth, "Where there is power, there is resistance, and yet, or rather consequently, this resistance is never in a position of exteriority in relation to power."[152] Many of these points are repeated by Foucault in his lectures. For example, he says:

> Power must, I think, be analysed as something that circulates, or rather as something that functions only when it is part of a chain. It is never localized here or there, it is never in the hands of some, and it is never appropriated in the way that wealth or a commodity can be appropriated. Power functions. Power is exercised through networks, and individuals do not simply circulate in those networks; they are in a position to both submit to and exercise this power. They are never the inert of consenting targets of power; they are always its relays. In other words, power passes through individuals. It is not applied to them.[153]

Or rather, power is manifest in all kinds of human relations, and especially those relations characterized by inequalities sometimes typified by claims to superior knowledge.

Foucault's exploration of power, between how power is understood to function both as a component of individual subjectivity and a constituent part of various external relations characterized by inequality and possibly by repression, has garnered significant criticism. The problem is that Foucault is in effect claiming that power is unavoidable and that it is everywhere, which in conceptual terms provides for a convoluted definition since if power is in all human relations and conditions of human subjectivity all the time, what distinguishes power from any other features that mark the social, political and economic parts of human life?

In this sense, Foucault is correct when he claims that he does not provide a theory of power, for as Lukes suggests, that was not his aim. Lukes writes:

> Foucault was a genealogist, concerned with the historical recovery of the formation of norms (such as define the mad, the sick, the criminal and the abnormal) and as such he had no interest in analysing such mechanisms by examining variations, outcomes and effects: he just asserted that there were such effects.[154]

It is for this reason that Lukes argues that Foucault's argument, which links the construction of human subjects to power, fails:

> Foucault's first way of interpreting the key idea central to his view of power – that power is "productive" through the social construction of subjects, rendering the governed governable – makes no sense. Taking this to mean that those subject to power are "constituted" by it is best read as a striking overstatement deployed in his purely ideal-typical depictions of disciplinary and bio-power, not as an analysis of the extent to which the various modern forms of power he identified actually succeed, or fail, in securing the compliance of those subjects to it.[155]

Foucault does broaden the concept of power so that it can easily be conflated with knowledge and identity. Identity is a part of power relations, although once this connection is acknowledged power can no longer be understood as a way to distinguish individuals acting on their own accord from those acting under the influence of others.[156] Lukes, however, is not dismissing Foucault's insight into how power features as a form of individual voluntary compliance, of self-regulation based on the discourses that define the parameters of a particular identity. Indeed, people often participate in relations of power without acknowledging the presence of power, and this wilful blindness is significant. As Foucault writes, "Power is tolerable only on condition that it mask a substantial part of itself. Its success is proportional to its ability to hide its own mechanism."[157]

Others, however, have also argued that there exists a close correlation between power and identity. For example, Manuel Castells argues that identity cannot be separated from power because "the social construction of identity always takes place in a context marked by power relationships."[158] He identifies three "forms and origins of identity building."[159] These include legitimizing, resistance and project identity. Legitimizing identities are those that serve the interests of dominant institutions and serve to "rationalize their domination."[160] Alternatively, "Resistance identities are generated by those actors who are in positions/conditions devalued and/or stigmatized by the logic of domination" and find their identity through resistance and opposition.[161] Finally, project identities are "when social actors, on the basis of whatever cultural materials are available to them, build a new identity that redefines their position in society and, by so doing, seek the transformation of overall social structures."[162] Castells notes that these identities can move across categories, especially from resistance to object identities. The main point, however, is that the construction of these identity-types is done via power relationships, and the same is true of Diaspora identity in relation to Israel.

Indeed, each of these three categories has a role to play, with the legitimizing identity discourse potentially referring to the role of either Israel or Diaspora Jewish institutions and how they push particular Zionist tropes that Diaspora Jews are expected to agree with or at least accept. Resistance identities could pertain to those who reject the Israelization of Jewish identity, and understand their sense of Jewishness as involving explicit challenges to Israeli policy if not Israel itself. Finally, project identities could refer to those Jews that seek to define their sense of self according to their normative judgments about Israel or about how they respond to Israel. A conflict emerges, however, because whereas the majority of Diaspora Jews most likely place themselves in this last identity construction, at least where Israel is concerned, there exists an underlying public and private expectation that they will belong to the first. Evidence of this conflict can be found in the main American Jewish organizations' response to the Pew Survey, with leaders bemoaning its findings and claiming that they lead, not represent, and that this leadership will return Jews to their rightful sense of Jewish peoplehood.[163]

The Muscle Jew: Power, Politics and Identity in Theory and Practice

Now that the political has been defined away from the state, and with discourses of power being understood as (1) the public life of coming together for a shared purpose and (2) the construction of the self and related practices of discipline and governmentality, political obligation can be dramatically redefined away from the state. Instead, we can suggest that a transnational political obligation exists when:

- A transnational or diaspora community acts together out of a shared sense of purpose or identity;
- A transnational or diaspora community is expected to hold a set of political commitments by virtue of its identity;
- A transnational or diaspora community's constituent members act in ways that simultaneously affirm and construct their individual and collective identities;
- The ties that set up these constructions are characterized by discourses of power reflective of both.

Transnational political obligations are framed by the discourses of power that bind a group together and shape their political discourse in ways that reaffirm and reflect their individual and collective identity. Transnational political obligations do not require collective agreement or any kind of solidarity. They are merely representative of the political commitments that are morally expected. As such, transnational political obligations are always in a state of contestation, and so debates over authority, tradition and legitimacy are regular points of debate in transnational political obligation. In addition, transnational political obligations tend to focus on questions about identity and security, widely construed. The security at stake could be physical but it could also be more abstract and refer, for example, to constructions of identity or feelings of fear and anxiety that emerge from belonging to the community.

In order to illustrate how some of these tenets of transnational political obligation function, with a focus on the security and identity element, I am going to turn to a rather bizarre element in Zionist and Diaspora discourse. The Zionist myth of the settler Jew was a masculine stereotype supported by an outlandish racial ideal type of the New Jews or Muscle Jews (*Muskeljudentum*).[164] This identity discourse brings together the different elements of power explored in this chapter, including the idea of power as the ability to compel another into submission, and the power of identity rooted in constructions of the self. This latter type of power is difficult to observe empirically for it is in how identity itself functions as a discourse that scripts the conditions of possibility for self-understanding and individual behavior. The New Jew, the Muscle Jew, the Strong Jew, was supposed to be the opposite of the Jew in the Diaspora. This view, which was clearly disparaging of Diaspora Jewish identity, nevertheless came to have an influential role in the Diaspora/Israel relationship. It illuminates an example of the power in and of identity, and it also sets up some of the themes about Diaspora Jewish identity and Israel that are explored in the next chapter.

The narrative of the strong Israeli Jew was an outgrowth of the scientific racial theories of modernity that placed great emphasis on how the body carried specific meaning. Donna Haraway has argued how from the eighteenth century onward, the body, and gender, became understood as social constructs that reflected the prejudices which sustained hierarchical power relations and discrimination.[165] It was the body that carried meaning and made someone an Other that could be discriminated against. The Zionist idea of the Strong Jew was built on this racial logic.

Examples in Zionism of such political-racial thought about the body can be found in a variety of sources. The revisionist Zionist Vladimir Jabotinsky bought into the logic of the strong muscular Jew that could tame a lion with his bare hands.[166] This mythology of the strong racial ideal type Jew, the *Muskeljudentum*, was, however, most famously articulated by Max Nordau, a cultural critic and political Zionist who was influenced by phrenology. Nordau was quite possibly the most influential Zionist to bring racial-scientific theory into Zionism.[167] As Jay Geller writes, "According to Nordau the civilized world thwarted the natural, progressive development of humanity by blindly ignoring evolutionary insight."[168] The Muscle Jew ideal involved the acceptance by some Jews of the anti-Semitic tropes of the Jew as weak and diseased, but it was also built on social Darwinism. As Todd Presner writes:

Power and Obligation

Nordau's muscle Jew not only built upon the heroism of Jewish history, but the concept was suffused by a social ethos of survival of the fittest, in which Jews, overcoming the extenuating circumstances that rendered them weak and adapting to the new challenges of nation building, could now become "true moderns" in order to thrive.[169]

This racial thinking did not disappear, but informed twentieth-century Zionism, including Israeli propaganda.[170]

The cover of *Life* magazine for June 23, 1967 is of an Israeli soldier, smiling, holding an AK-47 assault rifle, reveling in the success of the war.[171] Israel was not just about providing for the security of the Jews, it was about doing so in a way that redefined Jewish identity. This ostensibly new Jewish identity is curious not only because it accepts some of the historical anti-Semitic caricatures of Jewish identity, but also because it identifies pride in rejecting intellectual pursuits in favor of physical fitness. For example, note the following passage from a 1967 physical fitness book published by the Israeli army and used as a marketing tool in the USA:

> The Israeli army is producing a new type of man in this young, energetic Middle Eastern country. By means of tough, well-planned physical training, the army is contributing to the change in the physiognomy of the modern Israeli and to the transforming of the immigrants from seventy different countries into one, homogenous type. The "traditional Jew" of Eastern Europe was known, in the past, for his capability to bear mental sufferings and moral tortures and for his physical weakness. Subjected to racial discriminations, the Jew of Eastern Europe was not conscripted into the army, nor did he engage in manual work. His main activity was in commerce and the educational field. This had resulted in the Jew having weak arms and soft back and belly muscles ... But with the new Israeli it is quite different. The citizen is taller, he has broad shoulders and his muscles are stronger. The physical fitness of the average Israeli was one of the most important elements which led to the lightning victory of the Israeli army in the Six-Day War of June 1967.[172]

Compare the above Israeli government propaganda from 1967 with Nordau's writing on Jewish exercise in 1902, and there is a clear correlation:

> Our muscles are outstandingly capable of development ... No one need be satisfied with the muscles they are given. Everyone can have the muscles he wishes for. Methodological, persistent exercise is all that is necessary. Every Jew who is or believes himself to be weak can attain the musculature of an athlete.[173]

Equally fascinating and disturbing, the idea of the Muscle Jew became not just a product of Zionist propaganda but a part of wider Jewish culture in the Diaspora.[174] Providing a flavor of this Diasporic discourse is the Jewish Rambo, or "Rambowitz,"[175] a super-muscular heroic figure that started to appear in Jewish fiction post-1945, but more so post-1967, especially after the 1973 Yom Kippur War. To give a flavor of this literature: one of the novels offered up by Paul Breines in his study of this subject matter is by John Rowe (an Australian), whose 1979 novel *The Aswan Solution* involves an American Jew, David Laker, who moves to Israel and becomes recruited into the Mossad by a beautiful Israeli widow. He turns from an assimilated Jew into a committed Zionist and is sent on a top-secret mission to investigate the potential demolition of the Aswan Dam. En route to Tel Aviv, David starts to think about his fellow Jewish American passengers:

> "Were they members of the new Jewish warrior race?" Lake wonders. "Horseshit," he thinks to himself in response. "American Jews are fat asses with soft families rooting for a new kind of football team – the Israeli Defence Forces – and supporting these Jewish Green Bay Packers with cash contribution and a new chauvinism...."[176]

In the Diaspora, the motif of this strong New Jew was firmly evident in the 1967 military success, although as Breines argues, it is really after 1973 that this identity-type started to play a larger role in the Diaspora:

> As decisive as the 1967 Arab–Israeli War was in generating the Jewish American cult of both Israel and tough Jewish imagery, it left a small but significant gap, a gap then filled by the 1973 Arab–Israel War or Yom Kippur War. The Six Day War had placed Jewish power on the stage of world history, in the words of the *New Republic*; the 1973 war, in which Israel was nearly defeated, reasserted Jewish vulnerability. Jewish toughness appears to be all the more necessary and all the more

ethically grounded. And it is in the years following the Yom Kippur War that the Rambowitz novels begin to proliferate.[177]

The strong Muscle Jew had arrived and was vindicated not just in 1948, but then again with even greater emphasis in 1967. Israel's military accomplishments in 1967 were a public and powerful demonstration that the Jews could not be pushed around and Jews in the Diaspora gave exceedingly generously to support the Jewish State in its time of need. As Israel became more important for Diaspora Jews, Israel became increasingly reliant on Diaspora Jewish support – something that the 1973 war further cemented.

The idea of this New Jew not only helped shape Israeli mythology, it also contributed to Diaspora discourse about what Israel meant for the Jews. The new identity carried with it the promise of feeling a sense of pride that Jews had hitherto not experienced (according to the Zionist mythology), and it entrenched a sense of a shared fate between Diaspora Jewry and Israel, as evident in the incredible fundraising efforts that took place at that time. This new identity-type, and the military victories that were credited to this new identity, helped to condition what it meant to be Jewish in the age of Israel. Israel exported this ideal-type Muscle Jew into the Diaspora and Diaspora Jews readily accepted this new ideal and also the opportunity to help Jews in another country, and redress the perceived Diasporic weakness during the Second World War toward saving European Jewry.

Jewish identity in the Diaspora is regularly connected to Israel in some way. Individual Jews grow up learning this, and many non-Jews automatically presume that being Jewish presupposes some kind of commitment to Israel. In linking this new identity-type to Israel and the military victory of the Six Day War that cemented the Israelization of Diaspora identity, the exercise propaganda manual is one example of this connection that is easily overlooked because of its ostensibly mundane character. Yet the bizarreness of the example should not be overlooked, for it reveals the extent to which Israeli discourses about Jewish identity have gone to recreate a new identity for all Jews to connect with should they choose to. In this case, we have a scientific-racial ideal-type discourse of bodily aesthetics being used in the 1960s, the age of civil rights, to explain political and military success and invite other Jews to participate in it. Either the Israeli training manual quoted above is an example of how far removed Israel was from the political mood in the USA at that time, or it serves as an example of how Zionist identity-construction infiltrated Diaspora identity. The evidence suggests a bit of both.[178]

Conclusion

Political obligations are political not only because of the relation they have to supporting the institutions of the state, but because they function as a part of power relationships between particular members of a spatial community and the institutions of rule that they participate in and are subject to. The political obligation literature does not address in much detail what is meant by "political," relying instead on allusions to Weber and on what makes a state. It is, as a consequence, not just the particularity principle that limits the scope of political obligation. It is also the seemingly unresolvable quest to explain what it is about the state that justifies the normative expectations behind accepting political obligations. There clearly is a puzzle at stake in trying to explain political obligation, but the puzzle is also greater than the literature is prepared to accept. For it is not just the special characteristic of the state that matters; it is also the equally, if not more, complex problem of how political relationships transgress state borders to create similarly obligatory relationships.

Political theory has for years acknowledged the existence of such different types of obligations, addressing them as problems of minority politics, diasporic relationships, and/or transnational migrant networks. Yet the literature has rarely made the move that frames identity-based border crossing commitments, loyalties, duties and/or allegiances as a type of political obligation. The experience of such relations, however, is consistent with them being a form of obligation, even if obedience is not a requirement of the obligatory relationship. Exploring this intellectual geography, through Weber and away from the state as the condition under which political obligations are possible, is what I have tried to do in this chapter.

Central to this journey is providing a different theoretical language about power that sets out the parameters for understanding not just transnational political obligations more generally, but the

Jewish Diaspora's relationship with Israel in particular. As such, while definitions of power are complex and contested, the choice of Arendt and Foucault is made because they both highlight different facets of power that help reveal the various power dynamics at stake in transnational political obligations.

Arendt's account of power is influenced by a variety of factors. Steven Lukes accurately suggests that her definition of power is conditioned by her account of politics.[179] For Arendt, politics is a key part of the human condition of living a life among other people and of not being able to choose with whom we share our lives on this planet. To pretend that such choices are possible is a mistake, one of the many committed by Eichmann.[180] Arendt does not provide a clear definition of politics, yet she is a deeply inspiring thinker on this topic. As Craig Calhoun and John McGowan write:

> No thinker has argued more passionately that politics should transcend the play of mere instrumental concerns than Hannah Arendt. Brilliant, demanding, inspiring, original, and sometimes perverse, her writings offer an important resource for theorists who would conceptualize a politics in which questions of meaning, identity, and value take center stage.[181]

One of the most important aspects of Arendt's understanding of politics is the importance of human plurality. This condition of human plurality is central for politics, and is also important for her account of power. The two are closely related, but they are distinct. Calhoun and McGowan continue to explain that Arendt's theory of politics cannot be

> merely a matter of power, of divisions between ruler and ruled, or of distribution of economic resources. Politics has to be, among other things, a realm of self-creation through free, voluntary action undertaken in consort with and in relation to other people.[182]

Arendt framed her own discussion of politics as follows:

> For at the center of the politics lies a concern for the world, not for man – a concern, in fact, for a world, however constituted, without which those who are both concerned and political would not find life worth living.[183]

Politics, for Arendt, could never be instrumental, because it is central to the human condition, and to the empirical existence of life in the world.

In another passage, Arendt argues that "Wherever people come together, the world thrusts itself between them, and it is in this in-between space that all human affairs are conducted."[184] Politics, consequently, is not about the state or sovereignty any more than it can be about economy. Politics is more about the conditions of human existence than it is concerned with juridical discourses establishing boundaries for the maintenance of order. Arendt's definition of power is deeply suggestive of what political obligation is intended to explain: those socio-political phenomena that involve individuals acting within the scope of possibilities, the conditions of which emerge out of negotiations and public practices that define the boundaries of community membership. In this way, obligation involves moral choice as well as the potential for having to do what is necessary, and corresponds to how political obligations exist only insofar as they refer to expectations of conduct necessary for a life among others.

Arendt, however, also helps in other ways by distinguishing power from violence, and in explaining the differences between power, authority and tradition. Each of these distinctions is apparent in how Diaspora Jews articulate and understand their relationship with Israel and of the political challenges that characterize this relationship. Questions about tradition, legitimacy, power, authenticity, political space, and moral responsibilities all feature in the overly complex and often counter-intuitive discourses of the Diaspora/Israel relationship. The example of the Muscle Jews is just one illustration of how, in a search for authenticity and political might, a tradition is challenged and then created on the basis of an idea of the type of physicality a Jew possesses.

More generally, what Arendt is also implying is that it is clearly possible to think of obligations that are political but are not directed toward the sovereign state. In this regard, and building on Foucault, there is no sovereign authority in transnational political obligation, there is only a sharing of power that comes together in two ways: the power that is part of acting collectively and the power contained in, and produced by, constructions of the self.

Transnational political obligations are political not just in the Arendtian sense, but also in a Foucauldian sense of identity construction and self-discipline. The powerlessness that Diaspora Jews often feel is evidence not of an absence of power, but of a feeling of isolation, which features in how Diaspora Jewry (and Zionism) participates in the construction of Jewish identity. The point in turning to these thinkers is not that we have to agree with everything they say, but that they provide a counterpoint to how power and politics are conventionally assumed in the obligation literature. In the process they provide an opening for how to think differently. Consequently, it becomes not just easier but necessary to acknowledge that contra the stereotype that Rambowitz displaces, the Jews have always had power, just not necessarily political authority. The correlation between power and political authority is part of the Zionist narrative about Jewish political identity and is not representative of Jewish experience, whereas Jewish power is about Jews defining their sense of identity as a people and acting accordingly. These are important reflections that become increasingly significant as the Diaspora/Israel relationship is explored.

If one focuses on power in these ways, additional insights are possible that reveal new challenges. Indeed, part of the challenge in the Diaspora/Israel relationship is in navigating the tensions that exist between the differences that matter in searches for identity, authority and security. Martin Ben-Moreh, of the Reut institute, described this situation as follows:

> A person figuratively speaking has on his hand possibly four different watches. The first is his/her own personal watch – what is happening to him (age, physically, mentally, the perception of his/her place in the world we live in). The second is his/her community's watch (neighbourhood, town, kibbutz, synagogue, etc.). The third watch is his/her country's – whether it is Israel or some other country, and the fourth is the watch of the Jewish people. The basic "human condition" is that the watches have the same clock face but are they telling the same "time"? Are they synchronized?[185]

They are not always synchronized; there are tensions between the different watches. In Israel, where the early Zionist Pioneers (*Chalutzim*) of the *Second* and *Third Aliya* wanted to create a "New Jew – an Israeli," something may have been lost in the process of founding the State of Israel – the solidarity of the Jewish communities throughout the centuries. Paradoxically, it may be to the

Diaspora that Israel may need to turn to redefine what the essence is of a Jewish and democratic state in the twenty-first century:

> When you go to America and you see the different Jewish streams: Reform, Conservative, Reconstructionist, Modern Orthodox and Orthodox Jews, they are all encompassing different interpretations of Judaism. Jews in Israel see this and say this pluralism is missing in Israel. The Zionists wanted to build a Jewish State. Our socialist visionaries wanted a new Jew who works the land, fights in the army and is responsible for his/her own destiny. Now nearly 70 years on we are asking who are we? There is also the paradox of nearly a million Israelis living in the Diaspora.[186]

Part of the challenge today for Diaspora Jewry is in understanding its roles with regard to Israel. The search for identity, and the absence of clear authority in the Diaspora, all contribute to a state of political flux, where the Diaspora/Israel relationship is regularly contested, and may be less assured than commonly appears.

3 Between Zion and Diaspora: Internationalisms, Transnationalisms, Obligation and Security

Introduction

The purpose of this chapter is fairly simple: to further frame what is meant by transnational political obligation in a series of three moves, and then to demonstrate how security features in the transnational political obligation of Diaspora/Israel relations. The three moves that make up the first point of this chapter are as follows. First, I revisit how political obligation is not divorced from international considerations. Second, I reveal how the international implications of political obligation share some specific features of Jewish internationalist discourse. Third, I argue that Jewish transnationalism vis-à-vis Israel can be understood as a revision of the previous Jewish internationalism. This revision is somewhat paradoxical, however, as it also incorporates the previous discourse of Diaspora nationalism in its acceptance of Diaspora as an important part of Jewish continuity even in the age of Israel.[1] Said differently, what I am calling Jewish transnationalism between the Diaspora and Israel is a contemporary form of what used to be called Jewish internationalism. The other contribution of this chapter follows from the security element highlighted. This discussion explores how security features in the transnationalism of Diaspora/Israel relations.

In moving away from the statist discourses of political obligation, it will prove helpful to reveal how political obligation does have implications for international relations. The particularity principle involves ignoring the international implications of assuming a moral liberal character of a state. While the following may not be new to scholars of international relations[2] or to the history of colonialism and its close relationship with liberalism,[3] it is worth repeating here because it helps lay some doubt on the claim that political obligation is based on a moral relationship with one's polity. The doubt comes from how this ostensibly moral relationship ignores its immoral consequences. This point is also important because, first, it helps reveal a synergy between liberal discourses of political obligation and the liberal discourses of Jewish internationalism. Second, both political obligation and Jewish internationalism (and then today's Diaspora–Israel transnationalism) involve security dynamics that contribute to shaping their normative value. Moreover, what the raising of security also reveals is that one component of political obligation is not sovereignty or the state or the law, but security. Jewish internationalism and contemporary obligation discourses in Diaspora–Israel transnationalism are similarly framed by security concerns. What Lisa Moses Leff calls Jewish internationalism or international Jewish solidary,[4] and the international commitment of Jews in France and the UK to Jews in Damascus in the Damascus Affair,[5] are early examples of a form of political obligation that is tied to security and not to the state or to law.

Transnationalism

Some of the themes addressed in this book have been explored elsewhere under the rubric of transnationalism. This book also seeks to contribute to that body of literature by offering a theoretical approach to questions of transnational identities and transnational political spaces. There are various definitions of transnationalism, but what most of them share is a critical view of the nation-state in the contemporary global landscape. As Arjun Appadurai writes, in one of the primary texts on transnationalism:

> Nation-states, for all their important differences (and only a fool would conflate Sri Lanka with Great Britain), make sense only as parts of a system. This system (even when seen as a system of differences) appears poorly equipped to deal with the interlinked diasporas of people and images that mark the here and now. Nation-states, units in a complex interactive system, are not very likely to be the long-term arbiters of the relationship between globality and modernity.[6]

Appadurai may make reference to the international system, but structural realism[7] is not where he is going. His approach to transnationalism is different from that in the International Relations (IR)[8] literature, which unsurprisingly is less dismissive of the nation-state's future relevance.

Transnationalism in the IR literature is less about challenging the state than identifying additional actors that work with states or supplement state practice. One of the original and leading IR scholars of interdependence and transnationalism, James N. Rosenau, writes:

> By the transnationalization of world affairs I mean the processes whereby international relations conducted by governments have been supplemented by relations among private individual groups, and societies that can and do have important consequences for the course of events.[9]

For Rosenau, the main point is not that the nation-state is becoming less central an actor; in fact, the opposite is the case. He argues that the nation-state remains a, if not the, central actor in global affairs, but that changes in global politics have raised the profile of non-state actors and that our understanding of the state needs to change accordingly. "Transnational relations" is the term that he uses to refer to global politics that are not purely based on interactions between states in a system of nation-states. For Rosenau, transnational relations involve widening the net of actors that participate in global affairs and influence the policies and actions of states.

Transnationalism was thus a term used to address the confusion that Rosenau notes as having plagued IR scholars in the 1970s who were caught by surprise by "Nixon's trip to China, by the Arab oil embargo, by the collapse of U.S. efforts in Vietnam."[10] Studies of transnationalism in international relations have followed in Rosenau's path by using this term to represent a broadening of the field in order to accommodate the acknowledging reality that there are political actors and forces other than the state that the state must respond to. Transnationalism was thus about broadening the scope of who constitutes a political actor in international politics and can be read as an IR response to globalization. This literature remained concerned with state behavior, and sought to provide additional factors that could explain it, as well as the activities of non-state actors of significance to global politics. The transnationalism was, as such, a modification of earlier IR theories

125

and not the kind of radical rethinking of global politics envisioned by Appadurai.

In Appadurai's terms, the spatial framing in which transnational political obligations exist is not statist, but is described by the term "ethnoscapes," by which he means:

> The landscape of persons who constitute the shifting world in which we live: tourists, immigrants, refugees, exiles, guest workers, and other moving groups and individuals [who] constitute an essential feature of the world and appear to affect the politics of (and between) nations to a hitherto unprecedented degree.[11]

In this book, the primary ethnoscape is the Jewish Diaspora, and by definition diaspora communities are transnational communities. As Steven Vertovec writes in his introduction to transnationalism, "the dispersed diasporas of old have become today's 'transnational communities' sustained by a range of modes of social organization, mobility and communication."[12]

The transnational character of diasporas is one of the underlying features of diasporic identity, of belonging to a community living in exile in different places. There are, to be sure, different definitions of diaspora,[13] and its meaning has changed over the years from a historical description applicable to a relatively small number of minority communities, of which the Jewish Diaspora was an archetype, to a metaphor for contemporary conditions of displacement in a globalized, deterritorialized world. Diaspora as both a concept and a condition is seemingly in constant states of change, full of contradictions. As James Clifford notes in an especially insightful passage: "The empowering paradox of diaspora is that dwelling *here* assumes a solidarity and connection *there*. But *there* is not necessarily a single place or an exclusivist nation."[14] The Jewish Diaspora is also paradoxical.

Primarily, the Jewish Diaspora is both quite stable and, for historical reasons as well as Zionist ideology, is ideationally treated as insecure and unstable. Indeed, the Diaspora has historical connotations that frame it as a condition of homelessness and of Diaspora Jews living in a perpetual transitory state of migration by never being at home.[15] Yet, this historical narrative is refuted by how strongly Diaspora communities are and have been rooted in their places of residence. The Jewish Diaspora is perhaps better understood as an ethnoscape. To do so involves rejecting the Zionist negation of the Diaspora and its historical revisionism that seeks to dismiss the cultural wealth created by Jews in the Diaspora because they were not in their own state. Appadurai's concept of the ethnoscape is a starting point for understanding how identity politics become globalized, how the local forces that inform identity are influenced by global and international conditions and influences, and how there are important political spaces and identities that transcend the spatial boundaries of the state.[16] It is in this context that transnational political obligations come to pass. Whereas political obligations exist in a localized statist sense, transnational political obligations emerge out of a local identity-group's encounter with similar identity-groups in other places. Sometimes the obligations are imposed, as when the homeland tries to extract "obligations from the diaspora based on the presumption that emigrants owe loyalty to their nation-state of origin."[17] The transnational political obligations I am concerned with flow "through the cracks between states and borders."[18]

The kind of transnational relationship I am concerned with is different from both the IR version of transnationalism and the political obligation literature's version for the same reason: that what makes transnational political obligations political is different from how both the political obligation literature and the transnational IR literature conceptualize the political. The early IR transnational literature accepted a definition of politics based on power relations, in which power is understood in the Weberian terms adopted by the classical realist Hans Morgenthau.[19] The Weberian understanding of power is an often-unacknowledged assumption that guides the political obligation literature and it also served as a framing for politics in the main IR transnational literature from the 1970s.[20] Note, for example, the following passage written by Robert Keohane and Joseph Nye and published in 1972:

> We ... prefer a definition of politics that refers to relationships in which at least one actor consciously employs resources, both material and symbolic, including the threat or exercise of punishment, to induce other actors to behave differently than they would otherwise behave. Using this definition of politics, we define world politics as all political interactions between significant actors in a system in which a significant actor is any somewhat autonomous individual or organization that

controls substantial resources and participates in political relationship with other actors across state lines.[21]

While power has come to be understood in a variety of ways in the IR literature,[22] this framing of power remains influential both in IR and in the social sciences more generally.

It is, however, a way of framing power that ignores power as the ability to resist, which is an important part of transnational politics.[23] It also does not work with the kind of transnationalism I am concerned with, nor is it applicable to the understanding of either transnationalism or politics articulated elsewhere in the social sciences which frames transnationalism as "social morphology, as type of consciousness, as mode of cultural reproduction, as avenue of capital, as site of political engagement, and as (re)construction of 'place' or locality."[24] To be sure, transnationalism carries a variety of meanings, with texts focusing on diasporas, migrant communities, and different conceptions of political space. One leading scholar of transnationalism defines it as:

> A condition in which, despite great distances and notwithstanding the presence of international borders (and all the laws, regulations and national narratives they represent), certain kinds of relationships have been globally intensified and now take place paradoxically in a planet-spanning yet common – however virtual – arena of activity.[25]

Transnationalism refers to the social formation of a community across state borders, the creation of networks that span states and cannot be explained by them, shifting identities, and a spatial cartography informed by ideational and symbolic ties as opposed to legal state boundaries. Thus, literature on political space,[26] network societies,[27] social movements,[28] migrant communities,[29] diasporas,[30] and alternative models of citizenship[31] informs and contributes to the transnational research agenda.[32]

Political transnationalism has many manifestations, including the former mayor of New York City, Rudy Giuliani, making "regular trips to Santo Domingo, Dominican Republic, to campaign for elections. Under the aegis of various dual citizenship and dual nationality arrangements, political candidates from Guatemala, the Dominican Republic, Haiti, Columbia, Mexico and elsewhere return the favour."[33] To be sure, this kind of transnational politics is present when Israeli politicians travel to the USA, and the current Prime Minister, "Bibi" Netanyahu, has been very effective in the past at mobilizing American Jews on his behalf.[34] American politicians have also been known travel to Israel as a way of demonstrating their credentials as Israel supporters.[35]

Moreover, Naftali Bennett, the Israeli Jerusalem and Diaspora Affairs Minister, has recently suggested that Diaspora Jews should be offered a kind of "semi-citizenship."[36] Bennett, who has acknowledged a limited understanding of Diaspora Jewry, or at least American Diaspora Jewry, has said that "Jews outside Israel 'should have some sort of say' in the Israeli government's affair."[37] While it is not yet clear what he means by any of this, it is suggestive that a citizenship-informed account of political obligation could exist between a state and its Diaspora community. In this case, Bennett's vague proposal is part of the Government of Israel and World Jewry Joint Initiative, which is "an attempt to strengthen Jewish identity and connections between Israel and Jews around the world."[38] It is still too early to know what exactly Bennett has in mind with this initiative, let alone what the initiative's five-year budget of $1.4 billion will be spent on. Nevertheless it is significant, as the initiative suggests a potential revision to how Israel understands its relationship with Diaspora Jewry, and the semi-citizenship idea is intriguing as it could provide one form of a transnational political obligation that exists between a diaspora people and the homeland. For the time being, however, it is unclear what this kind of semi-citizenship transnational political obligation would entail. Thus, it remains important to explore the diaspora element in transnational relations that are not state-centric.[39]

In this regard, the diaspora element of transnationalism is especially pertinent. Diaspora communities are transnational communities. As the editors of the very first issue of the periodical *Public Culture* wrote, "Diasporas today run not against the grain of transnational cultural relationships but with them."[40] Writing in the same volume and issue of this periodical, Arjun Appadurai and Carol Breckenridge suggest that "Diasporas always leave a trail of collective memory about another place and time and create new maps of desire and attachment."[41] In this light, this book does speak to transnational theory. Why, then, do I not use this literature and instead take a seeming detour through political theory and political obligation? I do engage with the literature on diasporas and transnationalism respectively, but not in the main theoretical chapters.

Partly, the reason is accidental. When I began this project it was a reaction to how the political obligation literature does not seem to take identity, other than very general notions of citizenship or belonging, especially seriously. Moreover, political theory has traditionally "worked on models of 'closed societies' and exclusive loyalties of citizens toward a single state."[42] Political obligation is part of the exclusive loyalties this author is referring to. In this sense, the approach I take involves bringing political theory out of this traditional frame in a multi- and interdisciplinary combination of political theory, transnational studies and diaspora studies.

In this regard, the political obligation literature intrigued me as someone interested in expanding political theory to questions of political life that transcend the sovereign state. However, the transnational literature is heavily concerned with the global politics of migrants and can focus more on social practices than on the politics of consciousness that shape identity.[43] The Jewish Diaspora is historically a community of migrants, but for the most part settled ones who often no longer see themselves as migrants. In addition, the transnational literature tends to be about practice, whereas the political obligation literature is more theoretical. However, this book involves both, and thus combines select components of transnationalism, including sociological methodology, with political theory.

The citizenship-focused transnational literature could have been another route taken, as leading critical literature on citizenship studies has involved divorcing the concept of citizen from the nation-state.[44] This literature helpfully points out that there are transnational relations that are indicative of a different model of citizenship. Some of those interviewed for this book did use citizenship as a way of explaining their political relation with Israel, doing so in a curious way by arguing how citizenship in one country, the USA, gave them the opportunity to influence politics in another country, Israel. This is a view, however, that speaks the largest for Americans. Those Jews whom I interviewed in the UK did not share this view. Alternatively, it could be argued that because all Jews are potential citizens of Israel, and because Israel often speaks as if it represented all of world Jewry, there does exist a type of non-legal citizenship linking all Jews to Israel. However, this is not a view that I am comfortable assuming, as it requires dismissing the empirical condition of those Diaspora Jews who do not live in Israel, and it accepts uncritically a Zionist account of Israel's centrality for the Jewish world that is deeply troublesome for many Diaspora Jews.[45] In addition, to pursue the citizenship route poses ethical problems, as it necessitates an investigation into membership, which in the case I am concerned with is an especially difficult question, as it requires asking who is a Jew. This question was not one I was prepared to ask the participants, as it changes the focus of discussion away from the Diaspora/Israel relationship to moral, religious and political matters about who decides who is a Jew, and who recognizes different modes of being Jewish. Sometimes this identity question came up, but only with regard to the extent to which converted Jews are expected to also hold a relationship with Israel as a definitive or important part of their Jewish identity.[46] Whether or not their conversion is recognized across all Jewish communities was never asked.

Critical literatures on citizenship could have been used, and in some ways seem to offer a good fit. Surely, the concept of diasporic citizenship[47] seems apt for the present discussion. In the words of one author, diasporic citizenship emphasizes the "transnational," and moves "away from the territorial bound and sedentary versions of citizenship."[48] Yet the Jewish Diaspora is in many ways a sedentary diaspora, and to raise the term "citizenship" to help understand Diaspora/Israel relations is to invite a discussion about Israel's Law of Return, that any Jew anywhere can immigrate and be granted citizenship in Israel. This possibility, and the discourses surrounding it, are always looming in the Diaspora/Israel relationship. Diaspora Jews, however, are not legal citizens of Israel. They could claim to represent a different type of citizenship, but if that is the case, what binds them together as a community of diasporic citizens? The fact that they could all immigrate to Israel under the Law of Return? Yet while the Law of Return gives all Jews the right to immigrate to Israel, and as a mirror to the Nuremburg Laws is clear, there are debates about who is a Jew that nevertheless complicate matters. Inter-marriage across faiths and different forms of religious conversion to Judaism all raise challenges to traditional definitions of Jewish identity. Alternatively, could it be because Jews somehow all belong to a political community that exists across different states in the Diaspora? The historical literature on Jewish transnationalism[49] provides a fitting case for such an identity, but the equivalent of Jewish internationalism today is largely directed toward Israel, not the Diaspora.

Conceptions of Jewish peoplehood provide another option consistent with a diasporic citizenship model, but Jewish peoplehood is itself a problematic notion that marginalizes the differences across Diaspora communities, including those between the Israeli and Jewish Diasporas, and conveniently sidesteps the historiographical question of whether it makes more sense to speak in terms of either the Jewish people or specific Jewish communities. There are additional problems about the notion of Jewish peoplehood in which inclusion and exclusion depend on abstract senses of commitment that are rarely clear, as Hannah Arendt famously demonstrated in her debate with Gershom Scholem.[50] Providing an argument for how the Jewish Diaspora represents one example of diasporic citizenship is the topic for another book.

There are a variety of literatures and avenues by which I could have approached this subject, but it is often the journey and not the conclusion that is the primary learning experience. Thus, although the terminology I use is different from that used by Jasmin Habib, who defines the Diaspora/Israel relationship along the lines of Diaspora nationalism, both Habib and I are concerned with "understanding the relationships to Israel developed by [Diaspora Jews]."[51] In understanding this relationship, this book offers a journey including political theory, history, and sociology. Although the journey sometimes passes through dense terrain, the conclusion should be clear and of interest to anybody curious about the Jewish Diaspora's relationship with Israel, the transnational politics that shape this relationship, and the construction of contemporary Diaspora Jewish identity.

Liberalism, Obligation and Jewish Internationalism

Jewish internationalism was a product of Jews fighting for their security inside the state, and then projecting this fight into other states, often using the same language, as in the case of French colonial policy in Algeria and in the justification for involvement in the Damascus Affair.[52] Paradoxically, while the rise of Jewish internationalism was justified in liberal principles, Jewish internationalism was then attacked and used as an example of dual loyalty and contributed to the modern anti-Semitic belief in a world Jewish conspiracy.[53] The Jewish internationalism and the anti-Semitic response are both representative of the role played by discourses of obligation.

The connection between the domestic and the international is clear in the history of Jewish internationalism in France, where the domestic concerns of Jews became tied to their concerns for Jews in other countries. The Damascus Affair may be one of the more famous examples of Jewish internationalism, but according to Lisa Moses Leff, the history of Jewish internationalism cannot be understood without first appreciating the domestic forces that Jews were engaged with.[54] Building on the work of the historian Michael Graetz,[55] she argues that the development of Jewish internationalism/international solidary was, at least in the French case, part of the Jews' wider political activities within France. The rationale behind helping Jews in Damascus, or elsewhere such as in Algeria or Romania, was tied to their domestic arguments for Jewish rights.

The political struggles of the Jews in nineteenth-century France were largely influenced by the universal ideals of the French Revolution and of the subsequent struggles in France against Catholicism. The argument for Jewish emancipation was tied to the revolutionary ideals of integrating all peoples into the French nation, and the universalization of economic and civil rights was beneficial not just for the Jews, but for the whole nation. The Declaration of the Rights of Man and Citizen played an obviously important role in setting out this new universal discourse. Protecting the rights of Jews as equal French citizens was thus consistent with both the universalism of the Revolution and the progressive character of the argument for "civilization." This was not an anti-religious argument, even if it contained a kind of secular discourse with its framing of universal civil rights. Jews were not supposed to give up their religion. Rather, the argument's religious side had more to do with rejecting Catholicism, and replacing Catholicism with civilization.

This emphasis on the universal values of civilization meant that Jews found a worldview in which they could fight for their rights, do so with non-Jewish liberal allies, and at the same time be consistent with the wider international discourse of French political ambitions that supported France's colonial adventures. Indeed, by placing their discourse within a universal civilization worldview, French Jews were, unsurprisingly, often supportive of French colonial policy, and were quite active in trying to expand their ideas of political rights and universal freedoms in Algeria, and for that matter, in Damascus.[56] Jews in Algeria would be helped by the application of a French political and education system in Algeria, regardless of any indigenous concerns. The Jews in Damascus were similarly backward and needed the benevolent help of enlightened European Jewry to save them. In the process of helping these Jews in other countries, French Jewry felt not only that they were helping the cause of Jewish rights both locally and internationally, but that doing so was part of a larger moral mission to spread the universal values of France.

The *Alliance Israélite Universelle* (AIU) was founded in 1860 in support of this international focus, and it still exists.[57] The AIU was established as a synthesis of Judaism and the ideas of the 1789 Revolution. The development of modern Jewish internationalism, which is sometimes also referred to as solidarity, emerged out of the AIU. Previously, Jewish struggles for rights were articulated within the context of the state. For example, the arguments used in both the Damascus Affair and in the case of Jewish involvement in France's colonial policies in Algeria were both directed toward the universal values of 1789 and fell under the discourse of a European "civilizing mission."[58] Much of Adolphe Crémieux's discourse was consistent with this approach.

Crémieux, one of the leaders of French Jewry in the nineteenth century, a lawyer and politician who was involved in the Damascus Affair and the AIU, consistently argued for the rule of law that would protect all citizens. Thus in Algeria, French Jews argued for the expansion of French legal institutions into Algeria as both a means of helping Jewish rights and a way of conducting France's greater moral civilizing mission. A similar rhetoric was used during the Crimean War.

The early "Alliance leaders and liberal writers" witnessed "an inextricable link between the progress of religious tolerance, human rights, colonialism, and the French revolutionary tradition."[59] There was, consequently, little distinction between Jewish rights in France and those of Jews outside of France:

> Believing strongly in the need to secure Jewish rights, and also in the universalism of the ideology underpinning them, French Jewish leaders

mobilized to advocate for Jews elsewhere. Linking "Jewish interests" to "civilization" effectively rooted the question of Jewish rights in the extension of a religious policy based on ideals affirmed in 1789, but actualized only gradually over the course of the nineteenth century.[60]

Moreover, for liberals and Jews, protecting minority Jewish rights helped to show that there was nothing irreligious about their activities, merely that they were anti-Catholic. Keeping a religious element was important for wider public support, at least among Protestants.

Yet, the development of Jewish solidarity with the AIU was different from previous domestically focused activities. The AIU had no legal relationship to the state; its purpose was "to help Jews around the word to obtain national citizenship, achieve material security, and make 'moral progress.'"[61] The AIU used the term "solidarity" to frame its work, and also used the term "obligation" when soliciting for donations. Solidarity, however, had previously had a different meaning. It used to be a legal term traced back to Roman law (*in solidum*), that referred to how one person can be held legally responsible for the debts of another. What this meant was that Jews of a particular community could be held liable for the debts of any individual from that community. The political meaning of solidarity used by the AIU was noticeably different from this earlier legal meaning. The political sense of Jewish solidarity "denoted a feeling of mutual responsibility among Jews dispersed all over the world in the name of shared liberal values," and the AIU understood its work as being for the "good of all humanity."[62] As Lisa Moses Leff argues, "This new 'solidarity' was independent of any particular state, and yet it was based in the same modern ideals that French Jews had embraced in their earlier campaigns to achieve legal equality themselves . . . and for Jews elsewhere under French jurisdiction in the 1840s and 1850s."[63]

Solidarity was thus political and not legal, and once it became political the AIU started referring to obligation in its fundraising efforts. It was the twofold rhetoric of solidarity and obligation that provided the early basis for Jewish internationalism. Paradoxically, considering how political obligation today is so closely tied to the law, the use of the term obligation to refer to a political expectation was made possible only once the law was removed. Leff writes:

Let us keep in mind that this new meaning for *solidarity* developed only after the juridical "solidarity" of French Jews, their collective responsibility for each other's debts and transgressions, had finally been eradicated from French law. Alliance leaders encouraged donations by using the terms of "obligation" only when no actual obligations existed any longer.[64]

The combination of solidarity with obligation as a political discourse without any legal foundation (thus making it an obligation even though there is no political obligation in a technical sense) is partly what makes transnational political obligation unique. That the term obligation could be used in so clearly a political sense as opposed to a legal one helps to illuminate the very close relationship that exists between obligations and politics. What it also reveals is the close relationship between this kind of obligation and security.

There exist, then, two parallels in Jewish internationalism with the liberal obligation thinking of Klosko. There is the connection between liberal values and violence – either through colonialism or a preference for the security provided by stable international borders – and there is the close connection between a discourse of obligation and that of security. Jewish internationalism, which grew out of local fights for Jewish rights and the struggle against anti-Semitism, was always about the security of Jewish communities. It was a bitter irony that Jewish internationalism led to further anti-Semitic attack, although not an irony that is especially surprising.[65]

Diaspora–Israel Transnationalism: Between Zion and Diaspora

The literature on transnationalism is a relatively recent body of work concerned with the implications of increased migration and the displacement of statist identities across multiple geographies.[66] The development of transnational theory was largely about improving migration studies,[67] and as Patricia Clavin writes, "transnationalism, despite its early identification with the transfer or movement of money and goods, is first and foremost about people: the social spaces that they inhabit, the networks they form and the ideas they exchange."[68] It is no coincidence that she uses a German Jew to help in her definition, Julius Moriz Bonn, who had worked for the

League of Nations but had also been a government advisor, academic and economist, among other things. It was Jews who from the 1920s until after the Second World War were often border crossers whose horizontal movements could not escape the vertical political structures of national boundaries.[69] This example reveals another important feature of transnationalism, that it is not a new phenomenon.[70] In this sense, Jewish internationalism can be read as a precursor to today's Diaspora/Israel relationship, which I am using the term transnationalism to help explain. The one significant exception to my usage, however, is that transnationalism is often about migration, and Diaspora Jewish communities are not best understood as migrant communities – although one notable exception is the so-called Israeli Diaspora, which has been described as a transnational community.[71]

I use the term transnationalism because, in a sociological framing of the relationship, the Jewish Diaspora does demonstrate similarities with what the transnational literature is concerned with, including demographic, political, cultural, economic and familial ties across states. In essence, the Jewish Diaspora's relationship with Israel is transnational in everything except migration. In place of migration is a shared sociology, history and psychology of Diaspora. Jewish transnationalism is just like any other transnationalism in the sense that it crosses state borders, includes participation in the politics of multiple states and involves "overlapping boundaries of membership in political communities."[72]

While Jewish internationalism was a precursor to today's Diaspora/Israel relationship in the sense that both are about assisting Jewish communities in other countries, there are some differences. Whereas Jewish internationalism was largely uni-directional, led by Western European Jews, especially French Jews, and directed toward Jews in Eastern Europe, North Africa and the Middle East, today's Diaspora–Israel transnationalism is often bi-directional. Ideational cultural discourses from Israel often penetrate the Diaspora along with Israeli-based outreach toward Diaspora communities, and many Diaspora practices and discourses about Jewish identity and politics are geared toward Israel, ranging from greater Jewish religious pluralism to political lobbying.

Another difference has to do with what used to be called Diaspora nationalism. Jewish internationalism was closely tied to this variant of Jewish political thought in that it emphasized the importance of

Obligation in Exile

Diaspora for Jewish life and sought to protect and support Jewish life in the Diaspora. Zionism was obviously antithetical to this view, and contemporary Diaspora–Israel transnationalism includes a combination of both. Israel's centrality involves a rejection of Diaspora nationalism, but Diaspora has not disappeared, and it is not uncommon to find arguments to the effect that Diaspora is important for Israel. Diaspora nationalism, however, was conceived in the absence of the Jewish State. The condition of Diaspora life, while different for Jews in different communities and countries, was nevertheless generally speaking a shared experience. There was no State of Israel. Prior to Israel's creation in 1948, the condition of living in the Diaspora was an important point in defining the Jewish people. The creation of the Jewish State of Israel, however, changed everything.

In his classic text on the history and meaning of Diaspora for the Jews, *Galut: Modern Jewish Reflection on Homelessness and Homecoming*, Arnold Eisen argues that exile has been an important part of Jewish identity, and that while its meaning has changed over the years, its significance for Jewish identity is evident not just in the empirical experience of life in the Diaspora but also in Torah. As he writes, "In the beginning, there was exile."[73] Genesis hardly begins before Adam and Eve are exiled out of the Garden, thus setting the stage for future exiles. Yet, Diaspora became not a place of exile but a place of many homes, as Jews developed their lives, cultures and religious thought throughout this condition of exile.[74]

The traditions that Diaspora created are crucial to any understanding of Jewish identity, history, culture, politics and religion. Yet, in 1948 with the creation of the State of Israel, this tradition was faced with a revolution. After 1948 the meanings of Diaspora and of Diaspora Jewish identity changed. The few remaining anti-Zionist Jewish organizations, such as the Jewish Fellowship in Britain, shut down.[75] The American Council for Judaism, which fought hard against Zionism right until Israel's Declaration of Independence in May 1948, resigned to its failure, accepted the reality of the new Jewish State, but then sought to distance itself from Israel and focused its energies toward strengthening American Jewish communities. They acknowledged the risks of closely aligning Diaspora Jewry with Israel, bemoaned the "'Zionization' of Jewish philanthropy"[76] and still in 1953 were greatly concerned about the "'confusion of Judaism' with the nationalism of Israel."[77]

With Israel, one of the underlying shared meanings that brought Jews together changed. This shift is important for understanding the transnational political obligations of the Jewish Diaspora in its relationship with Israel, because it is representative of a fundamental change for the Jewish people. Most dramatically, Zionism often involved an ideological commitment against diaspora life. This commitment was certainly the case with the political Zionists. Cultural and spiritual Zionists varied on this point. Ahad Ha'Am, the spiritual leader of these variations of Zionist thought, was somewhat ambivalent about the potential for any immediate successes of Zionism and thus did not view Zionism as negating Diaspora life, although some of his followers did.[78] For the majority of Zionists, Diaspora was exile; a place of homelessness and weakness, a place where Jews died, while Israel is a place where Jews live. This negation of Diaspora is perhaps most visible and most disturbing in the work of the famous Israeli novelist A. B. Yehoshua, who argued:

> The Holocaust was not only the "final and absolute proof of the failure of *golah*," but a tragedy which "we forced upon ourselves … responsibility for our people's awful fate in this century is its own." Jews had failed to face up to the inevitable. They had not come home to Zion. Galut, before and after the Holocaust, was a "neurotic solution" to the Jewish problem. Health lay only in bringing that problem to an end.[79]

Yehoshua has described *golah* (the Diaspora) as being responsible for the Holocaust and as threatening Jewish life. In his essay *Exile as a Neurotic Condition* he writes:

> The *golah* was the source of the most terrible disasters to befall the Jewish people, that because of *golah* the nation was almost completely wiped out in our generation; that in spite of the existence of the State of Israel, the *golah* constitutes a threat to Jewish communities.[80]

Yehoshua's argument is problematic, for blaming the victims of the Holocaust for their fate is extreme and disturbing. Nevertheless, the negation of the Diaspora was central to Zionist mythology, and "the Holocaust fundamentally altered the facts of Jewish geography, and did so in a way that was deeply confirming of the tenets of political Zionism."[81] For Yehoshua it was important that Israel stand separate from Diaspora, and he was, along with the American

Council for Judaism, concerned about the Zionization of Diaspora Jews, although for different reasons, and was not in favour of the encroaching Israelization of Diaspora Jewish identity:

> Recently, Israel has become a too-familiar presence in the *golah*, especially in the USA. Paradoxically, it is no longer necessary to immigrate to Israel to live in Israel, and it is possible to acquire scraps of significant Israeli reality in *golah* itself. The aura of distance and mystery surrounding Israel has become blurred, if it has not vanished altogether... The constant deepening of relations between the *golah* and Israel has obscured the dividing line between them. Perhaps it was thought that in this way people's hearts would be prepared for *aliya*, but the reverse is true. What has been created is a legitimate reality of substitutes for *aliya* – of quasi-*aliya*. We must at all costs reestablish a certain feeling of alienation between *golah* and Israel – a controlled disagreement, as it were.[82]

For Yehoshua, Diaspora is a "virus."[83]

The Zionist negation of Diaspora was clear. Golda Meir once wrote, "We have nothing against Jews in the *galut*. It is against the *galut* itself that we protest."[84] Another example of Israel's radical reframing of Diaspora and Jewish identity is evident in Gershom Scholem's thought. He once wrote, in response to a challenging question about the "ethical and intellectual consequences of the Zionist project in life in Israel," that "the question is not *the price of Zionism but the price of exile*."[85] For Scholem and the political Zionists, the creation of the State of Israel brought the Jews back into history.[86] However, for Jews in the Diaspora who do not want to reject their lives as Diaspora Jews, Scholem's Israelization is insulting and demeaning. Yet, his is not an isolated voice. Diaspora life, a life in exile or *galut*, was framed by Zionists as an absence in opposition to the presence found in Israel, and a place where Jewish identity could never be realized, and, consistent with this risk, where Jewish security could never be actualized.

There is a lot of historical revisionism in the narratives that emphasize Israel's power at the expense of the Diaspora and that view Israel as a place of life and Diaspora as a place of death and disease. This revisionism problematically assumes that Nazi success was evidence of Jewish weakness. In addition, Jews in North American in particular posed a serious problem for the anti-Diaspora worldview in classical Zionism. Jews in North America were not subject to the same wartime experiences and Jewish life in North America was highly successful. Consequently, if the Zionist negation of the Diaspora was to be accepted, the successes of American Jews in particular in successfully integrating[87] into their country had to be an illusion.[88] Eisen writes, "Only American Jewry could credibly deny Israeli centrality in Jewish life or the wholesale negation of the diaspora."[89] Jewish leaders in North America who did become Zionists in their support of Israel had to define a different account of Zionism, one where emigration was not a necessary component. However, such an account posed some logical difficulties.

Regardless of the necessary support, especially financial, that a young Israel needed and that American Jews were often happy to give, there was an ideational tension. Put succinctly, the very idea of being a Zionist Jew in North America was an oxymoron. Certainly for Ben-Gurion and Golda Meir, to be a Zionist meant to live in Israel. Anything else was nonsense, or "pseudo-Zionism."[90] For American and Canadian Jews who defined themselves as Zionists but were not about to move to Israel, this rejection of their joint Jewish/Zionist identity posed a problem. Two leaders of American Jewry, Solomon Schechter (1847–1915) and Louis Brandeis (1856–1941), helped provide discourses that could help resolve this tension.

Brandeis equated being Jewish with being a Zionist.[91] This move has had subsequent repercussions for Jewish identity that have made many Diaspora Jews uncomfortable as it assumes an allegiance and loyalty to a state that they may not feel such attachments for,[92] and inadvertently provided an opening for the new anti-Semitism, whereby attacking Israel can be used as a seemingly politically correct way of attacking Jews (since all Jews support Israel, Jews and Israel can be conflated).[93] The point Brandeis made was that to be a good Jew and a good American, one should become a Zionist.[94] He argued that "loyalty to America demands ... that each American Jew become a Zionist."[95] He claimed that American Jews had a home, and did not need a new one, but many Jews did not have a home and for them there was Israel. As Eisen argues, for American Jews, for a time at least, "The Land's [Israel's] *existence* is accorded significance, then, but not its historical or physical *reality*."[96]

Schechter saw Zionism as an important factor in preventing

assimilation because it helped to maintain a sense of Jewish identity in the Diaspora.[97] As such Jews could live in the Diaspora without losing their Judaism. There was also the advantage that only in a Jewish State could Jewish culture be created. This kind of Ahad Ha'Am style of Zionism deeply influenced Mordecai Kaplan (1881–1983). For Ahad Ha'Am, the development of a Jewish community in Palestine was crucial for the regeneration of the Jewish spirit and Zionism was not primarily an exercise in national independence. Kaplan's Zionism was clear in its acceptance of the Diaspora. For him, American Jews should not disembark for Palestine (and later Israel); they needed to remain home in the USA and continue to develop Judaism there. Long-distance Zionism was, he argued, just as important for the success of Israel as those kinds that sought Jews' immigration into Palestine and Israel. As he argued in his text *A New Zionism*, "Zionism has to be redefined so as to assure a permanent place for Diaspora Judaism."[98]

Kaplan was greatly concerned with the Zionist preoccupation with negating the Diaspora. Writing at a time when Israel was still uncertain about its future prognosis, Kaplan argued that instead of Zionism negating the Diaspora in the hope of encouraging much needed immigration, it needed to affirm the Diaspora, and not alienate Diaspora Jewry. Yet, Jews in the Diaspora also needed to feel committed to the future of Israel. Kaplan was concerned not just about Diaspora Jewry, but also with the Jews in Israel. As products of a political or classical Zionism which in his eyes had little in it that was specifically Jewish, the political and classical Zionists settling in Israel were not specifically Jewish either. He argued that the destiny of both Israel and Diaspora are interconnected, and took seriously Franz Rosenzweig's warnings that were the Zionists to lose touch with the Diaspora, they too would become lost.[99] He wrote: "Should the Jewish civilization fail to be at home in Eretz Yisrael, it will disappear everywhere else. Should it disappear everywhere else, it is bound to give way to some new Levantine civilization in Eretz Yisrael."[100] His solution was a Zionism where being a Zionist meant reconstituting Jewish peoplehood both in Israel and in the Diaspora, and in strengthening the cultural and spiritual ties between them.

Part of the challenge for Zionist thought was in dealing with the fact that North American Jews were largely comfortable in their home countries and were not about to emigrate en masse to a Jewish State in Palestine. While Israel nevertheless became increasingly important for the construction of Jewish identity in the Diaspora, including North America, as Arthur Hertzberg's work clearly demonstrates,[101] its importance also led to tensions since there existed, all attempts to the contrary notwithstanding, a logical quandary in being a Zionist in the Diaspora with no intention of moving to Israel.

Kaplan's solution – to emphasize the importance of long-distance Zionism – provided one appealing approach to dealing with this problem, assuming that one could understand the metaphysical religious side to his argument, which associated his Diaspora Zionism with becoming more human.[102] The success of the Zionists in creating the new physical reality of Israel created some particularly Jewish problems that needed Diaspora help. In succeeding to build the Jewish State, the Zionists scored a major victory, but in the process they did not develop an account of what being Jewish meant in this new State.[103] The mere fact of Israel's existence was presumed to be enough, at least for the political Zionists. While Eisen suggests that the spiritual and religious Zionists could fill this void,[104] he also notes how Diaspora Jewry more generally is also important since part of the meaning of and for Israel requires that it play the role of being a center for Jews who still live in the Diaspora.

This importance of Israel for Diaspora Jews, when combined with the success of Jewish life in North America and the rest of the Diaspora, has led Diaspora Jews to publicly and vocally become involved in Israeli affairs. So long as Israel claims to be the homeland of the Jewish people, and claims to represent Jewish interests globally, Diaspora Jews have largely been unprepared to let Israel go it alone. They too have a voice, and they will use it to speak with Israeli officials. In other words, if Israel is going to try to represent Jewish interests globally, Diaspora Jewish organizations are not going to let Israel do so without their say.

What the success of Diaspora life in the age of Israel required was an ideational connection between Diaspora Jewry and Israel that could accommodate the political narratives of both. The solutions of Kaplan or Schechter, for example, provided one answer, and what eventually transpired was the Israelization of Jewish identity in the Diaspora. Israel became conceived of as a center of Jewish life to which all Jews could turn, and which, because of its centrality and the historical tensions that legitimated Zionism and delegitimized Diaspora, could always potentially overshadow Diaspora life. In this sense, there have always been tensions between the Diaspora and Israel, as the late Yitzhak Rabin's request that Diaspora Jews stay out of Israeli politics demonstrates, while Benjamin Netanyahu has regularly carried out the reverse and solicited certain segments of American Jewry for support.[105]

To further complicate matters, while the Zionist narrative is clearly hierarchical as regards to how the Diaspora is perceived, Israel has also needed Diaspora support, to varying extents and for varying reasons. Israel has always been careful, however, not to stray into the realm of asking Jews to choose between Israel and the USA, although the Pollard Affair is conceivably an exception. While the relationship is obviously complicated, it nevertheless reflects the precedent set by Jewish internationalism, of Jews coming to the aid of Jews in other countries. Both Israel and Diaspora success have involved an ongoing attempt at writing what being a Jew means in the Diaspora (its historical condition) in the age of Israel (a relatively new condition), and one way in which this has been done is by developing an obligation to be connected to Israel. In this way, Diaspora Jewish identity and the Jewish State could exist simultaneously without negating Diaspora, but enhancing it by connecting the Diaspora to the great success of Jewish national aspirations in Israel. In this way, the Jewish internationalism was refashioned into a Diaspora–Israel transnationalism.

Israel and Diaspora Security

Jewish internationalism was often directed toward supporting Jewish communities and making them more secure, and Zionism also has always been about Jewish security. It is, consequently, not surprising that security features as one of the ideational connections in the new Diaspora–Israel transnationalism. The Zionist success story is predicated on the idea that Israel exists to provide the Jews with security, and the transnational relationship between the Diaspora and Israel is regularly colored by this claim. Jewish internationalism was famously active in helping Jews in Damascus from anti-Semitic persecution and violent attack, and today's Jewish transnationalism between the Diaspora and Israel is also characterized by security. Indeed, Diaspora Jews have long been concerned about Israel's security, and over the years have become increasingly active in supporting Israel whenever its security is threatened, be the threat real or imagined. Much debate about Israel today is based on precisely this issue, and on that of how Israel has come to use violence as either a justifiable means to ensure its security or a disproportionate hammer wielded against another's people human and political rights. The obvious question then could be whether or not the obligation toward Israel that Diasporas Jews feel they have or are presumed to have involves supporting Israel's security policies. But the more important question is, how does security inform the transnational political obligation of Diaspora Jewry toward Israel today? The bombing of the Jewish community center in Buenos Aires, Argentina, on July 18, 1994, committed as an attack against Israel, serves to highlight the importance of this question.

It is April 4, 2011, and I am searching for a synagogue in London. Although I completed the first part of my graduate training in London, I never really became involved in the London Jewish community, and only went to one synagogue, which was something of a shock to the system. I had never been to a *shul* with an organ and a choir before. It is not raining, I have my A–Z map and I found the synagogue without too much difficulty. In the end I did not need the A–Z. The big nondescript building on the corner was obviously a synagogue. It had CCTV cameras facing down from every possible direction. Even for London, with its high number of closed-circuit cameras monitoring what seems to be every public space of the city, the high concentration of cameras on this building was a giveaway. Synagogues and Jewish community centers around the world have increased their security apparatus over the years. When I lived in Zurich, the synagogue there had a guard stationed outside every time there was a service. Speaking Hebrew served as a kind of password for foreigners to enter without hindrance.

If we are to believe the increasing security at synagogues, Jewish schools and Jewish community centers, security, or rather the fear of insecurity, has become a major part of Diaspora Jewish life, often to the chagrin of at least one London rabbi, who would rather spend money on childcare or Jewish education than on security guards.[106] As this rabbi said, "The idea that we need a security guard standing is ludicrous and is part of the victim mentality that the CST keeps up."[107] As one London Masorti rabbi said, the presence of security guards creates a sense of anxiety, suggesting that the "synagogue is a dangerous place and can discourage entrance. They also transmit insecurity. We need to make this security as invisible as possible."[108] The synagogue I was looking for this April 4 did not have security guards, but the CCTV cameras were very visible and gave the impression of a building perpetually under siege.

Organizations like the Community Security Trust (CST) in the UK help keep this fear of attack in the Jewish mind. The CST's 2012 annual report begins ominously: "640 anti-Semitic incidents were recorded by CST in 2012, a 5 per cent increase from the 608 anti-Semitic incidents recorded in 2011 and the third-highest annual total ever recorded by CST."[109] The year may not have been the worse, but the message is clear. The situation is bad, attacks on Jews are on the increase, and vigilance is required.

Insecurity and Diaspora identity seemingly go hand in hand. Indeed, the traditional Zionist narrative identifies Diaspora as the home of Jewish insecurity. Today, Israel plays its own role in this discourse. The 2012 CST Report includes a section on whether or not verbal attacks against Israel constitute anti-Semitic behavior. The report says:

> Clearly, it would not be acceptable to define all anti-Israel activity as anti-Semitic; but it cannot be ignored that contemporary anti-Semitism can occur in the context of, or be accompanied by, extreme feelings over the Israel/Palestine issue, or that discourse relating to the Israel/Palestine issue is used by offenders to abuse Jews. Drawing out these distinctions, and deciding on where the dividing lines lie, is one of the most difficult areas of CST's work in recording and analyzing hate crime.[110]

Challenging Israel is thus always potentially an attack against Jews, and it is not hard to fathom why. For the Jewish people, Israel is not just another country. While not all Jews share equally in their connection with Israel, Israel does play a significant role in the construction of contemporary Jewish identity, which is why the 2013 Pew Jewish Population Survey includes data about American Jews' relationship with Israel. It is also why the Orthodox London rabbi Barry Marcus told me "An attack on Israel is an attack on all Jews."[111] Thus, for many Jews, part of their identity involves an obligation to support Israel.

The general obligation that Jews who share a connection with Israel have toward Israel is one of support, although manifestations of support vary. One reason many Jews feel such an obligation an has to do with security and the sense that all Jews are in it together. As the London Masorti rabbi Chaim Weiner told me, "Attacks on Jews anywhere are a threat." However, he was clear about then saying that a "bomb in Argentina does not make my synagogue more dangerous."[112] Yet, the message that many Jews get is the opposite. For example, a British report published in 2010 noted that out of the 23 percent of Jews in Britain who had witnessed an anti-Semitic incident, 56 percent believed "that the incident was 'probably' or 'definitely' related to the abuser/assailant's views on Israel."[113] Of the 11 percent who said they had been subject to an anti-Semitic attack, verbal or physical, 56 percent also felt that the attack had been related to the attacker's views on Israel.

Another illustration is provided by the bi-weekly emails sent out by the European Jewish Congress. In addition to each email including a roundup of news from the Israeli press, during the period December 11, 2012–December 13, 2013, just over 23 percent of all headlines contained something about Israel or the Israeli–Palestinian conflict.[114] If we include the Israeli news roundup, well over a quarter of all headlines and stories have something to do with Israel, which contributes to Jews feeling that they are under attack because of threats to Israel.

The linkage between Israeli security, including both Israel's foreign policy and its policy in the Occupied Territories, and Diaspora security is controversial. Indeed, many Jews are deeply distraught by Israeli security policy to such an extent that they want nothing to do with Israel and tend to avoid any public debate or discussion about Israel. Perhaps more controversial are those who do speak out, and who do not feel any political obligation to support Israel because of their universal moral obligations.[115] Those Jews who do speak out are often verbally assaulted by other Jews. Brian Klug writes about his own experiences of being at the receiving end of such attacks. Placing these occasions in context, he quotes the British rabbi Dr Jeffrey Cohen: "There can be no more pathetic sight than that of a Jew-hating Jew, or to be a little more charitable, a Jew embarrassed by his own people and their historical aspirations."[116] That some Israelis, such as Amos Oz and David Grossman, are often also deeply critical of their government's security policies is always a problem for those who hold that undivided loyalty to Israel is a hallmark of being Jewish.

These issues all came up in the interviews I conducted, as the obligations that Jews do have toward Israel are not just political in the sense of involving relations of power (more on this later), but also moral. (Political obligation, it should not be forgotten, is also a moral discourse.) The moral sentiments that animate Jewish obligations to Israel vary from a sense of peoplehood to the concrete application of being able to help shape government policy. It is important to note that criticism of Israel can be a manifestation of a political obligation. However, what was common was how the obligations to Israel felt by Diaspora Jews were often a reaction both to how they understand Jewish identity generally and to their sense of individual identity. Their Jewish identity was closely tied up with Israel – this is the Israelization of Jewish identity. Jewish Diasporic identity often involves addressing the presumptions that accompany how to mitigate a connection with a land they do not live in but are often associated with.

The answers given to explain the feelings of obligation to Israel varied and reflected the usual historical justifications of Diaspora Zionists. They ranged from the safe-haven clause, that Israel provides a place of escape for the Jews should one be needed – or said differently, "a Zionist is a Jew who lives in the Diaspora with his bags eternally packed"[117] – to its corollary of historical necessity, to feelings of shared peoplehood, biblical history and pride. The Holocaust came up more than once, along with the argument that had Israel existed, the Holocaust would not have happened – a claim, incidentally that has been challenged since the Yishuv did not do much to help Jews in Europe, not that it had the resources to in any case and, even if it did, Israel's treatment of Holocaust survivors has been poor.[118]

Nevertheless, that many pointed out that Israel can provide security for the Jewish people is not surprising as this argument reflects how Zionists traditionally argued their case. Some of the interviewees even argued that the Diaspora matters for Israel's security. As one American Orthodox Jew told me, "Israel cannot exist without the Diaspora. Without major powers in Israel's corner it would not have made it sixty years."[119] In this view, Diaspora support matters hugely for Israel, and as Steven Gold notes in his book about the Israeli Diaspora, "There is little doubt that the Jewish

State would not have survived without the financial assistance of diaspora Jews..."[120] Moreover, in 2010, 77 percent of British Jews agreed that "Jews have a 'special responsibility to support Israel,'" and 87 percent agreed that "Jews are responsible for ensuring the 'survival of Israel.'"[121] That these beliefs help to increase the importance of the Diaspora is convenient as this provides an important source of legitimacy for Diaspora Jewish involvement in Israeli affairs.

The feelings behind Diaspora support for Israel are strong, although they are still open to interpretation and critique. As J. J. Goldberg told me in our second interview, "I'm not saying necessarily that Israel makes American Jews more secure. I do believe that most American Jews feel Israel makes them more secure."[122] In quite a few interviews, individuals found that the claims they made and the assumptions they held did not always stand up to as much scrutiny as they thought. As many of the interviewees acknowledged, the Diaspora relationship with Israel is often emotional, and this makes it difficult to critically analyze the connection. Hence Goldberg's point about Jews feeling that Israel makes them more secure. The emphasis is on how they feel, and the empirical reality that these feelings create for them. Because of the emotions involved, especially for older generations of Diaspora Jews, critical investigation about Israel and Diaspora support of Israel can be a touchy subject.

To conduct such a critique and to problematize the rationale behind Diaspora connections with Israel is not to dismiss the feelings that Jews have toward or about Israel. Rather, it is to help explore in greater depth the moral discourses by which obligations to Israel are understood. In this vein, some of the main claims for Diaspora support and engagement with Israel are not as strong as they may appear.

First, Jews in the Diaspora are perhaps safer now than ever before, and Jews in North America in particular have been exceptionally successful at integrating into wider society. Jews are not powerless to protect themselves or their interests.[123] It is a mistake to think that Diaspora Jews today still have their bags eternally packed, and while Israel may have the largest Jewish population of any country,[124] this demographic shift has only occurred within the past few years and does not reflect a growing commitment of young Jews from the Diaspora to immigrate. Indeed, the largest Diaspora

Jewish organizations are regularly concerned about a declining connection of young Jews with Israel.

Second, an additional and somewhat self-serving feature of the ability of Diaspora Jews to highlight Israel's existence as a Jewish safe haven makes it possible for Diaspora Jews not to have to fight for Jewish immigration into their hostlands. For Jews in the West, where immigration is a loaded political debating point (and let us not forget how bad the world was in allowing Jewish immigration prior to, during and after the Second World War), Israel provides a way of identifying a destination without minority Jewish populations needing to address and challenge immigration policy in their countries of residence. Consequently, there was no need for Jews in the USA, Canada, France, the UK or elsewhere to make a national case for allowing large numbers of Russian or Ethiopian Jews, for example, to immigrate into these countries. When American Jews were successful in helping Jews emigrate from the USSR to Israel, the argument was made in Cold War terms[125] and without having to request increasing immigration into the USA.

Third, the security argument is deeply problematic, since it is Israeli security practices that are often the reason for increasing alienation, manifested primarily as non-Zionist detachment and in some cases as anti-Zionism among Diaspora Jews. The type of security that Israel provides is ensured by means that are not acceptable to many Diaspora Jews. While this type of critique toward Israel is not new – Albert Einstein, among others, made such points in 1948[126] – it is becoming a more popular view among Jews who did not live through the Second World War and for whom Israel's wars, such as the 1982 war, were not of necessity but of choice.[127] Tony Judt has argued that Israel is actually bad for the Jews. As he wrote in 2003:

> Today, non-Israeli Jews feel themselves once again exposed to criticism and vulnerable to attack for things they didn't do. But this time it is a Jewish state, not a Christian one, which is holding them hostage for its own actions. Diaspora Jews cannot influence Israeli policies, but they are implicitly identified with them, not least by Israel's own insistent claims upon their allegiance. The behavior of a self-described Jewish state affects the way everyone else looks at Jews. The increased incidence of attacks on Jews in Europe and elsewhere is primarily attributable to misdirected efforts, often by young Muslims, to get back at

Israel. The depressing truth is that Israel's current behavior is not just bad for America, though it surely is. It is not even just bad for Israel itself, as many Israelis silently acknowledge. The depressing truth is that Israel today is bad for the Jews.[128]

It cannot be ignored that the association that exists between Jewish identity and Israel has also contributed to the misplaced view that identifies Jews as targets for attack because of Israeli policy. It has long been acknowledged that Jews in the Diaspora and Jews in Israel are heading in different directions,[129] and different experiences and understandings about security are one reason for Diaspora and Israeli Jews to be diverging.[130] As Judt points out, there is also the possibility that Israeli security policies have perversely had the effect of decreasing Jewish security, or at least of raising particular security risks.

One diplomat in the Israeli Ministry of Foreign expressed the view that although the existence of the State of Israel has increased the personal security of the Jewish Diaspora in Europe, in some Jewish Diaspora communities there can be feelings of insecurity because of developments in the Middle East: "anti-Semitic attacks against Jewish institutions might be triggered by events in the Middle East, maybe not in the USA, but yes in Europe."[131] Israeli security policy, particularly with regard to the Occupation, has often been a difficult matter for Diaspora Jews, especially since Jews tend to be on the left wing of the political spectrum.

Jacobson's award-winning novel *The Finkler Question* is largely about revealing this moral schism and presenting it as a divide between those who support Israel and those who support human rights. The two main characters in the novel, Finkler and Libor, regularly debate Israel and the Middle East. They cannot separate their Jewish identity from the security politics of Israel, or, for that matter, from the security politics of Jewish history. For Libor, whose bags are always packed, anything to do with Israel is an issue of conscience, but for Finkler it is about justice. Libor's views are informed by his particular conscience shaped by his experiences as a Jew, and Finkler's views are representative of a philosophical moral universalism. Neither of them is ever satisfied. Libor and Finkler represent the archetypes of contemporary debate around Israel. One non-fictional example that corresponds to these archetypes was the petition "For the sake of Zion," circulated online in May 2010. The petition is no longer online, but the reporter Josh Nathan-Kazis, writing for *The Jewish Daily Forward*, describes it as follows:

> The petition, posted at www.forthesakeofzion.org on May 13, claims inspiration from the European Jewish Call for Reason, otherwise known as JCall. A petition that JCall submitted to the European Parliament on May 3 condemned Israel's policy of establishing exclusively Jewish settlements in the occupied West Bank and in Palestinian-dominated East Jerusalem as "morally and politically wrong." The American group's petition cites and supports that characterization.[132]

Israel's security challenges have been a polarizing topic for Diaspora Jews who do feel committed to Israel.

Jonathan Kopp is a volunteer for J Street. He has ample political experience, having worked on Obama for America's national media team during President Obama's 2008 presidential campaign, and he later became involved in J Street. Founded in 2008, J Street was set up by Jeremy Ben-Ami as an alternative American Jewish voice about Israel. J Street comprises three different organizations, a registered lobby group, a political action committee that endorses federal candidates, and a non-profit education fund. Its website describes J Street as follows:

> the political home for pro-Israel, pro-peace Americans fighting for the future of Israel as the democratic homeland of the Jewish people. We believe that Israel's Jewish and democratic character depend [sic] on a two-state solution, resulting in a Palestinian state living alongside Israel in peace and security.
>
> Rooted in our commitment to Jewish and democratic values, J Street is redefining what it means to be pro-Israel in America. We are changing the U.S. political dynamics around Israel by mobilizing broad support for a two-state solution because it's in Israel's and America's interest. And we are expanding support for Israel by affirming – along with many Israelis – that being pro-Israel doesn't require supporting every policy of its government.
>
> We have the responsibility to fix the broken politics in America around Israel.[133]

Jonathan became involved with J Street because he did not feel represented by the main Jewish organizations. AIPAC, the American

Jewish Committee, and other incumbent Jewish organizations did not represent his views even while they claim to speak on behalf of the Jewish community. Speaking about his decision to become involved with J Street, Jonathan recalled:

> I grew up a Jewish American with a very strong and proud Jewish identity. I grew up very civically engaged; active in community and active in politics. I have lived in Israel as an exchange student and have very close family ties and consider myself a very strong supporter of Israel and am very proud of my connection to Israel. But at the same time in all my life I had never, ever been in any way involved in, or drawn to Jewish American advocacy, and I never even realized it until Jeremy planted a flag with J Street. It was then that I had this sort of questioning: "Wait a second, I'm an involved political, Jewish, Israel-loving guy. Why have I never been involved in Jewish American politics before?" I realized when Jeremy started J Street that it was because the incumbent Jewish American advocacy organizations never . . . I never felt they were speaking for me or to me. And so there was this void and all of a sudden I realized wait a second, all of the reasons why Jeremy was starting J Street resonated with me because I felt the same frustration and lack of voice but I hadn't ever recognized it. It's an overgeneralization I'm sure but for the most part the voice of Jewish Americans in the political discourse is always about Israel's right to self-defense. And, you know, there was always this litmus test: are you a friend of Israel and the "are you a friend of Israel" meant did you blindly support the Israeli government no matter what, no matter what their point of view is or actions are. It is a very hawkish perspective and I'm more of a leftie progressive and so I never felt like they spoke for me. I never felt aligned with that point of view. I know plenty of hawkish Jewish Americans; when it comes to Israel they are hawkish, they might be doveish on all sorts of other issues but when it comes to Israel they're hawks. And I never felt a connection there. So when Jeremy started advocating about a two state solution and peace and security for stability through two states, I thought oh my God, finally someone is saying what makes sense to me and I hadn't heard that in the Jewish American political discourse before.[134]

What resonated with Jonathan was the opportunity to engage with Israel politically in the USA, in no small part because of his views about Israeli security issues.

Conclusion

Jewish internationalism was a particular development in European Jewish history that combined the universal ideals of the Enlightenment and the French Revolution with political processes aimed at protecting Jewish security. It was very much a product of Diaspora Jews looking for political spaces in which to act as Jews. Jews in the Diaspora were not inactive in politically working to strengthen Jewish security and strengthen Jewish identity. The history of Jewish internationalism is the case in point that reveals the hollowness of how this myth refused to acknowledge the significant efforts undertaken by Diaspora Jews toward their brethren abroad. Jewish internationalism was largely a practice based on ensuring Jewish security, either security against anti-Semitic persecution (as in Damascus) or security to live an improved life based on Western European ideals. By identifying and acting upon an obligation to other Jewish communities in the Diaspora, Jewish internationalism foreshadowed the Diaspora/Israel transnationalist discourses of the twentieth and twenty-first centuries. Both were also animated by concerns pertaining to the connection between identity and security. Yet, with the creation of the State of Israel, Diaspora identity underwent a radical reframing, as there was now a political geography that was Jewish and not Diasporic.

Building up a connection between Diaspora and Israel became an especially important part of Jewish discourse. So much so that it eventually became the argument that to be a good Jew meant being a Zionist. This is a view that has been contested historically and continues to be. Yet what is interesting is not so much the position one takes in this regard as the fact that it, or responding to it, has become such an important issue in contemporary Jewish discourse. If anything, what the interviews suggest is that there is sufficient concern that reflects a sense that to be Jewish involves an obligation to have a relationship with Israel, and the debate is about what this obligation means in practice. A correlation is presenting itself involving identity, security and obligation, and involving debates over the Diaspora/Israel relationship raising questions about power and authority. Yet it is not clear how we are to understand this category of obligation, what makes it political, and why it makes sense to think of the relationship in terms of obligation. While it is often manifested politically (as well as religiously and culturally), what kind of political obligation is this? It is, consequently, to the experiences and self-understandings of this obligation that I turn to in the next chapter, and in the process reveal the relevance of the previous theoretical discussions.

4 From Eating Hummus to the Sublime

Introduction

The term "Jewish internationalism" is a historical reference to the mainly French and British Diaspora Jewry's international activities regarding other Jewish communities in the eighteenth and nineteenth centuries. Nevertheless, remnants of Jewish internationalism continue to influence Diaspora life. The activities of the Joint Distribution Committee represent one ongoing legacy of Jewish internationalism, and the AIU (*Alliance Israélite Universelle*) is still active. A connection with other Jewish communities, and coming to their aid, has been an ongoing part of Diaspora life. As Arnold Eisen demonstrates, Diaspora has for most of Jewish history been the spatial focus of Jewish life and Jewish identity,[1] and thus it is not surprising that Diaspora Jews have supported each other.[2] The creation of Israel, however, changed this focus. Jewish internationalism was forced to adapt to changing geopolitical contexts, especially with the simultaneous rise of both Zionism in Palestine and fascism in Europe.

These changes meant that internationalist-minded Jews had to make a choice. Act to help save Jewish communities in Europe or choose to support the Zionist mission. The two positions were ideologically incommensurable, and Jewish communities today remain faced with the challenge of how to mediate their Diasporic identity with the significance and successes of Israel. To be a Jewish internationalist today is something of a non sequitur in the age of Israel, when any internationalist Jewish activities ostensibly ought to flow into supporting the Jewish homeland, and if Jews in the Diaspora do need assistance, Israel, as the new center of Jewish life, culture and politics, ought to help them. The Israelization of Jewish identity has had a profound impact on the potential for Jewish internationalism.

One of the few remaining examples of a Diaspora-focused internationalism is the American Jewish World Service. In an interview with Aaron Dorfman, its Vice President for National Programs, I was told how, when he and his colleagues go to Washington DC to meet with politicians, the politicians automatically assume that because they are Jewish Israel will be the focus of discussion, and are surprised when it is not:

> When we walk in to sit down for the meetings in [Washington with government staff] and we've scheduled the meeting about the farm bill ... and the house staff or the senate staff isn't the agriculture person it's the Israel person cos they're like, "Oh, Jews, they always advocate about Israel" and they're surprised, like "oh, I'm in the wrong meeting" and they go and get the agriculture person to come in. It's been kind of fascinating to see the shift in consciousness on the part of members of congress and their staffs, who are like "oh, wow this is crazy, there are Jews out there who give a shit about poor people in sub-Saharan Africa and not just about Israel security and whatever."[3]

Nevertheless, the Washington politicians do have something right in their initial assumption, for most Jewish international activity is geared toward Israel, and the obligation to support Israel has largely taken over other Jewish internationalist commitments. How Jews understand their obligations to support Israel, and the presumption that is often directed at Jews that by virtue of being Jews they are expected to have an obligation to support Israel, is the focus of this chapter.

Even though the political obligation literature refers to an empirical phenomenon, citizens obeying the law, it rarely engages with how people understand their own political obligations.[4] This absence of empirical work reflects the by-definition abstract character of political theory. Empirical material in political theory texts usually involves anecdotal evidence, selected references to newspaper articles and/or secondary empirical research, often using sociology.[5] Instead of conducting primary empirical work, the tendency of the political obligation literature authors is to rely on abstractions pertaining to various accounts of consent or collective commitments. A significant exception is Klosko's work. Klosko examines US Supreme Court decisions and military service in Israel and Germany, as well as the findings from ten focus groups.[6] As he writes, "I believe that lived experience provides a test for moral theories."[7]

His findings from the focus groups are that individuals tend to distinguish different types or categories of laws (there is a lot of discussion about breaking traffic laws), that there is considerable confusion about how membership, consent and benefits function as independent categories (for example, one of the focus groups conflated receiving benefits provided by the state with consent), but that most agreed that there exists a moral obligation to obey the law. While the particularity principle was not discussed directly in the focus groups, the reference to the provision of state benefits suggests a connection, since a citizen in the USA does not benefit from the healthcare provisions in another country.

This American-centric example, which reflects how Klosko often frames the particularity principle, also reveals how problematic the particularity principle is. The particularity principle works best in a US-centered worldview. While the obligation to obey the law in other countries does not impact the USA, the reverse is not necessarily true. Domestic laws in the USA do have the potential to impact citizens in other countries in ways that are not reciprocal, and not just with regard to extradition treaties or extra-territoriality. US agricultural trade laws that require US farmers to buy specific types of seeds and grow specific crops carry repercussions felt across the globe by low-income farmers in industrializing countries who find the value of their crops lowered and are forced into growing cash crops for export and are unable to feed their families.[8] The particularity principle works best as a heuristic device in a Western-centered rationality, and specifically in the USA.

In any case, Klosko's book is one of the few exceptions in the relevant political theory literature that involves qualitative empirical research. Much more common in the political theory literature is the normative application of theoretical tools to empirical situations. For example, writing for the *New York Times*, the philosopher Michael Lynch provides one example of using important concepts for political obligation, including consent and commitment, in a critical piece about the US Government shutdown in October 2013.[9] Incidentally, the US Government shutdown helps illuminate how domestic matters ostensibly about consent and commitment can transcend the legal borders of the nation-state, as the shutdown was of global significance. Lynch provides an example in this accessible work of how political theory can be used to explore and critique specific empirical political situations.

Klosko's empirical work, however, provides one model for how political theory can involve empirical research within the analytical tradition. A few important examples provide additional and different models. Foucault's work involves political theory, and sociological and historical research. His archaeological and genealogical methods provide especially influential models for social-scientific research. Another example is provide by Arendt, whose early writings demonstrate a methodological reflexivity because of how they were informed by her direct involvement in Jewish politics, and because of her experience of being a refugee, and her later work on Eichmann involved first-hand observation.[10] Arendt's work was greatly inspired by her life experience, and not just her intellectual training. Her idiosyncratic work remains influential and the methods that she used, involving examinations of what is forgotten, provide a useful starting point for my investigation into Diaspora/Israel relations.

In previous chapters I conducted textual critiques and exegesis of the political obligation literature. I argued that power features importantly in political obligation and that power is a large part of what makes obligations political. By emphasizing power as opposed to the state, I suggest that political obligations can become transnational.

In this chapter I build on the theoretical and empirical discussions of the previous chapters. Adopting Arendt's distinctions pertaining to power, politics, authority and tradition, I explore how different discourses of public Diaspora engagement with Israel are reflective of an obligatory frame of mind regarding having a relationship with Israel. In addition, I explore how Diaspora Jewish involvement with Israel is often based not on agreement but on forgetting the differences that characterize Diaspora and Israeli life. The obligations that Diaspora Jews feel is a product of a sense of self more than it is a matter of consent or of belonging. In fact, there are many different ways of framing the obligation, with the differences often being highly contradictory. Religious Jews see Israel in terms that secular Jews do not, even if both use Torah in their narratives. Israel means different things to different Jews, and while Israel may be of great importance to most Jews, it is not for the same reasons. The significance that Israel has for Jewish identity in the Diaspora also leads to deeply problematic encounters, with Diaspora Jewish discourse about Israel often being characterized primarily by hysteria or awkward silence induced by hysteria. The discourse of power present in the obligations reflects a disciplinary mode of power whereby the power relations feature as constructions of self. What I found was that Jews self-governed their own sense of obligatory duties and commitments on the basis of how they understood Jewish identity.

Diaspora Jews who do feel themselves obligated to support Israel do so because of how Israel features in their sense of Jewish identity. As each Jew has a different sense of self, albeit one that includes belonging to a (fragmented) Jewish people, the way in which the obligation is understood and manifested varies. Some Jews take exception to the centrality Israel has in the construction of contemporary Jewish identity, but it remains plausible that even Jews who are ambivalent about Israel nevertheless would feel a tremendous sense of loss and/or crisis were Israel to disappear or if something terrible were to happen to the Jewish State that would threaten its existence. Diaspora Jews who do identify with Israel generally agree that a connection to Israel does not require Jews to support everything that Israel does, but this agreement does not spread into other areas that characterize the Israelization of Diaspora Jewish identity. What all those whom I interviewed generally shared, however, was the view that being Jewish should involve (what I am calling) an obligation to be connected to the Jewish State. In the words of the executive director of the Association of Reform Zionists of America, Rabbi Andrew Davids, "Prior to becoming to a citizen of the state of Israel I felt obligated to Israel."[11]

The Loyalty Problem

The political obligation discourse is closely connected to the potential for accusations of dual loyalty. Considering Jewish history, this connection has not gone unnoticed. The meaning of obligation, and not specifically political obligation, of being morally bound to act in a particular way, poses problems because of the problematic way in which Jewish identity and Israel have become linked in the public imagination about Jews as well as in internal Jewish discourse. This last point is one of the issues that many of those who are critical of the Israelization of Jewish identity highlight.[12] This point pertains to wider concerns about how Jews are understood, simply by virtue of being Jewish, to support Israel. One interviewee felt that such presumptions about Jewish identity and Israel are "extremely dangerous."[13] This assumed connection makes possible the "new" anti-Semitism, whereby critiques of Israel function as a proxy for attacking Jews, and thereby somehow make it acceptable to attack Jews.

The main literature on Diaspora/Israel relations uses the word loyalty and not obligation, largely because political obligation is a specific term in political theory, and because historically loyalty has been the term that has been used and continues to be used.[14] One of the main scholars in this area is Gabriel Sheffer,[15] who writes, "Loyalty to Israel and criticism of it by ... world Jewry is an important issue, and is more complex than usually thought."[16] The article just quoted is a survey or state-of-the-union piece about loyalty to and criticism of Israel by Diaspora Jews. Sheffer points to demographic changes in Diaspora Jewry, the increasingly successful integration by Diaspora Jews, the roles of different Jewish organizations, and other global forces:

> Accelerated processes of globalization, liberalization and democratization also affect the definition of Jewish identity, and the nature of the life of religious and secular Jews in the Diaspora and their contacts with Israel. In the beginning of the 21st Century Jews are expected to deal simultaneously with two opposite developments: living in pluralistic societies which are much more accessible compared to the previous century and dealing with hostility and even hatred towards foreigners and "others" including Jews. The result of these contradicting developments is that many Jewish groups are in a state of confusion with respect to their identity components, their identification with the Jewish nation and their contacts with Israel.[17]

The acknowledged growing criticism of Israel by Diaspora Jews does not, he states, involve a rejection of their loyalty:

> This growing criticism is not related to a complete cancellation of loyalty to the Jewish nation and the homeland – the land of Israel. Even the harshest critics do not completely detach themselves from the land of Israel and the Jews living in it. Thus one should not refer to the question of loyalty and criticism as one.[18]

Notice how Sheffer recognizes that loyalty can involve criticism, and as such there are different ways in which loyalty is manifest. Yet, it easy to imagine that Diaspora criticism of Israel is in fact an example of disloyalty, because it provides ammunition to enemies of Israel.

The exact ideational and rhetorical dynamic can be found when governments or politicians accuse newspapers of being disloyal to the state by questioning the decision to go to war or by revealing questionable surveillance practices. If anything, in such cases those who stand accused are not being disloyal but are merely acting out the obligations they feel they have to the country and the citizenry. Loyalty involves the possibility of disloyalty, and criticisms of Israel could be construed to be illustrative of one kind of disloyalty. Indeed, it often is by right-wing Jews. In this sense, it is difficult to use loyalty to clearly and fairly describe Diaspora/Israel relations because it makes difficult a recognition of the diversity of ways in which Jews feel and manifest their "loyalty" to Israel. The word loyalty carries connotations of disloyalty that may not be accurate, let alone appropriate. For these reasons, the general meaning of obligation, of involving a moral duty, as opposed to being loyal, seems to me be the most accurate way of making sense out of the Diaspora's relationship with Israel.

Part of the reason why the term "loyalty" is used is historical and is connected with what used to be and sometimes still is called dual loyalty.[19] The charge of dual loyalty involves the accusation that a minority group holds a political allegiance to another community, be it a state, foreign power, or some kind of foreign network (real or imagined), that makes this minority a national threat.[20] It is an accusation that Jews have historically been the victim of and remain sensitive to, even in the USA. The American solution, which followed from the internationalist discourse of French Jews in the eighteenth century,[21] was to argue that the interests of American Jews are the same as those of the USA. It is in this vein that AIPAC frames its activities – although even AIPAC has been suspected of dual loyalty.[22]

In 2008, when I was conducting the first round of interviews in New York City, one of the ongoing stories in the Jewish press was the controversy surrounding John Mearsheimer and Stephen Walt's article and then book about the Israel lobby.[23] A large part of the debate surrounding their book was whether or not it was anti-

Semitic in implying that Jews were guilty of dual loyalty because their activities in the Israel lobby (including AIPAC) were against the national interests of the USA. Their work attracted significant criticism from a range of sources, including the Anti-Defamation League,[24] the professor of Strategic Studies, Eliot Cohen,[25] and the Harvard law professor Alan Dershowitz.[26] The majority of those I interviewed were also at best deeply suspicious of the Walt and Mearsheimer argument. Consequently, at that time the topic of dual loyalty was at the front of people's minds when otherwise it probably would not have been.

The dual loyalty issue was not relevant to all, and some took a different approach to the terms used. Rabbi Jerome Epstein, the Executive Vice-President of the United Synagogue of Conservative Judaism between 1989 and 2009, said, "I don't feel obliged I feel committed."[27] He made the distinction that obligations are externally driven while commitments are internal. Both involve a reference to a moral duty. This distinction did, however, become confused, for he also argued that Israel has an obligation to inspire the commitment of Diaspora Jews. In this usage the Israeli state becomes the author of obligations, and individuals in the Diaspora should, he hopes, take up this obligation to have a commitment to Israel. By framing obligation in this way he acknowledged the close relationship involved in obligations and commitments. Another interviewee did not care. With regard to dual loyalty this person said, "I don't care. It's not a crime, there's nothing wrong with it." For him, living in a country full of migrants, most people have dual loyalties and so it was unfair to single out Jews. A further interviewee said, "Dual loyalty is a bogus issue. America withstood the test of dual loyalty incredibly well."[28] Nevertheless, in the words of yet another interviewee: "I wouldn't use the word loyalty because it has got too much baggage in this context ... Once you admit that word into the conversation then the dual loyalty issue has to come up."[29]

The Authority and Legitimacy Problem

Part of the complication in the Jewish Diaspora's relationship with Israel is a question of authority and legitimacy. It is on this point that Diaspora Jewish critics of Israel such as Jewish Voice for

Peace, ProZion, and Women in Black sometimes emerge. For these and similar groups, it is not just the human rights violations perpetrated by Israel against the Palestinians that is at issue; it is also the tendency on the part of the major Jewish organizations not to speak out against such crimes and claim that they represent Jewish voices. The authority problem pertains to who speaks for the Jewish Diaspora, which public body has the clout and the legitimacy to speak on behalf of Diaspora concerns about Israel. In political obligation, the question about authority and legitimacy is addressed normatively via liberal discourses of consent, agreement and the benefits provided by the state. None of these is present in transnational political obligations, and this absence is not lost on Jews who do feel an obligation to Israel. In fact, it was precisely because of this issue that J Street was created in the USA. It tries to be a fairly mainstream organization, and includes a political lobby group in its organizational structure.

Nevertheless, it is noteworthy that J Street has not been without controversy. It has even been attacked by the Israeli ambassador to the USA, Michael Oren, who called it a "unique problem in that it not only opposes one policy of one Israeli government, it opposes all policies of all Israeli governments. It's significantly out of the mainstream."[30] He continued:

> This is not a matter of settlements here [or] there. We understand there are differences of opinion. But when it comes to the survival of the Jewish state, there should be no differences of opinion. You are fooling around with the lives of 7 million people. This is no joke.[31]

Not all Israeli politicians share his view about J Street. Shimon Peres and Tzipi Livni have been supportive of J Street's existence and activities.

The experience of many American Jews, however, has been that the main organizations that Oren is more comfortable with, such as AIPAC or the Conference of Presidents of Major American Jewish Organizations, have not been representative of US Jews for quite a few years. In a response to the 2013 Pew Jewish Population Survey, Abe Foxman, the national director of the Anti-Defamation League, said, "You know who the Jewish establishment represents? Those who care. This is a poll of everybody. Some care, some don't care ... I don't sit and poll my constituency. Part of Jewish leadership is leadership. We lead."[32] In other words, the Jewish leadership does not represent and is not representative. In response to this statement by Foxman, *The Jewish Daily Forward* investigated some of the major Jewish organizations in an attempt to discover whom they represent, concluding that those who chose who leads are primarily "wealthy donors and local activists."[33]

J Street is also supported by wealthy donors and local activists, but it was nevertheless created to provide a voice for Jews who did not feel represented by the major Jewish organizations. J Street was created to fill a void, and to represent the increasing number of Jews who are supportive of Israel but are critical of both US policy toward Israel and Israel's own security policies. A younger volunteer for J Street said precisely this, about how J Street better reflected her views about Israel as an American Jew and that is why she volunteers for them.[34] In a sense, J Street was created so that liberal-thinking American Zionist Jews did not have to leave their values at the door when it comes to Israel.

For Jonathan Kopp, being active in J Street is part of an obligation that he feels as a Jew, but also as a committed American citizen. He does not claim that Israel has to accept his views, or those of J Street, but that it does have to listen, and that his views are probably not that far removed from what many Israelis think:

> The US government and US marketplace exerts influence all over the world. We impose sanctions and embargoes and we send drones and everything else so diplomacy seems to me to be a very legitimate form of engagement and expressing our interest, our concern, our support or our displeasure seems like an entirely reasonable thing to do. Particularly when, you know . . . from its founding Israel has always said we can't do this alone, we need the world's Jews and we represent the world's Jews and we are a homeland for the Jewish people. And so [Israel] needs our involvement; it needs our funding, our voice, our support, our tourism and we're happy to. I mean, I think the world's Jews are very happy to support Israel in all those ways but with that we also have a right to have a point of view. And that point of view can be ignored, it can be rejected, it can be debated, but there's nothing wrong with expressing a point of view and I think I know enough Israeli Jews who say that they need their government to understand that the world has a point of view on these issues. And just as there are some parties within the US, and maybe some other places around the world, that are joining their voice

to this call for a war against Iran and trying to push Israel to the brink of taking this very dangerous action, I think there are enough people within Israel that probably appreciate when groups outside of Israel say, "hold on a second, let's exhaust all manners of diplomacy before we go to war." I think we have an obligation and I think we also have a right to speak; there's nothing wrong with speaking. Jeremy's been invited to testify in front of the Knesset so he's been invited to share his point of view and he's doing that on behalf of J Street.[35]

The creation of J Street was designed to fill a void noticed not just because different viewpoints were not being sufficiently aired in public discourse between the Diaspora and Israel, but because they were not being aired within the US political system, and because for Jews it is important not to stay quiet but to get involved.

In addition, part of his argument, which is only alluded to here but which he acknowledged at other points in our conversation, is that as a US citizen he pays taxes and has a say in how these dollars are spent. His involvement in J Street is one way to influence the use of his tax dollars insofar as US policy is concerned. That he is also in effect acting not just to direct the efforts of his government, but also the domestic and international policy of another country, in this case Israel, raises an additional characteristic of his involvement, albeit one consistent with his sense of obligation as both a self-described left-wing Jew and a US citizen.

For Kopp and for others who are even more critical of Israeli policy, a question that animates their public engagement in Diaspora/Israel discourse is the question of who speaks for Diaspora Jews, why certain voices are heard above others, and how dissenting voices are responded to.[36] These are all issues that speak to the particular manifestations of how Diaspora Jews negotiate their relationship with Israel, of how these obligations are framed as a political process, of how authority is understood within this process, and of how certain authorities can claim legitimacy over others. Abe Foxman's rhetoric about not representing but leading is the perfect example of the detachment that can be found in the major American Jewish organizations, but can also be said to exist in other Diaspora bodies. That it is views about Israel that prove so polarizing and often raise the question of authority should not escape notice, as it only further demonstrates the centrality of Israel for contemporary Diaspora Jews.

From Hummus to the Sublime

The Institute for Jewish Policy Research (JPR) is the main body in the UK that researches contemporary Jewish life. In 2010, the JPR published its Israel survey in a report entitled *Committed, Concerned and Conciliatory: The Attitudes of Jews in Britain*. The report starts by referring to a previous JPR publication from 1997 that recorded that "81% of British Jews felt a strong or moderate attachment to Israel."[37] Nevertheless, that earlier report concluded that in the future Israel would come to have a significantly smaller role for British Jewry, that support for Israel would decline among non-Orthodox or Traditional Jews, that Zionism would become irrelevant, and that instead of Israel serving as a central feature of Jewish identity Zionism would become a source of increasing division in the Jewish community.

The 2010 JPR Israel Survey revealed a rather different outcome from the one predicted in 1997:

> This survey shows that the vast majority of respondents exhibit strong personal support for and affinity with Israel; 95% have visited the country; 90% see it as the "ancestral homeland" of the Jewish people, and 86% feel that Jews have a special responsibility for its survival.[38]

In addition, 82 percent felt that "Israel plays a 'central' or 'important but not central' role in their Jewish identities."[39] The survey also stated: "An overwhelming majority (87%) agrees that Jew are *responsible for ensuring 'the survival of Israel'* – over half (54%) the non-Zionist respondents also agree."[40]

In April 2011, I was able to sit down with Dr Jonathan Boyd, the executive director of the JPR, and talk about the JPR's Israel survey. Jonathan highlighted the generational issue: that the formative experience of Jewish life for those who witnessed the Holocaust was Jewish powerlessness, whereas it was Jewish power for those who witnessed the Israeli military victory of 1967 and its ability to survive in 1973. He also addressed the significant investment (he was speaking about the UK, but the same is true in North America) that had gone toward Israel programs that seek to educate young Jews about the centrality of Israel and Jewish peoplehood. Of particular interest, however, was his observation that for many Jews attacks or critiques of Israel "feel personal, that 'I am being told that a key bit of who I am is racist, anti-democratic,' and this is very difficult."⁴¹

Jonathan Boyd's comments illuminate an important element of the obligation felt by Jews to Israel, which is that the obligation is in part constitutive of these people's sense of self, and this subjective character of the obligation is consistent with the self-driven but externally supported discourses of power that characterize the transnational political obligation that many Diaspora Jews feel toward Israel.

Just as identity is not static, but is always fluid,⁴² so there exist a multiplicity of discourses by which Jews understand the rationale behind their obligations to Israel. Jon Benjamin, of the Board of Deputies of British Jews, highlighted a few such rationales, including the historical 2000-year longing for a return, regular daily prayers, the historical importance of the biblical land for Jews, that Israel can serve as a safe haven if necessary, that it makes it possible for Jews to be responsible for our own destiny in a way that had not been possible before, and that Israel allows the Jews to become a member of the community of nations.⁴³ One or more of these points was used by almost all of the interviewees in their self-reflections on Israel's importance to them. The similarity of reasons used is evidence of a shared collective narrative about Israeli centrality in the construction of contemporary Jewish life and identity. Jon Benjamin also said, in this same interview, that many Jews sense "that you cannot safely engage in public debate or critique of Israel, because it will encourage Israel's enemies."⁴⁴ However, he concluded, "But in some circumstances it is best to be honest."⁴⁵ These are all themes and issues that came up again and again in subsequent interviews. For example, the modern Orthodox Rabbi Saul Berman said:

> I may profoundly disagree with what had been Israel's policy of, say, destruction of the homes of suicide bombers or of terrorists. I may think personally that that constitutes a vicarious punishment which breaches Jewish values. But at the same time it's not likely that I'm going to speak to that issue with enormity, with great virulence, because my passionate sense of not wanting to say something that would give support to enemies of Israel is just there. It's just there and it's very powerful.⁴⁶

Steven Bayme is director of the Contemporary Jewish Life Department of the American Jewish Committee and one of the leading figures in the American Jewish community. He agreed to meet me in his office in September 2008, where he told me that "So much of being a Jew today is bound up with the State of Israel."[47] While he acknowledged that significant segments of American Jewry do not view Israel as central to Jewish identity, he nevertheless took the position that "Identification with Israel is a critical measure of Jewish identity. In that sense, I do find it difficult to say that 'I am a serious Jew but have no commitment to Israel.' I'm not saying it can't happen but this is a statement that I reject."[48]

This view reflects the widely held opinion in many Jewish organizations in the USA and beyond that irrevocably ties what it means to be Jewish with Israel and is representative of the Israelization of Jewish identity. This view was repeatedly expressed by, among others, an Orthodox rabbi in London and a member of the Board of Deputies of British Jews. For Bayme, Diaspora Jews do have an obligation, and the stronger one self-identifies as a Jew the stronger the connection with Israel. For him, Jews have an obligation to Israel because it represents a pivotal moment in Jewish history and it is the Jewish homeland. As he said, Israel represents a

> shift in paradigm from statelessness to statehood, which is the reversal of 2000 years of Jewish paradigmatic existence, and replaces the older paradigm of Diaspora with the much more positive paradigm of the Jews having a homeland of their own. So one level of obligation, which I call the intellectual one, is recognizing that the State of Israel, warts and all, is the single most positive development in 2000 years of Jewish history. Two, if one is true, that becomes translated as: that State of Israel and its welfare, defined broadly as its physical welfare, economic well-being and its place in the Jewish sun, that the welfare of the Jewish State is the concern for Jews everywhere. This gets translated as: I must do whatever I can to advance the welfare of the Jewish State, because the welfare of the Jewish State is the key embodiment of the welfare of the Jewish People.[49]

He did not then argue that to critique Israel is wrong, and as such the obligation to support Israel does not require that one support everything that Israel does. Nevertheless, he said:

> My obligations are real in terms of the Jewish people and one of them is a kind of moral obligation of when the Jewish people are doing something

wrong I need to take a stand on that, but if the impact of my making a stand on that is to weaken the relationship between Washington and Jerusalem, I'm going to be much more tepid, much more cautious.

In his view, it is not in American Jews' interests to give policy makers in Washington DC the idea that the Jewish community is not united with Israel. Bayme was quite clear that in his view, a strong Jewish sense of self requires an obligation to support Israel, and to keep dissent private.

Bayme is not alone in claiming that for those who feel an obligation toward Israel, doing so is very much part of their being Jewish and the implication is that if you do not share the obligation you may not be an equal member of the Jewish community. For example, one of the interviewees stressed that being committed to Israel does not require supporting whatever Israel does, but that the relationship is nevertheless one of all Jews belonging to a community, *kol Yisrael haverim*.[50] This individual did not address the inference that those who do not support Israel do not belong to this community.

This inference also begs the question about how criticism of Israel pertains to one's identity as a Diaspora Jew. If Israel is foundational in the construction of contemporary Jewish identity, what does it mean to criticize Israel? While Bayme and a few others felt it wise to limit public criticisms of Israel, nobody said that criticism should be silenced or not allowed, and for those whom I interviewed in Israel, criticism is openly acknowledged. A senior diplomat in the Israeli Ministry of Foreign Affairs told me: "There is a generational gap, and the younger generation of the diaspora tends to be more critical of policies. I think that's pretty evident."[51]

Shelley Kedar, who at the time of our interview worked at *Beit Hatfutsot*, helped place the Israeli perspective in context:

> I don't think Israelis care enough. I don't think Israelis know and feel connected toward the Diaspora. Israelis feel no commitment or obligation toward world Jewry. It is part of a natural process of being a majority, part of the Zionist revolution, which has done very well in making Israel the center of the Jewish people.[52]

In Israel, the Diaspora tends to matter the most when Diaspora Jewish organizations are in agreement with Israeli policy and can be turned to for support. It is very common to hear the refrain voiced in Israel that unless one lives there it is not possible to fairly offer any criticism, yet the Diaspora is the obvious place to turn for support when it is needed. As a diplomat of the Israeli Ministry of Foreign Affairs said:

> In the relations between Israel and the Diaspora there is a dilemma. You can hear the question: "You in the Diaspora, how the hell do you have the right to tell us what to do? If you are not a citizen, how dare you tell me, not living here, not suffering from all the fences and walls, tell me about the borders and not having to live with Palestinians ... You dare tell me what is right and what is wrong?!" This is another big question that influences the relationship. On the other hand, whenever we are in need, the first ones to go to are our brothers and sisters in the Diaspora. Whether it is a political attack over Israel and we need the Jewish advocacy, Lobby, assistance or Jewish solidarity, you name it, all over the world, or if we have some kind of economic problems like in the first 30–40 years of the State, the first people we went to ask for some intervention were the Jewish People and they were very keen to help us.[53]

For Shelley Kedar, the Diaspora serves an important role for Israel, and not just in terms of being there to support Israel. On the contrary, for her,

> Israelis need world Jewry as a constant reminder of what it means to be a minority and to preserve identity as a minority, to preserve creativity in non-Jewish societies ... Israelis need to be exposed to what it means to choose to be Jewish.[54]

Nevertheless, with regard to the construction of Jewish identity Israel matters more to Diaspora Jews than the Diaspora matters for Israeli Jews. This imbalance is yet another feature of how Diaspora Jewry and Israel are heading in different directions, and it creates a real problem or challenge for Diaspora Jewish identity. So long as the relationship is lopsided, it makes it difficult to fully understand and appreciate what exactly the connection to Israel means. If it means only that the Diaspora is there to help Israel every time Israel gets into trouble and needs help, it is not reciprocal and feeds into the Zionist negation of Diaspora and the inferior status of Jews living in ostensible exile. So long as Diaspora Jewry is there mainly to help Israel get its way while Israel is not prepared to hear

Diaspora concerns, the relationship remains more unstable than many would appreciate.

In more ways than most are prepared to openly acknowledge, the strength of the relationship between Diaspora Jewry and Israel does depend on the extent to which the Diaspora and Israel are prepared to listen and hear each other's voices. In the Diaspora, the issues vary and involve questions about conversion and different ways of practicing Judaism. The rights of women to pray at the Wailing Wall is one example of a largely Diaspora-led struggle for religious equality of Jews in Israel. The issue of Israel's ongoing military occupation is another contentious point of debate. Yet, however the relationship is understood it will always be unbalanced, as Diaspora voices will never carry the same weight in influencing Israeli policy as Israeli voices. This imbalance is to be expected, and so I was surprised to hear it being critiqued in Israel.

Shlomo Brom is a retired Brigadier General, who served from 1990 until 1998 as Deputy Chief and then Chief of the Strategic Planning Division of the Israeli Defense Forces (IDF). We met at his office in the Institute for National Security Strategy in Tel Aviv. He took an extremely open-minded approach to Diaspora involvement in Israeli affairs:

> All Jews can interfere ... anybody can interfere so long as he is not a clearly declared enemy of Israel ... But the question that I should be asked is: Do I, as an Israeli citizen, have to give the same weight to Jews from Brooklyn as to my fellow citizens, as an Israeli who is willing to sacrifice his life in the army? ... There is a tension, between being a citizen of the world but also a citizen of the nation-state. I am trying to work this tension out. So I give the right to everyone, and certainly Jews, to interfere. The issue is really the issue of the recipient and what weight is given to those who interfere.
>
> I would not invite involvement of Diaspora Jews in controversial issues, but I will accept it. I would not invite it because they are not well equipped to deal with controversial issue because they do not live here, and I mean this with regard to both sides, Left and Right. You need to live here. Residency does matter in how seriously I will take involvement. But I apply the same criteria to Israelis as to Diaspora Jews. If you are deeply involved, know a lot about it, et cetera ... I will take you seriously. I have no problems with most forms of intervention from the Diaspora. I think that I am unusual in this regard.[55]

Brom's insistence that Diaspora Jews do have a right to interfere by voicing publicly their views about Israeli policy is somewhat unusual. The tendency, rather, is either to try to keep dissent quiet by keeping it private, or to dismiss those who do not live in Israel as being unqualified to offer intelligent advice. Brom's argument is different, and not just because he thinks that others have a right to make their views heard, but also because such interference can be important, from a Zionist perspective, for Diaspora Jewry:

> But is the participation of Diaspora Jews important for Israel? It is important. It is important because as a Zionist I am interested in the survival of the Jewish people, and this activity helps sustain the identity of the Jewish people. Israel is to some extent the means, it is not the goal, it is the means for the survival of the Jewish people. There are other means. Israeli Jews have the right to interfere in Diaspora Jewish affairs. All has to be done legally. But Israel has an even greater right, because of the linkage between the nation-state of Israel and the Jewish people.[56]

Interestingly, even when the rights of Diaspora Jewry to participate in Israeli public debate are accepted, there remains the sense of hierarchy that still places Israel above the Diaspora. Brom, however, was (I felt) unusually open and honest about the reasons behind his views, and was one of the few to openly acknowledge that the logic of the issues surrounding the Diaspora/Israel relationship stem from the tensions of Israel being built on the explicit model of the nation-state. The logic of the nation-state and of Israel being the national homeland of the Jews necessarily provides Israel with a rank above the Diaspora. Brom did, however, provide general limits for the interference to remain legitimate. There are rules: "What are the rules of the game? (1) No illegal activity – not legitimate for American Jew to finance settlements in the Occupied Territories; 2 equality to all; 3 transparency, the activity should be known."[57]

The majority of the efforts made toward supporting Diaspora involvement in Israel, however, focus on the question of peoplehood, and of how a connection with Israel is an important part of being Jewish, and a lot of energy has gone toward fostering this connection. As a diplomat of the Israeli Ministry of Foreign Affairs (MFA) explained:

Many young Jews don't see themselves any longer as connected to the Jewish People (not to say to the state of Israel). This is dangerous for the strength of the Jewish People, but also for the safety of the state of Israel. We need the assistance and the contributions of the Jewish People to the State of Israel – to help keep the very existence of the State. If there are no Jewish People, or if they are weak, than the state of Israel will have a big problem.

There is the Birthright program: It aims to connect those persons to the State of Israel. It is very nice. It is connecting. It leaves you at least with a very good memory, in most cases, but it is far from being enough. You need to stay here for a longer time to be really connected. So there is the need to find some kind of program for young Jews that will allow them to come here for some months up to a year. And for that there is the other project: Masa. This is a program that belongs to the Jewish Agency (50%) and the government of Israel. It is shaped as a company which presents the young Jew many programs. People come to Israel to study, work, volunteer, intern, etc. for 4–12 months. To do their gap year or a one-year program in a college. It has had over 10 000 participants a year in the last few years. This makes the difference. After being here for such a long time you are connected. Not like the Birthright program, Masa is not a free ride. In Masa the applicants pay.[58]

One of the main points the diplomat made to me in our conversation is that the main question is where the center of world Jewry lies. As he tells it, the ancient centers of Babylon and Israel came to be replaced by Europe, which was destroyed in the Holocaust. There exist again two centers, Diaspora, especially the USA, and Israel. The question is which center is the more important one, since for many younger Jews who do not share in the historical memory of the Holocaust there is no clear center and no clear answer to this question. Consequently, the relationship between Diaspora Jewry and Israel is complicated. Nevertheless, as this diplomat told me, "Israel is the second home of every Jew around the world and the responsibility of the Jewish state is to be responsible for the safety of every Jew."[59] This view was supplemented by Shelley Kedar of *Beit Hatfutsot*: "World Jewry needs Israel because Israel is the most wonderful creation that has happened in the last 200 years, at least. It should be a source of pride and joy and ownership."[60] Israel has certainly come to the assistance of Jews in other countries in select cases, but is that enough to demand that all Jews feel obliged to

Israel? Moreover, how should Diaspora Jews relate to Israel when most of the time Israel is ambivalent about the extent to which it is prepared to listen to the Diaspora?

A senior diplomat in the MFA provides a different but related answer to these questions:

> Israel is important for the Diaspora, but what about the Diaspora for Israel? There are ambivalent feelings in Israel about this, and in Gov. as well. Classical Zionism negated the Diaspora, but the reality was that this was not the case. So now, that there is a certain reality and what do you do with that? Following 1948, with all the negation of Diaspora, the Jewish Agency with the support of the government of Israel developed quite an extensive effort to enhance, among other things, Jewish education in the Diaspora. It still does. But in all those years it was in a very uneasy situation. On one hand the Jewish Agency is there to promote Zionism and the "ingathering of the exiles," but on the other hand it does, and has for quite a long time, extensive work in the Diaspora to enhance Judaism, Jewish education, as well as Zionism. You can see the ambivalence here, as it was reflected in the policy and deeds of the Jewish Agency.
>
> And behind all that, or not behind, but on the basis of all this, you have this issue of loyalty too. The ambivalence remains. When Sharansky and other leaders of the JA have to decide where to spend their money, they are confronted year-in year-out with where are we spending all our money? Whether to enhance Jewish education in the Diaspora or to help new immigrants into the country with shelter and health care? This is not an acute issue, but is a live issue, and the JA has to confront it every year. It is certainly not a theoretical issue. It is a very practical issue.
>
> This practical issue, to add one other dimension, one other aspect: one Jewish community reaching out to another Jewish community: the work of the Joint Distribution Committee. They are not Israel focused, where one Jewish community is helping other communities, or perhaps "interfering" in supporting Jewish communities in need.[61]

The Joint Distribution Committee is a Jewish humanitarian organization that aids Jews in needs across the Diaspora and in Israel. As such, it does continue in the tradition of Jewish internationalism.

As Martin Ben-Moreh explained, there is a great deal of ambivalence surrounding the Diaspora/Israel relationship, which has constantly changed during the years of Israel's existence, and even when the presumption is not one of certainty, it is at least one of clarity of purpose. As he told me, "It is not by chance that you are writing a book on Israel–Diaspora relations, something that is very problematic and remains ambiguous – it's in the Jewish psyche."[62] Moreover: "The Zionist project has taken the Jews on a particular journey that many thought was jumping two thousand years from the *Tanah* to the *Palmah*."[63]

The diplomats at the MFA who were interviewed all held sophisticated views about the Diaspora. They recognized that Jews in the USA, France, the UK and Eastern Europe have different needs and experiences, and that the mere fact of their being Jewish does not mean that they can all be treated in the same way. However, these differences did not obviate the fact that they are all Jews and do belong to one larger community that Israel represents, or can represent if asked to. The Zionist account of Israel being the national home of the Jews provided these diplomats with a narrative by which they could frame Israel's role in helping Diaspora communities. Their main point was that Israel could help other Jews. Importantly, those with whom I spoke were not patronizing about Diaspora Jewish communities, and they recognized the important cultural role that Israel can play in helping, in particular, young Jews retain their Jewish sense of self:

> Israel is something that can be perceived as cool by young people. It has a vibrant Jewish culture. There is the success of Israeli high-tech. And visiting Israel can help you to feel that there is a big group of people that are also Jewish and can relate to you.[64]

While most Israelis are not especially concerned with supporting cultural and other connections to Diaspora Jews, a few in Israel are, and they speak to a wider sense of how Jews in Israel and the Diaspora can be understood as one people. Speaking about American Jewry, one diplomat at the MFA said:

> There should be more dialogue between US Jewry and Israel. Because if there is tension between the Diaspora and Israel this is not a good situation and dialogue can help resolve tension. Why is the tension bad? Israel needs a strong Diaspora and vice versa, and tensions do not help this. A strong relationship empowers both communities. You don't have

to be a citizen of the state of Israel to enjoy the benefits it gives. The fact that there is a Jewish State says something about the Jewish people, about normality [65]

Indeed, this normality does help to give some Jews a greater sense of self. While some of the interviewees were unsure about how important the Diaspora actually is for Israel, many Diaspora Jews noted, sometimes explicitly, how for them Israel is empowering.

"Anon" is an educated young woman who has lived in Israel but now lives in Chicago. She learned Hebrew in Israel, where she went on a young Jewish leader internship. We conducted our interview in New York, in a café of the only company to have bested Starbucks, an Israeli chain called Aroma (Starbucks has had no branches in Israel since 2003).[66] Amid the clatter of the café we went over her relationship with Israel. Diaspora Jews, she said, have an obligation to learn about Israel and ought to visit Israel. Israel, as the Jewish country, is important, and Diaspora Jews should have an understanding of the only Jewish country in the world. Its importance stemmed from Jewish history, and not just the Holocaust, but also biblical history. In Israel there are also more Jews than in any other country, and while it is easy to think of Israel in homogeneous terms, it is a diverse society. Diaspora Jews often have preconceived notions of what Israel is or should be, and it is important, she said, to dispel idealizations of Israel. However, perhaps the most significant reason for Israel's importance for her lay in how it made her feel. Much as had been the case for me, when she had gone to Israel it had been the first time that she had not been "the Other" who celebrated different holidays and stood out. She recalled how it had been embarrassing for her to be Jewish until she had been to Israel. Israel provided a sense of self and of confidence. Obligations to support Israel for her thus followed from Israel's importance in constructing Jewish identity.

This confidence, however, is often complicated by the historical sense of victimhood felt by most Jews, and by Israel. The victim-mentality is particularly problematic insofar as it makes it harder for Diaspora Jews to navigate their relationship with Israel whose very existence is a sign of Jewish strength and power.

Harry Brechner is the rabbi of Congregation Emanu-El, in Victoria, British Columbia, Canada. Emanu-El is a medium- to mid-sized Conservative congregation in the provincial capital of

British Columbia. It is where I was a bar mitzvah, and is also Canada's oldest synagogue that has been in continuous use. The origins of Congregation Emanu-El date back to the Gold Rush in the mid-1800s when Jews from San Francisco came to secure mining licenses from the government offices in the capital city before heading onto the mainland in search of buried treasure. Similarly in one small sense to the development of Tel Aviv, which was a cemetery before it was a city, a cemetery here was the first need of the Jewish community, and in 1860 one was established. This cemetery, on Cedar Hill Road, is still in use. The synagogue was founded two years later and has been in continuous use ever since. Rabbi Brechner, an American citizen who served as a medic in the Israel army, found some time in his busy schedule to talk, and we met in a quiet room in the Faculty Lounge of the University of Victoria, where we discussed the victim element in the Diaspora/Israel relationship:

> I think there is a real need to see yourself as the good guy. And it's too hard now. And there are no good guys. And the game also shifted into who is a greater victim, the Palestinians or the Jews, and so you're playing out who is the greater victim, there is that war of rhetoric that happens as well. So on one level I think that to admit that your government is doing something wrong is to give victory in the war of rhetoric as to who is the greater victim, because somehow the greater victim is the one who has the greater legitimate claim to the land – it's a crazy argument.
>
> I think that there is a sense that if you criticize Israel, you are disloyal. I think that it is allowing for that strange twist in the argument, where it has become a question of Israel's right to exist as opposed to a question about Israel's policies. And how we allowed that shift, and allowed it to happen . . . I can't put my finger on it. But I think it was a very dangerous shift. I also really think that we, as a people, worldwide Jewry, have a hard time seeing ourselves as powerful. There is a sense of feeling righteous in victimhood. Or seeing oneself as weak, there is a sense of being righteous in that. That it is very difficult to be righteous and powerful. But I think that this is the primary task of our people right now. That we are becoming powerful, we need to be powerful. And if we really are a light unto the nations, part of that is to teach the world how to be powerful and just and righteous at the same time. It's a hard one to do.[67]

From Eating Hummus to the Sublime

Rabbi Brechner also addressed the question of how Diaspora Jewry has struggled to come to terms not just with the complication of needing to be righteous and powerful, but also with Israel's own negative behavior:

> It's really complex. I really do think that what's happening from a political place, no matter what piece of truth you hold or don't hold, or how you view the escalating conflict, it creates a real problem for a lot of Diaspora Jews. Certainly a lot of Jews here are confronted on a regular basis with a view that doesn't see Israel as the "good guy." And I've talked with good Israel friends about this. We kind of grew up on this myth; it was the myth of being the good guys, and the settlement of the Land of Israel, and we didn't have to deal with the sense of expulsion, of violence. The revisionist history coming out now has an element of truth to it, as does the myth that we lived with and lives on had an element of truth to it [sic]. And we don't know what the truth is anymore. I think that's really hard for people.[68]

He pointed out what is often glossed over in understanding the Diaspora/Israel relationship. Israel is in many ways a strong country, and yet understanding Israel to be the victim plays into the familiar historical narrative of Jewish peoplehood more than it accurately reflects the ideational influences of Israel or Diaspora identity, or Israel's own abilities and capabilities. One of the reasons for Israel's importance for Diaspora identity is its success. Israel provides a source of pride and a sense of place – both of which are important to the anonymous woman from Chicago who was quoted above. These are powerful motifs. Yet at the same time, Israel is also understood to be a victim. In a sense, Diaspora Jewry understands Israel as strong for the Jewish world, but weak once it has to engage with the non-Jewish world. There is a paradox here, in which Israel is both strong and weak, a paradox that Israeli politicians foster and one that is not lost on diplomats in the MFA.

Israel often plays it both ways, claiming to be the victim of violence while simultaneously arguing how successful it is, especially militarily and economically. The idea of Israel being a "start-up" nation ties in with this economic success story.[69] Israel and many Diaspora Jews want to have it both ways. Israel needs to be a strong success story, but it is also perpetually at risk. As one MFA diplomat said:

> As for the contradictions between being a power and trying to portray the state as a victim when it is attacked, that's true in the relations with the West and the Diaspora, in different degrees. You cannot project yourself as a regional force and as a start-up nation while victimizing yourself all the time. There is no doubt that Israel can be paranoid, but that doesn't mean nobody is after you.[70]

This complicated element of Israel being both the victim and a great regional power features heavily in how Diaspora Jews understand obligations to Israel. The obligations exist because of Israel's victimhood and its need for strong allies that can help, and they exist too because Israel's success helps provide positive feelings of strength. The contradiction is rarely openly questioned, because it fits within a traditional historical narrative of victimhood, while also seeing a future that is both different given the scope of Jewish success and the same, in that Jewish victimhood remains a reality. As a consequence, Israel can play multiple and contradictory roles in the construction of Jewish identity.

As the Masorti rabbi Jeremy Gordon argues, Israel has become the focus of insecurity because of the perceived relationship between anti-Semitism and anti-Zionism.[71] In his view, the Jews' relationship with Israel is fed by an overriding narrative of victimhood. This narrative leads to the sense that "They want to attack us there [Israel], and here, and when they attack us there it gets worse for us here."[72] In his view, Israeli actions can frighten Diaspora Jews: he argues that "Israel has lost the moral debate," and Jewish insecurities lead to an "unwillingness to come to terms with significant issues."[73] He acknowledges that Israel is not as secure as had been hoped. However, "Judaism is more important than Israel. To place Israel first is idolatry."[74] Similarly, in a not-so-faint echo of what the American Council for Judaism was concerned about in the 1950s, Rabbi Tony Bayfield, President of the Movement for Reform Judaism in the UK, expressed to me his concern that the traditional and sacred order of "God, Torah, Israel" is being reversed into "Israel, Torah, God."[75]

Keith Kahn-Harris, the London-based sociologist, author of *Uncivil War: The Israel Conflict in the Jewish Community* and co-author of *Turbulent Times: The British Jewish Community Today*, confirmed and elaborated on some of these points in one of many discussions we had in central London about this topic. Israel is, he noted, a defining issue for being Jewish, and there exists a considerable amount of insecurity about Israel among British Jews. He suggested, however, that, "If Israel is increasing insecurities among Diaspora Jewry, there is no vocabulary for dealing with this."[76] Conceptually, Diaspora Jews' relationship with Israel is complicated not just by Israel having to be both strong and a victim simultaneously, but by the issue of whether or not what takes place in Israel has an impact on Diaspora Jewish life, especially with regard to matters of security. "The point of critiquing Israel," Keith told me over coffee and fruit juice at a café near Russell Square, "is that it affirms the belief that what happens in Israel does affect Diaspora Jewry. If Israel does not affect us, why does it matter if we defend it?"[77] While Rabbi Gordon said that "what goes on in Israel does have an effect on Diaspora Jewry,"[78] there nevertheless exists some uncertainty about how far Israel directly impacts Jewish life in the Diaspora. As Khan-Harris pointed out, if Israeli policies end up increasing Jewish insecurities because of a fear of violence against Jews, and so Jews become targeted because of Israeli actions, it means that Israel plays a part in increasing Diaspora Jewish insecurities, but this is a very uncomfortable realization to come to, because Israel is supposed to have the opposite effect. The development of the new anti-Semitism, whereby Jews are attacked under the masquerade of attacking Israel, especially in Europe where the historical Left has become increasingly critical of Israel,[79] has made it especially difficult for Jews to navigate their ideational and often existential as well as religious connection with Israel. Few Jews would agree that Israel is above criticism, but the close ties that Jews have with Israel means that, such openness to debate notwithstanding, "the devil is in the details."[80]

Yet the association that links anti-Semitism with criticism of Israel is quite strong. On January 20, 2014, Prime Minster Stephen Harper became the first Canadian Prime Minister to address the Knesset. Here is an excerpt from his speech:

> We all know about the old anti-Semitism.
> It was crude and ignorant, and it led to the horrors of the death camps.
> Of course, in many dark corners, it is still with us.
> But, in much of the western world, the old hatred has been translated into more sophisticated language for use in polite society.

> People who would never say they hate and blame the Jews for their own failings or the problems of the world, instead declare their hatred of Israel and blame the only Jewish state for the problems of the Middle East.
>
> As once Jewish businesses were boycotted, some civil-society leaders today call for a boycott of Israel.
>
> On some campuses, intellectualized arguments against Israeli policies thinly mask the underlying realities, such as the shunning of Israeli academics and the harassment of Jewish students.
>
> Most disgracefully of all, some openly call Israel an apartheid state.
>
> Think about that.
>
> Think about the twisted logic and outright malice behind that: a state, based on freedom, democracy and the rule of law, that was founded so Jews can flourish, as Jews, and seek shelter from the shadow of the worst racist experiment in history, that is condemned, and that condemnation is masked in the language of anti-racism.
>
> It is nothing short of sickening.
>
> But, this is the face of the new anti-Semitism.
>
> It targets the Jewish people by targeting Israel and attempts to make the old bigotry acceptable for a new generation.
>
> Of course, criticism of Israeli government policy is not in and of itself necessarily anti-Semitic.
>
> But what else can we call criticism that selectively condemns only the Jewish state and effectively denies its right to defend itself while systematically ignoring – or excusing – the violence and oppression all around it?
>
> What else can we call it, when Israel is routinely targeted at the United Nations, and when Israel remains the only country to be the subject of a permanent agenda item at the regular sessions of its Human Rights Council?
>
> Ladies and gentlemen, any assessment – any judgment – of Israel's actions must start with this understanding:
>
> In the sixty-five years that modern Israel has been a nation, Israelis have endured attacks and slanders beyond counting and have never known a day of true peace.[81]

Indeed, the devils are in the details, for Harper makes it exceptionally difficult to identify what would constitute a non-anti-Semitic critique.

For Jews, the "details" mean that so long as Israel remains a key element in the construction of contemporary Jewish identity, any challenge to or critique of Israel can feel like a personal attack. Nevertheless, even on this point there exist within world Jewry different approaches that seem to challenge the idea that critique is threatening. At one end of the spectrum, a Liberal rabbi in London said, "Liberal rabbis will say whatever needs to be said."[82] As Danny Rich, the Chief Executive of Liberal Judaism told me, "Not only is it legitimate to criticize Israel but it is supportive of Israel to do so."[83]

I did not come across one person who said that it was wrong to criticize Israel or that criticism of Israel automatically implied anti-Semitism. Nevertheless, if there is one conclusion that can be drawn from the interviews, it is that Jews are often deeply uncomfortable with criticisms of Israel, but are also highly active in making a variety of criticisms or critiques. It is just that they make different types of criticisms according to their different religiosity and political views. Thus, some types of critique are viewed by some as hurting Israel and as giving ammunition to its enemies, while other critiques are viewed by others as having the opposite effect. Which critiques have which effect depends on one's standpoint. But whatever standpoint is taken, the act of critiquing Israel is often a result of feeling obligated to Israel. While many criticisms are a product of various moral duties that have nothing to do with Israel's importance for Diaspora Jewry, it cannot be denied that a great deal of debate about Israel happens precisely because of this importance.

The young woman from Chicago whom I interviewed said: "Everyone who is Jewish has an obligation to learn to some extent about Judaism and Israel and not be totally ignorant, but then they have to decide for themselves what to do."[84] The same point was made independently by a Jewish male in his thirties who lives in Vancouver.[85] This similarity is not accidental. Israel has become a center of Jewish life in a way that worldwide Jewry has not experienced for over two thousand years. Yet this young woman also said "The religious part is not necessarily connected with Israel," and that "If you are thinking of Judaism as a culture, then without a doubt Israel is the centre of world Jewish culture."[86] While her argument for a connection to Israel was explicitly secular, she nevertheless used biblical history to explain the connection. This seeming confusion was not uncommon in my interviews with young Jewish adults, and represents the "multiple aspects of being Jewish:

religious and cultural."[87] This duality is yet another way in which Israel serves multiple and sometimes contradictory roles in the construction of Jewish identity. Secular Jews use religious history to justify their cultural attachment, without having much engagement with Judaism as it is practiced in Israel, where the Orthodoxy controls all regulations concerning such life events as marriage, divorce, and conversion.

Of course, religious connections to Israel are important, and in some senses, the more religious one is, the stronger the connection to Israel. This is what the Orthodoxy would have others believe, and it is confirmed by the Pew Jewish Population Survey (which says nothing about the content and reasons for their obligations). Consequently, if there is one group that can be clearly described as having an obligation to Israel it is the Orthodox Union (OU). In 2008, I interviewed an Orthodox Jew who worked at the OU.[88] Around halfway through our discussion, he raised an explicitly political point about the OU's relationship with Israel. He told me that the OU had changed its bylaws in 2006:

> Previously the bylaws stated that the OU could not oppose a decision of the government of Israel because we don't live there and don't send our sons to war, etc. The disengagement from Gaza changed this because we predicted that it would cause a catastrophe, which it certainly did, and the overwhelming majority of people that were removed forcibly were Orthodox Jews and the OU came under intense criticism in its US constituency for not opposing the disengagement from Gaza. Therefore when we met at the convention in 2006, we changed our bylaws to enable us in situations of great significance – not routinely – to oppose decisions made by the government of Israel. Our commitment to Israel is so great that even though we don't live there, we provide so much of the moral support, of those who go to Israel and pay, not those who go on free trips like Birthright, overwhelmingly they are Orthodox. When Israel is fighting wars or when their soldiers get kidnapped our people run to the synagogue and say psalms, day and night, for the success in the war, for the freedom of our soldiers. You might say what good does that do? But God is an important part of Judaism. In certain limited circumstances of great significance we can tell the government that it is wrong.[89]

It is not just that the Orthodox pay their way, as opposed to those who enjoy free trips to the Holy Land: what is particularly interesting about what he said was how, although in a purely moral sense the OU, as a group of non-citizens, does not have the right to inform a democratically elected government what it should do, nevertheless its commitment and its religious devotion are so great – greater than many other Jews' – that in practice it has the right to do so.

The OU's devotion is empirically manifest not just in acts of religious prayer, but also financially. That many Israelis are not Orthodox and that there exist significant political and social cleavages between the religious and the secular in Israel does not lessen the OU's sense of its own responsibility. Indeed, its solution to not being representative is to try to increase religiosity among Israeli Jews. The OU has for quite a few years now, been active in trying to turn "Israeli Jews into Jewish Israelis,"[90] which is one of the roles of the OU's Israel Center in Jerusalem.[91]

Not all Orthodox Jews, however, subscribe to this position whereby Diaspora Jewish organizations can question the Israeli government's decisions to the extent that the OU does. There is, of course, Neturei Karta, the anti-Zionist Orthodox group. However, there are other Orthodox Jewish voices that are supportive of Israel although not in the sense suggested by the OU. For example, the Orthodox London Rabbi Barry Marcus said in an interview, "We don't live there so we need to be cautious about advising on Israeli policy."[92] In New York, Rabbi Saul Berman had a related view.

Rabbi Berman is an adjunct professor in Law at Columbia University. He was ordained at Yeshiva University, studied law at New York University, and holds a graduate degree in Political Science from the University of California at Berkeley. He spent two years at Hebrew University and Tel Aviv University studying *mishpat ivri* (Jewish laws that pertain to such matters that would otherwise be contained in present-day legal systems). He has also been the director of Edah, the main body of modern Orthodox Jewry, and has contributed to the *Encyclopaedia Judaica*. Rabbi Berman did not share the OU's position. He said:

> There is often room for disagreement about how best to balance Israel's security needs with its other values and while I have opinions on what would be the best balance, I'm willing to sort of give the benefit of the doubt to the Israeli political process to make determinations in that regard that I will not condemn as evil, despite the fact that I reserve the right to disagree with them. So I think that there is a difference between

disagreeing with a particular position that the government of the State of Israel takes without thereby attempting to delegitimize the government or the State or the persons who represent the government and the State in relation to those decisions.

Continuing, he presented the Jewish State as being:

An instrumentality of the actualization of the Jewish vision, and there are minimum requirements that everyone needs to partake of, and that is to assure, to help assure the security and physical wellbeing of the State and of its citizenry. Beyond that, there are lots of other things that people can do to help maximize the capacity of this instrumentality to fulfil the Jewish vision. But that can take many different forms and for some people it is supporting museums in Israel so that the cultural vision can be enhanced. And for other people it's making large contributions to free loan organizations. There are infinite numbers of ways in which this can be done. So from my perspective there is a sort of a core duty that everybody has, but leaves to the individual the judgment about how far that gets carried and through what particular mechanism that gets furthered.[93]

There are a variety of different ways of understanding the connection that Diaspora Jewry has with Israel, and in typically Jewish fashion many of the arguments are alternative interpretations of the same underlying motif: that Israel contributes in a significant way to Jewish identity. Religious and secular Jews may both use Biblical history as one way of understanding this relationship, even if they have significantly different understandings of how to interpret and act upon this history. When the Orthodox Jew from the OU told me that Israel is "the sense of the Jewish soul,"[94] he might as well have been speaking, in general terms, for many non-Orthodox Jews, even if they would profoundly differ about what Jewish soul means and Israel represents.

Indeed, it is the meaning of Israel, of what it represents, that is becoming increasingly contested, even if the point about Israeli centrality remains a shared belief among many different Jews. In the words of this same Orthodox Jew:

The reality of Israel's existence is a glue that helps bind all Diaspora communities, across all different religious Jewish groups. Even for those who eat pork on Yom Kippur, Israel's destruction would entail a huge sense of loss. It unites Jews who *doven* three times a day with those who *doven* three times a year with those who don't *doven* at all.[95]

The Israelization of Jewish identity is perhaps most pronounced among the Jewish Orthodoxy, but it is a centrality that is shared by many secular Jewish organizations and other religious Jewish groups. In some areas, there is overlap between secular and religious discourse about Israel's importance. In words that were remarkably similar to those spoken to me by a young J Street volunteer four years later,[96] the same Orthodox Jewish man told me, "The Diaspora could exist without Israel in the sense that nobody is going to come to the US and deport American Jews or put us in concentration camps. But had there been an Israel, what happened in Germany would not have happened."[97]

I am sitting in a quiet Italian restaurant in Manhattan, having lunch with David Twersky. Twersky, like me, is a former *Habonim* member and was at that time director of international affairs of the American Jewish Congress. Sadly, he retired not long after our interview and he passed away a few years later. In his obituary, J. J. Goldberg wrote:

> In the course of more than 40 years in the public eye, Twersky was a nationally known student leader, a kibbutz member and Israel Labor Party leader, a Knesset aide, respected Israeli political analyst, Washington correspondent of the Forward and international affairs director of the American Jewish Congress. He was also a published poet and contributor to literary journals, including the Partisan Review. A charismatic figure with a quick wit, he left a profound impact in each of his varied careers.[98]

Twersky had a very active life as a Zionist, having lived in Israel, having helped settle Kibbutz Gezer, and having fought in the 1982 war. For him, supporting Israel was his life's work, but he noted:

> For most people [supporting Israel] means very little. It probably means that if a candidate for office, local or national office, doesn't pass some kind of pro-Israel threshold then they won't vote for them. It would be one of the reasons they would weigh about whether to vote for someone or not, but they are not active in anything . . .

Nevertheless, he also said, "I can't imagine what the American Jewish identity would be now, or Jews in any country really, without the space that is occupied by identification with Israel." He added, "From eating hummus to the sublime, I can't imagine what Jewish life would be without Israel."

Israel is, he said, integral to Jewish life; but if it is so integral, how are we to reconcile its centrality with his previous statement that for most Jews, supporting Israel actually involves very little? Other leaders in the American Jewish establishment shared similar thoughts, noting how it remains a challenge to ensure that Israel continues to play an important, and they hope positive, role in the lives of Diaspora Jews. Twersky suggested that this relationship's manifestations are often financial, such as the purchase of Israel bonds or supporting the Jewish Agency, for example. Indeed, any visitor to Israel will notice how much of the country has been funded by Diaspora donations, from yeshivas to kibbutzim to parks and sports centers (Israel's largest ice-skating rink is in the Canada Centre, in Metula). Another manifestation of Diaspora support is political, as there is a major effort in the USA to influence relevant foreign policy. Yet many Jews are involved in neither financial support nor political lobbying on behalf of Israel. Nevertheless, the centrality of Israel for Jewish identity remains, which is why Twersky said, "I think many, many Jews feel an obligation. I don't think all Jews feel an obligation."

Nevertheless, Twersky argued: "I think people should be familiar with Israeli literature and intellectual thought and what are the issues that Israelis are wrestling with on a deeper level. I think most American Jews stop at the level of the next war, or Palestinian terrorism, that's it." This viewpoint was one he shared with his friend, the famous Israeli diplomat Abba Eban, who referred to Israel's Jewish vocation. "Eban used to say, 'Israel has a Jewish vocation,' by which he meant, since he wasn't personally religious, that its concern and involvement with and commitment to the well-being of Judaism in the Diaspora is an essential component of the State of Israel."

Across all the interviews, the view that Israel is what defines being a Jew held as a common denominator, even though those who worked in major Jewish organizations all agreed that Israel means less to younger generations. The younger one is the less important Israel is.[99] Why younger Jews are increasingly distancing themselves from Israel, if that is the appropriate way to describe the shift, is a significant question for the major Jewish organizations. In the UK, Jonathan Boyd explained this shift by virtue of different historical experiences. Yet part of the challenge that Zionists face when trying to encourage younger generations to connect with Israel is, as Rabbi Harry Brechner pointed out, that there are no good guys in this story, and it is hard to identify with a militarily powerful country that is sustaining a military occupation described by many as illegal. Twersky eloquently described this situation as one of Jewish self-understanding, and of a familiar and thus comfortable historical narrative that sustains the Jewish paranoia of victimhood. In his own words:

> We don't always properly assess our strengths. We're very aware of our weaknesses and we anticipate disasters. We always anticipate disasters. We are a deeply traumatized people who have had a very difficult history in the last 100 years of being uprooted worldwide, of finding ourselves in a new culture and trying to adapt . . . We internalize the trauma and won't give it adequate expression.[100]

This inability to adequately express the political challenges the Jewish people face, and to recognize the strengths the Jewish people have, has led in part to the hysterical character of so much of the debate about Israel. Indeed, the tendency in Diaspora discourse about Israel is either to keep silent or to verge on the hysterical. As Twersky said in response to the fury surrounding the infamous book by John Mearsheimer and Stephen Walt, "We tend to get hysterical in the Jewish community."

The hysteria comes from the deep emotional commitment that Diaspora Jews often have toward Israel, even when the commitment is one laced with deep cynicism and a desire to alter Israeli policy and end the ongoing Israeli–Palestinian conflict. We ended our conversation on this point, discussing Jews who define the relationship with Israel in negative terms:

> There are people for whom what informs their relationship with Israel is criticism. Not that I don't have criticism, but the heart and soul and substance of their relationship is how many times a day can I criticise Israel, to prove that I am Jewish but not *that* kind of a Jew. Over time, people who were pro-Soviet, in the 20s and 30s, started to be less and less

> favourable to Stalin and the Soviet Union, and it is very interesting to draw a parallel, especially among Jews, between people who supported the Soviet Union but then broke away from it and became sharply critical, still affirming their Marxism but sharply critical of Stalin and then some of them kept going and became conservatives, a number did, prominent conservatives and certainly very anti-communist. So in my mind, there's a question if this thing drags on forever, this Israeli/Palestinian problem, and these people for whom the question of solving is the heart and soul of their Jewish identity . . . because the occupation is so immoral, I don't know what they are going to do . . .[101]

It is not my place here to assess whether or not Twersky's analysis in this regard is correct, but it does speak to an important part of the obligation felt by many Jews toward Israel.

Steven Bayme, of the American Jewish Committee, said:

> The distancing from Israel . . . among the younger generation is less a reflection of harsh criticism of Israeli policy than it is a distancing from Jewish matters generally. Therefore, Jewish organizations do need to be concerned about this, but they need to be concerned primarily about continuity and assimilation.[102]

The clear inference here is that the solution to the issue of increasing distancing from Israel by Jews lies in policies designed to prevent assimilation and support Jewish continuity in the Diaspora. While it is not surprising that senior members of the American Jewish establishment felt that being Jewish requires an obligation to support Israel, what is interesting is how this obligatory discourse is characterized and understood. Bayme's views could be challenged by arguing that the obligation to support Israel is best executed by not allowing Israel to get away with enacting morally questionable security policies. Indeed, for many younger Jews, what obligations toward Israel entail is not always clear, and the Jewish establishment's tendency to expect support above public criticism is alienating. Part of the problem is that the Israelization of Jewish identity involves the assumption of an obligation to support Israel, but with no clear answer as to what support means, coupled with significant dissonance between what Israel means (or rather, what it is expected to mean) and what it does, which creates moral and political problems for many Jews.

Conclusion

Ilan Zvi Baron. So do you think that there is an automatic presumption that being Jewish means that there should be some form of loyalty to Israel?
Rabbi Berman. Yes I do.
Baron. Loyalty meaning that Israel is important for these people, or in a different sense?
Berman. Loyalty in the sense that this is, and the nation-state of Israel is, an important instrumentality for the actualization of the Jewish vision in the world. And that in turn yields a sense of obligation that every Jew needs to have.

For those Jews who do feel an obligation to Israel, it is a product of their personal narrative, of their sense of self. The connection between Jewish identity and Israel, the Israelization of Jewish identity, is not something to be taken lightly, nor is it something that unites all Jews. While "For Jewish organizations, such as the Board of Deputies, to be a Jew means to support the state of Israel,"[103] this is not a view shared by all Jews.[104] Sometimes, Jews take great care to challenge and undermine many of the established myths that underpin the Israeli political narrative.[105] These range in scope and scale, and some of the classic texts in this regard are products of academics who live in Israel or who are Israeli by birth.[106] While supporting Israel may not always be how Diaspora Jews connect with that country, it is impossible to deny that Israel has altered Jewish identity in a variety of ways, from the political and cultural to the culinary.[107] It is now common to find Israeli fare, such as hummus and falafel, resting besides knishes and herring at a Kosher table, and the success of Yotam Ottolenghi and Sami Tamimi's cookbook *Jerusalem* owes partly to its idealized Israel, with Jerusalem food-ways imparting a comfortable identity-narrative.[108] Indeed, it is often easier to enjoy the gastronomic pleasures that Israel has helped Jews discover than to buy into the logic of Zionism. As the young woman from Chicago aptly said while sitting in an Israeli café in Manhattan, "Not wanting to go live in Israel is not the same as not wanting Israel to live."[109]

In this chapter, I have explored some of the mechanisms that shape the Diasporia's attachment to Israel and any ensuing obligations. Rabbi Chaim Weiner, director of the European region of Masorti, offered a dichotomous synopsis of these mechanisms. Israel's importance, he said, comes down to two general points. The first concerns how Israel has helped shape Jewish identity post-Holocaust, in that there "would have been ever greater despair without Israel in the aftermath of the Holocaust."[110] Following from this point, the second is that "Israel gave Jews hope for the future, offered the possibility to finish with hope – this is important for Jewish peoplehood. Israel is tied to a sense of Jewish strength. But today Diaspora Jews don't look to Israel to provide security. Diaspora Jewry is comfortable and confident."[111] Indeed, Diaspora Jews' confidence is partly illustrated by how they are able to manifest their obligations to Israel in so many ways, from donating money and time to public activism and political lobbying.

5 Obligation and Critique

Introduction

I have suggested that one way to understand the Diaspora's relationship with Israel is to think of it as a form of transnational political obligation. A transnational political obligation is a political relationship that exists across states, among Diaspora, transnational or trans-state communities, and which frames their relations and identity-practices. What makes them political is that transnational political obligations are characterized by multiple discourses of power. The first of these is a public account of power that associates it with people acting together in public. The roles of authority and of sovereignty are displaced in this reading of power. What unites people in relations of power is a shared purpose in their public lives. Even though the power relations among a transnational diaspora group remain tied to a like-group, the spatial character of this group reflects the fact that people who share ties do not necessarily live in the same geographical location.

The second discourse of power expands this public framing of power into the private sphere and into constructions of the self. In this regard, power in transnational political obligation is reflected and produced by the knowledge that makes up the self. Senses of identity carry with them expectations about how to behave, who to relate with, what to think and why, what community to belong to, who does not belong, and so on. All of these are clearly visible in the debates found in *The Finkler Question*, where Jewish identity is understood as requiring particular beliefs about Israel, and not to share in these beliefs is anathema to what it means to be Jewish. Here Jewish identity in a non-religious sense is framed by discourses of knowledge that privilege certain claims over others (which is what a discourse is), in this case about Jewish history and Israel, and then apply these discourses to constructions of identity. What matters here is not what the causes of these discourses are, but rather that identity carries with it a variety of power relations which are unseen but which are necessary for the construction of the self.

What my argument for transnational political obligation has not done is explain what one ought to do. The focus on the Jewish Diaspora is important here, because debates about Diaspora/Israel relations are regularly a flashpoint of debate, and so the point of my theoretical framework has not been to take sides, but to explain how this relationship can be such a flashpoint. While most texts about Diaspora/Israel relations simply argue about whether one ought to support Israel and what support means, what they do not address in a critical sense is why Diaspora Jews are expected to have a relationship with Israel and to support it. The relationship is simply assumed as a product of Jewish identity. However, this is not a satisfactory answer.

It is unsatisfactory because it relies on a tautology: being Jewish means supporting Israel, and one supports Israel because one is Jewish. When articulated, the argument is not always so obviously tautological, because of references to history, psychology or religion. Some of the arguments articulated, as is evident from the interviews and texts examined, are: to be Jewish is to have a relationship with Israel because Israel is the Jewish State; Israel provides Jews with a home should they need it; Israel offers Jews a sense of pride and a place at the international negotiating table, a seat at the United Nations and a return to global international history; Israel is the biblical homeland; and/or Israel is the cultural (and religious) center of Judaism. While all these arguments carry significant weight, they are also all easily problematized. Not only is there a tautological aspect to pretty much all of them, they are also problematic for political, historical, and ethical reasons. Many of these answers take uncritically a Zionist historiographical reading of Jewish history, and they ignore Israel's greater internal problems pertaining to civil rights, religious tolerance, racism, and of course national security and the Occupation. They dismiss the extent to which Diaspora has been a critical part of Jewish identity and not the disaster that Zionism wants it to be. They dismiss the extent to which Diaspora Jews have to sacrifice their moral commitments as minority populations in order to support a traditional majority-modeled nation-state. They also create questionable narratives about security and identity that many Jews are deeply uncomfortable with. In a sense, the historical default position is that Israel is exceptional, and that this justifies any discrepancies in what it may mean to have a relationship with Israel as a Diaspora Jew. (Of course, it is exceptional only for Jews; when it comes to Israel's relations in international politics, the argument is that Israel should not be held to be an exception but should treated like any other state.)

To use transnational political obligation is to provide a heuristic framework for understanding how these claims function and why they function to the extent they do. The incommensurable positions that are argued either for or against Israel, and that do so by way of claims to Jewish ethics and Jewish identity, are clearly illuminated by transnational political obligation, because it is not the normative conclusions that matter here so much as the heuristic that enables such debates to function and be so intense. This intensity exists because, as my theory of transnational political obligation demonstrates, Diaspora Jewish identity is now understood to require an obligation to have a connection with Israel. How this connection is mediated then becomes the terrain for debate, but because the connection is a constitutive part of Jewish identity, or is assumed to be one and largely functions as one, the debates implicitly involve challenging one's identity as a Jew. Thus, to question how one relates to Israel is not just a political, ethical or religious question, it is to question one's very identity as a Jew. Jacqueline Rose has illuminated how such discourses function psychoanalytically,[1] but what I have tried to offer is a political framework.

What transnational political obligation reveals is the tipping points for these discourses about the Diaspora/Israel relationship, where they become the flashpoints for debate, for hysteria, panic, anger or extreme consternation. They exist in the realm of security (of the relationship between Israel and Jewish security, both in the Jewish State and in the Diaspora), of political practice (of what it means to become publicly engaged with Israel as a Diaspora Jew), and of individual and collective identity (of how the relation with Israel conditions the construction of Jewish identity and what this means for public and private belief and action). Debate about Diaspora Jewry and Israel rests on how one reacts to each of these tipping points.

However, what I want to conclude on in this chapter is not what position one should take with regard to any of these. There is an ample literature that addresses these topics, and I have little to add to these debates. Rather, what transnational political obligation reveals is that underneath the ideological debates about Zionism and Jewish identity is the fundamental problem that contained within such debates are the conditions for the unmaking of contemporary Jewish Diaspora identity.

If the transnational political obligation of Diaspora Jewry toward Israel is to have a relationship with Israel, it follows that a normative discourse that can influence the terms of this relationship is necessarily required. Yet, all that can be said with any certainty is that there exists a prevailing pressure for Jews in the Diaspora to connect with Israel. While the Pew Survey in the USA reveals a decline in interest in Israel, this view is not shared by the Jewish establishment, which feels strongly that the connection with Israel is fundamental to Jewish identity. The statistics also cannot address the counter-factual question of how Diaspora Jews would react should Israel disappear from the map. The statistics in the USA are not universal, for Jews in the UK remain very closely connected with Israel (perhaps because Israel is so much closer geographically and easier to travel to, and because of greater levels of anti-Israel rhetoric and sentiment in Europe than in North America).

In this concluding chapter, I am going to argue that the underlying normative problem pertaining to Diaspora/Israel relations is not about Israeli policy or the Occupation or Israeli security (the usual flashpoints of debate). While these are obviously important and concern serious matters pertaining to human rights, international law, moral accountability and justice, what the rhetoric about Israel misses is that contained within the Diaspora/Israel relationship rests an immanent critique that poses a fundamental question mark over Jewish identity today. Thus, this chapter begins with an examination of the normative role of critique and then, using the work of Judith Butler, proceeds to focus on an immanent critique. It is the fundamental problem posed by critique, and what an immanent critique reveals, that makes it so difficult to clearly address the Diaspora/Israel relationship, which as David Twersky noted is a relationship all too often characterized by hysteria.[2]

Critique and Transnational Political Obligation

Unlike in situations of political obligation where the normative choice is one of resistance to the state, there is no such opportunity in transnational political obligation because there is no state to resist. Rather, there are only assumptions about loyalty or commitment that one can challenge – as Judith Butler and many others do.[3] Transnational political obligation thus seems to limit the opportunities for resistance, but in fact it does not.

As listed above, transnational political obligation reveals the tipping points on which to judge one's relationship with Israel. These are in the realms of security, of political practice, and of individual and collective identity. The only actual obligation that exists, and which is encouraged to exist,[4] is to have a relationship with Israel. Debate thus centers on the manifestations of this obligation. Some are uninterested and just get on with their lives, others are highly agitated one way or another and act accordingly, still others are involved publicly in fairly conventional platforms, and many are concerned but, other than reading the news and discussing the issues over coffee and dinner, do not get involved. What they all share, however, is that their main avenue for any kind of normative response to this obligation is critique.

Critique is the primary site in which transnational political obligations encounter their normative potential. It is in this light that we need to understand Gershom Scholem's antagonism toward Hannah Arendt's critical relationship with Zionism and Israel. In response to her writings about the Eichmann trial in Jerusalem, Scholem accused Arendt of being heartless and of having no love of the Jewish people. As he wrote:

> In the Jewish tradition there is a concept, hard to define and yet concrete enough, which we know as *Ahabath Israel*: "Love of the Jewish People ..." In you, dear Hannah, as in so many intellectuals who came from the German Left, I find little trace of this.[5]

The view that associates being Jewish with supporting Israel is a continuation of this debate between Scholem and Arendt, with the mainstream major Jewish Diaspora organizations, as well as some of my interviewees, siding closer to Scholem than Arendt. Scholem's attack is personal (although he and Arendt were friends) precisely because he believes that her critique is the greatest of all betrayals for it challenges the very idea of Jewish identity and Jewish continuity.

The significance of critique is also apparent in the somewhat schizophrenic character of how Diaspora Jewry (and Israel) are both regularly concerned about criticism of Israel, but are also deeply involved with it. There is so much debate about Israel that even if Diaspora organizations are keen to silence critical voices, the failure to do so is so great as to make any such attempts farcical. Rather, what exists is a deep anxiety about not letting criticism of Israel get out of hand or about not challenging critical voices deemed to be beyond the pale (the borders of the pale in this case can shift just as much as the old Eastern European borders used to). Thus, the usual Diaspora/Israel discourse emanating from the major Jewish organizations is one of commitment, sometimes laced with hypothetical disaster scenarios to reinforce the point and discourage too much criticism.

Indeed, the famous neo-conservative Jewish writer Norman Podhoretz once wrote in 1974, "The feeling was – and is – that if Israel were to be annihilated, the Jews of America would also disappear."[6] In 2005, Tony Bayfield wrote in *The Guardian* that "If the state of Israel were to cease to exist ... Judaism would, I believe also cease to exist."[7] While those interviewed for this project did not provide such an alarmist conclusion, more than one interviewee claimed that should Israel disappear it would be a tragedy, if not a catastrophe, for American and world Jewry.

However, recent Pew data about American Jewry suggests that the further to the left one is, the less centrally Israel plays in one's sense of identity and the less worried one is about Israel.[8] The data, however, are mixed. When asked whether or not caring about Israel is an essential part of being Jewish, 38 percent of Jewish Democrats agreed, as against 59 percent of Jewish Republicans. Yet 65 percent of Jewish Democrats (and 69 percent of Jewish independents) agreed that they feel somewhat attached to Israel, as against 84 percent of Jewish Republicans. The conclusion is not that Democratic Jews care less about Israel. Forty-eight percent of Jewish Democrats agreed that Israel is important but not essential. Part of the problem with such surveys is that they necessarily require the use of compartmentalized variables, which rarely reflects how individuals understand their own sense of self. As the sociologist Manuel Castells explains, in sociology identity is often conceived as an overarching category that organizes meaning, and within each identity an individual has multiple roles that often overlap and interact.[9] The different roles are treated as different independent variables, but roles can be influenced by each other, and their meaning is framed by one's sense of self. It is a sense of identity that gives the roles meaning, but the quantitative data implies that it is the other way round.

Nevertheless, those on the left do approach Israel without as much panic. As J. J. Goldberg said, "It's almost a definitional thing today that the further left you are the less alarmed you are about the status of Jews – you're sitting right here with living evidence."[10] Yet, being less alarmist does not mean that obligations disappear, just as rejecting Scholem's position does not mean there are no obligations – it is just that the obligations are felt and responded to differently. Whereas in political obligation the moral or ethical obligation comes down to a choice about obedience, in transnational political obligation the moral obligation centers on the ethics of critique.

In this regard, there is so much critique, so much that is written about Israel, that it is difficult to know where to start, or which texts best demonstrate the various poles of obligatory discourses. However, some limits can be placed. Of interest here are not those texts that seek to provide a justification or a "case for Israel"[11] or that attempt to strengthen the Zionist project by challenging critical histories of Israel, viewing such post-Zionist or revisionist scholarship as undermining the Jewish State.[12] These texts are not especially interesting, because they do not critically engage in what it means for Diaspora Jewry to share in obligations toward a country from which they are in many ways far removed. They merely assume the obligation. Moreover, what such texts ignore is that, as the Israelization of Jewish identity has changed, so there are more opportunities for critique, which is not to say that such critique is easy. It is easiest to support the establishment, easier to remain critical but to work within it, and hardest to fight from the outside.

While J. J. Goldberg says that the further to the left one is "the less alarmed you are about the status of Jews," the obverse is true, which is that the further to the left you are, the more you are concerned about the political character of Israel, as opposed to threats to its existence. To put it crudely, right-wing Jews care about protecting Israel's boundaries whereas left-wing Jews care about what takes place inside these boundaries. Notice, for example the following by Jay Michaelson, who has written on sexuality, religion and law. He writes how he has been losing his passion for Israel, for having to defend Israel. He is worth quoting at length:

> My love of Israel has turned into a series of equivocations: "I do not support the expansion of settlements, but the Palestinians bear primary responsibility for the collapse of the peace process in 1999." "The Israelis acted overzealously in Gaza, but they must be entitled to defend themselves against rocket attacks." "Yes, the separation wall is odious, but it is also effective and necessary." Yes, but; no, but; defend, but. At some point, the complexity and ambiguity wears one out, particularly when the visuals on the anti-Israel side are so compelling, and so stark: walls, tanks, checkpoints.
>
> I admit that my exhaustion is exacerbated because, in my social circles, supporting Israel is like supporting segregation, apartheid or worse. I know this is a sign of weakness of will on my part, and I hope that the *Times-Magazine*-sanctioned rise of J Street changes things, but I don't think advocates of Israel understand exactly how bad the situation is on college campuses, in Europe, and in liberal or leftist social-political circles. Supporting Israel in these contexts is like supporting repression, or the war in Iraq, or George W. Bush. It's gotten so bad, I don't mention Israel in certain conversations anymore, and no longer defend it when it's lumped in with South Africa and China by my friends. This is wrong of me, I know, but I've been defending Israel for years, and it's gotten harder and harder to do so.
>
> Part of the problem here is that the Israel I love is not the Disneyland most of my fellow Americans seem to adore ... Worse than that, the mythic Israel is now actively affecting – I would say harming – the real one. The handful of rich American conservatives who have influenced Israeli politics lately have tended to prefer grandiose myths to the messy realities that should govern pragmatic decision making – and eventually, all those simplifications add up to dangerous distortions in policy. The "fantasy Israel," the one many Americans seem largely to inhabit, doesn't compensate for the erosion of the real one. On the contrary, it causes it.[13]

This kind of alienation is one response to an obligation which offers few choices for action and which the vast literature on the Diaspora and Israel does not address in much detail if at all. Instead, the literature all too often tells its readers what to believe and what to do, who is right and who is wrong, who has fabricated history and who has a selective memory.

It is perhaps worth mentioning that considering how much is written about Israel it is remarkable how little is actually said. There exist websites dedicated to either defending or challenging Israel, and it is a full-time job to keep up with all that is published on the topic. The debate over Israel is always hotly contested, and most of the literature about Zionism and Israel today fits into easily identifiable categories that reflect one of the following views and that range from radical defense to radical critique. On one side of the spectrum there is the view famously (or infamously) articulated by the French Jewish sociologist Maxime Rodinson that Israel is a colonial-settler state (because of its following the settler model for state development and being sufficiently supported by Western powers).[14] Related critiques of Israel come from a variety of sources often accusing not just Israel but also Zionism of being inherently racist.[15] Heading toward the other side of the spectrum is the kind of Dershowitz text already mentioned that seeks to defend Israel. Other Zionist defenses of Israel are easily found in Yoram Hazony's critique of post-Zionist historiography and Benjamin Netanyahu's wide-ranging defense of Israel.[16] Another interesting example from the right of the political spectrum is Norman Podhoretz's text about why Jews are traditionally liberal, arguing that today the historical lesson is that the threat in fact comes from the left in the guise of anti-Zionism.[17] Some of the more influential historical literature also fits into the same categories. What much of the post-Zionist or revisionist literature sets out to do, even when it is ostensibly apolitical in its argument, is provide an intellectual grounding for one's political views about Israel.[18] It is in this light that Shlomo Sand's book *The Invention of the Jewish People* is best understood.[19] Other works, such as those by Yossi Klein Halevi, Gershom Gorenberg and Avi Shavit, provide different critiques of Israel that build on the post-Zionist revelations.[20] A kind of left-leaning middle ground are texts which remain committed to the Zionist idea but are unhappy with where it has gone and seek to secure a more just and moral Zionism within a state that recognizes its democratic principles.[21]

There are gray areas in all of these, but unfortunately, in public discourse the choice often tends to be set up as one of human rights versus Zionist property rights, and one is tasked to choose between Palestinian and Arab rights and Jewish Israeli rights – a blatantly false dichotomy. Sometimes the texts are quite extreme, such as Max Blumenthal's *Goliath: Life and Loathing in Greater Israel*,[22] a book described as one that could belong to the "Hamas Book-of-the-Month Club (if it existed)."[23]

One cannot help but think that the extreme language that characterizes debate about Israel has the effect of turning people off engaging with the issues. It may also be the case that the rhetoric is so heated because it is often so powerless to affect Israeli policy. Diaspora Jews protesting about human rights violations committed by the Israel military have so far had minimal or no impact in Israel. The Israeli government can continue to evade or ignore Diaspora voices when it chooses to because there are very few immediate implications in doing so. Of course, the long-term implications could be quite serious and include the eventual theocracization of Israel and a weakening of Israel on the international stage through its becoming a pariah state because of the ongoing Occupation and settlement-building. Yet in the immediate term, the main implications for Diaspora activism with regard to Israel have to do with the obligations that one feels are demanded of being a Jew, and not with the fact that the Israeli government will switch policy tracks.

While I am not suggesting that Diaspora Jews stop becoming involved, I am proposing that the immediate impact may not be on Israel, but on oneself. Arendt once remarked that the best moral argument against murder was the answer provided by Socrates: that one should not murder because to do so is to live in the presence of a murderer – oneself – and nobody wants to be in the presence of a murderer.[24] Whatever critique one takes, the person who has to live the longest with the decision made is the critic, and critique contributes to defining one's sense of self. It is one's identity that is primarily at stake in transnational political obligations.

Toward an Immanent Critique of Zionism

Even though she won the prestigious Adorno Prize, Judith Butler is not a Frankfurt School theorist, though she shares some intellectual history with the School. Her extensive use of Walter Benjamin, who was no stranger to the Frankfurt School, and of Hannah Arendt (a close friend of Benjamin, although not of Adorno), links Butler to the political-ethical concerns that animated the Frankfurt School project. Moreover, there is the possibility of a connection between the French poststructuralism to which Butler is heavily indebted and the Frankfurt School.[25] The Frankfurt School is mentioned here because I am going to suggest that contained within Butler's critique of Israel and Zionism there rests an immanent critique.

Immanent critique is often associated with the Frankfurt School Critical Theorists. While much has been written on the Frankfurt School, one important part of its intellectual and political impetus was the necessity to explain the rise of fascism. How could fascism (and totalitarianism for that matter) exist in an age under the historical influence of Enlightenment rationality?[26] In order to answer this question it was necessary to explore the extent to which this language of universal rationality and enlightenment contained within it the seeds of fascism and how the assault against democracy in the Weimer Republic was possible.[27] The early Critical Theorists of the Frankfurt School included Max Horkheimer, Theodor Adorno, Erich Fromm, Herbert Marcuse, Leo Löwenthal, Franz Neumann, Otto Kirchheimer and Friedrich Pollock. Walter Benjamin was not, strictly speaking, a member of the Frankfurt School but was a close friend of Adorno. Karl Wittfogell is also sometimes associated with the early Frankfurt School, and Jürgen Habermas is usually acknowledged as its last member.

While there is no single approach that can define the Frankfurt School, and while there exist ample and lengthy texts about it,[28] there are some clear breaks within the School, such as the early negative outlook on Enlightenment rationality and Habermas' more positive take. The early theorists also shared some intellectual dispositions, not least their being influenced by Karl Marx. They were also generally deeply critical of Kantian transcendentalism and Hegel's claims about history following a process of universal reason. Many of the early members of the Frankfurt School were not only German but also Jewish, which explains their concern with the rise of fascism and their skepticism.

In her articulation of a Jewish ethics toward Israel, Judith Butler suggests that "critique is obligatory."[29] She writes:

> Jewishness can and must be understood as an anti-identitarian project insofar as we might even say that being a Jew implies taking up an

ethical relation to the non-Jew, and this follows from the diasporic condition of Jewishness where living in a socially plural world under conditions of equality remains an ethical and political ideal.[30]

Her general point is that the historical condition of Jewish life has fostered an ethical obligation that Jews have to others in part because the character of Diaspora Jewish life necessarily involved a life among others who are not Jewish. Butler seeks to offer a theory of diasporic ethics, one influenced by Hannah Arendt, Martin Buber, Walter Benjamin, Edward Said, and the French Jewish philosopher Emmanuel Lévinas.[31] Her diasporic-ethical argument offers an alternative discourse in which to understand one's relationship with Israel, one where the obligation remains present, but requires critique.

What Butler is implicitly suggesting is that contained within the Diaspora/Israel relationship there exists an immanent critique. Immanent critique is to use a methodology or theoretical position against itself, and is often directed toward revealing hidden contradictions. The origins of immanent critique lie in Kant's use of reason to provide a critique of reason.[32] Hegel's dialecticism is also based on immanent critique. Marx further developed this methodology, and it became an important method in the Critical Theory of the Frankfurt School.[33]

What Butler does, which among other things has made her a controversial figure within the Jewish community, is use Jewish political and ethical thought against Israel. For those who see Israel as the pinnacle of Jewish political achievement, this method of critique in particular is tantamount to heresy (although Butler's sympathetic treatment of Hamas and her support for the Boycott, Divestment, and Sanctions movement have also made her a target). When she was nominated for the Adorno Prize, there was considerable anger that someone so critical of Israel could receive this accolade.[34]

Butler's most basic point, which she has been making for over a decade, is that "It will not do to equate Jews with Zionists or Jewishness with Zionism."[35] Her line of inquiry has been to criticize Israel "in the name of one's Jewishness, in the name of justice, precisely because such criticisms seem 'best for the Jews.'"[36] Part of her moral argument is to build on the ethical implications of what Franz Rosenzweig writes in *The Star of Redemption*, when he defines Jewish life as one of "wandering and waiting."[37] Butler

Obligation and Critique

takes this starting point and develops an ethical argument based on the absence of statehood and the ethical imperatives that come from not being privy to the powers of sovereignty over a political space. Somewhat problematically, since historically the condition of statelessness was part of what made the Jews a victim of nineteenth- and twentieth-century European anti-Semitism,[38] Butler also argues that Jews need to understand when the Jews are not victims but are in positions of strength:

> It seems, though, that historically we have now reached a position in which Jews cannot legitimately be understood always and only as presumptive victims. Sometimes we surely are, but sometimes we surely are not. No political ethics can start from the assumption that Jews monopolize the position of victim.[39]

The slight paradox here that cannot be ignored is that it is Israel, along with Jewish success at integration in North America, that has transformed the Jews into a people with the kind of political power that no longer makes them victims. Thus it is Israel's successful existence that is partly responsible for giving Jews the ability to escape their victimhood and which should then serve as the basis for pursuing a more ethical politics that is critical of the Zionist ethno-nationalism that Israel is built on.

In this regard, Butler is using a form of immanent critique, as Israel is both responsible for the ethical problems posed by the Occupation yet also an important source of Jewish inspiration that should serve to provide a progressive resolution to the Occupation. Jews should care about Israel because Israel represents a major political achievement in Jewish history, and as a product of Diaspora Jewry, Israel should act according to the ethical ideals that Jews learned in the Diaspora. Butler argues that "the very possibility of ethical relation depends upon a certain condition of dispossession from national modes of belonging."[40] Israel also provides Jews with a sense of strength that confirms that Jews are not helpless victims, and this strength can be used to criticize Israel without Israel thereby being a victim. We see this kind of paradox when Israel is viewed as both powerful and also a victim, and when Israel tries to have it both ways.

Butler does not directly acknowledge the positive force that Israel has had on Jewish Diaspora identity, but her argument implies as much. For the close tie between Jewish identity and Israel is precisely what she is concerned about, while she also feels troubled about what goes on in Israel because she is Jewish. The problem she is faced with is not just wanting to argue for justice for those who are the victims of Zionism (to borrow Edward Said's phrase),[41] but to make a Jewish case for justice because (1) she is a Diaspora Jew and (2) because since she is a Jew Israel is important to her (other not exclusively Jewish grounds no doubt also influence her). Consequently, what she is strongly implying is that Jewish success in Israel mediated via the Israelization of Jewish identity has created the problems that this new stronger Jew is meant to solve, namely, injustices conducted by the hand of the security services and military of the Jewish State. It is not just that Jews in Israel have created the problems they need to resolve. It is also that the problems themselves can only be resolved through being in the position that enables one to commit them in the first place. It is this problem that is so important, because it gets to the heart of what it means to be a Diaspora Jew in the age of Israel.

What makes the Diaspora/Israel relationship so fraught with emotional tension is that Israel was supposed to make the Jews safe and to create a new political geography in which Jews could carry their heads high as proud members of the community of nations. What has happened instead is that while Israel has contributed to making Jews feel proud as a community, it has also helped Jews to regularly feel as if they are under siege. If it is not some Arab state or Arab terrorist organization, it is the Left which regularly charges Israel with being a racist colonial state. Israel is viewed as strong for the Jews, but weak in the sense that it remains a victim regularly under attack. Yet, as is readily acknowledged, it is not as if Israel is completely innocent. Israel, like any other country, makes mistakes. The problem, however, is that Israel regularly behaves so badly that it becomes not a source of cohesion but of tension. Hannah Arendt was one of the more famous and vocal critics of the type of political and military force that the Zionists used and which many Diaspora Jews are deeply uncomfortable with. Butler's turn to Arendt in her critique is not surprising. Arendt's critique of the nation-state model of Zionism is well-known, although there are other important Jewish anti-Zionist or critical-Zionist voices who Butler does not engage with, but who struggled with similar issues with regard to Israeli centrality for Jewish identity and the potential fallout from this centrality.

For example, in 1954, Simon Rawidowicz, a Jewish Studies scholar at Brandeis, wrote to Ben-Gurion complaining about how Israel had come to mean the State of Israel and could no longer be used in a non-geographical sense.[42] Rawidowicz's point, which is related to those of other Jewish nationalists such as Simon Dubnow, was that Israel the State was overshadowing if not displacing Israel the People. While Arendt did not know what it meant to love a people,[43] Rawidowicz certainly did, and in a sense his critique is closer to what Butler is getting at when she identifies the Jewish people and its historical condition of Diaspora as an ethical framework by which to critique the State of Israel. Butler explicitly uses her Jewishness as a reason for her critique, in an overt and explicit way that is not quite as evident with Arendt. Arendt, for example, does not say that because she is Jewish she is obligated to critique Zionism or Israel, even if that sentiment was no doubt present in her earlier Jewish writings.[44]

There is an increasing interest in these alternative voices of Jewish nationalism and anti-Zionism,[45] because what such voices recognized, and which Butler misses in her critique of Israel, is that there exist profound implications in how the Zionist narrative of identity, power and place remolds Jewish identity. The alternatives reveal significant options by which to critique Israel. One such example is Arendt's retort about how for the Zionists violence and possibly even martyrdom have become an acceptable form of politics: "Now Jews believe in fighting at any price and feel that 'going down' is a sensible method of politics."[46]

In addition to Arendt, the nineteenth-century Jewish nationalists and the twentieth-century heirs of this tradition also are important. As the historian Noam Pianko writes:

> Expanding our vision of the past to include the wide range of state-seeking and counterstatist varieties ... inspires a more pluralistic approach to reconsidering what it means to be a Zionist today. Indeed, the future of Zionism, and a sustainable model of Jewish peoplehood, depends on reengaging the basic principles of Zionism's roads not taken – the distinction between the Jewish nation and the Jewish state – as well as the accompanying questions of what boundaries can substitute for the state in defining membership in Jewish national life.[47]

While Arendt was also all too aware of this problem, the voices of Simon Rawidowicz, Mordecai Kaplan, Hans Kohn, Simon Dubnow and others all in their own ways highlight that Jewish peoplehood remains important, if not crucial for sustaining the Jewish people and that Zionism was not necessarily a solution. For example, Dubnow felt:

> A single national policy must become the surrogate for territorial unity for a nation which, existing in the Diaspora, faces the threat of dissolution within the surrounding territorial nations. If the ruling peoples can turn national policy into a weapon of oppression, it can be a means of self-defence for minorities.[48]

However, it is not as if Dubnow was against Zionism in its entirety. He readily acknowledged that "It is self evident that if we had the power to transfer the entire Diaspora to a Jewish state we would do it with the greatest joy."[49] Nevertheless, since that is not possible, it is necessary that "In the Diaspora we must strive, within the realm of the possible, to demand and attain national-cultural autonomy for the majority of the nation."[50]

Dubnow demonstrates a kind of nineteenth-century pragmatism that had not yet realized the implications of the twentieth-century merger of nation and state. Nevertheless, he does offer some important foresight for he was concerned about how a relationship between a Jewish center in Palestine and the Diaspora would function. Moreover, in a direct repost to Ahad Ha'Am, who argued for a Jewish spiritual and cultural home in Palestine, Dubnow asked:

> If the Diaspora cannot endure and it is destined to disintegrate, what point is there to furthering the growth of a centre in Palestine? The very revival of the spiritual centre in the land of Israel depends on the healthy national material which will stream into Palestine from the Diaspora; and where is this material to come from if the external security for national development in the Diaspora will be lacking? If the Diaspora cannot live a full national life without the center in Palestine, then the latter cannot possibly exist without a national Diaspora.
>
> Only one thing can save the spiritual Zionists from the dilemma: they must recognize autonomism, or the idea of national rights in the Diaspora . . .[51]

Tragically, Dubnow was murdered by the Nazis in Riga in 1941.

What concerned Dubnow in fact happened. Israel remade Jewish identity by displacing Diaspora as the geographical center. In the process, the risk was run that the Jews would lose their unique moral place in the world as a Diaspora people[52] (which is also Butler's claim) and that critique of Israel could be nearly impossible to sustain, for doing so would involve challenging Jewish peoplehood because of the conflation of Israel the people with Israel the State.

It is, however, the lost voice of Simon Rawidowicz that reveals the extent to which Israel involves both a crisis for Diaspora Jewry and its hope. Rawidowicz, a self-described "lonely man," has largely been forgotten, which is probably because he withheld publication of his most critical text about Israel, *Between Jew and Arab*.[53] As I have argued, major problems that charge the Diaspora/Israel relationship are based on security, political practice, and identity. It is largely on these issues that Diaspora debate about Israel rests, with the exception of religious debate, which I am not concerned with here. What Rawidowicz already knew in 1957 (when he wrote *Between Jew and Arab*) was that these are not separate issues, but are closely connected, and their connection reveals the extent to which the Diaspora ought to be concerned about what goes on in Israel.

Rawidowicz was not an anti-Zionist. He wrote:

> I have always had faith in Israel. And I pray: may the remnant of Israel not commit acts of injustice. May the Guardian of Israel protect this remnant, which became the foundation of the State of Israel, from the injustice and destruction [*keliyah*] now associated with it.[54]

In *Between Jew and Arab*, Rawidowicz strongly challenged Israeli immigration policy toward the Arab refugees and took Israel to task for mistreating its Arab national minority. He astutely pointed out that it was wrong for Israel to discriminate against its national minority of Arab citizens and even worse for Israeli leaders to be concerned about minority populations as a threat:

> If it is not good for the State of Israel to have "an alien national minority" then it is not good for any country in the world to have a national minority. That is, every national minority should be eliminated ... But don't those who make this claim realize that it actually undermines the existence of the Jewish Diaspora?[55]

The answer is that they probably did not care, at least not if they accepted the Zionist negation of the Diaspora. Rawidowicz was, of course, aware of such Zionists. His argument was not directed toward them, but toward those who called for a relationship between Israel and the Diaspora.

Rawidowicz was taking Israel to task, calling upon it to resolve in an ethical way the refugee problem and to treat its national Arab minority properly. He argued that Israeli policy toward the Arabs and the challenge to critics of Israeli policy will

> make an enemy out of one who is not an enemy, as if he seeks to eliminate us from the world, as if he wants the life, limb, and property of Jews, though in fact he has no intention of doing so.[56]

He challenged Israeli policy explicitly, writing, "It is forbidden for Israel to adopt the laws of the Gentiles and expropriate the property of an enemy or combatant who was vanquished on the battlefield."[57] He continued to warn Israel against its questionable approach to Palestinian inhabitants of Israel and the Arab refugees: "Woe onto the Jew who has been rebuilt in the state of the Jews upon the ruins of the Arab!"[58] Moreover, he warned that Israel needed to accept criticism, for to do otherwise would be to continue to proclaim a kind of Jewish exceptionalism that was not in Jewish interests: "We want candour between 'Israel' and the nations. Let the Gentiles think of us without prejudice, but also without 'defending' or 'tolerating' us. They speak about and with us candidly, just as we approach them as free people, by right and not sufferance."[59]

Rawidowicz clearly appreciated that the Diaspora is impacted by Israel and that Israel in turn needed to recognize as much, lest it run the risk of harming both:

> If the State of Israel is responsible for the "fate and status" of the Jewish people outside of it, and if every act that the state and its citizens undertake concerns the well-being of the Jewish people in the world, then doesn't this affect the "fate and status," as well as the future, of the Jewish people in the wide world out there? Does not the responsibility placed on the state, according to Ben-Gurion, compel it to regard the plight of the refugees also from the standpoint of the status of Jews in the Diaspora, of their struggle for rights in Gentile countries, whether the rights be those of a citizen or a national minority? They should not

be deprived of their right to property and land, and their possessions should not be plundered.[60]

In essence, Rawidowicz knew that Israel ran the risk of causing serious harm not only to itself but to world Jewry. He believed that within Jewish thought and Jewish history were the lessons that Israel needed to hear, but for reasons that are not clear, he did not publish this critique – perhaps because he feared the reaction that it could cause, which in itself leads one to think of the power of critique. For if his reasoning was related to this concern, which it probably was,[61] it only reaffirms that what characterizes the normative character of any obligations between Diaspora and Israel is critique of Israel.

Interest in such critical Jewish voices about Israel is on the increase. For example, David Myers writes: "Like [Rawidowicz] I have become unsettled by the intoxicating effects of political power and sovereignty on the Jews."[62] Noam Pianko offers a similar commentary:

> Israel's increasing position as a flashpoint in popular and scholarly debates about the morality of nationalism further engenders rifts in theorizing shared grounds of Jewish national cohesion inside and outside the state. Liberal scholars and activists disproportionately selected Israel to illustrate the limits of national sovereignty and the excessive power of Jewish lobbying groups. These claims have generally failed to evaluate Israel in a comparative perspective or to appreciate the ways in which other states disenfranchise certain populations. Nevertheless, it has become a politically charged moment to think about the limits of the sovereign mold as the basis for envisioning Jewish collective identity.[63]

A few points stand out. The first is that much contemporary theoretical literature does precisely what Pianko is asking for in challenging the hegemony of sovereignty in our understanding of political space and related political claims to identity and ethical responsibility, including the influential work in Jewish Studies, *The Powers of Diaspora*.[64] The second is that Pianko is using history to suggest alternative models and discourses by which to suggest what future debates could make use of. However, in the absence of any theoretical engagement of the normative kind that he envisions is necessary in order to address today's charged environment, it is not exactly clear what the reader is to make of his normative inference. Theory is needed. It is in this vein that we can turn to Butler, whose own turn toward Arendt reflects a need among Diaspora Jews to find Jewish voices that can illuminate an ethical critique toward Israel. It is also for this reason that I have sought to provide an outline for a theory of transnational political obligation, for doing so supports an exploration of the types of spatial and ethical questions that the Diaspora needs to be asking in its relationship with Israel.

Conclusion: A New Diaspora/Israel Relationship

The significance of critique for the Diaspora/Israel relationship is that critique is at the heart of where the obligation to Israel is most readily manifested in an empirical normative choice. I have demonstrated how within the Diaspora/Israel relationship there exist fundamental contradictions that are most apparent once the relationship is conceptualized in terms of obligation. What the framework of obligation reveals above all else is why the character of debate about Israel is marked so regularly by incommensurable positions and general anxiety about undermining the Jewish State. Why does Israel matter for Diaspora Jews and the construction of contemporary Jewish identity? Because of the expectation that Diaspora Jews have an obligation toward Israel, and because this obligation is to have a relationship with Israel. In theory, every Jew can decide how to respond to this obligation. Yet we know that the more critical one is of Israel, the harder it is to publicly articulate this position without being attacked because of the expectation that to be Jewish is to have a supportive obligation to Israel. Here again the immanent critique is apparent, as Jews are expected to relate to Israel, but if the relationship is too critical or too lax one runs the risk of being accused of failing as a Jew.

Both Martin Buber and Hannah Arendt recognized that Zionism was built on a paradox, that it was the Zionists who were the most assimilated out of all the Jews. In their argument against assimilation, the Zionists wanted nothing less than to be assimilated into the community of nations. Thus when other states or other nations challenge Israeli policy the betrayal is huge. For how could Israel be condemned for acting like any other state, like any other assimilated national group who succeeded in their territorial aspirations to national self-determination? Such critiques could only be justified as anti-Semitic because with the successful assimilation of Israel into the community of nations there was ostensibly nothing left to distinguish the Jews from other nations. As Arendt writes in her essay *Zionism Reconsidered*:

> The ... struggles between Zionism and assimilationism have completely distorted the simple fact that the Zionists, in a sense, were the only ones who sincerely wanted assimilation, that is, "normalization" of the people ("to be a people like all other peoples"), whereas the assimilationists wanted Jewish people to retain their unique position.[65]

Jacqueline Rose identifies both Arendt and Buber as recognizing this contradiction in Zionism, although Buber also argued how Israeli injustices toward the Arabs could cause harm to Israel and the Jews.[66] Rose goes further, and argues that Zionist thinkers were not naïve about the violence that Zionism contained within itself.

This conclusion is certainly consistent with the revisionist historical scholarship, although it is also fairly obvious in the sense of Zionists coming to the realization that military force would be required to succeed in creating a state in Palestine.[67] Zionism was, Rose acknowledges, "not meant of course to be a military endeavour. It was not meant to be violent."[68] Yet, she argues that "to survive, or defy its own internal contradictions, Zionism had to get carried away with itself."[69] Most of Rose's book is about revealing that within Zionism there has always been doubt and critique about itself, and there has always been a concern over the acceptance of military power as a constitutive feature of the new Jewish identity in Israel. She notes how "in Israel, catastrophe has become an identity."[70]

Others have also expressed concern over the use and abuse of the victim mentality. Boas Evron writes:

> Jewish impotence created the illusion that the essential attribute of independent national existence is military might. It also fostered the view of Zionism and the state of Israel as a historical revenge rather than as a means of becoming integrated as equals in both history and the family of nations. Self-confident nations (and individuals) are not in a hurry to display force.[71]

Significantly, Evron also notes how there is a paradoxical relationship between how the messianic religious Right in Israel understands the international security discourses and the related role of the Diaspora:

> The thinking of the messianic Right in Israel fails to grasp the nature of international relations and is incapable of understanding the nature of an independent nation in the international arena. It imagines Israel's existence not in the world as it is but only in the Jewish world. The Jewish world is supposed to provide a sort of protective envelope around the state (in an ironic reversal of the Zionist aim of providing protection for the Jewish people). But even if the Jewish world were interested in providing such a shield, it is too small and weak to permit such a flight from the facts of international life. The state must function as a state in order to exist at all. And it follows that the acceptance of the responsibilities of political existence also implies the acceptance of the rules of international behaviour.[72]

While Evron's critique is seemingly directed primarily at a specific constituency within Israel, it nevertheless is relevant to the wider Diaspora's understanding of its own role and to how Diaspora features as a Jewish political space in its relations with Israel. Indeed, he argues that the Diaspora is manipulated by Israel.

To the extent that there is even a kernel of truth in Rose's and Evron's respective observations, they reveal a major shift. Israel was supposed to be the answer to the Jewish Question, to what political spaces exist for the Jews in modernity, and its development has rewritten what it means to be Jewish. I suspect that for most (with the notable exceptions of those addressed earlier), this revision was largely a positive development. Yet, with Israel becoming a lightning rod for dissent, and with its identity becoming informed by catastrophe and violence, it is not in Israel that a positive answer to the Jewish Question was provided. Instead, Israel has contributed to an ongoing mentality of victimhood. To the extent that Israel sustains such a Jewish identity, it poses a threat to the successes of Diaspora Jews in escaping the historical victimhood mentality.

Criticism about Israel from Diaspora Jews is nothing new.[73] The point of this chapter is not to suggest that it is. What is missed in all the debating about Israel in the Jewish press and elsewhere

Obligation and Critique

is that the question of obligation that Jews feel toward Israel is not just about Israeli policy or Israel's existence and Palestinian national aspirations. The question is not just about the human rights of Palestinians and the security of Israelis. The question is about what it means to be a Diaspora Jew today, and because the question is so bound up in Jewish identity, it is exceptionally difficult to approach the topic without seriously insulting those Jews who do feel obligated. It is not that critiques of Israel cannot be heard, but that because the idea of Israel features so significantly in the construction of Jewish identity, to question Israel can be threatening.

Chaim Potok, the famous novelist and rabbi, finishes his historical book *Wanderings* by emphasizing many of the points that have animated the discussions so far, and which speak to identity, history, place, power and politics. He writes:

> For many Jews there is a sense of constant struggle with frightening echoes of the past, a wariness that is the reflex of a battered people, a defensiveness after millennia of anti-Semitism, and a fear that once more we might lose hundreds of thousands, perhaps millions, of our people as we compete in the open marketplace of ideas during this confrontation with secularism. The Jew sees all his contemporary history refracted through the ocean of blood that is the Holocaust. But there is also a sense of renewal, a forced sharpening of our self-identity, a feeling that we are approaching some distant fertile plain, though we cannot clearly make out the paths leading to it.
>
> This is an early, troubled springtime for the Jewish people in the United States and Israel, in England, Canada, Australia, South America, in almost all the non-European lands to which Jews have wandered in the past two centuries. The chill of a winter death is still in the air.
>
> But Israel is a warmth for Jews everywhere despite the failures and disappointments felt when dreams are soiled by much of reality and the weaknesses of human beings. In the past few years I have wandered back and forth across oceans. Everywhere I go I meet Jews passionate with pride in Israel. They fear for her, tremble when her people are hurt, support her, are not yet certain what sort of nation-state they wish her to be, are concerned about the drain upon creative energies and the coarsening of moral fibre caused by endless military vigilance, and are dazed with disbelief and joy over an achievement like Entebbe. From Auschwitz to Entebbe in a single generation.[74]

Salo Baron, the famous Jewish historian, writes that both Diaspora and Israel are here to stay, and so there will remain a "continuing dialogue between the State of Israel and the Diaspora."[75] Yitzhak Rabin has written:

> I realize that in the foreseeable future the Jewish people will continue to be divided into Jews who live in the State of Israel and Jews who will continue to live in the Diaspora. People who reject this approach are on very slippery ground.[76]

There is no doubt that there exist significant ideational forces that link Diaspora and Israel. There exists an obligation felt by many Jews (and assumed by many non-Jews) that Diaspora Jews ought to have a relationship with the Jewish State, and there exists to a lesser extent the view that Israel should reciprocate. However, what is not explored in any of this literature, even the literature that recognizes that the Diaspora and Israel are heading in different directions, are the underlying political discourses that today require a radical rethinking of the terms under which the Diaspora/Israel relationship was conceived. It may be time to rethink what this relationship is about and what it means to be a Diaspora Jew in the age of Israel, and whether or not an obligation to have a relationship with Israel could be the undoing of the Jewish Diaspora.

Conclusion: Obligation in Exile, Critique and the Future of the Jewish Diaspora

This book has been driven by one large question: how are we to understand the Jewish Diaspora's relationship with Israel when it is no longer appropriate, if it ever was, to presume that to be a good Jew means being a Zionist? Answering this question has meant working out what is it about Jewish identity that ties it to Israel, and what theoretical framework can be used to explore this relationship. The language of political obligation raised the hope that political theory could provide a starting point for working out the complexities of a relationship that involved obligations and had clear political aspects to it, but was characterized by a transnational geography spreading across a Diaspora and involving a specific state. The political obligation literature provided some headway, but it became clear very quickly that because of its state-centric focus, this language of political theory was not appropriate.

At issue is a kind of obligatory framework that is difficult to explain. The closest that we have in political theory to explaining this kind of commitment is in Marxism, where state does not matter and class does instead. However, as neither class nor historical materialism, let alone ideological commitments, are the relevant factors here a different theoretical framework is required. Turning to political obligation made it possible to work out some of the underlying features of this relationship without having to adopt or begin with an uncritical acceptance of Zionist narratives or alternative normative positions. Political obligation made it possible to highlight the problematic nature of this relationship, as it is not statist but is nevertheless characterized by political relations and expectations of obligations. Moreover, by working out critically some of the unaddressed but underlying assumptions that guide theories of political obligation, in particular the role of power, this approach opened up new avenues for thinking about the

Diaspora/Israel relationship. Moreover, beginning with political obligation was useful, because it avoided both having to take Zionist claims for granted, and beginning by challenging normative beliefs about what it means to be a Diaspora Jew. What this path enabled is the idea that the relationship can be explained by what I have called a transnational political obligation.

A transnational political obligation is different from political obligation in the specific sense that there is no state that one is morally obligated to. In its place is a different locus of politics, one characterized by the power of people coming together in public in pursuit of a common cause, the power that informs and shapes the construction of individual identity, and the way in which this construction in turn shapes the conditions of possibility for behavior and belief. Transnational political obligations exist when:

- A transnational or diaspora community acts together out of a shared sense of purpose or identity;
- A transnational or diaspora community is expected to hold a set of political commitments by virtue of its identity;
- A transnational or diaspora community's members act in ways that simultaneously affirm and construct their individual and collective identities;
- The moral obligations are always in a state of contestation, and so debates over authority, tradition and legitimacy are regular points of debate in transnational political obligation;
- The key issues being contested primarily pertain to questions about identity and security, widely construed.

Using this theoretical framework, I have suggested that it is possible to review the Jewish Diaspora's relationship with Israel. The transnational political obligation that Diaspora Jews have with Israel is to have a relationship with Israel. Even those who reject this need to make a case why – because Israel has come to be so important for Diaspora Jewish identity.

Like theories of political obligation, transnational political obligation is about an identity-group and the moral ties that bind this group of people and link them in political activity. Political obligation rarely actually explores identity politics, relying instead on general references to membership and citizenship. Transnational political obligation, however, is all about identity, and the moral commitments that accompany identity-claims and are not a direct product of being a citizen under the spatial restrictions of national sovereignty. I have argued that the transnational political obligations of Diaspora Jewry are not in fact to support the state, but rather that the obligation is to have a relationship with Israel, even if the relationship is dysfunctional or one to avoid.

The point is that to be Jewish involves a relationship with Israel. This is the obligation in exile. Judith Butler notes as much, although she is surprised by how many people assume the relation[1] The assumptions surrounding this kind of connection between being a Jew and Israel provide much of the background in Howard Jacobson's award-winning novel *The Finkler Question*. It is a claim that animates religious and cultural discourses about Jewish peoplehood – and which came up, unsurprisingly, during interviews with employees in the Israeli Ministry of Foreign Affairs. Even when the relationship is marginalized or dismissed and the spatial identifier of Diaspora emphasized, it is still impossible to completely ignore Israel.[2] That Jews who want to have nothing to do with Israel or who are very critical of Israel feel the need to explain their position not solely in terms of a moral political decision but also in terms of Jewish identity is evidence of this obligatory discourse. Just as with the close relationship in political obligation between obedience and resistance so too do we see a similar dynamic being played out here. As the Jewish establishment continues to chant the need to maintain ties between the Diaspora and Israel, those who are critical of these ties are regularly pictured as outcasts, possibly even involved in some of kind of resistance because of their critiques. In the USA, Jews who marched alongside Martin Luther King and fought for civil rights at home have found themselves in a position where supporting Israel means leaving some of these moral values aside.[3]

So far, being able to make this point about obligation may not be that striking to readers familiar with the Jewish Diaspora and Israel. Indeed, many of the themes and examples raised in this book are not new. Most of them were raised in some fashion or other in 1994 in the political commentary and partial autobiography written by the Canadian author and *Habonim* alumnus Mordecai Richler, *This Year in Jerusalem*. Richler writes about the pride that Israel helps Jews to feel, but also expresses anxiety and concern over Israel's future, and some apprehension about what Israel has done to change Jewish identity:

> Certainly Israel is *a* source of Jewish pride, but hardly the only one. For generations, long before Israel was born again, a majority of Diaspora Jews, both Orthodox and secular, took pride in being members of our faith without brandishing it like a baseball bat.[4]

Yet, what a theory of transnational political obligation enables is a deeper critique than those which focus on what it means to be a Zionist today.

This shift of focus is especially important because what is lost in such Zionist debates is that the Diaspora has changed, and that the relationship with Israel is splintering the Diaspora. While many scholars have recognized that Jews in the Diaspora and Jews in Israel are heading in different directions (Richler also notes as much), what is often missed is that part of the reason has to do with how Diaspora Jewry has managed to successfully find a political space for itself in the age of the modern state. Jewish life in the Diaspora is now so strong, that even internal debates about what it means to be Jewish and to be connected to Israel can serve as plot lines in award-winning literature, as is the case in *The Finkler Question*.

There exist wide-ranging views about how Israel matters for Diaspora Jewish identity, and I have suggested that looking at the normative question of how one ought to approach the transnational political obligation to have a relationship with Israel causes the relationship to unravel. What is needed is a new discourse about Jewish identity that brings back the Diaspora into the transstate identity of Jewish peoplehood. It is not that we need to lessen Israel's importance or question it. Rather, we need to explore anew why Jews in the Diaspora are expected to have a relationship with Israel when the answers that Israel ostensibly provided have not been achieved only in Israel, but in the Diaspora also.

Jewish security is largely achievable in the Diaspora. Jews engage in politics, they contribute to culture, and participate in wider public life as Jews and as equal citizens. The main challenge for Jews in the Diaspora is often in maintaining a sense of Jewish community, especially a religious one. It is not as if Diaspora Jewish life is problem-free, but in many ways it is possible to be more culturally Jewish in the Diaspora than in Israel, where in one's daily life no choice is necessary about how to identify as a Jew. The reason debate about Israel is so heated has little to do with Israel itself, but

Conclusion

everything to do with the construction of Diaspora Jewish identity, and of concerns over what it means to be a Diaspora Jew now that the State of Israel exists. But this is a question about critique and identity, and not really about what much of this debate claims to be about, which is Israeli security.

Thus, when the major Jewish organizations raise their concerns about Jewish assimilation and bring up connectivity to Israel, Israel is readily acknowledged to serve as a device to help Jews reconnect with their Jewish identity. Israel is in this sense used in a very technical way, one that is quite curious because it means that Israel is used to strengthen the Diaspora. However, with the exception of Ahad Ha'Am's cultural Zionism, Zionism, especially political Zionism, was not about strengthening the Diaspora but negating it. This drastic revision of political Zionism was necessary because Diaspora Jews were not flocking to Israel and many were quite comfortable where they lived. But Israel's existence necessitated a reaction, and the reason it did so was the way in which a discourse of obligation came to permeate contemporary Diaspora Jewish identity, so that being Jewish obliged one to connect somehow with the Jewish State. There is an obligation in exile, in *galut*, although not because it is exile, but because there is Israel and a Diaspora.

If any of this sounds circular, it should. There is an inevitable circularity that governs the Diaspora's relationship with Israel, but being able to recognize this circularity is important because it makes possible a deeper level of engagement, from whichever direction one chooses to enter the circle. For what is required is not ideology, not certainty, but, in a traditional Jewish sense, a will to ask questions and to rarely be satisfied with the answer, to revel in critique and commentary, and to continue to explore the conditions that we find ourselves in and that we simultaneously produce.

In the process of researching this book, I heard many times how Diaspora Jews would all too often leave their values at the door when it came to Israel. For example, I heard concerns about how Canadian Jews were losing their moral character in their nearly unquestioned support for Israel, and about how the uncritical support for Israel by Stephen Harper, Canada's Conservative Prime Minister, has made him a friend of previously socially liberal Jews. In this sense, Israel is playing the part of an ideational political drive that displaces other interests, similar in structure to those who vote against their material interests in favour of ideological or faith-based commitments that politicians are not actually able to deliver.[5] I do not know whether, empirically speaking, any of this is true. I do not know how Jews will vote in the next Canadian election. But I do know that debate and concern on these points exist, and that they really matter to those who discuss them.

What I have tried to do is not just contribute to an understanding of these conditions, but also to set out a theoretical terrain that enables a critical engagement with them. It is in this regard that Arendt is so important, although not for the reasons for which she is usually turned to. The lengthy exploration of Arendt's thought on power identifies distinctions that are crucial to questioning the contemporary character of the Diaspora/Israel relationship.

First, by pointing to a different way of understanding power, it is possible to engage with the Diaspora/Israel relationship without having to buy into a statist account of power and political space that, once accepted, silences competing visions. In other words, if we understand power in the Weberian sense, there is no place for critique or for the Diaspora. All that matters is which actor is more powerful in its ability to force the other to submit, and according to the rules of this game the Diaspora will lose. So long as the Diaspora matters, we need to think differently about power and politics lest the Diaspora relegate itself to a dustbin of political irrelevance.

Second, Arendt's distinctions, which she makes in her discussion about power, also matter because they help us to know which questions we should be asking. She directs us to inquire into the practices, locations and constructions of authority and tradition, into how they function and their absences. Third, the Arendtian method of enquiring into what is forgotten also matters, by revealing that it is possible to think differently, and that it is only by forgetting different possibilities that the present begins to make sense. Yet, what kind of sense is this if it is based on collective amnesia? Arendt encourages us to ask this question, and to explore the limits of critique.

To conclude, I am going to go back to how I started this book, with a personal reflection. It is April 15, 2013. I just got back from a Yom Hatzmaut celebration in Ra'anana. I wonder, do all these people here realize that what they are celebrating, in fact what they are living, matters so much to the Jewish world? Israel is, as many people will attest, one of the greatest achievements in Jewish history. These Israelis are living this achievement. Their lives mean something to the Diaspora that most of them would not be aware of, let alone care about. It is a huge burden to place on these people, that every day they live and sustain the Israeli state they are playing a role for an entire people. It seems unfair.

There is little debate in Israel about its relationship with the Diaspora, although this may be changing.[6] Nevertheless, in a sense the relationship is one-sided. As Diaspora Jews continue to explore their relationship with Israel, will Israel do the same? And is the Diaspora comfortable with the one-sided character of the relationship? Should the Diaspora uncritically accept the Israelization of Diaspora Jewish identity, when there is no Diasporization of contemporary Israeli identity? Indeed, this very phrase, the Diasporization of contemporary Israeli identity, seems absurd. Yet, perhaps that is exactly what is needed. Perhaps what is required is not just that Jews in the Diaspora engage with what it means to have an obligation to connect with, to have a relationship with, Israel, but that, in looking to the Diaspora, Israelis ask this question too.

Appendix

What follows is a complete list of all those interviewed, along with copies of the different informed consent forms used. The variation is due to my having been at different institutions over the course of this project, and due to different legal guidelines operating at different times. It was not always possible to provide all participants with the forms, and in some cases, the interviewees were uninterested in the informed consent requirements. In all cases, however, a verbal explanation of the terms of the informed consent agreement was made.

Full list of interviews:
Anonymous 1 (August 16, 2012) New York.
Anonymous 2 (September 3, 2008) New York.
Anonymous 3 (April 18, 2013) Jerusalem.
Anonymous 4 (September 15, 2008) New York.
Anonymous 5 (February 19, 2014) Vancouver (group discussion)
Anonymous 6 (April 5, 2011) London.
Anonymous 7 (April 8, 2011) London.
Anonymous 8 (April 5, 2011) London.
Anonymous 9 (April 5, 2011) London.
Anonymous 10 (April 17, 2013) Jerusalem.
Anonymous 11 (April 18, 2013) Jerusalem.
Bayfield, Tony (April 7, 2011) London.
Barker, Jacob (May 24, 2008) Vancouver [Mr Barker also participated in subsequent informal conversations that were not recorded].
Bayme, Steven (September 3, 2008) New York.
Ben-Moreh, Martin (April 11, 2013) Tel Aviv.
Benamy, Talia (August 14, 2012) New York.
Benjamin, Jon (April 4, 2011) London.
Berger, Miriam (April 7, 2011) London.
Berman, Saul J. (September 2, 2008) London.
Boyd, Jonathan (April 5, 2011) London [I subsequently spoke with

Appendix

Dr Boyd about this project in multiple conversations that were not recorded].
Brechner, Harry (May 30, 2008) Victoria, BC, Canada [Rabbi Brechner participated in subsequent informal and unrecorded discussions].
Brom, Shlomo (April 10, 2013) Tel Aviv.
Davids, Andrew (August 29, 2008) New York.
Dorfman, Aaron (August 14, 2012) New York.
Epstein, Jerome (September 3, 2008) New York.
Friedrichs, Jonathan (May 27, 2008) Vancouver.
Goldberg, J. J. (February 13, 2009) (August 15, 2012) New York.
Goldstein, Aaron (April 6, 2011) London.
Gordon, Jeremy (April 5, 2011) London.
Horowitz, Bethamie (February 13, 2009) New York [Dr Horowtiz participated in subsequent informal and unrecorded discussions].
Holtz, Barry (February 19, 2009) New York.
Joselow, Ethan (May 24, 2008) Vancouver (resident of Washington DC).
Kahn-Harris, Keith (April 5, 2011) London.
Kedar, Shelley (April 14, 2013) Tel Aviv.
Kopp, Jonathan (August 16, 2012) New York.
Lepow, Jesse (September 2, 2008) New York.
Lis, Doron (September 1, 2008) New York (resident of Vancouver) [Mr Lis also participated in subsequent informal conversations that were not recorded].
Marcus, Barry (April 4, 2011) London.
Rich, Danny (April 7, 2011) London.
Twersky, David (September 2, 2008) New York.
Weiner, Chaim (April 4, 2011) London.
Wernick, Steven (August 22, 2012) New York.
Weinstein, Barbara (August 17, 2012) Washington DC (video conference from New York).

INFORMED CONSENT

This form is to make sure that as a participant in this academic research project you are fully aware of what the project involves and consent to being interviewed as part of this research project.

This research project explores the relationship between the Jewish Diaspora and Israel. The focus of the project is on how an account of obligation can help make sense out of the spatial, security and ideational ties that contribute toward the role that Israel plays in the construction of contemporary Jewish identity in the Diaspora. These interviews are concerned with exploring the [Diaspora or Israeli] perspective on the (political) connection between Diaspora

Jews and Israel. Topics of relevance that may be discussed include but are not limited to Jewish identity, Israel/Diaspora relations, Israel's security, the security of the Jewish people, the security of the state where Diaspora Jews reside, their duties, obligations, loyalties and/or allegiances as Jews and citizens toward Israel.

By signing and dating this document you agree with the following:

- The research project has been satisfactorily explained to you;
- You are familiar with the general aims of the research project;
- That you are participating voluntary;
- That you may at any time during the interview end the interview and withdraw from the research project;
- After the completion of the interview, you may decide, for any reason, to withdraw from the research project and have all data collected as a part of the interview deleted *provided* that such a request is made in writing, either by email or post, within one month of the interview date;*
- That your participation in the research project is restricted to being interviewed;
- That personal information will be treated as strictly confidential and will not be made publicly available;
- If recorded, and if requested by you, the recording of the interview will remain anonymous;
- That you agree to data emerging from this interview to be used in the production of research papers/monographs that will be submitted for publication and/or presented at academic conferences.

Please mark the appropriate box:

- Do you agree to a possible follow-up interview, if possible, at a date to be jointly scheduled:
  Yes ☐   No ☐

- Do you agree to the interview being recorded:
  Yes ☐   No ☐

- Do you request anonymity:
  Yes ☐   No ☐

- Are your views those of yourself or are you speaking on behalf of an organization or someone else:
  Yourself ☐   Organization/Someone else ☐
  Who: _____

  Both ☐ (depending on context)

Printed name of Interview participant: _____
Signature of Interview participant: _____
                                    Date: _____

Name of Interviewer: <u>Dr Ilan Zvi Baron</u>
Signature of Interviewer: _____
                                    Date: _____

(If recorded – Audio file name:)

Interview conducted in:
City: _____
Country: _____
Date: _____

* Requests made after this time has past will be considered *provided* that relevant material has *not* been submitted for publication or already been published or submitted as a working paper as part of a conference proceeding.

INFORMED CONSENT

This form is to make sure that as a participant in this academic research project you are fully aware of what the project involves and consent to being interviewed as part of this research project.

This research project explores the spatial linkages between identity and security. These interviews are concerned with how Diaspora Jews understand the connection (if there is one) between their Jewish identity, the State of Israel, and the security dynamics pertaining to: their Jewish identity, Israel's security, the security of the Jewish people, the security of the state where they reside, their duties, obligations, loyalties and/or allegiances as Jews and citizens.

By signing and dating this document you agree with the following:

- The research project has been satisfactorily explained to you;
- You are familiar with the general aims of the research project;
- That you are participating voluntarily;
- That you may at any time during the interview end the interview and withdraw from the research project;
- After the completion of the interview, you may decide, for any reason, to withdraw from the research project and have all data collected as a part of the interview deleted *provided* that such a request is made in writing, either by email or post, within one month of the interview date;*
- That your participation in the research project is restricted to being interviewed;
- That personal information will be treated as strictly confidential and will not be made publicly available;
- If recorded, and if requested by you, the recording of the interview will remain anonymous;
- That you agree to data emerging from this interview to be used in the production of research papers/monographs that will be submitted for publication and/or presented at academic conferences.

Please mark the appropriate box:

- Do you agree to a possible follow-up interview, if possible, at a date to be jointly scheduled:
  Yes ☐   No ☐

- Do you agree to the interview being recorded:
  Yes ☐   No ☐

- Do you request anonymity:
  Yes ☐   No ☐

- Are your views those of yourself or are you speaking on behalf of an organization or someone else:
  Yourself ☐   Organization/Someone else ☐
  　　　　　　　Who: _____

  Both ☐ (depending on context)

Appendix

Printed name of Interview participant: _____
Signature of Interview participant: _____
                                    Date: _____

Name of Interviewer: <u>Dr Ilan Zvi Baron</u>
Signature of Interviewer: _____
                                    Date: _____

(If recorded – Audio file name:)

Interview conducted in:
City: _____
Country: _____
Date: _____

* Requests made after this time has past will be considered *provided* that relevant material has *not* been submitted for publication or already been published or submitted as a working paper as part of a conference proceeding.

CONSENT FORM

Title of Project: "Why Occupy a Square? 18 Days in Cairo"
Name of Researchers: Dr Jeroen Gunning and Dr Ilan Baron

Please initial box

1. I confirm that I have read and understand the information sheet dated 18 May 2011 for the above project and its aims	
2. I have had the opportunity to consider the information and ask any questions	
3. I understand that my participation is voluntary and that I am free to withdraw at any time without giving any reason	
4. I consent to the interview being audio recorded on the understanding that the recordings will be stored securely and will only be accessible to those working on the project	
5. I understand that my data will be treated as strictly confidential and will only be accessed by those working on the project and not be made available to third parties	
6. I request that my data will be anonymised prior to publication/ will *not* be anonymised prior to publication (ie you will be referred to with your full name). Please delete as appropriate	
7. I agree to the publication of verbatim quotes or references to the content of this interview in research papers, books or articles emerging from this project	
8. I agree to the transfer of my data (by those working on the project) to countries outside the European Economic Area	
9. I am willing to be contacted in the future regarding this project/ future projects	
10. I agree to be interviewed for the above project	

Name of Participant   Signature   Date

Name of Researchers   Signatures   Date

Notes

Introduction

1 Whenever I am referring specifically to the Jewish Diaspora, an upper case "D" will be used. References to the concept more generally will use a lower case "d."
2 Peter Beinart, "The Failure of the American Jewish Establishment," *New York Review of Books*, June 10, 2010.
3 Ibid.
4 Yosef Grodzinsky, *In the Shadow of the Holocaust: The Struggle between Jews and Zionists in the Aftermath of World War II* (Monroe, ME: Common Courage Press, 2004).
5 Hilary Rose and Steven Rose, "Stephen Hawking's Boycott Hits Israel Where It Hurts: Science," *The Guardian*, May 13, 2013; "Stephen Hawking Boycotts Major Israeli Conference," BBC, http://www.bbc.co.uk/news/uk-22446054, accessed January 30, 2014.
6 S. W. Hawking, *A Brief History of Time: From the Big Bang to Black Holes* (New York: Bantam, 1988, 1996), 1.
7 Quoted in J. J. Goldberg, *Jewish Power: Inside the American Jewish Establishment* (Reading, MA and Harlow: Addison-Wesley, 1996), 134.
8 Naomi W. Cohen, *American Jews and the Zionist Idea* ([New York]: Ktav, 1975), 139.
9 Ibid.
10 Goldberg, *Jewish Power*, 135.
11 Ibid.
12 Haim Hillel Ben-Sasson, *A History of the Jewish People* (London: Weidenfeld & Nicolson, 1976), 1096.
13 Ofira Seliktar, *Divided We Stand: American Jews, Israel, and the Peace Process* (Westport, CT: Praeger, 2002).
14 Stephen J. Whitfield, "Declarations of Independence: American Jewish Culture in the Twentieth Century," in *Cultures of the Jews: Modern Encounters*, ed. David Biale (New York: Schocken Books, 2002), 414.

15 Goldberg, *Jewish Power*.
16 Related quantitative research texts that, although dated in some respects, examine the different ways in which American Diaspora Jews understand their relationship with Israel are: Steven Martin Cohen, *American Modernity and Jewish Identity* (New York and London: Tavistock, 1983); Charles S. Liebman and Steven Martin Cohen, *Two Worlds of Judaism: The Israeli and American Experiences* (New Haven, CT: Yale University Press, 1990).
17 David Vital, *The Future of the Jews: A People at the Crossraods?* (Cambridge, MA: Harvard University Press, 1990), 47.
18 See also Ilan Zvi Baron, "Diasporic Security and Jewish Identity," *Modern Jewish Studies* 13, 2 (2014).
19 Vital, *The Future of the Jews*, 46.
20 "Israeli Ministry of Foreign Affairs," http://www.mfa.gov.il/MFA/Foreign+Relations/Israel+Among+the+Nations/ISRAEL+AMONG+THE+NATIONS-+World+Jewry.htm, accessed October 22, 2012. [Webpage no longer online.]
21 The term used to refer to Jewish immigration into Israel. It literally means to ascend.
22 Cnann Liphshiz, "Natan Sharansky to Haaretz: Assimilation Is 'Eating' the Jews," *Haaretz*, November 6, 2009.
23 Ilene Prusher, "Jewish Agency Chairman: No Women of the Wall Arrests Next Month," *Haaretz*, November 11, 2013, http://www.haaretz.com/jewish-world/jewish-ga/jewish-ga-news-and-features/.premium-1.557505, accessed January 23, 2014. "Women of the Wall," http://womenofthewall.org.il, accessed January 23, 2014.
24 Vital, *The Future of the Jews*, 89. Emphasis added.
25 Ibid.
26 Ibid., 42.
27 Ibid.
28 Donniel Hartman, *The Boundaries of Judaism* (London and New York: Continuum, 2007), 170.
29 Ibid., 178.
30 Ibid., 1.
31 Ibid., 6.
32 Michel Foucault, *The History of Sexuality: An Introduction*, trans. Robert Hurley, Vol. 1 (New York: Vintage Books, 1990), 89.
33 Ibid., 88–9.
34 See Jonathan Boyarin and Daniel Boyarin, *Powers of Diaspora: Two Essays on the Relevance of Jewish Culture* (Minneapolis, MN and London: University of Minnesota Press, 2002); Judith Butler, *Parting Ways: Jewishness and the Critique of Zionism* (New York: Columbia University Press, 2012).
35 Noam Pianko, *Zionism and the Roads Not Taken: Rawidowicz,*

Kaplan, Kohn (Bloomington, IN: Indiana University Press; Chesham: Combined Academic [distributor], 2010).
36 Vital, *The Future of the Jews*, 103.
37 Ibid., 43.
38 See Goldberg, *Jewish Power*. See also David Biale, *Power and Powerlessness in Jewish History* (New York: Schocken Books, 1986).
39 Vital, *The Future of the Jews*, 89.
40 Ibid., 44.
41 J. J. Goldberg, "Prisoner X Case Signals Moment of Crisis for Israel and Jewish Diaspora: Israel Isolation Spawns 'Dual Loyalty' Charge Worldwide," *The Jewish Daily Forward*, March 1, 2013. (Pub. February 26, 2013).
42 Ibid.
43 Hody Nemes, "Feud over Israel Erupts at Jewish Institutions," *The Jewish Daily Forward*, February 26, 2014.
44 Ibid.
45 Steven Wernick, interview by Ilan Zvi Baron and Yael Baron, August 22, 2012, New York.
46 "About Taglit Birthright," http://www.birthrightisrael.com/Taglit BirthrightIsraelStory/Pages/default.aspx, accessed October 17, 2012. A study based on the 1990 National Jewish Population Survey which explores and confirms the thesis that American Jews who travel to Israel on education trips remain better connected to their Jewish history, to Israel and to the future of the Jewish people is David Mittelberg, *The Israel Connection and American Jews* (Westport, CT and London: Praeger, 1999).
47 Pew Research Center, "A Portrait of Jewish Americans," in *Pew-Templeton Global Religious Futures Project* (October 2013).
48 Bethamie Horowitz, "And Now for Some Good News About the Pew Survey," *The Jewish Daily Forward*, 2013.
49 Jerry Silverman and Michael Siegal, "4 Things to Do About Pew Survey Findings on #Jewishamerica," ibid. The Jewish Federation also compiled a list of media coverage of the survey: "The Federation Connection: Media Coverage of the Pew Study," The Jewish Federations of North America, http://www.jewishfederations.org/blog_post.aspx?id=7314, accessed January 20, 2014.
50 David Graham and Jonathan Boyd, "Committed, Concerned and Conciliatory: The Attitudes of Jews in Britain," (London: Institute for Jewish Policy Research, 2010), 3.
51 Pianko, *Zionism and the Roads Not Taken*, 2.
52 Howard Jacobson, *The Finkler Question* (London: Bloomsbury, 2010), 25.
53 Anonymous 1, interview by Ilan Zvi Baron and Yael Baron, August 16, 2012, New York.

54 Talia Benamy, interview by Ilan Zvi Baron and Yael Baron, August 14, 2012, New York.
55 Jacobson, *The Finkler Question*, 24.
56 Ibid., 25.
57 Ibid.
58 Ibid., 118.
59 Ibid., 189.
60 http://www.campus-watch.org
61 Norman G. Finkelstein, *Beyond Chutzpah: On the Misuse of Anti-Semitism and the Abuse of History* (Berkeley, CA: University of California Press, 2005), 17.
62 Alan Dershowitz, "Is Norman Finkelstein in Tehran?," *The Huffington Post*, December 12, 2006.
63 John K. Wilson to Academe Blog, June 8, 2012, http://academeblog.org/2012/06/08/an-interview-with-alan-dershowitz/, accessed January 20, 2014.
64 Ilan Zvi Baron, "Not My Grandfather's Israel: The Growing Racism of the Modern Israeli Public," *Tikkun Daily* (2012).
65 MITVIM: The Israeli Institute for Regional Foreign Policies, "Findings of a Mitvim Poll on Israel's Foreign Policy" (Ramat Gan: MITVIM, 2013).
66 The extremity of views in the Diaspora is unsurprising. Diaspora, exile and migrant communities often take more extreme positions regarding the homeland than do those that live there. Robin Cohen, *Global Diasporas: An Introduction*, 2nd edn (London: Routledge, 2008); Gabriel Sheffer, *Diaspora Politics: At Home Abroad* (Cambridge: Cambridge University Press, 2003); Yossi Shain, *Kinship and Diasporas in International Affairs* (Ann Arbor, MI: University of Michigan Press, 2007); Paul Hockenos, *Homeland Calling: Exile Patriotism and the Balkan Wars* (Ithaca, NY and London: Cornell University Press, 2003).
67 Norman G. Finkelstein, *Knowing Too Much: Why the American Jewish Romance with Israel Is Coming to an End* (New York and London: OR Books, 2012).
68 Gershom Gorenberg, *The Unmaking of Israel* (New York: Harper, 2011).
69 Beinart, "The Failure of the American Jewish Establishment."
70 Ilan Zvi Baron, "The Problem of Dual Loyalty," *Canadian Journal of Political Science* 42, 4 (2009).
71 Paul Koring, "Canadian Passports: The Disguise of Choice for International Dirty Deeds," *The Globe and Mail*, February 5, 2013.
72 Goldberg, "Prisoner X Case Signals Moment of Crisis for Israel and Jewish Diaspora."
73 Irving M. Zeitlin, *Jews: The Making of a Diaspora People* (Cambridge: Polity, 2012).

74 Ben Zion Dinur, *Israel and the Diaspora* (Philadelphia, PA: Jewish Publication Society of America, 1969), 186.
75 Eliezer Schweid, "The Rejection of the Diaspora in Zionist Thought: Two Approaches," *Studies in Zionism* 5, 1 (1984). Repr. in Jehuda Reinharz and Anita Shapira, *Essential Papers on Zionism* (London: Cassell, 1996), 133–60.
76 Arnold Eisen, *Galut: Modern Jewish Reflection on Homelessness and Homecoming* (Indianapolis, IN: Indiana University Press, 1986).
77 Herbert Butterfield, *The Whig Interpretation of History* (New York and London: Norton, 1965).
78 Caryn Aviv and David Shneer, *New Jews: The End of the Jewish Diaspora* (New York: New York University Press, 2005).
79 See Simon Rabinovitch, *Jews & Diaspora Nationalism: Writings on Jewish Peoplehood in Europe and the United States* (Hanover, NH: University Press of New England, 2012), 23–44.
80 Martin Sicker, *Judaism, Nationalism, and the Land of Israel* (Boulder, CO: Westview Press, 1992), 124. A history of Jewish nationalism up to 1917 is David Aberbach, *Jewish Cultural Nationalism: Origins and Influences* (London: Routledge, 2008). See also Simon Dubnow, *Nationalism and History: Essays on Old and New Judaism* (New York: Meridian Books, 1958).
81 Inderpal Grewal, *Transnational America: Feminisms, Diasporas, Neoliberalisms* (Durham, NC: Duke University Press, 2005), 10.
82 David Ward, "Bradford MP Condemns Israel for Treatment of Palestinians," http://davidward.org.uk/en/article/2013/654457/bradford-mp-condemns-israel-for-treatment-of-palestinians-on-the-day-he-signs-the-holocaust-memorial-day-book-of-commitment, accessed February 7, 2013. [This webpage has since been removed.]
83 Alda Edemariam, "David Ward: 'The Solid Ground I Stand on Is That I Am Not a Racist,'" *The Guardian*, February 6, 2013.
84 Jasmin Habib, *Israel, Diaspora and the Routes of National Belonging* (Toronto: University of Toronto Press, 2004), 160.
85 Jennifer Lipman, "David Ward Digs Deeper, Backed by Chomsky," *The Jewish Chronicle*, February 11, 2013. Jews have also made such claims, but of course it is different when Jews do it, just as it is different when First Nations peoples in Canada call themselves Indian or when African Americans use the word "nigger." Jerry Seinfeld once used this problematic as the punchline for an episode of his TV show, in which a dentist, who is not Jewish, converts for the jokes because that way he can make Jewish jokes without being anti-Semitic.
86 The Church of Scotland also came into a related controversy when it published a report that suggested that the Church boycott Israel; it questioned the extent of the religious connection between the Jews and the land of Israel, and suggested that some Jews view the right to the land in Israel as a form of compensation for the Holocaust. JTA,

"Church of Scotland Backs Away Denial of Jewish Claim to Land of Israel," *The Jewish Daily Forward*, May 11, 2013.
87 Peter Beinart, *The Crisis of Zionism* (New York: Times Books, 2012). There is also the related argument that it is wrong to expect Israel to act to a higher standard than any other country would, a view that tries to establish a kind of moral equivalence ("I may be just as bad as anyone else, so why pick on me and not them?"), which is a problem in its own right. It also uncritically accepts a moral realism that understands the relations between states to be based on power politics. The most famous articulation of this view of international affairs is Hans J. Morgenthau, *Politics among Nations: The Struggle for Power and Peace*, ed. Kenneth W. Thompson and W. David Clinton, 7th edn (London: McGraw-Hill, 2006). This is a view that has been exceptionally influential and has also been widely critiqued in the IR literature. The idea that Israel should not be held to the same standard as any other country is questioned by Jay Michaelson, "There's a Good Reason for 'Singling out' Israel," *The Jewish Daily Forward*, January 25, 2014.
88 Butler, *Parting Ways*.
89 Lisa Moses Leff, *Sacred Bonds of Solidarity: The Rise of Jewish Internationalism in Nineteenth-Century France* (Stanford, CA: Stanford University Press, 2006).
90 Yossi Shain, "Ethnic Diasporas and U.S. Foreign Policy," *Political Science Quarterly* Winter, 5 (1994–5); *Kinship and Diasporas in International Affairs*; "Ethnic Diasporas and U.S. Foreign Policy;" Yossi Shain and Aharon Barth, "Diasporas and International Relations Theory," *International Organization* 57, 3 (2003); Yossi Shain and Barry Bristman, "Diaspora, Kinship and Loyalty: The Renewal of Jewish National Security," *International Affairs* 78, 1 (2002).
91 "Diaspora, Kinship and Loyalty," 77.
92 Ibid., 78.
93 Shain and Barth, "Diasporas and International Relations Theory," 93.
94 Butler, *Parting Ways*, 3.
95 Aviv and Shneer, *New Jews*.
96 Jacqueline Rose, *The Question of Zion* (Princeton, NJ: Princeton University Press, 2005).
97 John Rose, *The Myths of Zionism* (London: Pluto Press, 2004); Max Blumenthal, *Goliath: Life and Loathing in Greater Israel* (New York: Nation Books, 2013).
98 Rose, *The Question of Zion*.
99 Max Weber, *The Methodology of the Social Sciences*, trans. Henry A. Finch and Edward Albert Shils (London: Transaction, 2011 [1949]), 72.

100 Ibid. Emphasis in original.
101 Wolfgang J. Mommsen, *The Political and Social Theory of Max Weber: Collected Essays* (Cambridge: Polity, 1992, 1989), 122.
102 In the field of international relations this turn is often identified by pointing to a distinction between understanding and explaining. See Martin Hollis and Steve Smith, *Explaining and Understanding International Relations* (Oxford: Clarendon Press, 1990).
103 Michael J. Shapiro, "Metaphor in the Social Sciences," in *Michael J. Shapiro: Discourse, Culture, Violence*, ed. Terrell Carver and Samuel A. Chambers (New York: Routledge, 2012), 16–17.
104 Aviv and Shneer, *New Jews*, 137.
105 Ibid., 141.
106 I had contacted AIPAC repeatedly prior to both American field trips, but they never returned my requests for an interview.
107 Karpf et al., *A Time to Speak Out*.
108 Janet Smith, "Finding Israel's Finest Export," *The Georgia Straight*, February 13–20, 2014.
109 Clifford Geertz, *The Interpretation of Cultures: Selected Essays* (New York: Basic Books, 2000 [1973]).
110 James Clifford and George E. Marcus, *Writing Culture: The Poetics and Politics of Ethnography* (Berkeley, CA and London: University of California Press, 2010).
111 George Klosko, *Political Obligations* (Oxford: Oxford University Press, 2005).
112 A more detailed exploration that helps to locate Arendt's work in its Jewish context, including her critiques of Zionism, is Richard J. Bernstein, *Hannah Arendt and the Jewish Question* (Cambridge, MA: MIT Press, 1996).

Chapter 1: The Limits of Political Obligation

1 Jonathan Frankel, *The Damascus Affair: "Ritual Murder," Politics, and the Jews in 1840* (Cambridge: Cambridge University Press, 1997).
2 Robin Cohen, "Diasporas and the Nation-State: From Victims to Challengers," *International Affairs* 72, 3 (1996): 510.
3 Baron, "The Problem of Dual Loyalty."
4 For an introduction to political obligation see Dudley Knowles, *Political Obligation: A Critical Introduction* (London: Routledge, 2010).
5 Richard Dagger, "Political Obligation," in *Stanford Encylcopedia of Philosophy*, ed. Edward N. Zalta, Uri Nodelman, and Colin Allen (Stanford, CA: The Metaphysics Research Lab, Stanford University, 2010).

6. George Klosko, "Multiple Principles of Political Obligation," *Political Theory* 32, 6 (2004).
7. John Horton, *Political Obligation*, 2nd edn (Basingstoke: Palgrave Macmillan, 2010), 1–2.
8. Ibid., 135.
9. Ibid.
10. Ibid., 51.
11. On consent and political obligation see Harry Beran, *The Consent Theory of Political Obligation* (London, New York and Sydney: Croom Helm, 1987).
12. Ronald Dworkin, "The Original Position," in *Reading Rawls: Critical Studies on Rawls' A Theory of Justice*, ed. Norman Daniels (Oxford: Basil Blackwell, 1975).
13. Horton, *Political Obligation*, 146.
14. Ibid., 148.
15. Ibid.
16. Ibid., 149.
17. Klosko, "Multiple Principles of Political Obligation;" *Political Obligations*.
18. H. L. A. Hart, "Are There Any Natural Rights?," *The Philosophical Review* 4, 2 (April 1955): 175–91.
19. George Klosko, *The Principle of Fairness and Political Obligation*, new edn (Lanham, MD and Oxford: Rowman & Littlefield, 2004), xi.
20. Hanna Pitkin, "Obligation and Consent – I," *The American Political Science Review* 59, 4 (1965): 991.
21. Klosko, *Political Obligations*.
22. Margaret Gilbert, *A Theory of Political Obligation: Membership, Commitment, and the Bonds of Society* (Oxford: Clarendon Press, 2006), 44.
23. Gilbert, *A Theory of Political Obligation*, 95.
24. Hedley Bull, *The Anarchical Society: A Study of Order in World Politics*, 2nd edn (New York: Columbia University Press, 1977, 1995).
25. Gilbert, *A Theory of Political Obligation*, 95.
26. Thomas Hobbes, *Leviathan*, ed. Richard Tuck, rev. student edn (Cambridge: Cambridge University Press, 1996), Ch. 13.
27. Which makes Gilbert's argument an interesting reversal of how the domestic analogy usually functions. On the domestic analogy see Hidemi Suganami, *The Domestic Analogy and World Order Proposals* (Cambridge: Cambridge University Press, 1989).
28. J. J. Goldberg, "David Twersky, Political Journalist and Peace Activist, Dies at 60," *The Jewish Daily Foward*, July 18, 2010.
29. Horton, *Political Obligation*, 151, 52.
30. Gilbert, *A Theory of Political Obligation*, 104.

Notes

31 Ibid.
32 Ibid., 106. Emphasis in original.
33 Ibid., 185.
34 Ibid., 239.
35 Horton, *Political Obligation*, 151–2.
36 Gilbert, *A Theory of Political Obligation*, 209.
37 Richard Dagger, "Membership, Fair Play, and Political Obligation," *Political Studies* 48, 1 (2000): 106.
38 A. John Simmons, "Associative Political Obligations," *Ethics* 106, 2 (1996): 256–7.
39 Ibid., 257.
40 Ibid.
41 Horton, *Political Obligation*, 154.
42 Simmons, "Associative Political Obligations."
43 Who perhaps not coincidentally was also very influential for Hedley Bull, and this may explain the similarity between Gilbert's very brief and Bull's extensive presentation of international society.
44 Hart, "Are There Any Natural Rights?", 180.
45 A. John Simmons, *Moral Principles and Political Obligation* (Princeton, NJ: Princeton University Press, 1980).
46 Gilbert, *A Theory of Political Obligation*, 8, 15–17.
47 Simmons, *Moral Principles and Political Obligation*, 3.
48 Ibid.
49 As famously argued by Martin Wight, "Why Is There No International Theory," *International Relations* 21, 1 (1960).
50 For example, Jean Bethke Elshtain, *Women and War: With a New Epilogue* (London and Chicago, IL: University of Chicago Press, 1995); Will Kymlicka, *Multicultural Odysseys: Navigating the New International Politics of Diversity* (Oxford and New York: Oxford University Press, 2007); John Rawls, *The Law of Peoples; with, "The Idea of Public Reason Revisited"* (Cambridge, MA and London: Harvard University Press, 1999); Michael Walzer, *Just and Unjust Wars: A Moral Argument with Historical Illustrations*, 3rd edn (New York: Basic Books, 2000); *Arguing About War* (New Haven, CT and London: Yale University Press, 2004).
51 Klosko, *Political Obligations*, 21; *The Principle of Fairness and Political Obligation*, 1.
52 *The Principle of Fairness and Political Obligation*, 8.
53 See Richard K. Dagger, "What Is Political Obligation?," *The American Political Science Review* 71, 4 (1977); Carole Pateman, *The Problem of Political Obligation: A Critical Analysis of Liberal Theory* (Chichester: Wiley, 1979); Simmons, *Moral Principles and Political Obligation*; Dagger, "Membership, Fair Play, and Political Obligation."
54 In this regard Klosko is influenced by H. L. A. Hart and John Rawls.

55 Klosko, *The Principle of Fairness and Political Obligation*, 11.
56 Ibid., 12.
57 Ibid., 21.
58 He does acknowledge the difficulty of his liberal theory accurately reflecting government practice, but nevertheless remains committed to this viewpoint, and uses the USA as an example. Ibid., 127–30.
59 Ibid., 21.
60 Quoted in ibid., 33.
61 The fair play principle is also based on practice, which means, according to David Miller, that "in the absence of practice I clearly have no obligation . . . even if the practice would be beneficial to me and others if it did exist . . ." David Miller, "The Ethical Significance of Nationality," *Ethics* 98, 4 (1988): 652. Klosko's many examples touch on this objection.
62 Quoted in Klosko, *The Principle of Fairness and Political Obligation*, 39.
63 Ibid.
64 Ibid., xv, 40. See also pp. 39, 41,43, 113, and 114.
65 *Political Obligations*, 21-2, 26–36, 41.
66 Ibid., 3, 17.
67 Ibid., 20.
68 In the preface to this classic he states how he began thinking about morality and war largely because of the Vietnam War. Walzer, *Just and Unjust Wars*.
69 *Obligations: Essays on Disobedience, War and Citizenship* (Cambridge, MA: Harvard University Press, 1970).
70 These metrics are, at the time of writing, available in the JStor beta search function. In terms of 5-year intervals, the increase in research articles published on political obligation rises in the 1960s and generally kept on increasing until 2006 when a drop in the numbers of research articles published starts. Here is a sampling of the 5-year data: 1946–50, 3023 articles published; 1951–5, 3837 articles published; 1956–60, 4174 articles published; 1961–5, 5194 articles published; 1966–70, 5621 articles published; 1971–5, 6910 articles published; 1976–80, 7889 articles published.
71 Klosko, *Political Obligations*, 3.
72 Immanuel Kant, *Kant: Political Writings*, ed. Hans Reiss, trans. H. B. Nisbet, 2nd edn (Cambridge: Cambridge University Press, 1991), 59.
73 Walzer, *Obligations*, 17.
74 Ibid.
75 Fred Halliday, *Revolution and World Politics: The Rise and Fall of the Sixth Great Power* (New York: Palgrave, 1999).
76 The regularity of international relations is important in the construction of what Brent Steele defines as ontological security. Brent J.

Steele, *Ontological Security in International Relations: Self-Identity and the IR State* (London: Routledge, 2008).
77 He did eventually modify his position. Walzer, *Just and Unjust Wars*; "The Moral Standing of States: A Response to Four Critics," *Philosophy and Public Affairs* 9, 3 (1980); *Arguing About War*.
78 See for example Ania Loomba, *Colonialism/Postcolonialism*, 2nd edn (London: Routledge, 2005); Anne McClintock, Aamir Mufti, and Ella Shohat, *Dangerous Liaisons: Gender, Nations, and Postcolonial Perspectives*, Cultural Politics; V.11 (Minneapolis, MN and London: University of Minnesota Press, 1997).
79 There are many attempts in International Relations to address the question of justice so that it remains consistent with the philosophically liberal discourses behind the modern state. See in particular Andrew Linklater, *Men and Citizens in the Theory of International Relations*, 2nd edn (London: Macmillan in association with London School of Economics and Political Science, 1990); *The Transformation of Political Community: Ethical Foundations of the Post-Westphalian Era* (Oxford: Polity, 1998).
80 Although some have demonstrated an alternative narrative. See in particular Nicholas J. Wheeler, *Saving Strangers: Humanitarian Intervention in International Society* (Oxford: Oxford University Press, 2000).
81 A key text here on the relationship between political theory and international relations is R. B. J. Walker, *Inside/Outside: International Relations as Political Theory* (Cambridge: Cambridge University Press, 1993).
82 Klosko, *Political Obligations*, 162–80.
83 *The Principle of Fairness and Political Obligation*, 71–2.
84 Ibid., 67.
85 *Political Obligations*, 108.
86 Robert E. Goodin, "What Is So Special About Our Fellow Countrymen?," *Ethics* 98, 4 (1988): 682.
87 David Miller, "The Ethical Significance of Nationality," ibid.: 647.
88 Simmons, *Moral Principles and Political Obligation*, 194.
89 Horton, *Political Obligation*.
90 Simmons, *Moral Principles and Political Obligation*, 23.
91 Ibid., 14.
92 Ibid.
93 Ibid.
94 Ibid.
95 Ibid.
96 Ibid.
97 Ibid.
98 Ibid., 15.
99 Ibid.

100 Ibid., 31.
101 Ibid.
102 Ibid., 32.
103 Ibid., 36.
104 Grodzinsky, *In the Shadow of the Holocaust.*
105 Walzer, *Obligations.*
106 See Ilan Zvi Baron, *Justifying the Obligation to Die: War, Ethics and Political Obligation, with Illustrations from Zionism* (Lanham, MD: Lexington Books, 2009).
107 Walzer, *Obligations*, 7.
108 Charles S. Maier, "'Being There:' Place, Territory, and Identity," in *Identities, Affiliations, and Allegiances*, ed. Seyla Benhabib, Ian Shapiro, and Danilo Petranović (Cambridge: Cambridge University Press, 2007).
109 Melissa S. Williams, "Nonterritorial Boundaries of Citizenship," ibid., ed. Seyla Benhabib, Ian Shapiro, and Danilo Petranović, 228.
110 For more on the relationship between transnationalism and cosmopolitanism see Victor Roudometof, "Transnationalism, Cosmopolitanism and Glocalization," *Current Sociology* 53, 1 (2005). It is worth noting here that Roudometof identifies power relations as important in transnationalism, although what he identifies are structural power relations, and not the kind that I explore in the next chapter.
111 Sheffer uses the term "trans-state." Gabriel Sheffer, "Ethno-National Diasporas and Security," *Survival* 36, 1 (1994).
112 Baron, "Diasporic Security and Jewish Identity." The different usage in terms is partly because my thinking on this subject has changed, but also because there is no generally agreed fixed meaning for either. In that article I used "trans-state" because I wanted to emphasize a cross-border dynamic without emphasizing the importance of ethnicity. In this book I have chosen "transnational," because I am engaging with a much wider literature, including the political obligation literature, and this has led me to choose a different term, in no small part for stylistic reasons. Even though I use the term "transnational," I do not mean that the political relations exist across different ethnic national groups, but that they exist across the same group, albeit one located in different states. In this sense, "trans-state" would be a more correct term, even though in the literature "transnational" is used to mean these kinds of cross-border relations among a like-group.
113 Habib, *Israel, Diaspora and the Routes of National Belonging*, 25.
114 Warren Magnusson, *The Search for Political Space* (Toronto: University of Toronto Press, 1996).
115 Pianko, *Zionism and the Roads Not Taken.*
116 Adam Shatz, ed., *Prophets/Outcast: A Century of Dissident Jewish*

Writing About Zionism (New York: Nation Books, 2004); Pianko, *Zionism and the Roads Not Taken*.
117 Hannah Arendt, *The Human Condition* (London and Chicago, IL: Chicago University Press, 1958), 7.

Chapter 2: Power and Obligation

1 Horton, *Political Obligation*.
2 Hannah Arendt, *On Violence* (London: Harcourt Brace, 1970), 6.
3 Clarissa Rile Hayward, "Binding Problems, Boundary Problems: The Trouble with "Democratic Citizenship," in *Identities, Affiliations, and Allegiances*, ed. Seyla Benhabib, Ian Shapiro, and Danilo Petranović (Cambridge: Cambridge University Press, 2007).
4 See in particular Hannah Arendt, *The Promise of Politics*, ed. Jerome Kohn (New York: Schocken Books, 2005); *Jewish Writings*.
5 Bertrand Russell, *Power: A New Social Analysis* (London: Allen & Unwin, 1938), 10.
6 Ibid., 35.
7 Michael Mann, *The Sources of Social Power: A History of Power from the Beginning to A.D. 1760*, vol. 1 (Cambridge: Cambridge University Press, 1986), 7–8.
8 Ibid., 6.
9 Klosko, *Political Obligations*, 21.
10 Ibid.
11 Max Weber, Peter Lassman, and Ronald Speirs, *Political Writings* (Cambridge and New York: Cambridge University Press, 1994), 310. Emphasis in original.
12 Ibid., 310–11.
13 Max Weber, *Economy and Society*, ed. Guenther Roth and Claus Wittich, vol. 1 (Berkeley, CA: University of California Press, 1978); Weber, Lassman, and Speirs, *Political Writings*.
14 Weber, *Economy and Society*, 1, 54. Emphasis in original.
15 Weber, Lassman, and Speirs, *Political Writings*, 311.
16 Ibid.
17 Ibid.
18 Horton, *Political Obligation*.
19 Charles Tilly, "War Making and State Making as Organized Crime," in *Bringing the State Back In*, ed. Peter B. Evans, Dietrich Rueschemeyer, and Theda Skocpol (Cambridge: Cambridge University Press, 1985).
20 Weber, Lassman, and Speirs, *Political Writings*, 311. Emphasis in original.
21 Mommsen, *The Political and Social Theory of Max Weber: Collected Essays*.

22 Weber, Lassman, and Speirs, *Political Writings*, 287.
23 See, Randall Collins, *Weberian Sociological Theory* (Cambridge: Cambridge University Press, 1986).
24 Weber, *Economy and Society*, 1, 53.
25 Magnusson, *The Search for Political Space*, p. 36.
26 Mann, *The Sources of Social Power Vol. 1*, 1, 2.
27 Horton, *Political Obligation*; Klosko, *Political Obligations*; Simmons, *Moral Principles and Political Obligation*.
28 Gilbert, *A Theory of Political Obligation*.
29 Walzer, *Obligations*.
30 Ibid., xii, 7, 9, 10, 11, 12, 13, 15, 16, 19, 21, 22, 24, 27, 30, 31, 35, 36, 37, 48, 52, 54, 61, 62, 63, 70, 71, 72, 75, 82, 83, 87, 89, 99, 105, 205.
31 Ibid., xii, 7, 9, 10, 11, 12, 16, 21, 24, 35, 62, 73, 99, 109, 205.
32 Ibid., 27, 37.
33 Ibid., 31, 175.
34 Robert A. Dahl, "The Concept of Power," *Behavioural Science* 2, 3 (1957).
35 Steven Lukes, *Power: A Radical View*, 2nd edn (Basingstoke and New York: Palgrave Macmillan, 2005).
36 Dahl, "The Concept of Power," 202–3.
37 Lukes, *Power: A Radical View*.
38 Ibid., 21.
39 Ibid., 25.
40 Walzer, *Obligations*, 31, 36, 87, 215.
41 Ibid., 87. See Plato, *The Last Days of Socrates: Euthyphro, Apology, Crito, Phaedo*, trans. Hugh Tredennick and Harold Tarrant (London: Penguin, 2003).
42 Walzer, *Obligations*, 83.
43 Ibid., 222.
44 James Tully, *Public Philosophy in a New Key, Vol. 1.* (Cambridge: Cambridge University Press, 1986): 121.
45 See for example Foucault, *The History of Sexuality: An Introduction*, 1.
46 Jürgen Habermas, "Hannah Arendt's Communications Concept of Power," *Social Research* 44, 1 (1977).
47 John O'Neill, "The Disciplinary Society: From Weber to Foucault," *British Journal of Sociology* 37, 1 (1986).
48 Amy Allen, "Power, Subjectivity, and Agency: Between Arendt and Foucault," *International Journal of Philosophical Studies* 10, 2 (2010).
49 An introduction to the literature is Mark Haugaard, ed., *Power: A Reader* (Manchester and New York: Manchester University Press, 2002).

50 Manuel Castells, *The Power of Identity*, 2nd edn, with a new preface (Oxford: Wiley-Blackwell, 2010), 12.
51 Dahl, "The Concept of Power;" Morgenthau, *Politics among Nations*.
52 Peter Morriss, *Power: A Philosophical Analysis* (Manchester: Manchester University Press, 1987, 2002).
53 Ibid., 13.
54 Ibid.
55 On methodology and the social sciences see Shapiro, "Metaphor in the Social Sciences."
56 Nicos Poulantzas, *State, Power, Socialism* (London: Verso, 2000 [1980]).
57 Anthony Giddens, *The Constitution of Society: Outline of the Theory of Structuration* (Cambridge: Polity, 1984, 1986).
58 Arendt, *The Jew as Pariah*; *Jewish Writings*; Bernstein, *Hannah Arendt and the Jewish Question*.
59 Promise of Politics, 106.
60 See and compare Seyla Benhabib, *The Reluctant Modernism of Hannah Arendt*, new edn (New York: Rowman & Littlefield, 2003); Craig Calhoun and John McGowan, eds, *Hannah Arendt & the Meaning of Politics* (Minneapolis, MN: University of Minnesota Press, 1997); Margaret Canovan, "The Contradictions of Hannah Arendt's Political Thought," *Political Theory* 6, 1 (1978); *Hannah Arendt: A Reinterpretation of Her Political Thought* (Cambridge: Cambridge University Press, 1995); Bonnie Honig, "The Politics of Agonism: A Critical Response to 'Beyond Good and Evil: Arendt, Nietzsche and the Aestheticization of Political Action' by Dana R. Villa," *Political Theory* 21, 3 (1993); Anthony F. Lang Jr. and John Williams, eds, *Hannah Arendt and International Relations: Reading across the Lines* (New York: Palgrave Macmillan, 2005); Walter Laqueur, "The Arendt Cult: Hannah Arendt as Political Commentator," *Journal of Contemporary History* 33, 4 (1998); John McGowan, "Must Politics Be Violent? Arendt's Utopian Vision," in *Hannah Arendt and the Meaning of Politics*, ed. Craig Calhoun and John McGowan (Minneapolis, MN and London: University of Minnesota Press, 1997); Patricia Owens, *Between War and Politics: International Relations and the Thought of Hannah Arendt* (Oxford: Oxford University Press, 2007); Dana Villa, ed., *The Cambridge Companion to Hannah Arendt* (Cambridge: Cambridge University Press, 2000); Elisabeth Young-Bruehl, *Why Arendt Matters* (New Haven, CT and London: Yale University Press, 2006).
61 Habermas, "Hannah Arendt's Communications Concept of Power," 3.
62 Hobbes, *Leviathan*.
63 Jean Bodin and Julian H. Franklin, *On Sovereignty: Four Chapters*

from the Six Books of the Commonwealth (Cambridge: Cambridge University Press, 1992).
64 Arendt, *The Origins of Totalitarianism*, 269–70.
65 Dahl, "The Concept of Power."
66 Arendt, *On Violence*, 38.
67 Bauman, *Modernity and the Holocaust*.
68 Arendt, *The Origins of Totalitarianism*; *Eichmann in Jerusalem: A Report on the Banality of Evil*, rev. and enlarged edn, Penguin Twentieth-Century Classics (New York and London: Penguin, 1994).
69 Some of the IR literature would disagree. See in particular Toni Erskine, ed., *Can Institutions Have Responsibilities?: Collective Moral Agency and International Relations* (Basingstoke: Palgrave Macmillan, 2003). The earlier IR transnationalism literature also would challenge Arendt's argument on this point. See Keohane and Nye, *Transnational Relations in World Politics*.
70 Foucault, *The History of Sexuality: An Introduction*, 1; Michel Foucault and Paul Rabinow, *The Essential Works of Michel Foucault, 1954–1984. Vol. 3, Power* (London: Allen Lane, 2001); Giddens, *The Constitution of Society: Outline of the Theory of Structuration*; Lukes, *Power: A Radical View*.
71 Arendt, *The Human Condition*, 200.
72 Ibid.
73 Ibid., 201.
74 Ibid., 175–6.
75 Ibid., 7.
76 Ibid. Italics in original.
77 *On Violence*, 44.
78 Ibid., 44–5.
79 Talcott Parsons, "On the Concept of Political Power," in *Power: A Reader*, ed. Mark Haugaard (Manchester: Manchester University Press, 2002), 87.
80 Hannah Arendt, *On Revolution* (New York: Penguin Books, 1965), 179.
81 *Between Past and Future: Eight Exercises in Political Thought* (New York: Penguin Books, 2006), 102.
82 *On Violence*, 45.
83 Ibid.
84 *Between Past and Future*, 104.
85 Ibid., 105–6.
86 Ibid., 118.
87 Aristotle, *The Politics and the Constitution of Athens*, ed. Stephen Everson (Cambridge: Cambridge University Press, 1996).
88 Plato, *The Republic of Plato*, trans. Allan Bloom (New York: Basic Books, 1968); *The Laws*, trans. Trevor J. Saunders (London and New York: Penguin Books, 2004).

Notes

89 Non-political in a specific sense that is consistent with Arendt's understanding of politics.
90 Arendt, *Between Past and Future*, 108.
91 Ibid., 109.
92 Ibid., 115–16.
93 See Aristotle, *The Politics*; Arendt, *Between Past and Future*, 116.
94 Aristotle, *The Politics*, 185 (1332b5). p. 185 (1332b5).
95 Ibid., 186 (1332b35).
96 Ibid., 186 (1333a1).
97 Arendt, *Between Past and Future*, 118, 20.
98 Ibid., 122. *Potestas* is also rooted in *possum*. However, *potestas* has more meanings than "potential," for unlike "potential," *potestas* involves legal inferences.
99 Ibid.
100 Between Past and Future, 123.
101 See, Baron, *Justifying the Obligation to Die*.
102 See, Plato, *The Last Days of Socrates*.
103 See, Aristotle, the Politics.
104 Arendt, *The Promise of Politics*, 81.
105 Ibid. See in particular the foreword by Villa. See also Canovan, *Hannah Arendt*.
106 Elisabeth Young-Bruehl, *Hannah Arendt: For Love of the World*, 2nd edn (New Haven, CT and London: Yale University Press, 2004).
107 Hannah Arendt, *The Life of the Mind* (New York: Harcourt, 1978).
108 *The Promise of Politics*, 82.
109 Ibid., 82–3.
110 Ibid., 83.
111 *Between Past and Future*, 136.
112 *On Violence*, 44.
113 Ibid., 52.
114 Owens, *Between War and Politics*. See also Lang Jr. and Williams, *Hannah Arendt and International Relations*.
115 Arendt, *The Promise of Politics*, 93, 95 (emphasis in original).
116 Quoted in *On Violence*, 35.
117 Quoted in ibid.
118 Ibid., 35 6.
119 Ibid., 37.
120 Ibid., 4.
121 Carl von Clausewitz et al., *On War* (Princeton, NJ and Guildford: Princeton University Press, 1976).
122 Arendt, *On Violence*, 56.
123 *The Human Condition*, 202.
124 *On Revolution*, 18,19, 21–58.
125 Canovan, *Hannah Arendt*, 186.
126 Arendt, *On Violence*, 41.

127 See, Lukes, *Power: A Radical View*.
128 Arendt, *On Violence*, 44.
129 Habermas, "Hannah Arendt's Communications Concept of Power," 3.
130 Aristotle, *The Politics*.
131 See in particular all the discriminations required for a life of philosophical contemplation in Plato, *The Republic*.
132 See in particular Simone de Beauvoir, *The Second Sex*, trans. Constance Border and Sheila Malvony-Chevallier (London: Vintage Books, 2009 [1949]).
133 Michel Foucault, *Society Must Be Defended: Lectures at the Collège De France, 1975–76*, ed. Arnold I. Davidson, trans. David Macey (New York: Picador, 2003), 19.
134 Anthony Giddens, *Modernity and Self-Identity: Self and Society in the Late Modern Age* (Cambridge: Polity Press, 1991), 57.
135 Morriss, *Power*, xvi–xvii.
136 Foucault, *Society Must Be Defended*; *The History of Sexuality: An Introduction*, 1; Michel Foucault, Michel Senellart, and Arnold I. Davidson, *Security, Territory, Population: Lectures at the College De France, 1977–78*, Michel Foucault: Lectures at the Collège De France (Basingstoke: Palgrave Macmillan, 2007).
137 Michel Foucault, *Discipline and Punish: The Birth of the Prison*, trans. Alison Sheridan (London: Penguin Books, 1991).
138 Ibid., 170.
139 Ibid.
140 See for example Tim Cole, *Selling the Holocaust: From Auschwitz to Schindler: How History Is Bought, Packaged, and Sold* (New York: Routledge, 1999); Norman G. Finkelstein, *The Holocaust Industry: Reflections on the Exploitation of Jewish Suffering* (London and New York: Verso, 2000); Segev, *The Seventh Million*; Idith Zertal, *Israel's Holocaust and the Politics of Nationhood* (Cambridge: Cambridge University Press, 2005).
141 Cohen, *Global Diasporas: An Introduction*, 9.
142 Stéphane Dufoix, *Diasporas*, trans. William Rodarmor (Berkeley, CA: University of California Press, 2003), 2.
143 See Biale, *Cultures of the Jews*.
144 I am aware of two published versions in English of his governmentality lecture. The older version is in Michel Foucault, *The Essential Works of Michel Foucault, 1954–1984. Vol. 3, Power*. James D. Faubion (ed.), London: Penguin: 201–22. A newer version can be found in Michel Foucault, *Security, Territory, Population: Lectures at the College De France, 1977–78*, Michael Senellart (ed.), Graham Burchell (trans.), New York: Palgrave Macmillan, 2007: 87–114.
145 Foucault, *The History of Sexuality: An Introduction*, 1.
146 Ibid., 86, 87.

147 Ibid., 89.
148 Ibid., 92.
149 Ibid., 93.
150 Ibid., 94.
151 Ibid., 95.
152 Ibid.
153 *Society Must Be Defended*, 29.
154 Lukes, *Power: A Radical View*, 98.
155 Ibid.
156 Ibid., 106. An interesting and related discussion about power and students is Clarissa Riles Hayward, *De-Facing Power* (Cambridge: Cambridge University Press, 2000).
157 Foucault, *The History of Sexuality: An Introduction*, 1, 86.
158 Castells, *The Power of Identity*, 7.
159 Ibid.
160 Ibid., 8.
161 Ibid.
162 Ibid.
163 Josh Nathan-Kazis, "Jews Express Wide Criticism of Israel in the Pew Survey but Leaders Dismiss Findings," *The Jewish Daily Foward*, October 2, 2013.
164 Max Nordau was the Zionist thinker who was the most famous articulator of this identity-type. For more on Nordau, degeneration, race theory, Zionism, and the idea of the Muscle Jew see Todd, Samuel Presner, "'Clear Heads, Solid Stomachs, and Hard Muscles:' Max Nordau and the Aesthetics of Jewish Regeneration," *Modernism/ modernity* 10, 2 (2003). See also Michael Stanislawski, *Zionism and the Fin De Siècle: Cosmopolitanism and Nationalism from Nordau to Jabotinsky* (Berkeley, CA, Los Angeles and London: University of California Press, 2001).
165 Donna Haraway, *Simians, Cyborgs and Women: The Reinvention of Nature* (New York: Routledge, 1991).
166 Ze'ev (Vladimir) Jabotinsky, *Samson*, trans. Cyrus Brooks (New York and Miami: Judea Publishing, 1986). This book was also published as *Judge and Fool* (1930) and *Prelude to Delilah* (1945).
167 Stanislawski, *Zionism and the Fin de Siècle*.
168 Jay Geller, *The Other Jewish Question: Identifying the Jew and Making Sense of Modernity* (New York: Fordham University Press, 2011), 215.
169 Todd Samuel Presner, *Muscular Judaism: The Jewish Body and the Politics of Regeneration* (London and New York: Routledge, 2007), 59.
170 A history of the racialization of the body by Jews is Geller, *The Other Jewish Question*.
171 Presner, *Muscular Judaism*, xvi.

172 Ibid., xvii–xix.
173 Quoted in ibid., 59. The gendered language should be immediately obvious here.
174 Paul Breines, *Tough Jews: Political Fantasies and the Moral Dilemma of American Jewry* (New York: Basic Books, 1990); Warren Rosenberg, *Legacy of Rage: Jewish Masculinity, Violence and Culture* (Amherst, MA: University of Massachusetts Press, 2001).
175 Breines, *Tough Jews*.
176 Quoted in ibid., 173.
177 Ibid., 175.
178 Ibid.; Rosenberg, *Legacy of Rage*.
179 Lukes, *Power: A Radical View*.
180 Arendt, *Eichmann in Jerusalem*.
181 Calhoun and McGowan, *Hannah Arendt and the Meaning of Politics*, 1.
182 Ibid., 9.
183 Arendt, *The Promise of Politics*, 10.
184 Ibid., 106.
185 Martin Ben-Moreh, interview by Ilan Zvi Baron, April 11, 2013, Tel Aviv.
186 Ibid.

Chapter 3: Between Zion and Diaspora: Internationalisms, Transnationalisms, Obligation and Security

1 See, Ben Halpern, "The Americanization of Zionism, 1880–1930," *American Jewish History* 69, 1 (1979). Repr. in Reinharz and Shapira, *Essential Papers on Zionism*, 318–36.
2 Mustapha Kamal Pasha and Craig N. Murphy, eds, *International Relations and the New Inequality* (Oxford: Blackwell Publishing, 2002). One text on colonialism and transnationalism is Masao Miyoshi, "A Borderless World? From Colonialism to Transnationalism and the Decline of the Nation-State," *Critical Inquiry* 19, 4 (1993).
3 This relationship is already evident in the racism that could be found in Enlightenment thought. See Emmanuel Chukwudi Eze, *Race and the Enlightenment: A Reader* (Cambridge: Blackwell, 1997).
4 Leff, *Sacred Bonds of Solidarity*.
5 Frankel, *The Damascus Affair*.
6 Arjun Appadurai, *Modernity at Large: Cultural Dimensions of Globalization* (Minneapolis, MN: University of Minnesota Press, 1996), 19.
7 Kenneth Neal Waltz, *Theory of International Politics*, Addison-Wesley Series in Political Science (Reading, MA, New York and London: Addison-Wesley; McGraw-Hill, 1979).

8 Following convention, I use upper case (International Relations) to refer to the academic field or discipline and lower case (international relations) to refer to the subject. I will be using "international relations" and "international politics" interchangeably in this regard.
9 James N. Rosenau, *The Study of Global Interdependence: Essays on the Transnationalization of World Affairs* (London: Pinter, 1980), 1.
10 Ibid., 13. Reprint of "International Studies in a Transnational World," *Millennium: Journal of International Studies* 5, 1 (1976).
11 Appadurai, *Modernity at Large*, 33.
12 Steven Vertovec, *Transnationalism* (London: Routledge, 2009), 5.
13 See Cohen, *Global Diasporas: An Introduction*.
14 James Clifford, "Diasporas," *Cultural Anthropology* 9, 3 (1994): 322. Emphasis in original.
15 See for example Zygmunt Bauman, *Modernity and the Holocaust* (Ithaca, NY: Cornell University Press, 1991).
16 Appadurai, *Modernity at Large*, 41.
17 Vertovec, *Transnationalism*, 98.
18 Appadurai, *Modernity at Large*, 41. Iris Young's social connection model of responsibility provides another approach that enables a type of moral obligation to cross state borders. Yet because of her critique of Arendt, at this time I am not using her theory of responsibility and justice in the construction of my argument. See Iris Marion Young, *Responsibility for Justice* (Oxford: Oxford University Press, 2011).
19 Morgenthau, *Politics among Nations*.
20 For a related discussion see Patricia Clavin, "Defining Transnationalism," *Contemporary European History* 14, 4 (2005).
21 Robert O. Keohane and Joseph S. Nye, eds, *Transnational Relations in World Politics* (Cambridge, MA: Harvard University Press, 1972), xxiv–xxv.
22 Felix Berenskoetter and Michael J. Williams, eds, *Power in World Politics* (London: Routledge, 2007).
23 Michael Peter Smith and Luis Eduardo Guarnizo, eds, *Transnationalism from Below* (London: Transaction, 1998).
24 Vertovec, *Transnationalism*, 4.
25 Ibid., 3.
26 Peter Jackson, Phil Crang, and Claire Dwyer, *Transnational Spaces* (London: Routledge, 2004).
27 Manuel Castells, *The Rise of the Network Society*, 2nd edn, *The Information Age: Economy, Society and Culture* (Oxford: Blackwell, 2000).
28 Cyrus Ernesto Zirakzadeh, *Social Movements in Politics: A Comparative Study*, expanded edn (Basingstoke: Palgrave Macmillan, 2006); Donatella Della Porta, Hanspeter Kriesi, and Dieter Rucht,

Social Movements in a Globalizing World (Basingstoke: Macmillan, 1999).

29 Alejandro Portes, "Globalization from Below: The Rise of Transnational Communities," in *Latin America in the World Economy*, ed. W. P. Smith and R. P. Korczenwicz (Westport, CT: Greenwood Press, 1996).

30 Rubin Patterson, "Diaspora–Homeland Development," *Social Forces* 84, 4 (2006).

31 Joe Painter, "Multi-Level Citizenship, Identity and Regions in Contemporary Europe," in *Transnational Democracy: Political Spaces and Border Crossings*, ed. James Anderson (London and New York: Routledge, 2002). For an introduction to the contemporary literature on citizenship see Part III (Chs 8–11) in Seyla Benhabib, Ian Shapiro, and Danilo Petranović, eds, *Identities, Affiliations, and Allegiances* (Cambridge: Cambridge University Press, 2007).

32 A useful and very thorough compendium on transnationalism that addresses both migration and diasporas is Steven Vertovec and Robin Cohen, *Migration, Diasporas, and Transnationalism* (Cheltenham: Edward Elgar, 1999).

33 Michael Peter Smith, "Transnationalism and Citizenship," in *Approaching Transnationalisms: Studies on Transnational Societies, Multicultural Contacts, and Imaginings of Home*, ed. Brenda S. A. Yeoh, Michael W. Charney, and Tong Chee Kiong (Boston, Dordecht and London: Kluwer Academic, 2003), 27.

34 Goldberg, *Jewish Power*.

35 Lazar Berman, "US Lawmakers Flocked to Israel in August, Figures Show," *The Times of Israel*, September 25, 2013.

36 Ben Sales, "Naftali Bennett: 'Semi-Citizenship' for Diaspora Jews," *Jewish Telegraphic Agency*, February 17, 2014.

37 Ibid.

38 Ibid. See also Joel Braunold, "Paying for Diaspora Jews Won't Save Israel," *Haaretz*, February 19, 2014.

39 Gershom Gorenberg also emphasizes that the Diaspora has an important role to play in advising Israel, although most likely not in the same way that Bennett has in mind. Gorenberg, *The Unmaking of Israel*.

40 The Editors and Editorial Community, "On Moving Targets," *Public Culture* 2, 1 (1989).

41 Quoted in Vertovec, *Transnationalism*, 12.

42 Rainer Bauböck, "Towards a Political Theory of Migrant Transnationalism," *International Migration Review* 37, 2 (2003): 700.

43 Nina Glick Schiller, Linda G. Basch, and Cristina Blanc-Szanton, *Towards a Transnational Perspective on Migration: Race, Class, Ethnicity, and Nationalism Reconsidered: Workshop: Papers* (New York: New York Academy of Sciences, 1992).

44 See for example Veit Bader, "The Cultural Conditions of Transnational Citizenship: On the Interpretation of Political and Ethnic Cultures," *Political Theory* 25, 6 (1997); Etienne Balibar, "Propositions on Citizenship," *Ethics* 98, 4 (1988); Will Kymlicka, "Immigration, Citizenship, Multiculturalism: Exploring the Links," in *The Politics of Migration: Managing Opportunity, Conflict and Change*, ed. Sarah Spencer (Oxford: Blackwell, 2003); David Thelen, "How Natural Are National and Transnational Citizenship? A Historical Perspective," *Indiana Journal of Global Legal Studies* 7, 2 (2000); Benhabib, Shapiro, and Petranović, *Identities, Affiliations, and Allegiances*.
45 See for example Butler, *Parting Ways*; Anne Karpf et al., eds, *A Time to Speak Out: Independent Jewish Voices on Israel, Zionism and Jewish Identity* (London: Verso, 2008).
46 I do, however, address some of these issues in passing in Baron, "Diasporic Security and Jewish Identity."
47 Michel S. Laguerre, *Diasporic Citizenship: Haitian Americans in Transnational America* (New York: Palgrave Macmillan, 1998).
48 Grewal, *Transnational America*, 12.
49 Leff, *Sacred Bonds of Solidarity*.
50 Hannah Arendt, *The Jew as Pariah*, ed. Ron H. Feldman (New York: Grove Press, 1978); *Jewish Writings*, ed. Jerome Kohn and Ron H. Feldman (New York: Schocken Books, 2007).
51 Habib, *Israel, Diaspora and the Routes of National Belonging*, 4.
52 Leff, *Sacred Bonds of Solidarity*.
53 Ibid.
54 Ibid.
55 Michael Graetz and Jane Marie Todd, *The Jews in Nineteenth-Century France: From the French Revolution to the Alliance Israelite Universelle* (Stanford, CA: Stanford University Press; Cambridge: Cambridge University Press, 1996).
56 On the Damascus Affair see Frankel, *The Damascus Affair*.
57 http://www.aiu.org/
58 Leff, *Sacred Bonds of Solidarity*, 117–53.
59 Ibid., 153.
60 Ibid., 155.
61 Ibid., 159.
62 Ibid., 158.
63 Ibid., 157.
64 Ibid., 182.
65 Cohen, "Diasporas and the Nation-State;" Leff, *Sacred Bonds of Solidarity*. See also Hannah Arendt, *The Origins of Totalitarianism* (London: Deutsch, 1986).
66 See for example Luis Eduardo Guarnizo, Alejandro Portes, and William Haller, "Assimilation and Transnationalism: Determinants

of Transnational Political Action among Contemporary Migrants," *American Journal of Sociology* 108, 6 (2003); M. Kearney, "The Local and the Global: The Anthropology of Globilization and Transnationalism," *Annual Review of Anthropology* 24 (1995); Peggy Levitt and B. Nadya Jaworsky, "Transnational Migration Studies: Past Developments and Future Trends," *Annual Review of Sociology* 33 (2007); José Itzigsohn and Silivia Giorguli Saucedo, "Immigrant Incorporation and Sociocultural Transnationalism," *International Migration Review* 36, 3 (2002); José Itzigsohn, "Immigration and the Boundaries of Citizenship: The Institutions of Immigrants' Political Transnationalism," ibid. 34, 4 (2000); Alejandro Portes, "Conclusion: Theoretical Convergengies and Empirical Evidence in the Sutyd of Immigrant Transnationalism," ibid. 37, 3 (2003); "Globalization from Below;" Nina Glick Schiller, Linda Basch, and Cristina Szanton Blanc, "From Immigrant to Transmigrant: Theorizing Transnational Migration," *Anthropological Quarterly* 68, 1 (1995); Roger Waldinger and David Fitzgerald, "Transnationalism in Question," *American Journal of Sociology* 109, 5 (2004).
67 Steven J. Gold, "Transnationalism and Vocabularies of Motive in International Migration: The Case of Israelis in the United States," *Sociological Perspectives* 40, 3 (1997): 410.
68 Clavin, "Defining Transnationalism," 422.
69 Ibid.
70 Portes, "Conclusion."
71 Gold, "Transnationalism and Vocabularies of Motive in International Migration."
72 Bauböck, "Towards a Political Theory of Migrant Transnationalism," 703.
73 Eisen, *Galut*, xi.
74 See David Biale, ed., *Cultures of the Jews* 3 vols (New York: Schocken Books, 2002).
75 Rory Miller, *Divided against Zion: Anti-Zionist Opposition in Britain to a Jewish State in Palestine, 1945–1948* (London: Frank Cass, 2000).
76 Thomas A. Kolsky, *Jews against Zionism: The American Council for Judaism, 1942–1948* (Philadelphia, PA: Temple University Press, 1990), p. 190.
77 Ibid., p. 191.
78 Eisen, *Galut*. See also Arthur Hertzberg, *The Zionist Idea: A Historical Analysis and Reader* (Westport, CT: Greenwood Press, 1975); Walter Laqueur, *The History of Zionism*, 3rd edn (London and New York: I. B. Tauris, 2003).
79 Quoted in Eisen, *Galut*, 155.
80 A. B. Yehoshua, "Exile as a Neurotic Condition," in *Diaspora: Exile*

and the Jewish Conditions, ed. Étan Levine (New York and London: Jason Aronson, 1983), 16.
81 Eisen, *Galut*, 117.
82 Yehoshua, "Exile as a Neurotic Condition," 32.
83 Ibid., 33.
84 Golda Meir, "What We Want of Diaspora," in *Diaspora: Exile and the Jewish Condition*, ed. Étan Levine (New York and London: Jason Aronson, 1983), 220.
85 Gabriel Piterberg, *The Returns of Zionism* (London: Verso, 2008), 155–6.
86 Ibid.
87 Goldberg, *Jewish Power*.
88 Eisen, *Galut*, 119.
89 Ibid.
90 Ibid., 118–19.
91 Melvin I. Urofsky, *American Zionism from Herzl to the Holocaust* (New York: Anchor Press/Doubleday, 1975).
92 See for example Karpf et al., *A Time to Speak Out*.
93 Unsurprisingly, Binyamin Netanyahu has declared the BDS (Boycott, Divestment, Sanctions) movement to be anti-Semitic. Ian Black, "Israel Boycott Movement Is Antisemitic, Says Binyamin Netanayhu," *The Guardian*, Tuesday February 18, 2014.
94 Louis Dembitz Brandeis, "The Jewish Problem and How to Solve It," in *The Zionist Idea: A Historical Analysis and Reader*, ed. Arthur Herzberg (Westport, CT: Greenwood Press).
95 Eisen, *Galut*, 157.
96 Ibid., 149.
97 Ibid. See Solomon Schechter, "Zionism: A Statement," in *Seminary Addresses and Other Papers* (New York: Burning Bush Press, 1959), 91–7.
98 Mordecai M. Kaplan, *A New Zionsm*, 2nd enlarged edn (New York: The Herzl Press and the Jewish Reconstructionist Press, 1959), 40.
99 Ibid., 18.
100 Ibid., 42.
101 Arthur Hertzberg, *Being Jewish in America: The Modern Experience* (New York: Schocken Books, 1979); Arthur Hertzberg and Aron Hirt-Manheimer, *Jews: The Essence and Character of a People* (San Francisco: HarperSanFrancisco, 1998).
102 Kaplan, *A New Zionsm*, 44.
103 The creation of the New Jew, the Muscle Jew, which I explore in Chapter 2, is one attempt at doing so, although not of the kind of cultural or religious identity that Kaplan had in mind.
104 Eisen, *Galut*, 142.
105 Goldberg, *Jewish Power*. Rabin has, however, also argued for Diaspora involvement.

106 Miriam Berger, interview by Ilan Zvi Baron, April 7, 2011, London.
107 Berger, "Interview." The CST is the Community Security Trust.
108 Chaim Weiner, interview by Ilan Zvi Baron, April 4, 2011, London.
109 "Antisemitic Incident Report 2012" (London: Community Security Trust, 2013), 3.
110 Ibid., 28.
111 Barry Marcus, interview by Ilan Zvi Baron, April 4, 2011, London.
112 Weiner, "Interview."
113 Graham and Boyd, "Committed, Concerned and Conciliatory," 11.
114 This statistic was compiled by counting all headlines across 100 of the emails between 11.12.2012 and 13.12.2013. The count does not include stories about Iran (which while often related to Israel do speak to wider geopolitical and international issues).
115 A brief discussion of these different viewpoints in this context is Baron, "Diasporic Security and Jewish Identity."
116 Brian Klug, "The Climate of Debate About Israel in the Jewish World," in *Being Jewish and Doing Justice: Bringing Argument to Life* (London and Portland, OR: Vallentine Mitchell, 2011), 122.
117 Norman Podhoretz, "Now, Instant Zionism," *New York Times*, February 3, 1974.
118 Israeli treatment of Holocaust survivors is an ongoing issue. Some recent reports from the Jewish and Israeli press that raise this issue are, Ron Friedman, "You Treat Us Disgracefully, Holocaust Survivor Fumes at MKs," *Times of Israel*, April 29, 2013; Talia Nesher, "92% of Israeli Holocaust Survivors Upset at Treatment by State," *The Jewish Daily Forward*, April 3, 2013; Amos Rubin, "Israel Is Waiting for Its Holocaust Survivors to Die," *Haaretz*, February 6, 2013; Ben Sales, "Holocaust Survivors Struggle to Survive on Pittance in Israel," *The Jewish Daily Forward*, November 25, 2013. See also Tom Segev, *The Seventh Million: The Israelis and the Holocaust* (New York: Hill & Wang, 1993).
119 Anonymous 2, interview by Ilan Zvi Baron, September 3, 2008, New York.
120 Steven J. Gold, *The Israeli Diaspora* (Seattle, WA: University of Washington Press, 2002), 5. An earlier book examining the phenomenon of Israelis immigrating to the USA is Zvi Sobel, *Migrants from the Promised Land* (New Brunswick, NJ; Oxford Transaction Books, 1986).
121 Graham and Boyd, "Committed, Concerned and Conciliatory," 9.
122 J. J. Goldberg, interview by Ilan Zvi Baron and Yael Baron, August 15, 2012.
123 See in particular Goldberg, *Jewish Power*. See also Biale, *Power and Powerlessness in Jewish History*; Hertzberg, *Being Jewish in America*.
124 This demographic claim is problematic. First, it depends largely

on how Jews are counted in Diaspora countries, which requires an assessment of who is a Jew. The various demographic statistics here vary just enough to warrant some skepticism about the extent to which Israel has overtaken the USA as the country with the largest Jewish population – a claim, incidentally, that is not a politically neutral observation about demographics, but a political point about the success of Zionism. According to a December 12, 2012 report by the American-based Pew Research Center, there are 14 million Jews in the world (0.2% of the global population). The USA has 5 690 000 Jews (1.8% of the US population), which is 41.1 percent of the global Jewish population. Israel has 5 610 000 Jews, or 40.5 % of the global Jewish population. Canada, France, and the UK are the next top three countries. However, on March 30, 2013, the British newspaper the *Daily Mail*, reported that Israel overtook the USA as having the largest Jewish population. It based its numbers on the Israeli census that reported a Jewish population of over 6 million. In September 2013, the Jewish Virtual Library reported a Jewish Israeli population of 6 066 000. In April 2013, however, the Israeli government's Central Bureau of Statistics reported an Israeli Jewish population of 6.042 million. Pew Research Center, *The Global Religious Landscape*, http://www.pewforum.org/2012/12/18/global-religious-landscape-exec/, accessed October 20, 2012; *Daily Mail*, "Israel Overtakes America as the World's Largest Jewish Population Centre for the First Time," *Daily Mail*, March 30, 2013; Jewish Virtual Library, "Vital Statistics: Latest Population Statistics for Israel," http://www.jewishvirtuallibrary.org/jsource/Society_&_Culture/newpop.html , accessed October 20, 2012; Central Bureau of Statistics, "Press Release: 65th Independence Day – More Than 8 Million Residents in the State of Israel," ed. State of Israel (Jerusalem 2013).

125 Goldberg, *Jewish Power*.
126 Shatz, *Prophets/Outcast*.
127 See, Karpf et al., *A Time to Speak Out*.
128 Tony Judt, "Israel: The Alternative," *New York Review of Books* (2003).
129 Hertzberg, *Being Jewish in America*.
130 Seliktar, *Divided We Stand: American Jews, Israel, and the Peace Process*.
131 Anonymous 3, interview by Ilan Zvi Baron, April 18, 2013, Jerusalem.
132 Josh Nathan-Kasiz, "Prominent Jewish Liberals Answer the Jcall," *The Jewish Daily Forward*, May 19, 2010.
133 "About J Street," http://jstreet.org/about, accessed October 28, 2013.
134 Jonathan Kopp, interview by Ilan Zvi Baron and Yael Baron, August 16, 2012, New York.

Chapter 4: From Eating Hummus to the Sublime

1. Eisen, *Galut*.
2. Which is not to ignore the fact that Jewish internationalism in the eighteenth and nineteenth centuries was influenced by imperial notions of Western superiority.
3. Aaron Dorfman, interview by Ilan Zvi Baron and Yael Baron, August 14, 2012, New York.
4. One example that is based on empirical work is Jason Sunshine and Tom Tyler, "Moral Solidarity, Identification with the Community, and the Importance of Procedural Justice: The Police as Prototypical Representatives of a Group's Moral Values," *Social Psychological Quarterly* 66, 2 (2003).
5. For an example of political theory text relying on sociological research for empirical evidence see James Tully, *Public Philosophy in a New Key: Democracy and Civic Freedom*, vol. I, Ideas in Context (Cambridge; New York: Cambridge University Press, 2008); James Tully, *Public Philosophy in a New Key: Imperialism and Civic Freedom*, vol. II (Cambridge: Cambridge University Press, 2008).
6. Klosko, *Political Obligations*.
7. Ibid., 188.
8. Marion Nestle, *Food Politics: How the Food Industry Influences Nutrition and Health* (Berkeley, CA; London: University of California Press, 2007); Robert L. Paarlberg, *Food Politics: What Everyone Needs to Know* (New York and Oxford: Oxford University Press, 2010); Raj Patel, *Stuffed and Starved: From Farm to Fork: The Hidden Battle for the World Food System*, updated edn (London: Portobello, 2007); Kelsey Timmerman, *Where Am I Eating* (Hoboken, NJ: John Wiley, 2013).
9. Michael P. Lynch, "Democracy after the Shutdown," *New York Times*, October 15, 2013.
10. Hannah Arendt, *Responsibility and Judgment*, ed. Jerome Kohn (New York: Schocken Books, 2003); *The Jew as Pariah*; *Eichmann in Jerusalem*; *Jewish Writings*.
11. Andrew Davids, interview by Ilan Zvi Baron, August 29, 2008, New York.
12. See, Karpf et al., *A Time to Speak Out*; Aviv and Shneer, *New Jews*.
13. Jesse Lepow, interview by Ilan Zvi Baron, September 2, 2008, New York.
14. Most recently, see Jay Michaelson, "Does the Iran Deal Force American Jews to Choose between Dual Loyalties," *The Jewish Daily Forward*, December 4, 2013.
15. Gabriel Sheffer, "Loyalty and Criticism in the Relations between

World Jewry and Israel," *Israel Studies* 17, 2 (2012); "Ethno-National Diasporas and Security."
16 "Loyalty and Criticism in the Relations between World Jewry and Israel," 77.
17 Ibid., 80.
18 Ibid., 84.
19 "Ethno-National Diasporas and Security." See also Steven Vertovec, "Migrant Transnationalism and Modes of Transformation," *International Migration Review* 38, 3 (2004).
20 Baron, "The Problem of Dual Loyalty."
21 For more on this internationalist discourse see Leff, *Sacred Bonds of Solidarity*.
22 There was a dual loyalty case against AIPAC, but it was dismissed in 2011. Neila A. Lewis and David Johnston, "U.S. To Drop Spay Case against Pro-Israel Lobbysts," *New York Times*, May 1, 2009. One of the plaintiffs subsequently brought about a defamation suit against his former employer AIPAC, which was granted a summary judgment on February 23, 2011. See Eric P. Christian, "Steven Rose V. American Israel Public Affairs Committee," in *Civil Action No. 2009 CA 001256 B*, ed. Superior Court of the District of Columbia (Washington DC, 2011). In our interview, David Twersky noted that one of the reasons the major Jewish organizations did not get involved on behalf of the convicted spy Jonathan Pollard was dual loyalty. As he told me, in 2008: "Some people were very scared, let's not go down that road towards the dual loyalty thing. Just because it was for Israel does not mean that we owe him anything, and other people would say precisely because it was for Israel we owe him something."
23 John Mearsheimer and Stephen Walt, "The Israel Lobby," *London Review of Books*, March 23, 2006; John J. Mearsheimer and Stephen M. Walt., *The Israel Lobby and U.S. Foreign Policy* (London: Allen Lane, 2007).
24 *A Review of Mearsheimer and Walt's "The Israel Lobby and U.S. Foreign Policy:" an Anti-Jewish Screed in Scholarly Guise*, Anti-Defamation League, http://www.adl.org/israel-international/anti-israel-activity/c/mearsheimer-and-walts.html., accessed January 30, 2014.
25 Eliot A. Cohen, "Yes, It's Anti-Semitic," *Washington Post*, Wednesday, April 5 2006.
26 Alan M. Dershowitz, *The Case against Israel's Enemies: Exposing Jimmy Carter and Others Who Stand in the Way of Peace* (Hoboken, NJ: John Wiley, 2008).
27 Jerome Epstein, interview by Ilan Zvi Baron, September 3, 2008, New York.
28 Steven Bayme, interview by Ilan Zvi Baron, September 3, 2008, New York.

29 David Twersky, interview by Ilan Zvi Baron, September 2, 2008, New York.
30 Josh Nathan-Kazis, "In a Shift, Oren Calls J Street 'a Unique Problem'," *The Jewish Daily Foward*, December 9 (issue of December 18, 2009), 2009.
31 Ibid.
32 "Jews Express Wide Criticism of Israel in the Pew Survey but Leaders Dismiss Findings."
33 "Who Do Jewish Leaders Really Represent," *The Jewish Daily Forward*, October 3, 2013.
34 Benamy, "Interview."
35 Kopp, "Interview."
36 Karpf et al., *A Time to Speak Out*.
37 Graham and Boyd, "Committed, Concerned and Conciliatory," 3.
38 Ibid., 7.
39 Ibid., 9.
40 Ibid.
41 Jonathan Boyd, interview by Ilan Zvi Baron, April 5, 2011, London.
42 This is not the place to get into the fluidity and contingency by which identity is understood and or constructed. However, important works of relevance here include: William E. Connolly, *Identity, Difference: Democratic Negotiations of Political Paradox*, expanded edn (Minneapolis, MN and London: University of Minnesota Press, 2002); Giddens, *Modernity and Self-Identity*; Charles Taylor, *Sources of the Self: The Making of the Modern Identity* (Cambridge: Cambridge University Press, 1989).
43 Jon Benjamin, interview by Ilan Zvi Baron, April 4, 2011, London.
44 Ibid.
45 Ibid.
46 Saul J. Berman, interview by Ilan Zvi Baron, September 2, 2008, New York.
47 Bayme, "Interview."
48 Ibid.
49 Ibid.
50 Epstein, "Interview."
51 Anonymous 10, interview by Ilan Zvi Baron, April 17, 2013, Jerusalem.
52 Shelley Kedar, interview by Ilan Zvi Baron, April 14, 2013, Tel Aviv.
53 Anonymous 12.
54 Kedar, "Interview."
55 Shlomo Brom, interview by Ilan Zvi Baron, April 10, 2013, Tel Aviv.
56 Ibid.
57 Ibid.
58 Anonymous 12. See http://www.masaisrael.org, accessed January

20, 2014. Repeated attempts to meet representatives of the Jewish Agency went unfulfilled.
59 Anonymous 12.
60 Kedar, "Interview."
61 Anonymous 11, interview by Ilan Zvi Baron, April 18, 2013, Jerusalem.
62 Ben Moreh, "Interview."
63 Ibid.
64 Anonymous 3, "Interview."
65 Ibid.
66 *Facts About Starbucks in the Middle East*, http://news.starbucks.com/news/facts-about-starbucks-in-the-middle-east, accessed October 17, 2013.
67 Harry Brechner, interview by Ilan Zvi Baron, May 30, 2008, Victoria, British Columbia.
68 Ibid.
69 Dan Senor and Saul Singer, *Start-up Nation: The Story of Israel's Economic Miracle* (New York: Twelve, 2009).
70 Anonymous 10, "Interview."
71 Jeremy Gordon, interview by Ilan Zvi Baron, April 5, 2011, London.
72 Ibid.
73 Ibid.
74 Ibid.
75 Tony Bayfield, interview by Ilan Zvi Baron, April 7, 2011, London. On the trilogy of God, Israel, Torah see David Biale, *Not in the Heavens: The Tradition of Jewish Secular Thought* (Princeton, NJ: Princeton University Press, 2011); Mordecai M. Kaplan, *Judaism as a Civilization: Toward a Reconstruction of American-Jewish Life* (Philadelphia, PA: Jewish Publication Society, 2010 [1934]); Leo Trepp, *A History of the Jewish Experience* (Springfield, NJ: Behrman House, 2001).
76 Keith Kahn-Harris, interview by Ilan Zvi Baron, April 5, 2011, London.
77 Ibid.
78 Gordon, "Interview."
79 Colin Shindler, *Israel and the European Left: Between Solidarity and Delegitimization* (New York: Continuum, 2012).
80 Kahn-Harris, "Interview."
81 Stephen Harper, "Prime Minister Stephen Harper's Speech to the Knesset," http://globalnews.ca/news/1094114/prime-minister-stephen-harpers-speech-to-the-knesset/, accessed February 3, 2014. http://www.cbc.ca/news/politics/stephen-harper-s-speech-to-the-israeli-knesset-1.2503902, accessed February 3, 2014.
82 Aaron Goldstein, interview by Ilan Zvi Baron, April 6, 2011, London.
83 Danny Rich, interview by Ilan Zvi Baron, April 7, 2011, London.

84 Anonymous 4, interview by Ilan Zvi Baron, September 15, 2008, New York.
85 Doron Lis, interview by Ilan Zvi Baron, September 1, 2008, New York.
86 Anonymous 4, "Interview."
87 Ibid.
88 He spoke as an individual, and not as a representative of the OU. A second appointment was scheduled, but when I turned up with my research assistant I was told by the receptionist that he would not see me.
89 Anonymous 2, "Interview."
90 Ibid.
91 http://www.ouisrael.org/about/, accessed July 2, 2014.
92 Marcus, "Interview."
93 Berman, "Interview."
94 Anonymous 2, "Interview."
95 Ibid. *Doven* means to pray (Yiddish).
96 Benamy, "Interview."
97 Anonymous 2, "Interview."
98 Goldberg, "David Twersky, Political Journalist and Peace Activist, Dies at 60."
99 "A Portrait of Jewish Americans."
100 Twersky, "Interview."
101 Ibid.
102 Bayme, "Interview."
103 Benjamin, "Interview."
104 Klug, "The Climate of Debate About Israel in the Jewish World."
105 Rose, *The Myths of Zionism*.
106 Avi Shlaim, *The Iron Wall: Israel and the Arab World* (London: Penguin, 2000); Benny Morris, *Righteous Victims: A History of the Zionist–Arab Conflict 1881–2001* (New York: Random House, 2001); *The Birth of the Palestinian Refugee Problem Revisited*, 2nd edn (Cambridge; New York: Cambridge University Press, 2004); Ilan Pappe, *The Ethnic Cleansing of Palestine* (Oxford: Oneworld, 2006).
107 The connection between Jewish identity and food is longstanding and food was how Heinrich Heine defined his Jewishness. Biale writes, "While food is certainly bound up with the religious practices of Judaism, Heine emphasizes instead cuisine as a symbol for the *secular* culture of the Jews." Biale, *Not in the Heavens: The Tradition of Jewish Secular Thought*, 136.
108 Julia Moskin, "'Jerusalem' Has All the Right Ingredients," *New York Times*, July 30, 2013.
109 Anonymous 4, "Interview."
110 Weiner, "Interview."
111 Ibid.

Chapter 5: Obligation and Critique

1 Rose, *The Question of Zion.*
2 Twersky, "Interview."
3 Butler, *Parting Ways*; Karpf et al., *A Time to Speak Out*; Rose, *The Question of Zion*. Often this work is influenced by the thought of Hannah Arendt, Martin Buber, and Emmanuel Lévinas. Arendt's and Buber's most relevant works in this regard are, Arendt, *Jewish Writings*; Martin Buber, *A Land of Two Peoples*, ed. Paul Mendes-Flohr (Chicago, IL: University of Chicago Press; first published 1983 by Oxford University Press, 2005). A survey of Jewish dissenting voices about Israel is Shatz, *Prophets/Outcast*. A recent historical text that addresses dissenting Jewish voices is Pianko, *Zionism and the Roads Not Taken.*
4 *Zionism and the Roads Not Taken*, 202.
5 Quoted in Arendt, *The Jew as Pariah*, 241.
6 Podhoretz, "Now, Instant Zionism."
7 Quoted in Arthur Neslen, *Occupied Minds: A Journey through the Israeli Psyche* (London: Pluto Press, 2006), 1.
8 "A Portrait of Jewish Americans."
9 Castells, *The Power of Identity.*
10 Goldberg, "Interview."
11 Alan M. Dershowitz, *The Case for Israel* (Hoboken, NJ: John Wiley, 2003).
12 Yoram Hazony, *The Jewish State: The Struggle for Israel's Soul* (New York: Basic Books, 2001).
13 Jay Michaelson, "How I'm Losing My Love for Israel," *The Jewish Daily Forward*, September 16, 2009.
14 Maxime Rodinson, *Israel: A Colonial-Settler State?* ([S.l.]: Anchor Foundation/Monad Pathfinder Press, 1973). For different approaches to the question of territory, Zionism and colonialism compare Baylis Thomas, *The Dark Side of Zionism: Israel's Quest for Security through Dominance* (New York: Lexington Books, 2009); Baruch Kimmerling, *Zionism and Territory: The Socio-Territorial Dimensions of Zionist Politics* (Berkeley, CA: Institute of International Studies, University of California, 1983).
15 Most recently, the Presbyterian Church in the USA has described Zionism as racism. See Lauren Markoe, "Jewish Critics: Presbyterian Study Guide Equates Zionism with Racism," *Washington Post*, February 15, 2014. The Church of Scotland has also come into related controversy over a report it published that questioned the use of religious scripture for political purposes pertaining to territorial control. See Marcus Dysch, "Scottish Church to Debate Jewish Right to Land of Israel," *The Jewish Chronicle*, May 2, 2013; Ira Glunts and

Adam Horowitz, "Church of Scotland Accepts Controversial Report on Israel/Palestine," Mondoweiss, http://mondoweiss.net/2013/05/scotland-controversial-israelpalestine.html, accessed February 18, 2014; JTA, "Church of Scotland Backs Away Denial of Jewish Claim to Land of Israel."

16 Hazony, *The Jewish State: The Struggle for Israel's Soul*; Benjamin Netanyahu, *A Durable Peace: Israel and Its Place among the Nations* (New York: Warner Books, 1993, 2000).
17 Norman Podhoretz, *Why Are Jews Liberals?* (New York: Doubleday, 2009).
18 This political bias was especially relevant with regard to the research of the so-called post-Zionist historians, although the direction of the bias varied. See the postscript in Alain Dieckhoff, *The Invention of a Nation: Zionist Thought and the Making of Modern Israel* (London: Hurst, 2001). For a methodological critique of the new historians see Efraim Karsh, *Fabricating Israeli History: The "New Historians,"* 2nd (rev.) edn (London: Frank Cass, 2000).
19 Shlomo Sand, *The Invention of the Jewish People* (London: Verso, 2009).
20 Yossi Klein Halevi, *At the Entrance to the Garden of Eden: A Jew's Search for Hope with Christians and Muslims in the Holy Land* (New York: Perennial, 2002); Gorenberg, *The Unmaking of Israel*; Avi Shavit, *My Promised Land: the Triumph and Tragedy of Israel* (New York: Spiegel & Grau, 2013).
21 For example, Chaim Gans, *A Just Zionism: On the Morality of the Jewish State* (New York and Oxford: Oxford University Press, 2008).
22 Blumenthal, *Goliath*.
23 J. J. Goldberg, "Max Blumenthal's 'Goliath' Is Anti-Israel Book That Makes Even Anti-Zionists Blush," *The Jewish Daily Foward*, October 31, 2013; Eric Alterman, "The 'I Hate Israel' Handbook," *The Nation*, October 16, 2013.
24 Hannah Arendt, Mary McCarthy, and Carol Brightman, *Between Friends: The Correspondence of Hannah Arendt and Mary Mccarthy 1949–1975* (London: Secker & Warburg, 1995), 22–9.
25 David Couzens Hoy and Thomas McCarthy, *Critical Theory* (Oxford: Blackwell, 1994). For an examination of Critical Theory and Poststructuralism see Beatrice Hanssen, "Critical Theory and Poststructuralism: Habermas and Foucault," in *The Cambridge Companion to Critical Theory*, ed. Fred Rush (Cambridge: Cambridge University Press, 2004). See also Peter M. R. Stirk, *Critical Theory, Politics and Society* (London: Continuum, 2000), 59.
26 *Critical Theory, Politics and Society*.
27 Ibid.
28 For example, David Held, *Introduction to Critical Theory: Horkheimer to Habermas* (London: Hutchinson, 1980).

29 Butler, *Parting Ways*, 117.
30 Ibid.
31 As she notes, Lévinas is known as the philosopher of the Other, but even though he emphasized an ethics based on otherness, he nevertheless was not prepared to include Palestinians as the ethical other to the Israeli. For an introduction to Lévinas and ethics see Simon Critchley, *The Ethics of Deconstruction: Derrida and Levinas* (Oxford: Blackwell, 1992). See Emmanuel Lévinas, *Totality and Infinity: An Essay on Exteriority*, trans. Alphonso Lingis (Pittsburgh, PA: Duquesne University Press, 1969); *The Levinas Reader* (Oxford: Blackwell, 1989); *God, Death, and Time*, trans. Bettina Bergo (Stanford, CA: Stanford University Press, 1993); *Otherwise Than Being: Or Beyond Essence*, trans. Alphonso Lingis (Pittsburgh, PA: Duquesne University Press, 1993); *Is It Righteous to Be?*, trans. Jill Robbins (Stanford, CA: Stanford University Press, 2001).
32 Immanuel Kant, *Critique of Pure Reason*, ed. Paul Guyer and Allen W. Wood, trans. Paul Guyer and Allen W. Wood (Cambridge: Cambridge University Press, 1998). See Philip Turetzky, "Immanent Critique," *Philosophy Today* 33, 2 (1989).
33 Held, *Introduction to Critical Theory*.
34 See for example Richard A. Landes, "Judith Butler, Renounce the Adorno Prize," *The Times of Israel*, September 6, 2012; JTA, "Israel Critic Judith Butler Honored in Germany," *The Jewish Daily Forward*, September 6, 2012.
35 Judith Butler, "No, It's Not Anti-Semitic," *London Review of Books*, August 2003.
36 Ibid.
37 *Parting Ways*, 37, 120. See Franz Rosenzweig, *The Star of Redemption*, trans. William W. Halo (Notre Dame, IL: University of Notre Dame Press, 1985).
38 Bauman, *Modernity and the Holocaust*.
39 Butler, "No, It's Not Anti-Semitic."
40 *Parting Ways*, 129.
41 Edward W. Said, "Zionism from the Standpoint of Its Victims," *Social Text* 1 (1979).
42 Pianko, *Zionism and the Roads Not Taken*, 61.
43 Arendt, *The Jew as Pariah*, 246; *Jewish Writings*, 466–7.
44 Which is not to say that Arendt was not a Jewish thinker. In many intellectual ways she was. See Bernstein, *Hannah Arendt and the Jewish Question*. My view is that Arendt is best understood as a Jewish thinker both because of her biography (which clearly influenced her writing) and because the types of issues she explored in her work resonate deeply with significant questions about what it means to be a Jew in the modern world. Arendt, *Jewish Writings*. The edited

book *Jewish Writings* is a revised and expanded version of *Jew As Pariah*.

45 Pianko, *Zionism and the Roads Not Taken*; David N. Myers, *Between Jew & Arab: The Lost Voice of Simon Rawidowicz* (Waltham, MA: Brandeis University Press; Hanover, NH and London: University Press of New England, 2008).

46 Arendt, *The Jew as Pariah*, 182; *Jewish Writings*, 391.

47 Pianko, *Zionism and the Roads Not Taken*.

48 Sophie Dubnov-Erlich, *The Life and Work of S. M. Dubnow: Diaspora Nationalism and Jewish History*, trans. Judith Vowles (Bloomington and Indianapolis, IN: Indiana University Press, 1991), 137.

49 Dubnow, *Nationalism and History*, 186.

50 Ibid.

51 Ibid., 188–9.

52 See also Boyarin and Boyarin, *Powers of Diaspora: Two Essays on the Relevance of Jewish Culture*.

53 Myers, *Between Jew & Arab: The Lost Voice of Simon Rawidowicz*; Pianko, *Zionism and the Roads Not Taken*.

54 Myers, *Between Jew & Arab: The Lost Voice of Simon Rawidowicz*, 180.

55 Ibid., 154.

56 Ibid., 152–3.

57 Ibid., 143.

58 Ibid., 150.

59 Ibid., 153.

60 Ibid., 155.

61 Ibid.

62 Ibid., 17.

63 Pianko, *Zionism and the Roads Not Taken*, 208.

64 Boyarin and Boyarin, *Powers of Diaspora: Two Essays on the Relevance of Jewish Culture*.

65 Arendt, *Jewish Writings*, 357.

66 Buber, *A Land of Two Peoples*.

67 Here we venture in the history of Zionism and Israel. The literature is too vast to list, but a good range of texts includes: Shlaim, *The Iron Wall: Israel and the Arab World*; Morris, *Righteous Victims*; Laqueur, *The History of Zionism*; Gideon Shimoni, *The Zionist Ideology* (Hanover, NH and London: Brandeis University Press, 1995). See also Anita Shapira, *Land and Power: The Zionist Resort to Force, 1881–1948* (Oxford: Oxford University Press, 1992; repr., Stanford, CA: Stanford University Press, 1999).

68 Rose, *The Question of Zion*, 122.

69 Ibid.

70 Ibid., 8. See also Juliana Ochs, *Security and Suspicion: An*

Ethnography of Everyday Life in Israel (Philadalphia, PA: University of Pennsylvania Press, 2011).
71 Boas Evron, *Jewish State or Israeli Nation?* (Bloomington and Indianapolis, IN: Indiana University Press, 1995), 242.
72 Ibid., 242–3.
73 Michael Selzer, ed., *Zionism Reconsidered: The Rejection of Jewish Normalcy* (New York: Macmillan, 1970); Shatz, *Prophets/Outcast*.
74 Chaim Potok, *Wanderings: Chaim Potok's History of the Jews* (New York: Fawcett Crest, 1978), 516.
75 Salo W. Baron, "A New Outlook for Israel and the Diaspora," in *Diaspora: Exile and the Jewish Condition*, ed. Étan Levine (New York and London: Jason Aronson, 1983), 199.
76 Yitzhak Rabin, "American Jews and Israel: Strengthening the Bonds," ibid., 213.

Conclusion: Obligation in Exile, Critique and the Future of the Jewish Diaspora

1 Butler, *Parting Ways*.
2 See for example Aviv and Shneer, *New Jews*.
3 An explanation of the traditional character of Diaspora Jews as being politically on the left, followed by a critique arguing why this is bad for the Jews, is Podhoretz, *Why Are Jews Liberals?*
4 Mordecai Richler, *This Year in Jerusalem* (Toronto: Knopf, 1994). Emphasis in original.
5 Thomas Frank, *What's the Matter with Kansas?* (New York: Holt, 2005).
6 Ethan Bronner, "Israel Reaches out to the Diaspora," *New York Times*, March 15, 2014.

Bibliography

Aberbach, David, *Jewish Cultural Nationalism: Origins and Influences*. London: Routledge, 2008.
Allen, Amy, "Power, Subjectivity, and Agency: Between Arendt and Foucault," *International Journal of Philosophical Studies* 10, 2 (2010): 131–49.
Alterman, Eric, "The 'I Hate Israel' Handbook," *The Nation*, October 16, 2013.
Anonymous 1, "Interview." By Ilan Zvi Baron and Yael Baron (August 16, 2012).
Anonymous 2, "Interview." By Ilan Zvi Baron (September 3, 2008).
Anonymous 3, "Interview." By Ilan Zvi Baron (April 18, 2013).
Anonymous 4, "Interview." By Ilan Zvi Baron (September 15, 2008).
Anonymous 10, "Interview." By Ilan Zvi Baron (April 17, 2013).
Anonymous 11, "Interview." By Ilan Zvi Baron (April 18, 2013).
Anti-Defamation League, *A Review of Mearsheimer and Walt's "The Israel Lobby and U.S. Foreign Policy:" An Anti-Jewish Screed in Scholarly Guise*, http://www.adl.org/israel-international/anti-israel-activity/c/mearsheimer-and-walts.html, accessed January 30, 2014.
Appadurai, Arjun, *Modernity at Large: Cultural Dimensions of Globalization*. Minneapolis, MN: University of Minnesota Press, 1996.
Arendt, Hannah, *Between Past and Future: Eight Exercises in Political Thought*. New York: Penguin, 2006.
Arendt, Hannah, *Eichmann in Jerusalem: A Report on the Banality of Evil*. Penguin Twentieth-Century Classics, rev. and enlarged edn. New York and London: Penguin, 1994.
Arendt, Hannah, *Jewish Writings*, ed. Jerome Kohn and Ron H. Feldman. New York: Schocken Books, 2007.
Arendt, Hannah, *On Revolution*. New York: Penguin, 1965.
Arendt, Hannah, *On Violence*. London: Harcourt Brace, 1970.
Arendt, Hannah, *Responsibility and Judgment*, ed. Jerome Kohn. New York: Schocken Books, 2003.
Arendt, Hannah, *The Human Condition*. London and Chicago, IL: Chicago University Press, 1958.

Bibliography

Arendt, Hannah, *The Jew as Pariah*, ed. Ron H. Feldman. New York: Grove Press, 1978.
Arendt, Hannah, *The Life of the Mind*. New York: Harcourt, 1978.
Arendt, Hannah, *The Origins of Totalitarianism*. London: André Deutsch, 1986.
Arendt, Hannah, *The Promise of Politics*, ed. Jerome Kohn. New York: Schocken Books, 2005.
Arendt, Hannah, Mary McCarthy, and Carol Brightman, *Between Friends: The Correspondence of Hannah Arendt and Mary Mccarthy 1949–1975*. London: Secker & Warburg, 1995.
Aristotle, *The Politics and the Constitution of Athens*, ed. Stephen Everson. Cambridge: Cambridge University Press, 1996.
Aviv, Caryn, and David Shneer, *New Jews: The End of the Jewish Diaspora*. New York: New York University Press, 2005.
Bader, Veit, "The Cultural Conditions of Transnational Citizenship: On the Interpretation of Political and Ethnic Cultures," *Political Theory* 25, 6 (December 1997): 771–813.
Balibar, Etienne, "Propositions on Citizenship," *Ethics* 98, 4 (July 1988): 723–30.
Baron, Ilan Zvi, "Diasporic Security and Jewish Identity," *Modern Jewish Studies* 13, 2 (forthcoming, 2014). Published online at http://www.tandfonline.com/doi/abs/10.1080/14725886.2013.824231?journalCode=cmjs20#.U8Ou8LH-m8D
Baron, Ilan Zvi, *Justifying the Obligation to Die: War, Ethics and Political Obligation, with Illustrations from Zionism*. Lanham, MD: Lexington Books, 2009.
Baron, Ilan Zvi, "Not My Grandfather's Israel: The Growing Racism of the Modern Israeli Public," *Tikkun Daily* (November 27, 2012).
Baron, Ilan Zvi, "The Problem of Dual Loyalty," *The Canadian Journal of Political Science* 42, 4 (2009): 1025–44.
Baron, Salo W., "A New Outlook for Israel and the Diaspora," Ch. 18 in *Diaspora: Exile and the Jewish Condition*, ed. Étan Levine, 199–201. New York and London: Jason Aronson, 1983.
Bauböck, Rainer, "Towards a Political Theory of Migrant Transnationalism," *International Migration Review* 37, 2 (Fall 2003): 700–23.
Bauman, Zygmunt, *Modernity and the Holocaust*. Ithaca, NY: Cornell University Press, 1991.
Bayfield, Tony, "Interview." By Ilan Zvi Baron (April 7, 2011).
Bayme, Steven, "Interview." By Ilan Zvi Baron (September 3, 2008).
BBC. *Stephen Hawking Boycotts Major Israeli Conference*. BBC, May 8, 2013, http://www.bbc.co.uk/news/uk-22446054, accessed January 30, 2014.
Beauvoir, Simone de, *The Second Sex*, trans. Constance Border and Sheila Malvony-Chevallier. London: Vintage Books, 2009 [1949].

Beinart, Peter, *The Crisis of Zionism*. New York: Times Books, 2012.
Beinart, Peter, "The Failure of the American Jewish Establishment," *New York Review of Books*, June 10, 2010.
Benamy, Talia, "Interview." By Ilan Zvi Baron and Yael Baron (August 14, 2012).
Benhabib, Seyla, *The Reluctant Modernism of Hannah Arendt*, new edn. New York: Rowman & Littlefield, 2003.
Benhabib, Seyla, Ian Shapiro, and Danilo Petranović (eds), *Identities, Affiliations, and Allegiances*. Cambridge: Cambridge University Press, 2007.
Benjamin, Jon, "Interview." By Ilan Zvi Baron (April 4, 2011).
Ben Moreh, Martin, "Interview." By Ilan Zvi Baron (April 11, 2013).
Ben-Sasson, Haim Hillel, *A History of the Jewish People*. London: Weidenfeld & Nicolson, 1976.
Beran, Harry, *The Consent Theory of Political Obligation*. London, New York and Sydney: Croom Helm, 1987.
Berenskoetter, Felix, and Michael J. Williams (eds), *Power in World Politics*. London: Routledge, 2007.
Berger, Miriam, "Interview." By Ilan Zvi Baron (April 7, 2011).
Berman, Lazar, "US Lawmakers Flocked to Israel in August, Figures Show," *The Times of Israel*, September 25, 2013.
Berman, Saul J., "Interview." By Ilan Zvi Baron (September 2, 2008).
Bernstein, Richard J., *Hannah Arendt and the Jewish Question*. Cambridge, MA: MIT Press, 1996.
Biale, David (ed.), *Cultures of the Jews*. 3 vols. New York: Schocken Books, 2002.
Biale, David, *Not in the Heavens: The Tradition of Jewish Secular Thought*. Princeton, NJ: Princeton University Press, 2011.
Biale, David. *Power and Powerlessness in Jewish History*. New York: Schocken Books, 1986.
Birthright Israel, "About Taglit Birthright," http://www.birthrightisrael.com/TaglitBirthrightIsraelStory/Pages/default.aspx, accessed October 17, 2012.
Black, Ian, "Israel Boycott Movement Is Antisemitic, Says Binyamin Netanayhu," *The Guardian*, February 18, 2014.
Blumenthal, Max, *Goliath: Life and Loathing in Greater Israel*. New York: Nation Books, 2013.
Bodin, Jean, and Julian H. Franklin, *On Sovereignty: Four Chapters from the Six Books of the Commonwealth* [translation of selections from *Six livres de la République*]. Cambridge: Cambridge University Press, 1992.
Boyarin, Jonathan, and Daniel Boyarin, *Powers of Diaspora: Two Essays on the Relevance of Jewish Culture*. Minneapolis MN and London: University of Minnesota Press, 2002.
Boyd, Jonathan, "Interview." By Ilan Zvi Baron (April 5, 2011).
Brandeis, Louis Dembitz, "The Jewish Problem and How to Solve It,"

in *The Zionist Idea: A Historical Analysis and Reader*, ed. Arthur Herzberg, 517–23. Westport, CT: Greenwood Press.
Braunold, Joel, "Paying for Diaspora Jews Won't Save Israel," *Haaretz*, February 19, 2014.
Brechner, Harry, "Interview." By Ilan Zvi Baron (May 30, 2008).
Breines, Paul. *Tough Jews: Political Fantasies and the Moral Dilemma of American Jewry*. New York: Basic Books, 1990.
Brom, Shlomo, "Interview." By Ilan Zvi Baron (April 10, 2013).
Bronner, Ethan, "Israel Reaches out to the Diaspora," *New York Times*, March 15, 2014.
Buber, Martin, *A Land of Two Peoples*, ed. Paul Mendes-Flohr. Chicago, IL: University of Chicago Press, 2005. [First published 1983 by Oxford University Press.]
Bull, Hedley, *The Anarchical Society: A Study of Order in World Politics*, 2nd edn. New York: Columbia University Press, 1977, 1995.
Butler, Judith, "No, It's Not Anti-Semitic," *London Review of Books*, August 2003, 19–21.
Butler, Judith, *Parting Ways: Jewishness and the Critique of Zionism*. New York: Columbia University Press, 2012.
Butterfield, Herbert, *The Whig Interpretation of History*. New York and London: Norton, 1965.
Calhoun, Craig, and John McGowan (eds), *Hannah Arendt and the Meaning of Politics*. Minneapolis, MN: University of Minnesota Press, 1997.
Canovan, Margaret, *Hannah Arendt: A Reinterpretation of Her Political Thought*. Cambridge: Cambridge University Press, 1995.
Canovan, Margaret, "The Contradictions of Hannah Arendt's Political Thought," *Political Theory* 6, 1 (February 1978): 5–26.
Castells, Manuel, *The Power of Identity*, 2nd edn, with a new preface. Oxford: Wiley-Blackwell, 2010.
Castells, Manuel, *The Rise of the Network Society. The Information Age: Economy, Society and Culture*, 2nd edn. Oxford: Blackwell, 2000.
Central Bureau of Statistics, *Press Release: 65th Independence Day – More than 8 Million Residents in the State of Israel*, ed. State of Israel. Jerusalem, 2013.
Christian, Eric P., "Steven Rose V. American Israel Public Affairs Committee." In *Civil Action No. 2009 CA 001256 B*, ed. Superior Court of the District of Columbia. Washington DC, 2011.
Clausewitz, Carl von, Michael Eliot Howard, Peter Paret, and Bernard Brodie, *On War*. Princeton, NJ and Guildford: Princeton University Press, 1976.
Clavin, Patricia, "Defining Transnationalism," *Contemporary European History* 14, 4 (November 2005): 421–39.
Clifford, James, "Diasporas," *Cultural Anthropology* 9, 3 (August 1994): 302–38.

Cohen, Eliot A., "Yes, It's Anti-Semitic," *Washington Post*, Wednesday, April 5 2006.
Cohen, Naomi W., *American Jews and the Zionist Idea*. [New York]: Ktav, 1975.
Cohen, Robin, "Diasporas and the Nation-State: From Victims to Challengers," *International Affairs* 72, 3 (July 1996): 507–22.
Cohen, Robin, *Global Diasporas: An Introduction*, 2nd edn. London: Routledge, 2008.
Cohen, Steven Martin, *American Modernity and Jewish Identity*. New York and London: Tavistock, 1983.
Cole, Tim, *Selling the Holocaust: From Auschwitz to Schindler: How History Is Bought, Packaged, and Sold*. New York: Routledge, 1999.
Collins, Randall, *Weberian Sociological Theory*. Cambridge: Cambridge University Press, 1986.
Community Security Trust, "Antisemitic Incident Report 2012," London: 2013.
Connolly, William E., *Identity, Difference: Democratic Negotiations of Political Paradox*, expanded edn. Minneapolis, MN and London: University of Minnesota Press, 2002.
Critchley, Simon, *The Ethics of Deconstruction: Derrida and Levinas*. Oxford: Blackwell, 1992.
Dagger, Richard, "Political Obligation." In *Stanford Encylcopedia of Philosophy*, ed. Edward N. Zalta, Uri Nodelman and Colin Allen. Stanford, CA: Metaphysics Research Lab, Stanford University, 2010.
Dagger, Richard K., "What Is Political Obligation?," *The American Political Science Review* 71, 4 (March 1977): 86–94.
Dagger, Richard, "Membership, Fair Play, and Political Obligation," *Political Studies* 48, 1 (2000): 104–17.
Dahl, Robert A., "The Concept of Power," *Behavioural Science* 2, 3 (1957): 201–15.
Davids, Andrew, "Interview." By Ilan Zvi Baron (August 29, 2008).
Della Porta, Donatella, Hanspeter Kriesi, and Dieter Rucht, *Social Movements in a Globalizing World*. Basingstoke: Macmillan, 1999.
Dershowitz, Alan M., *The Case against Israel's Enemies: Exposing Jimmy Carter and Others Who Stand in the Way of Peace*. Hoboken, NJ: John Wiley, 2008.
Dershowitz, Alan M., *The Case for Israel*. Hoboken, NJ: John Wiley, 2003.
Dershowitz, Alan, "Is Norman Finkelstein in Tehran?," *The Huffington Post*, December 12, 2006.
Dieckhoff, Alain, *The Invention of a Nation: Zionist Thought and the Making of Modern Israel*. London: Hurst, 2001.
Dinur, Ben Zion, *Israel and the Diaspora*. Philadelphia, PA: Jewish Publication Society of America, 1969.
Dorfman, Aaron, "Interview." By Ilan Zvi Baron and Yael Baron (August 14, 2012).

Dubnov-Erlich, Sophie, *The Life and Work of S. M. Dubnow: Diaspora Nationalism and Jewish History*, trans. Judith Vowles. Bloomington and Indianapolis, IN: Indiana University Press, 1991.
Dubnow, Simon, *Nationalism and History: Essays on Old and New Judaism*. New York: Meridian Books, 1958.
Dufoix, Stéphane, *Diasporas*, trans. William Rodarmor. Berkeley, CA: University of California Press, 2003.
Dworkin, Ronald, "The Original Position." In *Reading Rawls: Critical Studies on Rawls' A Theory of Justice*, ed. Norman Daniels, 16–52. Oxford: Basil Blackwell, 1975.
Dysch, Marcus, "Scottish Church to Debate Jewish Right to Land of Israel," *The Jewish Chronicle*, May 2, 2013.
Edemariam, Alda, "David Ward: 'The Solid Ground I Stand On Is That I Am Not a Racist,'" *The Guardian*, February 6, 2013.
Editors, the, and Editorial Community, "On Moving Targets," *Public Culture* 2, 1 (1989), http://publicculture.org/articles/view/2/1/editors-comment, accessed July 14, 2014.
Eisen, Arnold, *Galut: Modern Jewish Reflection on Homelessness and Homecoming*. Indianapolis, IN: Indiana University Press, 1986.
Elshtain, Jean Bethke, *Women and War: With a New Epilogue*. London and Chicago, IL: University of Chicago Press, 1995.
Epstein, Jerome, "Interview." By Ilan Zvi Baron (September 3, 2008).
Erskine, Toni (ed.), *Can Institutions Have Responsibilities?: Collective Moral Agency and International Relations*. Basingstoke: Palgrave Macmillan, 2003.
Evron, Boas, *Jewish State or Israeli Nation?* Bloomington and Indianapolis, IN: Indiana University Press, 1995.
Eze, Emmanuel Chukwudi, *Race and the Enlightenment: A Reader*. Cambridge: Blackwell, 1997.
Finkelstein, Norman G., *Beyond Chutzpah: On the Misuse of Anti-Semitism and the Abuse of History*. Berkeley, CA: University of California Press, 2005.
Finkelstein, Norman G., *Knowing Too Much: Why the American Jewish Romance with Israel Is Coming to an End*. New York and London: OR Books, 2012.
Finkelstein, Norman G., *The Holocaust Industry: Reflections on the Exploitation of Jewish Suffering*. London; New York: Verso, 2000.
Foucault, Michel, *Discipline and Punish: The Birth of the Prison*, trans. Alison Sheridan. London: Penguin, 1991.
Foucault, Michel, *Security, Territory, Population: Lectures at the College de France, 1977–78*, ed. Michel Senellart, trans. Graham Burchell. New York: Palgrave Macmillan, 2007.
Foucault, Michel, *Society Must Be Defended: Lectures at the Collège De France, 1975–76*, trans. David Macey, ed. Arnold I. Davidson. New York: Picador, 2003.

Foucault, Michel, *The Essential Works of Michel Foucault, 1954–1984. Vol. 3, Power*, ed. James D. Faubion. London: Allen Lane, 2001.

Foucault, Michel, *The History of Sexuality: An Introduction*, trans. Robert Hurley. Vol. 1, New York: Vintage Books, 1990.

Frank, Thomas, *What's the Matter with Kansas?* New York: Holt, 2005.

Frankel, Jonathan, *The Damascus Affair: "Ritual Murder," Politics, and the Jews in 1840*. Cambridge: Cambridge University Press, 1997.

Friedman, Ron, "You Treat Us Disgracefully, Holocaust Survivor Fumes at Mks," *Times of Israel*, April 29, 2013.

Gans, Chaim, *A Just Zionism: On the Morality of the Jewish State*. New York and Oxford: Oxford University Press, 2008.

Geller, Jay, *The Other Jewish Question: Identifying the Jew and Making Sense of Modernity*. New York: Fordham University Press, 2011.

Giddens, Anthony, *The Constitution of Society: Outline of the Theory of Structuration*. Cambridge: Polity Press, 1984, 1986.

Giddens, Anthony, *Modernity and Self-Identity: Self and Society in the Late Modern Age*. Cambridge: Polity Press, 1991.

Gilbert, Margaret, *A Theory of Political Obligation: Membership, Commitment, and the Bonds of Society*. Oxford: Clarendon Press, 2006.

Gold, Steven J., "Transnationalism and Vocabularies of Motive in International Migration: The Case of Israelis in the United States," *Sociological Perspectives* 40, 3 (1997): 409–27.

Gold, Steven J., *The Israeli Diaspora*. Seattle, WA: University of Washington Press, 2002.

Goldberg, J. J., *Jewish Power: Inside the American Jewish Establishment*. Reading, MA and Harlow: Addison-Wesley, 1996.

Goldberg, J. J., "David Twersky, Political Journalist and Peace Activist, Dies at 60," *The Jewish Daily Foward*, July 18, 2010.

Goldberg, J. J., "Interview." By Ilan Zvi Baron and Yael Baron (August 15, 2012).

Goldberg, J. J., "Max Blumenthal's 'Goliath' Is Anti-Israel Book That Makes Even Anti-Zionists Blush," *The Jewish Daily Foward*, October 31, 2013.

Goldberg, J. J., "Prisoner X Case Signals Moment of Crisis for Israel and Jewish Diaspora: Israel Isolation Spawns 'Dual Loyalty' Charge Worldwide," *The Jewish Daily Forward*, March 1, 2013. (Published February 26, 2013.)

Goldstein, Aaron. "Interview." By Ilan Zvi Baron (April 6, 2011).

Goodin, Robert E., "What Is So Special About Our Fellow Countrymen?" *Ethics* 98, 4 (July 1988): 663–86.

Gordon, Jeremy, "Interview." By Ilan Zvi Baron (April 5, 2011).

Gorenberg, Gershom, *The Unmaking of Israel*. New York: Harper, 2011.

Graetz, Michael, and Jane Marie Todd, *The Jews in Nineteenth-Century*

France: From the French Revolution to the Alliance Israelite Universelle [translated from the French]. Stanford, CA: Stanford University Press; Cambridge: Cambridge University Press, 1996.

Graham, David, and Jonathan Boyd, "Committed, Concerned and Conciliatory: The Attitudes of Jews in Britain," London: Institute for Jewish Policy Research, 2010.

Grewal, Inderpal, *Transnational America: Feminisms, Diasporas, Neoliberalisms*. Durham, NC: Duke University Press, 2005.

Grodzinsky, Yosef, *In the Shadow of the Holocaust: The Struggle between Jews and Zionists in the Aftermath of World War II*. Monroe, ME: Common Courage Press, 2004.

Guarnizo, Luis Eduardo, Alejandro Portes, and William Haller, "Assimilation and Transnationalism: Determinants of Transnational Political Action among Contemporary Migrants," *American Journal of Sociology* 108, 6 (May 2003): 1211–48.

Habermas, Jürgen, "Hannah Arendt's Communications Concept of Power," *Social Research* 44, 1 (Spring 1977): 3–24.

Habib, Jasmin, *Israel, Diaspora and the Routes of National Belonging*. Toronto: University of Toronto Press, 2004.

Halliday, Fred, *Revolution and World Politics: The Rise and Fall of the Sixth Great Power*. New York: Palgrave, 1999.

Halpern, Ben, "The Americanization of Zionism, 1880–1930," *American Jewish History* 69, 1 (September 1979): 15–33.

Hanssen, Beatrice, "Critical Theory and Poststructuralism: Habermas and Foucault," Ch. 11 in *The Cambridge Companion to Critical Theory*, ed. Fred Rush, 280–309. Cambridge: Cambridge University Press, 2004.

Haraway, Donna, *Simians, Cyborgs and Women: The Reinvention of Nature*. New York: Routledge, 1991.

Harper, Stephen, *Prime Minister Stephen Harper's Speech to the Knesset*, http://globalnews.ca/news/1094114/prime-minister-stephen-harpers-speech-to-the-knesset/; http://www.cbc.ca/news/politics/stephen-harper-s-speech-to-the-israeli-knesset-1.2503902, accessed February 3, 2014.

Hart, H. L. A., "Are There Any Natural Rights?," *The Philosophical Review* 4, 2 (April 1955): 175–91.

Hartman, Donniel, *The Boundaries of Judaism*. London and New York: Continuum, 2007.

Haugaard, Mark (ed.), *Power: A Reader*. Manchester and New York: Manchester University Press, 2002.

Hawking, S. W., *A Brief History of Time: From the Big Bang to Black Holes*. New York: Bantam, 1988, 1996.

Hayward, Clarissa Rile, "Binding Problems, Boundary Problems: The Trouble with 'Democratic Citizenship,'" Ch. 8 in *Identities, Affiliations, and Allegiances*, ed. Seyla Benhabib, Ian Shapiro and

Danilo Petranović, 181–205. Cambridge: Cambridge University Press, 2007.
Hayward, Clarissa Riles, *De-Facing Power*. Cambridge: Cambridge University Press, 2000.
Hazony, Yoram, *The Jewish State: The Struggle for Israel's Soul*. New York: Basic Books, 2001.
Held, David, *Introduction to Critical Theory: Horkheimer to Habermas*. London: Hutchinson, 1980.
Hertzberg, Arthur, *Being Jewish in America: The Modern Experience*. New York: Schocken Books, 1979.
Hertzberg, Arthur, *The Zionist Idea: A Historical Analysis and Reader*. Westport, CT: Greenwood Press, 1975.
Hertzberg, Arthur, and Aron Hirt-Manheimer, *Jews: The Essence and Character of a People*. San Francisco: HarperSanFrancisco, 1998.
Hobbes, Thomas, *Leviathan*, ed. Richard Tuck, rev. student edn. Cambridge: Cambridge University Press, 1996.
Hockenos, Paul, *Homeland Calling: Exile Patriotism and the Balkan Wars*. Ithaca, NY and London: Cornell University Press, 2003.
Hollis, Martin, and Steve Smith, *Explaining and Understanding International Relations*. Oxford: Clarendon Press, 1990.
Honig, Bonnie, "The Politics of Agonism: A Critical Response to 'Beyond Good and Evil: Arendt, Nietzsche and the Aestheticization of Political Action' by Dana R. Villa," *Political Theory* 21, 3 (August 1993): 528–33.
Horowitz, Bethamie, "And Now for Some Good News About the Pew Survey," *The Jewish Daily Forward*, 2013.
Horowitz, Ira Glunts and Adam, "Church of Scotland Accepts Controversial Report on Israel/Palestine," Mondoweiss, http://mondoweiss.net/2013/05/scotland-controversial-israelpalestine.html, accessed February 18, 2014.
Horton, John, *Political Obligation*, 2nd edn. Basingstoke: Palgrave Macmillan, 2010.
Hoy, David Couzens, and Thomas McCarthy, *Critical Theory*. Oxford: Blackwell, 1994.
Israeli Ministry of Foreign Affairs, *Israeli Ministry of Foreign Affairs*, http://www.mfa.gov.il/MFA/Foreign+Relations/Israel+Among+the+Nations/ISRAEL+AMONG+THE+NATIONS-+World+Jewry.htm, accessed October 22, 2012. [Webpage no longer online.]
Itzigsohn, José, "Immigration and the Boundaries of Citizenship: The Institutions of Immigrants' Political Transnationalism," *International Migration Review* 34, 4 (Winter 2000): 1126–54.
Itzigsohn, José, and Silivia Giorguli Saucedo, "Immigrant Incorporation and Sociocultural Transnationalism," *International Migration Review* 36, 3 (Autumn 2002): 766–98.

Jabotinsky, Ze'ev (Vladimir), *Samson*, trans. Cyrus Brooks. New York and Miami: Judea Publishing, 1986.
Jackson, Peter, Phil Crang, and Claire Dwyer, *Transnational Spaces*. London: Routledge, 2004.
Jacobson, Howard, *The Finkler Question*. London: Bloomsbury, 2010.
Jewish Federations of North America, *The Federation Connection: Media Coverage of the Pew Study*, http://www.jewishfederations.org/blog_post.aspx?id=7314, accessed January 30, 2014.
J Street *About J Street*, http://jstreet.org/about, accessed October 28, 2013.
JTA, "Church of Scotland Backs Away Denial of Jewish Claim to Land of Israel," *The Jewish Daily Forward*, May 11, 2013.
JTA, "Israel Critic Judith Butler Honored in Germany," *The Jewish Daily Forward*, September 6, 2012.
Judt, Tony, "Israel: The Alternative," *New York Review of Books* (October 23, 2003).
Kahn-Harris, Keith, "Interview." By Ilan Zvi Baron (April 5, 2011).
Kant, Immanuel, *Critique of Pure Reason*, trans. Paul Guyer and Allen W. Wood, ed. Paul Guyer and Allen W. Wood. Cambridge: Cambridge University Press, 1998.
Kant, Immanuel, *Kant: Political Writings*, trans H. B. Nisbet, ed. Hans Reiss, 2nd edn. Cambridge: Cambridge University Press, 1991.
Kaplan, Mordecai M., *A New Zionsm*, 2nd, enlarged, edn. New York: The Herzl Press and the Jewish Reconstructionist Press, 1959.
Kaplan, Mordecai M., *Judaism as a Civilization: Toward a Reconstruction of American-Jewish Life*. Philadelphia, PA: Jewish Publication Society, 2010 (1934).
Karpf, Anne, Brian Klug, Jacqueline Rose, and Barbara Rosenbaum (eds), *A Time to Speak Out: Independent Jewish Voices on Israel, Zionism and Jewish Identity*. London: Verso, 2008.
Karsh, Efraim, *Fabricating Israeli History: The "New Historians,"* 2nd, rev., edn. London: Frank Cass, 2000.
Kearney, M., "The Local and the Global: The Anthropology of Globalization and Transnationalism," *Annual Review of Anthropology* 24 (1995): 547–65.
Kedar, Shelley, "Interview." By Ilan Zvi Baron (April 14, 2013).
Keohane, Robert O., and Joseph S. Nye (eds), *Transnational Relations in World Politics*. Cambridge, MA: Harvard University Press, 1972.
Kimmerling, Baruch, *Zionism and Territory: The Socio-Territorial Dimensions of Zionist Politics*. Berkeley, CA: Institute of International Studies, University of California, 1983.
Klein Halevi, Yossi, *At the Entrance to the Garden of Eden: A Jew's Search for Hope with Christians and Muslims in the Holy Land*. New York: Perennial, 2002.
Klosko, George, "Multiple Principles of Political Obligation," *Political Theory* 32, 6 (December 2004): 801–24.

Klosko, George, *Political Obligations*. Oxford: Oxford University Press, 2005.

Klosko, George, *The Principle of Fairness and Political Obligation*, new edn. Lanham, MD and Oxford: Rowman & Littlefield, 2004.

Klug, Brian, "The Climate of Debate About Israel in the Jewish World," Ch. 7 in *Being Jewish and Doing Justice: Bringing Argument to Life*, 121–35. London; Portland, OR: Vallentine Mitchell, 2011.

Knowles, Dudley, *Political Obligation: A Critical Introduction*. London: Routledge, 2010.

Kolsky, Thomas A., *Jews against Zionism: The American Council for Judaism, 1942–1948*. Philadelphia, PA: Temple University Press, 1990.

Kopp, Jonathan, "Interview." By Ilan Zvi Baron and Yael Baron (August 16, 2012).

Koring, Paul, "Canadian Passports: The Disguise of Choice for International Dirty Deeds," *The Globe and Mail*, February 5, 2013.

Kymlicka, Will, "Immigration, Citizenship, Multiculturalism: Exploring the Links." In *The Politics of Migration: Managing Opportunity, Conflict and Change*, ed. Sarah Spencer, 195–208. Oxford: Blackwell, 2003.

Kymlicka, Will, *Multicultural Odysseys: Navigating the New International Politics of Diversity*. Oxford and New York: Oxford University Press, 2007.

Laguerre, Michel S., *Diasporic Citizenship: Haitian Americans in Transnational America*. New York: Palgrave Macmillan, 1998.

Landes, Richard A., "Judith Butler, Renounce the Adorno Prize," *The Times of Israel*, September 6, 2012.

Lang Jr., Anthony F., and John Williams (eds), *Hannah Arendt and International Relations: Reading across the Lines*. New York: Palgrave Macmillan, 2005.

Laqueur, Walter, "The Arendt Cult: Hannah Arendt as Political Commentator," *Journal of Contemporary History* 33, 4 (October 1998): 483–96.

Laqueur, Walter, *The History of Zionism*, 3rd edn. London and New York: I. B. Tauris, 2003.

Leff, Lisa Moses, *Sacred Bonds of Solidarity: The Rise of Jewish Internationalism in Nineteenth-Century France*. Stanford, CA: Stanford University Press, 2006.

Lepow, Jesse, "Interview." By Ilan Zvi Baron (September 2, 2008).

Lévinas, Emmanuel, *God, Death, and Time*, trans. Bettina Bergo. Stanford, CA: Stanford University Press, 1993.

Lévinas, Emmanuel, *Is It Righteous to Be?*, trans. Jill Robbins. Stanford, CA: Stanford University Press, 2001.

Lévinas, Emmanuel, *Otherwise Than Being: Or Beyond Essence*, trans. Alphonso Lingis. Pittsburgh, PA: Duquesne University Press, 1993.

Lévinas, Emmanuel, *Totality and Infinity: An Essay on Exteriority*, trans. Alphonso Lingis. Pittsburgh, PA: Duquesne University Press, 1969.
Lévinas, Emmanuel (ed.), *The Levinas Reader*, ed. Seán Hand. Oxford: Blackwell, 1989.
Levitt, Peggy, and B. Nadya Jaworsky, "Transnational Migration Studies: Past Developments and Future Trends," *Annual Review of Sociology* 33 (2007): 129–56.
Lewis, Neila A., and David Johnston, "U.S. To Drop Spy Case against Pro-Israel Lobbysts," *New York Times*, May 1, 2009.
Library, Jewish Virtual, "Vital Statistics: Latest Population Statistics for Israel," http://www.jewishvirtuallibrary.org/jsource/Society_&_Culture/newpop.html, accessed October 30, 2013.
Liebman, Charles S., and Steven Martin Cohen, *Two Worlds of Judaism: The Israeli and American Experiences*. New Haven, CT: Yale University Press, 1990.
Linklater, Andrew, *Men and Citizens in the Theory of International Relations*, 2nd edn. London: Macmillan in association with London School of Economics and Political Science, 1990.
Linklater, Andrew, *The Transformation of Political Community: Ethical Foundations of the Post-Westphalian Era*. Oxford: Polity, 1998.
Liphshiz, Cnann, "Natan Sharansky to Haaretz: Assimilation Is 'Eating' the Jews," *Haaretz*, November 6, 2009.
Lipman, Jennifer, "David Ward Digs Deeper, Backed by Chomsky," *The Jewish Chronicle*, February 11, 2013.
Lis, Doron, "Interview." By Ilan Zvi Baron (September 1, 2008).
Loomba, Ania, *Colonialism/Postcolonialism*, 2nd edn. London: Routledge, 2005.
Lukes, Steven, *Power: A Radical View*, 2nd edn. Basingstoke and New York: Palgrave Macmillan, 2005.
Lynch, Michael P., "Democracy after the Shutdown," *New York Times*, October 15, 2013.
Magnusson, Warren, *The Search for Political Space*. Toronto: University of Toronto Press, 1996.
Maier, Charles S., "'Being There:' Place, Territory, and Identity," Ch. 3 in *Identities, Affiliations, and Allegiances*, ed. Seyla Benhabib, Ian Shapiro and Danilo Petranović, 67–84. Cambridge: Cambridge University Press, 2007.
Mail, Daily, "Israel Overtakes America as the World's Largest Jewish Population Centre for the First Time," *Daily Mail*, March 30, 2013.
Mann, Michael, *The Sources of Social Power: A History of Power from the Beginning to A.D. 1760*. Vol. 1, Cambridge: Cambridge University Press, 1986.
Marcus, Barry, "Interview." By Ilan Zvi Baron (April 4, 2011).
Markoe, Lauren, "Jewish Critics: Presbyterian Study Guide Equates Zionism with Racism," *Washington Post*, Saturday, February 15, 2014.

McClintock, Anne, Aamir Mufti, and Ella Shohat, *Dangerous Liaisons: Gender, Nations, and Postcolonial Perspectives*. Cultural Politics, Vol.11. Minneapolis, MN and London: University of Minnesota Press, 1997.
McGowan, John, "Must Politics Be Violent? Arendt's Utopian Vision." In *Hannah Arendt and the Meaning of Politics*, ed. Craig Calhoun and John McGowan, 263–96. Minneapolis, MN and London: University of Minnesota Press, 1997.
Mearsheimer, John, and Stephen Walt, "The Israel Lobby," *London Review of Books*, March 23, 2006.
Mearsheimer, John J., and Stephen M. Walt, *The Israel Lobby and U.S. Foreign Policy*. London: Allen Lane, 2007.
Meir, Golda, "What We Want of Diaspora," Ch. 20 in *Diaspora: Exile and the Jewish Condition*, ed. Étan Levine, 219–25. New York and London: Jason Aronson, 1983.
Michaelson, Jay, "Does the Iran Deal Force American Jews to Choose between Dual Loyalties," *The Jewish Daily Forward*, December 4, 2013.
Michaelson, Jay, "How I'm Losing My Love for Israel," *The Jewish Daily Forward*, September 16, 2009.
Michaelson, Jay, "There's a Good Reason for 'Singling out' Israel," *The Jewish Daily Forward*, January 25, 2014.
Miller, David, "The Ethical Significance of Nationality," *Ethics* 98, 4 (July 1988): 647–62.
Miller, Rory, *Divided against Zion: Anti-Zionist Opposition in Britain to a Jewish State in Palestine, 1945–1948*. London: Frank Cass, 2000.
Mittelberg, David, *The Israel Connection and American Jews*. Westport, CT and London: Praeger, 1999.
MITVIM: The Israeli Institute for Regional Foreign Policies, "Findings of a Mitvim Poll on Israel's Foreign Policy." Ramat Gan: MITVIM, 2013.
Miyoshi, Masao, "A Borderless World? From Colonialism to Transnationalism and the Decline of the Nation-State," *Critical Inquiry* 19, 4 (Summer 1993): 726–51.
Mommsen, Wolfgang J., *The Political and Social Theory of Max Weber: Collected Essays* [in translations from the German]. Cambridge: Polity Press, 1992, 1989.
Morgenthau, Hans J., *Politics among Nations: The Struggle for Power and Peace*, ed. Kenneth W. Thompson and W. David Clinton, 7th edn. London: McGraw-Hill, 2006.
Morris, Benny, *The Birth of the Palestinian Refugee Problem Revisited*, 2nd edn. Cambridge; New York: Cambridge University Press, 2004.
Morris, Benny, *Righteous Victims: A History of the Zionist–Arab Conflict 1881–2001*. New York: Random House, 2001.
Morriss, Peter, *Power: A Philosophical Analysis*. Manchester: Manchester University Press, 1987, 2002.

Moskin, Julia, "'Jerusalem' Has All the Right Ingredients," *New York Times*, July 30, 2013.
Myers, David N., *Between Jew & Arab: The Lost Voice of Simon Rawidowicz*. Waltham, MA: Brandeis University Press; Hanover, NH and London: University Press of New England, 2008.
Nathan-Kazis, Josh, "In a Shift, Oren Calls J Street 'A Unique Problem,'" *The Jewish Daily Foward*, December 9, 2009 (issue of December 18, 2009), National News.
Nathan-Kazis, Josh. "Jews Express Wide Criticism of Israel in the Pew Survey but Leaders Dismiss Findings," *The Jewish Daily Foward*, October 2, 2013.
Nathan-Kazis, Josh, "Prominent Jewish Liberals Answer the Jcall," *The Jewish Daily Forward*, May 19, 2010.
Nathan-Kazis, Josh, "Who Do Jewish Leaders Really Represent," *The Jewish Daily Forward*, October 3, 2013.
Nemes, Hody, "Feud over Israel Erupts at Jewish Institutions," *The Jewish Daily Forward*, February 26, 2014.
Nesher, Talia, "92% of Israeli Holocaust Survivors Upset at Treatment by State," *The Jewish Daily Forward*, April 3, 2013.
Neslen, Arthur, *Occupied Minds: A Journey through the Israeli Psyche*. London: Pluto Press, 2006.
Nestle, Marion, *Food Politics: How the Food Industry Influences Nutrition and Health*. Berkeley, CA and London: University of California Press, 2007.
Netanyahu, Benjamin, *A Durable Peace: Israel and Its Place among the Nations*. New York: Warner Books, 1993, 2000.
Ochs, Juliana, *Security and Suspicion: An Ethnography of Everyday Life in Israel*. Philadelphia, PA: University of Pennsylvania Press, 2011.
O'Neill, John, "The Disciplinary Society: From Weber to Foucault," *The British Journal of Sociology* 37, 1 (March 1986): 42–60.
Owens, Patricia, *Between War and Politics: International Relations and the Thought of Hannah Arendt*. Oxford: Oxford University Press, 2007.
Paarlberg, Robert L., *Food Politics: What Everyone Needs to Know*. New York and Oxford: Oxford University Press, 2010.
Painter, Joe, "Multi-Level Citizenship, Identity and Regions in Contemporary Europe," In *Transnational Democracy: Political Spaces and Border Crossings*, ed. James Anderson, 93–110. London and New York: Routledge, 2002.
Pappe, Ilan, *The Ethnic Cleansing of Palestine*. Oxford: Oneworld, 2006.
Parsons, Talcott, "On the Concept of Political Power," Ch. 5 in *Power: A Reader*, ed. Mark Haugaard, 70–112. Manchester: Manchester University Press, 2002.
Pasha, Mustapha Kamal, and Craig N. Murphy (eds), *International Relations and the New Inequality*. Oxford: Blackwell, 2002.

Patel, Raj, *Stuffed and Starved: From Farm to Fork: The Hidden Battle for the World Food System*, updated edn. London: Portobello, 2007.
Pateman, Carole, *The Problem of Political Obligation: A Critical Analysis of Liberal Theory*. Chichester: Wiley, 1979.
Patterson, Rubin, "Diaspora–Homeland Development," *Social Forces* 84, 4 (June 2006): 1891–907.
Pew Research Center, *The Global Religious Landscape*. December 2012, http://www.pewforum.org/2012/12/18/global-religious-landscape-exec/, accessed October 20, 2012.
Pew Research Center, *A Portrait of Jewish Americans*. October 2013, http://www.pewforum.org/2013/10/01/jewish-american-beliefs-attitudes-culture-survey/, accessed July 17, 2014.
Pianko, Noam, *Zionism and the Roads Not Taken: Rawidowicz, Kaplan, Kohn*. Bloomington, IN: Indiana University Press; Chesham: Combined Academic [distributor], 2010.
Piterberg, Gabriel, *The Returns of Zionism*. London: Verso, 2008.
Pitkin, Hanna, "Obligation and Consent – I," *American Political Science Review* 59, 4 (December 1965): 990–9.
Plato, *The Last Days of Socrates: Euthyphro, Apology, Crito, Phaedo*, trans. Hugh Tredennick and Harold Tarrant. London: Penguin, 2003.
Plato, *The Laws*, trans. Trevor J. Saunders. London and New York: Penguin, 2004.
Plato, *The Republic of Plato*, trans. Allan Bloom. New York: Basic Books, 1968.
Podhoretz, Norman, "Now, Instant Zionism," *New York Times*, February 3, 1974.
Podhoretz, Norman, *Why Are Jews Liberals?* New York: Doubleday, 2009.
Portes, Alejandro, "Conclusion: Theoretical Convergences and Empirical Evidence in the Study of Immigrant Transnationalism," *International Migration Review* 37, 3 (Fall 2003): 874–92.
Portes, Alejandro, "Globalization from Below: The Rise of Transnational Communities." In *Latin America in the World Economy*, ed. W. P. Smith and R. P. Korczenwicz, 151–68. Westport, CT: Greenwood Press, 1996.
Portes, Alejandro, *Muscular Judaism: The Jewish Body and the Politics of Regeneration*. London and New York: Routledge, 2007.
Portes, Alejandro, *The Study of Global Interdependence: Essays on the Transnationalization of World Affairs*. London: Frances Pinter, 1980.
Potok, Chaim, *Wanderings: Chaim Potok's History of the Jews*. New York: Fawcett Crest, 1978.
Poulantzas, Nicos, *State, Power, Socialism*. London: Verso, 2000 [1980].
Presner, Todd Samuel, "'Clear Heads, Solid Stomachs, and Hard Muscles': Max Nordau and the Aesthetics of Jewish Regeneration," *Modernism/modernity* 10, 2 (April 2003): 269–96.

Prusher, Ilene, "Jewish Agency Chairman: No Women of the Wall Arrests Next Month," *Haaretz*, November 11, 2013, http://www.haaretz.com/jewish-world/jewish-ga/jewish-ga-news-and-features/.premium-1.557505, accessed January 23, 2014.

Rabin, Yitzhak, "American Jews and Israel: Strengthening the Bonds," Ch. 19 in *Diaspora: Exile and the Jewish Condition*, ed. Étan Levine, 211–17. New York and London: Jason Aronson, 1983.

Rabinovitch, Simon, *Jews and Diaspora Nationalism: Writings on Jewish Peoplehood in Europe and the United States*. Hanover, NH: University Press of New England, 2012.

Rawls, John, *The Law of Peoples; with, "The Idea of Public Reason Revisited."* Cambridge, MA and London: Harvard University Press, 1999.

Reinharz, Jehuda, and Anita Shapira, *Essential Papers on Zionism*. London: Cassell, 1996.

Rich, Danny, "Interview." By Ilan Zvi Baron (April 7, 2011).

Richler, Mordecai, *This Year in Jerusalem*. Toronto: Knopf, 1994.

Rodinson, Maxime, *Israel: A Colonial-Settler State?* [S.l.]: Anchor Foundation/Monad Pathfinder Press, 1973.

Rose, Hilary, and Steven Rose, "Stephen Hawking's Boycott Hits Israel Where It Hurts: Science," *The Guardian*, May 13, 2013.

Rose, Jacqueline, *The Question of Zion*. Princeton, NJ: Princeton University Press, 2005.

Rose, John, *The Myths of Zionism*. London: Pluto Press, 2004.

Rosenau, James N., "International Studies in a Transnational World," *Millennium: Journal of International Studies* 5, 1 (Spring 1976): 1–20.

Rosenberg, Warren, *Legacy of Rage: Jewish Masculinity, Violence and Culture*. Amherst, MA: University of Massachusetts Press, 2001.

Rosenzweig, Franz, *The Star of Redemption*, trans. William W. Halo. Notre Dame: University of Notre Dame Press, 1985.

Roudometof, Victor, "Transnationalism, Cosmopolitanism and Glocalization," *Current Sociology* 53, 1 (2005): 113–35.

Rubin, Amos, "Israel Is Waiting for Its Holocaust Survivors to Die," *Haaretz*, February 6, 2013.

Russell, Bertrand, *Power: A New Social Analysis*. London: Allen & Unwin, 1938.

Said, Edward W., "Zionism from the Standpoint of Its Victims," *Social Text* 1 (Winter, 1979): 7–58.

Sales, Ben, "Holocaust Survivors Struggle to Survive on Pittance in Israel," *The Jewish Daily Forward*, November 25, 2013.

Sales, Ben, "Naftali Bennett: 'Semi-Citizenship' for Diaspora Jews," *Jewish Telegraphic Agency*, February 17, 2014.

Sand, Shlomo, *The Invention of the Jewish People* [translated from the Hebrew]. London: Verso, 2009.

Schiller, Nina Glick, Linda Basch, and Cristina Blanc-Szanton, "From Immigrant to Transmigrant: Theorizing Transnational Migration," *Anthropological Quarterly* 68, 1 (January 1995): 48–63.

Schiller, Nina Glick, Linda G. Basch, and Cristina Blanc-Szanton, *Towards a Transnational Perspective on Migration: Race, Class, Ethnicity, and Nationalism Reconsidered: Workshop: Papers*. New York: New York Academy of Sciences, 1992.

Schweid, Eliezer, "The Rejection of the Diaspora in Zionist Thought: Two Approaches," *Studies in Zionism* 5, 1 (Spring 1984): 43–70.

Segev, Tom, *The Seventh Million: The Israelis and the Holocaust*. New York: Hill & Wang, 1993.

Seliktar, Ofira, *Divided We Stand: American Jews, Israel, and the Peace Process*. Westport, CT: Praeger, 2002.

Selzer, Michael (ed.), *Zionism Reconsidered: The Rejection of Jewish Normalcy*. New York: Macmillan, 1970.

Senor, Dan, and Saul Singer, *Start-up Nation: The Story of Israel's Economic Miracle*. New York: Twelve, 2009.

Shain, Yossi, *Kinship and Diasporas in International Affairs*. Ann Arbor, MI: University of Michigan Press, 2007.

Shain, Yossi, and Aharon Barth, "Diasporas and International Relations Theory," *International Organization* 57, 3 (2003): 449–79.

Shain, Yossi, and Barry Bristman, "Diaspora, Kinship and Loyalty: The Renewal of Jewish National Security," *International Affairs* 78, 1 (2002): 69–95.

Shain, Yossi, "Ethnic Diasporas and U.S. Foreign Policy," *Political Science Quarterly* Winter, 5 (1994–5): 811–41.

Shapira, Anita, *Land and Power: The Zionist Resort to Force, 1881–1948*. Oxford: Oxford University Press, 1992. Stanford, CA: Stanford University Press, 1999.

Shapiro, Michael J., "Metaphor in the Social Sciences," Ch. 1 in *Michael J. Shapiro: Discourse, Culture, Violence*, ed. Terrell Carver and Samuel A. Chambers, 15–32. New York: Routledge, 2012.

Shatz, Adam (ed.), *Prophets/Outcast: A Century of Dissident Jewish Writing About Zionism*. New York: Nation Books, 2004.

Shavit, Avi, *My Promised Land: the Triumph and Tragedy of Israel*. New York: Spiegel & Grau, 2013.

Sheffer, Gabriel, *Diaspora Politics: At Home Abroad*. Cambridge: Cambridge University Press, 2003.

Sheffer, Gabriel, "Ethno-National Diasporas and Security," *Survival* 36, 1 (1994): 60–79.

Sheffer, Gabriel, "Loyalty and Criticism in the Relations between World Jewry and Israel," *Israel Studies* 17, 2 (Summer 2012): 77–85.

Shimoni, Gideon, *The Zionist Ideology*. Hanover, NH and London: Brandeis University Press, 1995.

Shindler, Colin, *Israel and the European Left: Between Solidarity and Delegitimization*. New York: Continuum, 2012.
Shlaim, Avi, *The Iron Wall: Israel and the Arab World*. London: Penguin, 2000.
Sicker, Martin, *Judaism, Nationalism, and the Land of Israel*. Boulder, CO: Westview Press, 1992.
Silverman, Jerry, and Michael Siegal, "4 Things to Do About Pew Survey Findings on #Jewishamerica," *The Jewish Daily Forward*, 2013.
Simmons, A. John, "Associative Political Obligations," *Ethics* 106, 2 (January 1996): 247–73.
Simmons, A. John, *Moral Principles and Political Obligation*. Princeton, NJ: Princeton University Press, 1980.
Smith, Janet, "Finding Israel's Finest Export," *The Georgia Straight*, February 13–20, 2014, 31–2.
Smith, Michael Peter, "Transnationalism and Citizenship," Ch. 2 in *Approaching Transnationalisms: Studies on Transnational Societies, Multicultural Contacts, and Imaginings of Home*, ed. Brenda S. A. Yeoh, Michael W. Charney and Tong Chee Kiong, 15–38. Boston, Dordecht and London: Kluwer Academic, 2003.
Smith, Michael Peter, and Luis Eduardo Guarnizo (eds), *Transnationalism from Below*. London: Transaction, 1998.
Sobel, Zvi, *Migrants from the Promised Land*. New Brunswick, NJ: Oxford Transaction Books, 1986.
Stanislawski, Michael, *Zionism and the Fin De Siècle: Cosmopolitanism and Nationalism from Nordau to Jabotinsky*. Berkeley, CA, Los Angeles and London: University of California Press, 2001.
Starbucks, *Facts About Starbucks in the Middle East*, http://news.starbucks.com/news/facts-about-starbucks-in-the-middle-east, October 17, 2013.
Steele, Brent J. *Ontological Security in International Relations: Self-Identity and the IR State*. London: Routledge, 2008.
Stirk, Peter M. R., *Critical Theory, Politics and Society*. London: Continuum, 2000.
Suganami, Hidemi. *The Domestic Analogy and World Order Proposals*. Cambridge: Cambridge University Press, 1989.
Sunshine, Jason, and Tom Tyler, "Moral Solidarity, Identification with the Community, and the Importance of Procedural Justice: The Police as Prototypical Representatives of a Group's Moral Values," *Social Psychological Quarterly* 66, 2 (June 2003): 153–65.
Taylor, Charles, *Sources of the Self: The Making of the Modern Identity*. Cambridge: Cambridge University Press, 1989.
Thelen, David, "How Natural Are National and Transnational Citizenship? A Historical Perspective," *Indiana Journal of Global Legal Studies* 7, 2 (Spring 2000): 549–65.

Thomas, Baylis, *The Dark Side of Zionism: Israel's Quest for Security through Dominance*. New York: Lexington Books, 2009.
Tilly, Charles, "War Making and State Making as Organized Crime." In *Bringing the State Back In*, ed. Peter B. Evans, Dietrich Rueschemeyer and Theda Skocpol, 169–91. Cambridge: Cambridge University Press, 1985.
Timmerman, Kelsey, *Where Am I Eating?* Hoboken, NJ: John Wiley, 2013.
Trepp, Leo, *A History of the Jewish Experience*. Springfield, NJ: Behrman House, 2001.
Tully, James, *Public Philosophy in a New Key: Democracy and Civic Freedom. Ideas in Context*. Vol. I, Cambridge and New York: Cambridge University Press, 2008.
Tully, James, *Public Philosophy in a New Key: Imperialism and Civic Freedom*. Vol. II, Cambridge: Cambridge University Press, 2008.
Turetzky, Philip, "Immanent Critique," *Philosophy Today* 33, 2 (Summer 1989): 144–58.
Twersky, David, "Interview." By Ilan Zvi Baron (September 2, 2008).
Urofsky, Melvin I., *American Zionism from Herzl to the Holocaust*. New York: Anchor Press/Doubleday, 1975.
Vertovec, Steven, "Migrant Transnationalism and Modes of Transformation," *International Migration Review* 38, 3 (2004): 970–1001.
Vertovec, Steven, *Transnationalism*. London: Routledge, 2009.
Vertovec, Steven, and Robin Cohen, *Migration, Diasporas, and Transnationalism*. Cheltenham: Edward Elgar, 1999.
Villa, Dana (ed.), *The Cambridge Companion to Hannah Arendt*. Cambridge: Cambridge University Press, 2000.
Vital, David, *The Future of the Jews: A People at the Crossroads?* Cambridge, MA: Harvard University Press, 1990.
Waldinger, Roger, and David Fitzgerald, "Transnationalism in Question," *American Journal of Sociology* 109, 5 (March 2004): 1177–95.
Walker, R. B. J., *Inside/Outside: International Relations as Political Theory*. Cambridge: Cambridge University Press, 1993.
Waltz, Kenneth Neal, *Theory of International Politics*. Addison-Wesley Series in Political Science. Reading, MA, New York and London: Addison-Wesley; McGraw-Hill, 1979.
Walzer, Michael, *Arguing About War*. New Haven, CT and London: Yale University Press, 2004.
Walzer, Michael, *Just and Unjust Wars: A Moral Argument with Historical Illustrations*, 3rd edn. New York: Basic Books, 2000.
Walzer, Michael, *Obligations: Essays on Disobedience, War and Citizenship*. Cambridge, MA: Harvard University Press, 1970.
Walzer, Michael, "The Moral Standing of States: A Response to Four Critics," *Philosophy and Public Affairs* 9, 3 (Spring 1980): 209–29.

Ward, David, "Bradford MP Condemns Israel for Treatment of Palestinians," http://davidward.org.uk/en/article/2013/654457/bradford-mp-condemns-israel-for-treatment-of-palestinians-on-the-day-he-signs-the-holocaust-memorial-day-book-of-commitment, accessed February 7, 2013. [This webpage has since been removed.]
Weber, Max, *Economy and Society*, ed. Guenther Roth and Claus Wittich. Vol. 1. Berkeley, CA: University of California Press, 1978.
Weber, Max, *The Methodology of the Social Sciences*, trans. Henry A. Finch and Edward Albert Shils. London: Transaction, 2011 [1949].
Weber, Max, Peter Lassman, and Ronald Speirs, *Political Writings*. Cambridge and New York: Cambridge University Press, 1994.
Weiner, Chaim, "Interview." By Ilan Zvi Baron (April 4, 2011).
Wernick, Steven, "Interview." By Ilan Zvi Baron and Yael Baron (August 22, 2012).
Wheeler, Nicholas J., *Saving Strangers: Humanitarian Intervention in International Society*. Oxford: Oxford University Press, 2000.
Whitfield, Stephen J., "Declarations of Independence: American Jewish Culture in the Twentieth Century," Ch. 9 in *Cultures of the Jews: Modern Encounters*, ed. David Biale, 377–424. New York: Schocken Books, 2002.
Wight, Martin, "Why Is There No International Theory," *International Relations* 21, 1 (April 1960): 35–48.
Williams, Melissa S., "Nonterritorial Boundaries of Citizenship," Ch. 10 in *Identities, Affiliations, and Allegiances*, ed. Seyla Benhabib, Ian Shapiro and Danilo Petranović, 226–56. Cambridge: Cambridge University Press, 2007.
Wilson, John K., "An Interview with Alan Dershowitz," in *Academe Blog*, 2012.
Women of the Wall, *Women of the Wall*, http://womenofthewall.org.il, accessed January 23, 2014.
Yehoshua, A. B., "Exile as a Neurotic Condition," Ch. 1 in *Diaspora: Exile and the Jewish Conditions*, ed. Étan Levine, 15–36. New York and London: Jason Aronson, 1983.
Young, Iris Marion, *Responsibility for Justice*. Oxford: Oxford University Press, 2011.
Young-Bruehl, Elisabeth, *Hannah Arendt: For Love of the World*, 2nd edn. New Haven, CT and London: Yale University Press, 2004.
Young-Bruehl, Elisabeth, *Why Arendt Matters*. New Haven, CT and London: Yale University Press, 2006.
Zeitlin, Irving M., *Jews: The Making of a Diaspora People*. Cambridge: Polity Press, 2012.
Zertal, Idith, *Israel's Holocaust and the Politics of Nationhood*. Cambridge: Cambridge University Press, 2005.
Zirakzadeh, Cyrus Ernesto, *Social Movements in Politics: A Comparative Study*, expanded edn. Basingstoke: Palgrave Macmillan, 2006.

Index

Adorno, Theodor, 203
agency, 89–90; *see also* leadership
Ahabath Israel, 197
Algeria, 132, 133, 134
aliya, 33, 121, 140; *see also* immigration
Alliance Israélite Universelle (AIU), 134–5, 156
Alternative Jewish Voices, 32
American Council for Judaism, 138, 139–40, 180
American Israel Public Affairs Committee (AIPAC), 2, 42, 152, 162, 163, 164
American Jewish Committee, 12, 31, 152–3, 168–9, 190
American Jewish Congress, 3, 12, 32, 187
American Jewish World Service, 32, 157
American Revolution, 88
anarchist theories (political obligation), 44, 45, 50–1, 62–3
Anti-Defamation League, 163, 164
anti-Semitism, 114–15, 133, 136, 141, 144, 146–7, 154, 161–3, 180–3, 205, 213
anti-Zionism, 4–5, 33, 138, 150, 180, 201, 206–7
Appadurai, Arjun, 87, 124–5, 126, 127, 129
Arendt, Hannah, 2, 36–7, 69, 72–3, 87–105, 119–20, 132, 159, 197–8, 202–4, 206, 207, 212, 213, 222
Argentina, 21, 145
Aristotle, 53, 93–4, 95–6, 97, 98, 105
assimilation, 7, 141–2, 190, 212–13, 221; *see also* integration

Association of Reform Zionists in America (ARZA), 32, 160
associative theories (political obligation), 44, 45–6
Aswan Solution (Rowe), 116
Augustine, St, 53
authenticity, 120
authoritarianism, 98–9
authority
 and boundaries, 8, 9
 and legitimacy, 46, 47, 55, 163–6
 and political obligation, 46, 47, 51, 55, 80, 81–2, 93–9, 113, 120, 218
 and power, 78–83, 87, 91, 93–9, 103–4, 120, 121, 154, 159, 193, 222
 of the state, 46, 55, 78–80, 81–2
Aviv, Caryn, 29, 31

Baron, Salo, 216
Bauman, Zygmunt, 89–90
Bayfield, Tony, 180, 198
Bayme, Steven, 168–70, 190
Beinart, Peter, 1–2, 21
Ben-Aviv, Shoshana, 25
Ben-Gurion, David, 141, 207, 210
Ben Moreh, Martin, 121, 175–6
Ben-Sasson, H. H., 4, 22
Benjamin, Jon, 168
Benjamin, Walter, 202–3, 204
Bennett, Naftali, 129
Berman, Saul, 168, 185–6, 191
Bernard, Daniel, 19
Black, Conrad, 19
Blumenthal, Max, 29, 202
Board of Deputies of British Jews, 32, 168, 169, 191
Bodin, Jean, 88

Index

body, the, 106, 114–18
Bonn, Julius Moriz, 136–7
boundaries, 8, 9, 62, 64, 120, 137, 207
Boycott, Divestment and Sanctions movement, 204
Boyd, Jonathan, 167–8, 189
Brandeis, Louis, 2, 141
Brechner, Harry, 177–9, 189
Breckenridge, Carol, 129
Breines, Paul, 116
Bristman, Barry, 27
Brom, Shlomo, 172–3
Buber, Martin, 2, 204, 212, 213
Buenos Aires bombing, 145
Bull, Hedley, 48
bureaucracy, 89–90, 92
Butler, Judith, 11, 26, 27–8, 29, 196, 197, 202–7, 212, 219

Calhoun, Craig, 119
Campus Watch, 19
Canada, 31, 33–4, 140–3, 150, 177–9, 181–3, 189, 215, 221–2
Canovan, Margaret, 102
Castells, Manuel, 112, 199
Catholicism, 133, 135
Chicago, 34, 177
citizenship, 7, 24, 42, 61–2, 65–7, 71–2, 75, 129–32, 171–2, 218–19; *see also* membership
civil rights, 109, 117, 133, 194, 219
classical Zionism, 141, 142, 175
Clausewitz, Carl von, 101
Clavin, Patricia, 136
Clifford, James, 126
Cohen, Eliot, 163
Cohen, Jeffrey, 147
Cohen, Robin, 26, 108–9
Cohen, Steven M., 11
Cold War, 61, 88, 150
colonialism, 60, 123, 132, 133–4, 136, 201
Community Security Trust (CST), 146
Conference of Presidents of Major Jewish Organizations, 2, 12, 164
conscription (military), 57, 65–6
consent, 44–5, 54, 158–9, 164
contract theory, 50, 52
conversion, 131, 172, 184
Crémieux, Adolphe, 41, 42, 134
Crimean War, 134

critique, 29–30, 37–9, 147–8, 150, 161–2, 167–73, 178, 181–6, 189–90, 196–216, 219–22
cultural Zionism, 139, 142, 221

Dagger, Richard, 50
Dahl, Robert, 82, 86, 88, 89
Damascus Affair, 41–3, 124, 132–3, 134, 144
Davids, Andrew, 160
Declaration of the Rights of Man and Citizen, 133
D'Entrèves, A. P., 100
deontological theories (political obligation), 44–5
Dershowitz, Alan, 19–20, 163, 201
deterritorialization, 72, 126
Diaspora, negation of, 109, 127, 139–44, 171, 175, 210, 221
Diaspora nationalism, 68, 123, 132, 137–8
diaspora politics, 26–7, 41–2, 66, 108–9, 126–7, 129–30
Diaspora security, 6, 27, 140, 144–51, 154, 174–5, 180–1, 195, 208, 220
Dinur, Ben Zion, 22
disciplinary power, 106, 107–8, 160
division of labour, 105
divorce, 5, 184
donations *see* fundraising
Dorfman, Aaron, 157
dual loyalty, 21, 42, 67, 133, 160, 162–3
Dubnow, Simon, 2, 23, 207–8
Dufoix, Stéphane, 26
duty, distinguished from obligation, 63–4
Dworkin, Ronald, 45

Eban, Abba, 188
education, 11, 94, 95, 96, 104, 167, 175
Eichmann, Adolf, 90, 119, 159, 197
Einstein, Albert, 150
Eisen, Arnold, 23, 138, 141, 143, 156
Enlightenment, 154, 203
Epstein, Jerome, 163
espionage, 42
ethnoscapes, 87, 126–7
European Jewish Congress, 12, 147
Evron, Boas, 213–14

289

exile, 109, 126, 138, 139, 140, 171, 219, 221

fairness, 46, 54, 55–6
Fanon, Franz, 88
fascism, 156, 203
feminism, 105–6
Finkelstein, Norman, 19–21
Finkler Question (Jacobson), 15–19, 151, 193–4, 219, 220
food, 15, 16, 188, 191
"For the sake of Zion" petition, 151–2
force
   monopoly on legitimate use of, 54, 61, 75, 76, 77–9, 100
   and power, 83, 84, 88–9, 91, 92–3, 100–1, 107, 109–10
   see also violence
foreign policy
   Israel, 20, 147–8, 150–1, 165–6; *see also* Israeli security
   and liberalism, 60–1
   United States, 61, 165–6, 188
Foucault, Michel, 9, 37, 72, 74, 84, 85, 87, 90, 106–12, 119–21, 159
Foxman, Abe, 164–5, 166
France, 34, 41–2, 124, 132–6, 150, 156, 162, 176
Frankfurt School, 202–3, 204
French Revolution, 133, 134, 154
Fromm, Erich, 203
fundraising, 3–4, 117, 135, 141, 188

galut, 139, 140, 221; *see also* exile
Gaza, 24, 25, 184, 200
Geertz, Clifford, 34–5
Geller, Jay, 114
gender roles, 105
Germany, 61, 157
Giddens, Anthony, 87, 90, 106
Gilbert, Margaret, 47–53, 81
Giuliani, Rudy, 128
globalization, 125–7, 161
golah, 139–40
Gold, Steven, 26, 148–9
Goldberg, J. J., 10, 21, 149, 187, 199
Goodin, Robert E., 62
Gordon, Jeremy, 180
Gorenberg, Gershom, 201
Government of Israel and World Jewry Joint Initiative, 129

governmentality, 74, 109–10
Graetz, Michael, 133
Grewal, Inderpal, 24
Grossman, David, 147

Ha'Am, Ahad, 139, 142, 208, 221
Habermas, Jürgen, 87, 103, 203
Habib, Jasmin, 25, 68, 132
Habonim Dror, 33, 187, 219
Haiti, 61, 128
halakha (*halakhic*), 8, 9
Halevi, Yossi Klein, 201
Halliday, Fred, 59
Hamas, 202, 204
Haraway, Donna, 114
Harper, Stephen, 181–2, 221–2
Hart, H. L. A., 46, 52, 55, 56, 64
Hartmann, Donniel, 8–9
Hawking, Stephen, 3
Hazony, Yoram, 201
Hegel, Georg Wilhelm Friedrich, 53, 203, 204
Heidegger, Martin, 97
Hertzberg, Arthur, 143
Hobbes, Thomas, 48, 53, 59, 83, 88
Holocaust, 15–17, 24–6, 108, 139, 148, 167, 174, 177, 187, 192, 215
Horkheimer, Max, 203
Horowitz, Bethamie, 12–13
Horton, John, 43–6, 48, 50–1, 53, 63, 71, 78, 81
human rights, 2, 20, 60, 108, 145, 151, 164, 182, 201–2
Hume, David, 58
Hungarian uprisings, 88

identity construction, 37, 85, 104–14, 120–1, 160, 176–7, 193–4, 199, 218
immanent critique, 196, 202–12
immigration
   to Israel, 2, 33, 121, 131, 140, 142
   policies on, 131, 150, 209
   see also migration
Institute for Jewish Policy Research (JPR), 167
integration, 69, 141, 149, 161, 205; *see also* assimilation
international politics, 48, 53–4, 59–61, 123–6

Index

International Relations (IR), 48, 59–61, 86, 125–6, 127–8
international society, 48
Israel, empirical data, 31, 34, 170–7, 179–80
Israeli Defence Forces (IDF), 172
Israeli Diaspora, 137, 149
Israeli identity, 25, 121, 213, 214
Israeli security, 5, 21, 27, 145, 147–53, 165, 180, 186–7, 194, 195, 206, 214, 215, 221
Israelization, 27, 112, 117, 138, 139–44, 148, 156, 160, 169, 187, 190, 191–2, 199, 206

J Street, 17, 32, 42, 152–3, 164–6, 200
Jabotinsky, Vladimir, 114
Jacobson, Howard: *The Finkler Question*, 15–19, 151, 193–4, 219, 220
Jerusalem, 2, 7, 152, 191
Jewish Agency, 6–7, 10, 174, 175, 188
Jewish Call for Reason (JCall), 152
Jewish Daily Forward, 11, 152, 165
Jewish Federation of North America, 13
Jewish Fellowship, 138
Jewish history, 22–3, 169, 177, 186, 193–4, 201, 215
Jewish identity, 3–5, 9, 12–15, 22–3, 26–9, 33, 39, 69, 107–9, 112–18, 121–2, 130–2, 138, 140–4, 146–8, 151–4, 156, 159–61, 167–71, 176–7, 179–80, 184, 186–8, 190–6, 198–9, 205–9, 212, 215, 217–21
Jewish Institute for Policy Research, 32
Jewish internationalism, 23, 26, 28, 34, 37, 67, 123–4, 132–7, 144, 154, 156–7, 162, 175
Jewish law, 8, 12, 185
Jewish nationalism, 2, 9, 23, 28–9, 69, 207
Jewish Voice for Peace, 163–4
joint commitments, 49–51
Joint Distribution Committee, 32, 156, 175
Judis, John, 11
Judt, Tony, 150–1
justification, 96, 99, 102–3

Kahn-Harris, Keith, 180–1
Kant, Immanuel, 45, 53, 59, 203, 204
Kaplan, Mordecai, 142–3, 207
Kedar, Shelley, 170, 171, 174
Keohane, Robert, 127–8
Khalidi, Rashid, 11–12
King, Martin Luther, 219
Kirchheimer, Otto, 203
Klosko, George, 35, 43, 46, 54–7, 58, 60–2, 76, 81, 136, 157–9
Klug, Brian, 147
Kohn, Hans, 207
kol Yisrael haverim, 170
Kopp, Jonathan, 152–3, 165–6

Law of Return, 131
leadership, 76–80, 89–90, 164–5
Lebanon War, 150, 187
Leff, Lisa Moses, 26, 124, 133, 135–6
legitimacy, 46, 47, 56, 77, 90, 99–100, 113, 120, 163–6, 218; *see also* force: monopoly on legitimate use of
legitimizing identities, 112
Lévinas, Emmanuel, 204
Levine, Jacqueline, 3
Liberal Judaism, 183
liberal Zionism, 1–2, 165
liberalism, 46, 55–7, 58–61, 80, 123, 124, 132–6, 161
Livni, Tzipi, 164
Locke, John, 58, 59, 65
London, 31, 32–3, 145–7, 169, 180–1, 183, 185
Löwenthal, Leo, 203
loyalty, 7–8, 10, 21, 26, 29, 38, 42, 127, 130, 141, 160–3, 175, 191
Lukes, Steven, 82, 90, 111, 119
Lynch, Michael, 158–9

McGowan, John, 119
Magnes, Judah, 2
Magnusson, Warren, 80
Mann, Michael, 74, 80, 106
Marcus, Barry, 146, 185
Marcuse, Herbert, 203
marriage, 5, 131, 184
Marx, Karl, 53, 79, 98, 100, 203, 204, 217
Masa project, 174
Mearsheimer, John, 162–3, 189

media, 5, 108, 147
Meir, Golda, 140, 141
membership, 8–9, 44–5, 47–53, 66–7, 71, 131–2, 158, 170, 207, 218; *see also* citizenship
Michaelson, Jay, 200
migration, 136–7, 149–50; *see also* immigration
Milgrom, Shira, 20–1
Mill, John Stuart, 58
Miller, David, 62
Mills, C. Wright, 100
Ministry of Foreign Affairs (Israel), 6, 34, 151, 170, 171, 173–4, 175, 176–7, 179, 219
Montefiore, Sir Moses, 41
moral obligation, 38, 63–5, 147, 148, 158, 169–70, 218
Morgenthau, Hans, 86, 88, 127
Morris, Benny, 3
Morriss, Peter, 86, 106
Mossad, 21
Movement for Reform Judaism, 180
Muscle Jews, 37, 113–18, 120
Myers, David, 211

Nathan-Kazis, Josh, 152
national loyalty, 7, 10, 21, 42, 127, 130
nationalism *see* Diaspora nationalism; Jewish nationalism
Netanyahu, Benjamin, 129, 144, 201
Neumann, Franz, 203
New York, 31–2, 34, 128, 162–3, 177, 185, 187
Nordau, Max, 114–16
Noriega, Manuel, 61
Nozick, Robert, 58
nuclear weapons, 88, 89
Nye, Joseph, 127–8

obligation *see* moral obligation; political obligation; transnational political obligation
Occupation, 1, 3, 25, 151, 172, 189, 190, 194, 196, 202, 205; *see also* Palestine
Oren, Michael, 164
Orthodox Union (OU), 32, 184–5, 186–7
Orthodoxy, 7, 8–9, 19, 184–5, 186–7

Ottolenghi, Yotam, 191
Oz, Amos, 147

Palestine, 19, 24–5, 65–6, 142–3, 146–7, 151–3, 156, 164, 172, 178–9, 184, 189–90, 194, 200, 202, 205, 208–11, 213, 215
Panama, 61
Parsons, Talcott, 93
particularity principle, 44, 53–4, 61–7, 71, 75, 76, 118, 123, 158
Peres, Shimon, 27, 164
Pew Survey, 12–16, 112, 146, 164, 184, 196, 198
Pianko, Noam, 14, 207, 211–12
Pitkin, Hannah, 45, 46–7
Plato, 93–5, 97, 105
plurality, 88, 91–2, 100, 104, 119
Podhoretz, Norman, 198, 201
political obligation
    and authority, 46, 47, 51, 55, 80, 81–2, 93–9, 113, 120, 218
    and citizenship, 24, 42, 61–2, 65–7, 71, 75, 129–32
    and critique, 148, 197–216
    defining, 43–53
    and empirical data, 157–9
    and the law, 135–6, 158
    and liberalism, 58–61
    and loyalty, 7–8, 26, 29, 42, 161–2
    and the particularity principle, 44, 53–4, 61–7, 71, 75, 76, 118, 123, 158
    and power, 36–7, 46, 69, 72–104, 107–9, 113, 118–21, 127–8, 154, 159–60, 193–4, 217–18
    and rights, 52, 54, 64
    and security, 36, 37, 41–3, 53–61, 113, 123–4, 136, 147–9, 154, 174–5, 218
    and solidarity, 135–6
    and the state, 24, 43–8, 52, 53–69, 71–2, 74–81, 118, 123–4, 127, 217
    transnational, 28–30, 33, 36, 38–9, 46, 66, 68–9, 72–3, 84–7, 103–4, 107–9, 113, 118–21, 123–4, 127–31, 136, 193–202, 212, 218–20
political societies, 47–53

Index

political Zionism, 4, 139–40, 142, 143, 221
Pollard, Jonathan, 42, 144
Pollock, Friedrich, 203
post-colonial theory, 60
post-Zionism, 199, 201
Potok, Chaim, 215
Poulantzas, Nicos, 87
power
  and agency, 89–90
  Arendt on, 36–7, 69, 72–3, 85–105, 119–20, 159, 222
  and authority, 78–83, 87, 91, 93–9, 103–4, 120, 121, 154, 159, 193, 222
  disciplinary, 106, 107–8, 160
  and force, 83, 84, 88–9, 91, 92–3, 100–1, 107, 109–10
  Foucault on, 37, 72, 106–12, 120–1
  and identity, 37, 72, 85, 104–14, 120–1, 160, 176–7, 193–4, 199, 218
  in International Relations (IR) literature, 86, 127–8
  and the particularity principle, 73–6
  and plurality, 88, 91–2, 100, 104, 119
  and political obligation, 36–7, 46, 69, 72–104, 107–8, 113, 118–21, 127–8, 154, 159–60, 193–4, 217–18
  in political obligation literature, 81–5
  and the public realm, 90–1, 99, 103, 105, 113, 193, 218
  and strength, 91, 92, 177–80, 205, 211
  and violence, 72, 91, 99–103, 120
  Walzer on, 81–3, 84, 85
  Weber on, 36, 72, 76–81, 84–5, 86, 88, 89, 127
Presner, Todd, 114–15
Prisoner X scandal, 21
private realm, 105
progress, 88
project identities, 112
propaganda, 19, 108, 115–16, 117–18
Protestantism, 135
ProZion, 164
public goods, 56, 58, 61

public realm, 90–1, 99, 103, 105, 113, 193, 218

Rabin, Yitzhak, 27, 144, 216
"Rambowitz" figures, 116–17
Rawidowicz, Simon, 207, 209–11
Rawls, John, 45, 56, 58
resistance, 38, 47, 56, 59–60, 63, 75, 78–9, 95, 110, 197, 219
resistance identities, 112
revisionist history, 3, 127, 140–1, 179, 201, 213
Rich, Danny, 183
Richler, Mordecai, 219–20
rights
  civil, 109, 117, 133, 194, 219
  human, 2, 20, 60, 108, 145, 151, 164, 182, 201–2
  and obligation, 52, 54, 64
Rodinson, Maxime, 201
Romania, 133
Rose, Jacqueline, 29–30, 194, 213, 214
Rose, John, 29
Rosenau, James N., 125
Rosenweig, Franz, 142, 204
Rowe, John: *The Aswan Solution*, 116
Russell, Bertrand, 3, 73–4
Russia, 150, 189–90
Russian Revolution, 79

Said, Edward, 204, 206
Sand, Shlomo, 201
Sartre, Jean-Paul, 88
Schechter, Solomon, 141–2
Scholem, Gershom, 132, 140, 197–8
Second World War, 100, 117, 150; *see also* Holocaust
security
  Diaspora, 6, 27, 140, 144–51, 154, 174–5, 180–1, 195, 208, 220
  Israeli, 5, 21, 27, 145, 147–53, 165, 180, 186–7, 194, 195, 206, 214, 215, 221
  and political obligation, 36, 37, 41–2, 53–61, 113, 123–4, 136, 147–9, 154, 174–5, 218
self, constructions of, 37, 72, 85, 104–14, 120–1, 160, 176–7, 193–4, 199, 218
self-discipline, 106, 107–8, 111, 121, 160

Shain, Yossi, 26–7
Shapiro, Michael, 30–1
Sharansky, Natan, 7, 10, 175
Sharon, Ariel, 27
Shavit, Avi, 201
Sheffer, Gabriel, 26, 161–2
Shlaim, Avi, 3
Shneer, David, 29, 31
Siegal, Michael, 13
Silverman, Jerry, 13
Simmons, A. J., 45, 50–1, 53, 62–6, 81
Six Day War, 3–5, 115, 116–17, 167
Socrates, 82, 94, 95, 97, 105, 202
solidarity, 27, 121, 126, 134–6; *see also* Jewish internationalism
sovereignty, 30, 47, 60, 69, 72, 88, 193, 205, 211, 219
Soviet Union *see* Russia
spiritual Zionism, 139, 143, 208
strength, 91, 92, 113–18, 177–80, 189, 205–6
submission, 78–80, 88, 104, 114, 222

Taglit-Birthright program, 12, 174, 184
Tamimi, Sami, 191
technology, 88, 89, 102
Tel Aviv, 31, 172, 178
teleological theories (political obligation), 44
territoriality, 46, 53, 76–7, 78
Tilly, Charles, 78
Torah, 138, 159, 180
totalitarianism, 88, 89–90, 102–3
tradition, 96–8, 103–4, 113, 120, 159, 218, 222
transnational political obligation, 28–30, 33, 36, 38–9, 46, 66, 68–9, 72–3, 84–7, 103–4, 107–8, 113, 118–21, 123–4, 127–31, 136, 193–202, 212, 218–20
transnationalism, 123–32, 136–44, 154
Tully, James, 84
Twersky, David, 187–8, 189–90, 196
tyranny, 94, 102–3

Uganda, 61
Union for Reform Judaism, 32
United Jewish Appeal, 3–4

United Kingdom, 13, 42, 124, 130, 145–7, 150, 156, 196, 215
empirical data, 31–3, 167–9, 176, 180–1, 183, 185, 189
United Nations, 182, 194
United States, 1–4, 11–12, 27, 42, 57, 61, 109, 115, 118, 122, 128–30, 140–4, 149, 150, 152–3, 188, 205, 215, 219
empirical data, 31–2, 34, 157–9, 162–6, 168–70, 174, 176–7, 185–90
Pew Survey data, 12–16, 112, 146, 164, 184, 196, 198
United Synagogue of Conservative Judaism, 12, 32, 163

Vancouver, 33–4, 183
Vertovec, Steven, 126
victimhood, 25, 29, 146, 177–80, 189, 205–6, 213
Victoria, 33, 177–8
Vietnam War, 57
violence
  and liberalism, 60, 136
  monopoly on legitimate use, 54, 61, 75, 76, 77–9, 100
  and power, 72, 91, 99–103, 120
  and Zionism, 207, 213
  see also force
Vital, David, 5–6, 7–8, 9–10
voluntarist theories (political obligation), 44

Wailing Wall, 7, 172
Walt, Stephen, 162–3, 189
Walzer, Michael, 54, 57, 59–60, 61, 66, 81–3, 84, 85
Ward, David, 24–6
Washington DC, 34, 157, 170
weaponry, 88, 89
Weber, Max, 30, 54, 57, 61, 72, 74–81, 84–6, 87, 88, 89, 100, 118, 127, 222
Weiner, Chaim, 147, 192
Wernick, Steven, 12
West Bank, 24, 25, 152
Whitfield, Stephen J., 4–5
Wight, Martin, 53
Williams, Melissa S., 66
Wittfogell, Karl, 203

294

Index

Women in Black, 164
Women of the Wall, 7
World Zionist Organization, 6

Yehoshua, A. B., 139–40
Yishuv, 148
Yom Kippur War, 4, 116–17, 167
young people, 2, 11, 20–1, 32, 33, 149–50, 165, 167, 170, 174, 176, 177, 183–4, 188–9, 190

Zeitlin, Irving M., 22–3
Zionism
  anti-, 4–5, 33, 138, 150, 180, 201, 206–7
  and Arendt, 72, 87, 103
  classical, 141, 142, 175
  critique of, 26, 27–8, 37, 72, 199, 201–2, 204–14, 220
  cultural, 139, 142, 221
  defense of, 201–2
  and Jewish history, 22, 126–7, 194, 199
  and Jewish identity, 27–8, 69, 112, 114–18, 121–2, 131, 148, 173, 196, 206–7
  and Jewish internationalism, 156
  liberal, 1–2, 165
  and the Muscle Jew, 114–18
  as necessary for being a good Jew, 1–2, 141, 154, 217
  negation of Diaspora, 109, 127, 139–44, 171, 175, 210, 221
  political, 4, 139–40, 142, 143, 221
  post-, 199, 201
  and security, 15–17, 27, 144, 146, 148
  as source of division, 167
  spiritual, 139, 143, 208
  and violence, 207, 213
  and young people, 189

EU representative:
Easy Access System Europe
Mustamäe tee 50, 10621 Tallinn, Estonia
Gpsr.requests@easproject.com

www.ingramcontent.com/pod-product-compliance
Lightning Source LLC
Chambersburg PA
CBHW050203240426
43671CB00013B/2238